Vikram Seth was born in India and educated in India and in England, California and China. He has written acclaimed books in several genres: verse novel, *The Golden Gate*; travel book, *From Heaven Lake*; animal fables, *Beastly Tales*; epic novel, *A Suitable Boy*. His most recent novel, *An Equal Music*, was published in 1999.

'*Two Lives* is yet another unexpected development in [Seth's] dazzling polymathic career . . . Written as an act of love and duty, it is a testament to his modesty and familial affection'
Lucy Hughes-Hallett, *Sunday Times*

'More than once, Seth worries that he has betrayed them, by making their private lives public . . . But his motives are generous, and the breadth of the canvas is ample justification . . . Henny and Shanti had no children. But they did have an author for a great-nephew. And his *Two Lives* is a stay against their oblivion'
Blake Morrison, *Guardian*

'If, as Ernest Hemingway wrote, prose is architecture, then this memoir-cum-biography houses its characters in a way that allows readers to look in without feeling that they are gawping. Mr Seth is a sensitive, intelligent man. He combines an attention to detail and a willingness to let the source material speak for itself – most chillingly the banal documentation detailing Henny's family's deportation to the concentration camps'
Economist

'One of the most remarkable biographies since, well, the eighteenth century, when James Boswell profiled Samuel Johnson'
Donald Morrison, *Time Magazine*

'Seth's memory of the place remains as burnished as a fine piece of cherished family silver . . . Living in this close and private world he could enter into the dark heart of the story'
Anita Desai, *New York Review of Books*

'Seth's triumph here is that he takes the complex trace and communicates the almost incommunicable, he pins down and weaves a beautiful pattern out of the almost irrecoverable'
Sydney Morning Herald

'Both poignant and painfully revelatory . . . *Two Lives* is the most tender of Mr Seth's works'
Somini Sengupta, *New York Times*

'Extraordinary . . . unsentimental . . . a beautiful, loving, clear-eyed book [that] bears tough testimony . . . translucent, telling prose delicately unveils facet after facet of Shanti and Henny, until they stand before us poignantly, yet with humour to them, too'
Michael Upchurch, *Seattle Times*, Book of the Year

'That Seth is a gifted novelist is everywhere in evidence in *Two Lives*, which is both beautifully written and fluently expansive. If Shanti and Henny were lucky to find each other, they were doubly lucky to have a nephew as talented as Seth'
The Monthly (Australia)

'Sensitive and compassionate . . . [Seth's] prose fulfils the obligation Primo Levi once defined for writers on the Holocaust: it is unadorned and clear'
Pankaj Mishra, *New York Times Book Review*

'[Seth has the] uncanny ability to write glorious prose that communicates effortlessly and flows seamlessly but is devoid of distracting brushstrokes'
Herald Sun (Australia)

'A thoughtful, evocative, moving book'
Jonathan Yardley, *Washington Post Book World*

'Equally at home producing a novel in sonnets or a cornucopian family saga, Seth has few equals as a literary technician . . . his quiet tone has cumulative power'
The New Yorker

'Seth is a meticulous biographer . . . having set Shanti and Henny's lives out, unvarnished and un-prettified, in robust health and decrepit decay, Seth makes them better than great. He makes them human. It's the wealth of detail that makes the horror so gut-wrenching. These are not characters. They become people we know . . . We even know what they didn't know about each other, about the shadows of old loves'
San Francisco Chronicle, Book of the Year

'*Two Lives* is a moving examination of lives buffeted by great evils of the twentieth century'
The Age (Australia)

'An intricate study of the way lives and worlds can intertwine . . . tells the story of the Holocaust from a new angle . . . The heart of *Two Lives* – and its most resonant material – concerns World War II and the upheavals it wreaked on Shanti and Henny and everyone they knew'
Los Angeles Times Book Review

'An affecting story, especially because the lives of these two individuals encompass a large sweep of twentieth century history with all its cataclysmic ruptures'
Siddhartha Deb, *Times Literary Supplement* (USA)

'Profoundly moving . . . Seth's heart is in the right place and it is this quality, so apparent throughout *Two Lives*, which makes it on the whole as palatable as it is admirable'
Washington Times

Also by Vikram Seth

Mappings (poems)

From Heaven Lake: Travels Through Sinkiang and Tibet

The Humble Administrator's Garden (poems)

The Golden Gate: A Novel in Verse

All You Who Sleep Tonight (poems)

Three Chinese Poets (translations)

Beastly Tales From Here and There (fables in verse)

A Suitable Boy (novel)

Arion and the Dolphin (libretto)

An Equal Music (novel)

VIKRAM
SETH
TWO
LIVES

ABACUS

First published in Great Britain in 2005 by Little, Brown
This paperback edition published in 2006 by Abacus
Reprinted in 2006 (four times)

Copyright © Vikram Seth 2005

The moral right of the author has been asserted.

Ther author gratefully acknowledges permission to quote from *The
Destruction of the European Jews* by Raul Hilberg, copyright © 1961,
1985, 2003 Raul Hilberg, published by Yale University Press.

A CIP catalogue record for this book is available
from the British Library.

ISBN-13: 978-0-349-11798-0
ISBN-10: 0-349-11798-4

Typeset in Sabon by M Rules
Printed and bound in Great Britain by
Clays Ltd, St Ives plc

Abacus
An imprint of
Little, Brown Book Group
Brettenham House
Lancaster Place
London WC2E 7EN

A Member of the Hachette Livre Group of Companies

www.littlebrown.co.uk

TO SHANTI UNCLE AND AUNTY HENNY

Some words of yours to me suggested
How, through the fog of peace and war,
A pulse beat on, that, strained and tested,
No loss could mute, nor sorrow mar.
To trace this pulse through its confusions,
Illusions, allusions, elusions,
And limn its complex graph of love,
No skein of words is fine enough.
Does this half-filial endeavour
Hold half a chance of half-success –
Even to track your lives, much less
Not to let these recede for ever?
No, if I'd hoped to grasp the whole;
Yes, if some shard may touch the soul.

PART
ONE

1.1

When I was seventeen I went to live with my great-uncle and great-aunt in England. He was Indian by origin, she German. They were both sixty. I hardly knew them at the time.

It was August 1969 – the monsoon season in Calcutta. A few days before I left, Mama had taken me to a temple to be blessed, which was most unlike her. She and Papa came to see me off at Dumdum Airport. I arrived at Heathrow in the afternoon. My great-uncle and great-aunt were still away on their annual holiday in Switzerland and, as I recall, I was met at the terminal by someone in the firm for which my father worked. My first impression was of the width of the road that led (under grey skies) to London. I was housed for a night in a drab hotel somewhere near Green Park.

That evening Shanti Uncle and Aunty Henny returned from Switzerland, and the following day I and my luggage arrived at their door.

I looked at the house that was to be my home for the next few years. There was a red pillar-box not far from the gate of 18 Queens Road, Hendon; this was to be my beacon whenever I trudged up from the tube station. In front of the house was a small, low-walled, immaculately maintained garden with a few rosebushes in full bloom. A path led to the door. To the right of the path, slanted on a stand, was a burnished brass plaque that read:

I set down my luggage on the front step. The thought of meeting people whom I had not seen for years and did not really know, and whose home I would be sharing, made me nervous. I was, in any case, fearfully shy. After a minute I rang the bell.

Aunty Henny appeared. Lean, tall, sharp-featured and attractive, she didn't look sixty. She greeted me with enthusiasm rather than warmth, and led me down the linoleum-floored hallway where three or four people were seated, browsing through old magazines. 'Shanti's patients,' she explained. She poked her head into the surgery to exclaim in her high voice, 'Shanti, Vicky is here,' before opening the door to the drawing-room. 'No, leave the luggage in the corridor, by the stairs,' said Aunty Henny. 'Now sit down and I shall make some tea.'

Since I had been told by Mama not to give any trouble and to be helpful at all times, I offered to help. Aunty Henny would have none of it. I sat down and surveyed the room. Everything seemed inordinately tidy, down to the nested set of varnished side-tables and a polished cabinet for the television.

Aunty Henny brought tea with three cups, and soon afterwards Shanti Uncle took a break from his work. He was still dressed in his white dental jacket. As soon as he came in, he hugged me, then stood back and said, 'Now let me look at my little Vicky. It has been so many years since I saw you. Now you must tell me how your parents are, and what your journey was like. Have you got all your kit for school? Have you eaten? Henny, the boy's starving, you can tell. We must feed him up. Let's open a tin of peanuts. Have you shown him his room?' Aunty Henny looked on impatiently. Suddenly Uncle glanced at his watch, gulped his tea down and rushed back to the surgery.

In those days I was very sensitive about my height and cringed whenever anyone called me little. Shanti Uncle, however, was even

4

shorter than I was, and Aunty Henny towered over him. Nor did I like being called Vicky, even though in India it would not be taken for a feminine diminutive. But my overwhelming sense was that of relief. Uncle's talk filled in, indeed flooded, all my awkward silences. And his hug had made me feel welcome, though it was made with only one arm. His right arm, being artificial, was withheld from the embrace.

1.2

I had been to England twice before. When I was two and a half years old, I travelled by sea with an uncle and aunt who happened to be going there. I was to join my parents, who had left a year or so earlier: the Bata Shoe Company, for which my father worked, had transferred him to head office in London. My widowed grandmother – my mother's mother (whom I called Amma) – had been left in charge of me at home, and I grew very attached to her. When I began to speak, Amma insisted that it be in Hindi and only in Hindi. She herself was perfectly bilingual, but had decided that I would get more than enough English in England. As a result, when I was delivered to my parents in London, they found that I couldn't speak or understand a word of the local language.

Shortly after my arrival, I was taken to see Shanti Uncle and Aunty Henny. During the time my mother had been in England, she had become very fond of Shanti Uncle, and he of her. Both Aunty Henny and he were keen on children, and were looking forward eagerly to my arrival.

I don't know whether it was Shanti Uncle's effusiveness or Aunty Henny's European colour and features, but I quickly became uncomfortable. 'I don't like it here, I want to go home,' I stated firmly in Hindi. Shanti Uncle looked startled. When Aunty Henny asked him what I'd said, he told her that I was enjoying myself and would come again, but that I was tired and needed to go home and rest.

The foreign Aunty Henny, whatever she represented to me, did pose a puzzle to the whole of Shanti Uncle's extended family in India. Uncle had married late, in his forties, and had not brought her to India to be shown around in the proper way. They had no children. She was known to be a German, tall, quite brusque, and with no time for clan commitments in the Indian style. As Aunty Henny said, years later: 'It's very difficult to be enthusiastic about all these adults, these total strangers, who turn up every so often and call themselves your nieces and nephews.' Even my mother, whom Aunty Henny liked, never graduated to being her niece. Whenever my parents called, she would open the door, survey the visitors standing on the top step and shout out, in a view-halloo sort of voice, 'Shanti, your relations are here.'

After a year and a half, I was sent back to Calcutta with my grandmother, who had suddenly and unexpectedly arrived in London on a chartered flight. My parents remained in England for another year. When they returned to Calcutta, my baby brother Shantum was with them.

My second visit to England took place when I was nine, and lasted only a month. One memory of that visit was of Jackie, the plump and pretty au pair at 18 Queens Road, who was very huggable and on whom I had a crush.

But the event of which my memory is strongest, and perhaps has grown even stronger over time, took place at one of the bridge parties that Shanti Uncle and Aunty Henny used to hold from time to time on a Saturday evening. Shanti Uncle took his bridge very seriously, and my father had made a folding leather stand for him so that he could arrange his cards conveniently and play with his left hand. I was bored with watching this strange, intense game, which consisted of almost complete silence followed by incomprehensible, even acrimonious, volubility. It was late. I was leafing through a pile of magazines in another room. One of them – I think it was *Life* – contained an illustrated article about Adolf Eichmann. I cannot now remember much about it, but it must have covered his crimes, his capture and his trial. At one stage, either at a break in the game or while she was dummy, Aunty Henny stepped into the room, saw what I was reading, and said to me, 'So, Vicky, what do you think of him?' My reply was that he was an evil, horrible man. This seemed a natural enough reaction, but it had a strong effect on Aunty Henny. 'You think so? You think so?' she said, and looked at me searchingly. But instead of discussing matters further, she left the room and I went back to my reading.

1.3

Now, at the age of seventeen, I was once again in Shanti Uncle and Aunty Henny's home, reacquainting myself with them and with my surroundings.

18 Queens Road was a large semidetached house about five minutes' walk from the Hendon Central underground station on the Northern Line, a couple of stations after it emerged from its tunnel into the daylight. Apart from two small attics, the house was spread over two floors. Each floor had four main rooms. Downstairs, the sunniest room, with a large south-facing window, was Uncle's surgery. He spent more than eight hours there each day, and needed the light. The surgery faced the front garden with its roses and gleaming professional plaque, and, beyond the busy road, the green expanse of Hendon Park and the hills of Hampstead to the south.

Across the corridor, which acted as a sort of waiting-room for the patients, was the drawing-room. This was divided from the small dining-room by a sliding glass door, which was left open whenever there was a party. The dining-room led to the large linoleum-floored kitchen, Aunty Henny's sacred space; and that gave on to the long, narrow back garden where a couple of gnarled apple trees produced malformed but deliciously tart fruit.

A flight of stairs led up from the L-shaped corridor. Upstairs, above the kitchen was the so-called X-ray room, still used occasionally for developing X-rays, but now mainly a storage space for everything from dental gold to yellowing newspapers to dozens of bottles of Schweppes tonic water. Shanti Uncle was something of a pack-rat. There was also an upstairs drawing-room directly above the surgery which, though filled with sunlight, was, for some reason, almost never used. Its main ornament was a huge, colourful porcelain cockatoo. The other two rooms were Uncle and Aunty's bedroom and a guest bedroom. Everywhere there was a profusion of net curtains. The only toilet and the only bathroom in the house were on this upstairs floor.

Up a flight of narrow stairs, directly under the slanted roof, were the two attics, each with a small window. One of these attics was to be renovated for me, so that I could have a room of my own and privacy for study. It was, however, directly above Shanti Uncle and Aunty Henny's bedroom, and occasionally at night I would hear them talking or quarrelling in German.

My room had not yet been done up, so I stayed in the guest bedroom. I was there for only a few days in the first instance, because term at Tonbridge School was about to begin.

I had won a scholarship to study for my A-levels at Tonbridge on the basis of my final exams at Doon, my boarding-school in India. But my mother was not at all keen that I go to England on my own: sex, drugs and general dissipation were what she feared. My father, however, prevailed; he told her that if she prevented me from going, I would hold it against her all my life. Perhaps it was to preserve me from the temptations of English ways that Mama took me to the temple. The other preservative would be Shanti Uncle. He would keep a watchful eye on me, report back to them, and act, in general, *in loco parentis*. Had he not been in England, I doubt Mama would have let me go; and Papa was right – I doubt I would have forgiven her.

1.4

A few days after going to stay with Shanti Uncle and Aunty Henny, I packed a suitcase and took the train to Tonbridge. I was to be a boarder, but had to report regularly by letter and phone to Uncle and Aunty, as well as, of course, to my parents.

Two large boars' heads made of stone greeted me at the entrance. I was lodged in School House, and in a cavernous hall had a small wooden cubicle of my own to work and sleep in. Students were permitted record-players, and the sound of 'Bridge over Troubled Water' in particular wafted over my first term. Though I had come in at a late stage of school life, when friendships were already formed, the boys were not unwelcoming. Nor, for that matter, were the masters, though I found my housemaster (who was also the headmaster) daunting.

Mr McCrum was tall and distinguished-looking – indeed, at that stage I thought of him more as a personage than a person – and was later to become headmaster of Eton. Shortly after my arrival, he gave a lunch for some of the students in School House; I was one of the invitees. Everything was decorous and measured; after sherry we repaired to the dining-room. A surreptitious glance or two told me which implement everyone else was using, and I followed suit. But at some stage of the meal, I relaxed my vigilance. Shrimps were served inside scooped-out apples. I ate both. As I ate, I became aware that the conversation around me had grown muted. People were staring at me, and when I turned to look at them I noticed something else. On each plate, the shrimps had all been extracted and consumed; the enclosing apples, however, had been left intact. A shocked silence had descended upon the table. My fellow schoolboys glanced anxiously towards Mr McCrum. I looked down at my plate. After a pause, he said, 'Yes, I've always thought it rather wasteful not to eat the apple,' and in due course, the plates and my mortification were cleared unpainfully away.

My subjects at Tonbridge were Pure Mathematics, Applied Mathematics and Physics, but shortly after my arrival, I decided that this diet was too unvaried. I dropped Physics and took up English Literature. We read Chaucer, Shakespeare, Ben Jonson, George Herbert and Samuel Beckett. My teachers were excellent and I was happy in my studies, but Shanti Uncle was anxious about my anomalous mix of subjects.

In due course, Mr McCrum called me in for a serious chat about my future. It was decided, with some little input from me, that I should take the special entrance exams for Oxford. A little later, however, I discovered that one had to have studied a European language to O-level standard to be accepted at the university. I wrote to the authorities, requesting an exemption, explaining that I had studied Hindi to the required level but that I would never have had the opportunity to study European languages at my school in India even if I had wished to. I was told that no waiver would be granted.

I was now in a panic. Learning any language to the required standard in the ordinary way entailed about four or five years' work, and it was a mere six months to the O-level exams. Worse, there was a translation paper for the Oxford exams, which required a more advanced level of the foreign language. When I explained my problem to Shanti Uncle and Aunty Henny, they were worried for me, especially since they could see how dispirited I was. But shortly afterwards Aunty Henny sat me down in the drawing-room with a cup of tea and said firmly that there was nothing for it but to accept things as they were, unfair as they might seem. This is what life was sometimes about. I would have to fulfil the requirement. In addition, it was clear that German was the right language for me, because in the holidays she and Uncle would be able to help me where the school had left off.

Immediately she'd announced that I would have to learn German, Aunty Henny began to speak to me in the language. 'Was ist das, Vicky?' she asked, pointing at a picture, and I had to respond, 'Das ist ein Bild, Tante Henny.' I didn't much care for the sound of the language. After a while, German spread to the dining-table, and I would have to ask for bread or butter or whatever it was in German before it was offered to me. It was a game, sometimes interesting, sometimes tedious, but Aunty Henny was determined that I should have some grounding in the language before term began and all my various studies descended on me simultaneously.

Uncle used to have a hurried lunch with us, and return to the surgery shortly afterwards. While I washed the dishes and Aunty Henny dried them, she would sing songs she remembered from her youth. Her voice was penetrating, even strident, but very much in key. 'Röslein, Röslein, Röslein rot,' she would sing, pausing dramatically on the final word, before descending at last to 'Röslein auf der Heiden'. If she noticed a speck still remaining on a plate, she would return it to me with the word 'Retourkutsche [round trip]!'.

Lessons were also arranged for me with the German wife of an Indian friend of Uncle's, who lived nearby. She baked delicious biscuits, talked to me about left-wing politics and taught me the rudiments of grammar. Back at Tonbridge, a scholarly and somewhat frail teacher gave me private lessons at his house, since it was clear that I would have to be force-fed the language at high speed. As for German itself, after my initial resentment that I had to learn it at all and the shock of the genders and declensions, I began to enjoy it, though it was stressful every month or so to have to vault into the next year's course.

By the time I returned to Queens Road for the holidays, I found I could speak the language a little. I could understand the quarrels between Uncle and Aunty at the breakfast table; they were of surpassing triviality. At night, though, when they bickered, I would occasionally catch 'der Junge', and realised they were discussing me.

Now that I knew what their altercations were about, I was less concerned when there was an explosion of irritation between them. They made up by simply ignoring the fact that they had quarrelled and getting on with their work or chores. Each mentioned to me in

11

private that they were worried that the other was working too hard.

It was through my study of German that my relationship with them deepened. They were proud of my progress. Every day, Aunty would spend a long time on the phone with her friends, speaking mainly in German; now, when they visited, I was told to demonstrate that I too could speak to them: to Mia and Peter Schwab, to Auntie Rosie, to Sonja. I found the experience embarrassing.

Uncle's friend and fellow dentist, Fred Götte, was a different matter. With him I talked more freely, unmindful of my mistakes. He and Uncle would walk in Sunny Hill Park and discuss the world and their colleagues and friends. Fred was cheerful and foul-mouthed and a great deal of fun. 'Ach, die blöde Kuh!' – Oh, the stupid cow! – was one of his favourite expressions.

Whenever I returned for an exeat or for the holidays, Uncle would question me in detail about my activities (and inactivities) at Tonbridge – my course of studies, my social life, my avoidance of chapel, rugby and Corps, my contacts with my teachers and house-master. He approved of my early-morning cross-country runs, warned me against bad company, reproved me for not writing or telephoning often enough, and kept telling me to eat more.

My chronic untidiness distressed Aunty Henny, who could not stand the smallest bit of paper, thread or dust on the carpet. She came upstairs to inspect my room, said, in German, 'I can't stand it, Vicky, I'll faint,' and ceased to bother me as long as I confined my mess there. In general, though, Shanti Uncle was inclined to be strict with me, Aunty Henny lenient. 'Where have you been? What did you do? How much did it cost?' followed by 'Shanti, let the boy be!' was a constant refrain during the holidays.

After a while, I stopped being a guest for Aunty Henny, or a project, but became a sort of companion. I was still 'my husband's nephew' when introduced to strangers. One evening, however, she introduced me as 'my nephew', paused, but did not correct herself. After that, she used the terms interchangeably.

For Shanti Uncle, I became 'Söhnchen', or little son.

1.5

Of the two, Aunty Henny was my main correspondent. She was a demon at the typewriter, an old Remington that she had owned for many years and that I now keep in its case as a sort of low bedside table. When she did write, her handwriting, based as it was on the old German script, was neat but virtually illegible; it once took me half an hour to work out that a series of twelve loops ending in a squiggle was the word 'Mummy'. Uncle, owing to his long working hours, rarely found time to write; besides, it was physically less comfortable for him. His handwriting too was difficult to read and, what with pain in his arm and increasing feebleness, it became still more difficult as the years passed.

Aunty Henny's letters were somewhat staccato.

17th September, 1969

Dear Vicky,

Many thanks for your letter. We are so glad to hear that you settled down nicely. How very nice of your Headmaster to invite you twice. We understand from our friend, who is Headmaster from Mill Hill School (which is near us), what an efficient Man Mr. McCrum is. Hope you are successful in doing your room up. We have started having your room decorated and hope it will be finished before your half term. Could you please find out *when* you arrive on Sunday October 5th and at what time you have to be back. We re-directed a letter from your mother to you and trust you have meanwhile received same . . .

Your Aunty Usha's brother who got married in Switzerland 'phoned. He and his wife are coming for lunch to us on Sunday next. Wished you would be able to join us. I could also employ you as my 'mate' to help me cooking.

Auntie Rosie sends her love to you. My woman, Mrs. Cheers, wishes you all the best, so does Lesley.

We suppose you are quite busy with your work. Please write to us again, so that we know how you are getting on.

Fondest love to you and hope to see you (wir hoffen, Dich bald wieder zu sehen) soon.

Yours aff'ly,

Uncle Shanti and Aunty Henny

Best wishes from Auntie Mila, Uncle Henry and Auntie Nita, Uncle Peter and Auntie Mia.

What underlay Aunty Henny's slightly odd use of English was not only her German background (which accounted for her idiosyncratic use of prepositions) but also the fact that from her previous work she was used to the language of business. I discovered much later, after her death, a book among her belongings entitled (in German) *A Hundred English Letters for Export and Import*. These are a series of meticulously annotated little commercial gems. Letter no. 29, from a firm in Lübeck, requests from a firm in Barcelona a list of the most important olive oil exporters in the district and ends with 'Thanking you in anticipation, and always ready to reciprocate, I remain, Yours faithfully, Sigmund Friedrichsen.' I suspect that this book, an invaluable resource for insomniacs, is the likely origin of 'trust you have meanwhile received same'.

The next few letters contain news of Uncle's health – his back had given him a lot of trouble and he was undergoing manipulation – together with bulletins such as, 'The weather is still perfect though quite foggy' or, on a postcard from their holiday in Mallorca, a February fixture: 'We had ideal weather till now, hope it will improve and the sun will come out again.' Was this obsession with the weather an attempt at self-anglicisation? On the whole, I don't think so. Aunty Henny and Shanti Uncle both loved the outdoors – whether in the back garden or the mountains of Switzerland. 'Wie herrlich leuchtet/ Mir die Natur' – How marvellous nature appears to me – she would quote in a sort of ecstasy as

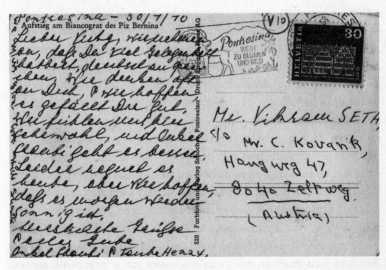

Tel : 202 6330

18 QUEENS ROAD,
HENDON, NW4 2TL

Dr. S. B. Seth,

L.D.S., R.C.S. (Edin.) B.Sc., D.M.D. (Berlin)

presents his compliments

AND WISHES TO STATE THAT YOU ARE NOW DUE FOR

CHECK UP/TREATMENT

YOU FAILED TO RETURN ON.....................................

PLEASE TELEPHONE OR CALL TO MAKE AN APPOINTMENT

ANY DAY EXCEPT WEDNESDAY.

Two cards: (top) Shanti's professional card. (bottom) A postcard from Henny and Shanti, displaying their distinctive handwriting.

she vigorously ground up nuts for a hazelnut cake. I also remembered the 'plume de ma tante' sentence in my first German reader: 'It often rains and sometimes snows.' Perhaps a preoccupation with the weather was not just an English but a European trait.

1.6

I took my German O-level in the spring of my first year in England, and decided to spend part of the summer hitch-hiking with an Indian friend around the German-speaking countries. It would be an adventure, I'd use my German, I would just about be able to afford it, and I wouldn't be stuck in London, glum and alone, while Shanti Uncle and Aunty Henny were on their annual holiday in Switzerland. Uncle, who was answerable to my parents for my welfare, tried to dissuade me and, when my friend had to pull out at the last moment, told me point blank that I could not go on my own.

I had already bought my rucksack and other gear, had booked my reduced-fare train ticket to Braunschweig and had written to the few people my parents knew in Austria, Germany and Switzerland to tell them that I might land up on their doorstep at short notice or none. Uncle's refusal reduced me almost to tears of anger and frustration.

Aunty Henny took my part. 'Shanti,' she said impatiently, 'let the boy alone. Let him go.' She reminded him that he himself had enjoyed wandering around the German countryside as a student. When he replied that he had been twenty-five, not eighteen, she clicked her tongue irritably and, rather than address the point, simply told him that he was talking 'quatsch'. They got into a shouting match in English and German; then Uncle angrily put on his coat and muffler and beret and went for a long walk around Hendon Park. When he returned, he had calmed down. He told me, 'Don't worry about me, darling, I'm just your old Uncle, I'll soon be gaga,' veered off into a philosophical disquisition about how the future belonged to youth, and gave me twenty pounds to help me on my way.

I had a wonderful holiday. My father's business friend in Braunschweig met me at the station. After a few days at his place, I got a ride with him up the Rhine, Mosel and Saar valleys (drinking much white wine en route) to the French border, where he had to take possession of a car he had just bought. On his way back, he dropped me off at Mannheim, and I hitch-hiked in stages to the Austrian border via Nuremberg, Regensburg and Passau, on one occasion getting a ride from a generous young man in a red sports car who later took me up in a glider. From Passau to Linz I decided to splash out on a steamer down the Danube. There I met a girl called Helga to whom I wrote for a year or more afterwards in a sort of romantic haze. She was travelling with her parents and was obviously unhappy about something; this made her seem even prettier. I also found that, shy though I was in English, I could be bold in German.

I caught a train to Vienna, where a distant relative took me under her wing and fed me schnitzel. In Graz, the wife of one of my father's Czech colleagues from Bata took charge of me: we made little forays out of the town, sunned ourselves by a lake and gathered berries in the woods. Next I hitch-hiked along swollen streams under pouring rain towards Salzburg and the Swiss border. A goggled motorcyclist, who assured me that my loaded rucksack posed no problem of balance, gave me a lift to Berne. Almost everyone I met was friendly and hospitable and tolerant of my German. All this was a world different from anything I had known.

I had no timetable and no responsibilities. I sent bland postcards filled with weather reports to Shanti Uncle and Aunty Henny and – at my known addresses – found similar postcards from them waiting for me.

In Berne, I stayed with an Indian diplomat, who was my mother's brother's wife's brother's wife's father, and therefore 'family' in the Indian sense. Rain was replaced with sunshine,

17

German with English and Hindi, adventure with comfort, and wurst with curry. But after a few days I grew restless and moved on towards Zurich, where I arrived in the early evening.

But here I faced a problem. There was no room in the youth hostel or in any of the hotels that I could afford. Then suddenly it struck me that Shanti Uncle and Aunty Henny might be in Zurich; their clockwork schedules in Switzerland always took them from Pontresina to Zurich before they returned to London, and they always stayed at the Hotel Seidenhof. I burst in upon them, wild hair, backpack and all, as they sat taking tea with friends in the drawing-room of the hotel.

Uncle started up in surprise, then came forward to embrace me; Aunty Henny, teacup poised, looked amazed. A chair was brought up, and I wolfed down vast quantities of cake while they questioned me about my journey. If their friends Oskar and Trüdchen and the staid-looking guests all around were puzzled by this extra-galactic incursion, they did not show it. I was plied with yet more cake, and the manager was asked if there was a vacant room in the hotel. When it became clear that not only this hotel but several others that he got in touch with were fully occupied, Oskar and Trüdchen invited me to stay at their home.

After Zurich came Geneva, Lyon, a night in Sète when I slept in a cupboard, which for some reason was lying on the beach, a stay with some of my father's friends in a small village in the Pyrenees, a journey to Paris where I heard a Bach concert in a church, and an almost reluctant return to the greyness of London, the routine of 18 Queens Road and the start of my second year at Tonbridge. Those few weeks had been a time of such intensity and independence that I often daydreamed about them then, and even now, decades later, when entire years of my intervening life have become a blur, they remain alive in my memory. Perhaps it is true that, for all the evidence of the mirror, one pictures oneself in some deep niche of the mind as forever eighteen.

1.7

Uncle and Aunty left Zurich for London the day after we met. But on the strength of our meeting in this unusual context and my evident competence in making my way on my own, I gained a useful reputation for intrepidity which stood me in good stead whenever Uncle was instinctively disinclined to permit something in the future. It was a reputation cheaply gained; all I had used was my thumb and a series of letters and introductions. But Aunty Henny had had faith in me all along.

She was not pleased, however, with a remark in one of my school reports. Mr McCrum had written: 'The one criticism I would make is of his appearance, which lately has grown rather slovenly.' Aunty Henny, who was always stylishly turned out, had recently taken to criticising the length of my hair. Now here was confirmation from the world that I was letting the side down. Nor was my father, who was very smart, delighted with the report. I was shorn in short order and given money for some new clothes.

I did well in my English A-level. But what delighted Aunty Henny was not this so much as my results in the more elementary German exam. She wrote to me in German to congratulate me, and when I replied in German, meticulously corrected my numerous mistakes, crossing out words, relocating phrases and inserting commas.

After the Oxford entrance exam, I was called in December for an interview at Corpus Christi College. Uncle was nervous and gave me lots of advice about being myself, being deferential, being bold, seizing the nettle and the reins and the moment and the bull by the horns. Aunty Henny hugged me and wished me luck.

The interview, which took place by candlelight during a power cut, lasted for more than half an hour. Rather than sitting as an inquisitorial board, the tutors who conducted the interview, two

19

men and a woman, were sprawled out casually in armchairs in a comfortable room. When, in the course of the interview, I asked them how I'd done in the German translation paper, they looked blank. One of the two men, who had a slight stutter, said, 'Oh, we don't know.'

'But didn't anyone look at it?' I asked.

'Oh, not really,' he continued. 'The translation paper's just a formality. But we notice you have a German O-level. Why, as a matter of interest, did you study German?'

'I didn't want to,' I replied. 'I had to – and at quite short notice. As you know, it's a requirement to have a European language.'

'Oh, is it? I suppose it is.'

I paused for a second, then told them of my attempt to get an exemption.

'Oh, you needn't have bothered with the university authorities,' said the don. 'You should have come to us. We'd have told you we didn't care – and unofficially ignored it.'

'So, in a sense, my study of German has been entirely unnecessary?'

'Entirely.'

Perhaps noticing, even by candlelight, the look on my face, he quickly added: 'In a sense, that is.'

1.8

Before I left the room, my interviewers told me that they looked forward to seeing me the next year. That night I could hardly sleep for excitement. It was too late to phone Shanti Uncle and Aunty Henny, but when I told them the news the next morning they were delighted.

The nine months between the interview and the start of the university year I spent back home in India, some of it teaching at my old school, Doon. Upon receiving official confirmation of my being accepted at Oxford, Aunty Henny wrote to me with her typical mixture of affection and efficiency.

8th January, 1971

Dear Vicky,

I am herewith enclosing the letter from U.C.C.A. [University Central Council on Admissions] together with the decision card for your immediate action. Uncle has written as per copy herewith.

I hope you are having a wonderful time and hast uns nicht ganz vergessen [haven't completely forgotten us].

Our love to the whole family.

> With fondest love,
> Yours aff'ly,
> Tante Henny
> (Sekretärin)

P.S. Uncle sends his love to you all.

Bitte schreibe eine Karte an Auntie Rosie. [Please send a card to Auntie Rosie.]

I went up to Oxford in autumn 1971. Though I had got in to read English, I decided that it didn't suit me and changed to Philosophy, Politics and Economics.

There were three eight-week terms each year. This meant that more than six months of the year were holidays, and I spent most of these in London with Shanti Uncle and Aunty Henny. Even during the term I would go down to see them a couple of times.

It was a wonderfully fruitful if not really happy time for me. The unhappiness came from my lack of ease, my lack of aim, a deep general sense of melancholy, and the fact that I was always falling unrequitedly in love. But these were years filled with a sense of freedom, largely because my time belonged to me. I walked a great deal, largely on my own, along streams and rivers and through woods. I wrote poetry imbued with the traumas of life and love and vast philosophical questions about existence and purpose. It was bad poetry, not insincere exactly, but desperately inflated.

Shanti Uncle and Aunty Henny knew little of my turmoil, but gave me that family anchor, so far away from home, that prevented me from sinking completely into the black vortices of my delayed adolescence. It was in the garden of 18 Queens Road, sitting in a deckchair under one of the apple trees that, week after week and weather permitting, I read dozens of Penguins bought at the Paperback Bookshop on Broad Street: novels, philosophy, history, poetry, psychology, science, plays, whatever took my fancy. The afternoon would pass into evening, I'd be called in for dinner, Uncle would expound his views on life and politics, Aunty Henny and I would wash the dishes afterwards and talk companionably about not very much.

Uncle loved to talk about the family, about who had been born and who had got engaged and who had fallen sick, who was good at making money and who had a weakness for gambling. He asked me dozens of questions about my parents, my brother Shantum and my sister Aradhana, and my mother's three brothers. Again and again he repeated how much he owed to my maternal grandfather, his eldest brother Raj, who had loved him so much and sent him abroad to study.

Aunty Henny never spoke about her family. I had heard from my parents that they had all been killed in Germany.

1.9

My studies continued. Despite the fact that I was reading Politics, I was not much interested at the time in contemporary British politics. Events in India in the aftermath of the Bangladesh War, the division of Pakistan and the re-election of Mrs Gandhi interested me far more. But in Britain this was the time of the miners' strike, and Aunty Henny's letters reflect the circumstances throughout the country. She writes on 20 February 1972:

When are your 'High Risk' days for the black-out? Ours are Tuesday and Friday, but we had a black-out on Sunday evening which is our 'Medium Risk' day. This week-end Saturday and Sunday are our 'Medium Risk days'. Uncle has to send the patients home, as he cannot use his machine and in the afternoon it is too dark to do anything. Well, we cannot do anything about it and it is no good grumbling . . . We love to see you again, but at present with the black-outs there is not much point for you to come. Let us hope an agreement will be reached *soon*.

Uncle, who had voted Liberal in every election since the war, began darkly contemplating the possibility of voting Conservative, so bothered was he by the strikes and by what he saw as growing laziness and lawlessness. But so conservative was he in his habits that it was to be a few more years before he finally took the plunge.

A week into my second year at Oxford, I wandered into the Oriental Institute on something of a whim, thinking I might sit in on a Japanese class. Entering the wrong room, I found myself in a Chinese class instead. This proved to be fascinating, and I enjoyed a couple of weeks of lessons until I was thrown out as an interloper from another faculty by the teacher. Meanwhile, I had begun learning Welsh because I was besotted with a friend whose family came from Wales – and I had also started to learn the flute, for no reason that I can remember. Shanti Uncle found all these enthusiasms dilettantish and troubling, in that they took my eye off my studies. He tried to dissuade me from expending my energy in this way, and was not happy when he heard that my tutors were displeased with my lack of progress. Aunty Henny, on the other hand, was more philosophical and assured me that she had confidence in me. 'But you must work hard, darling,' she would be careful to add.

After my second year, I did something which in those days was unusual: I took a year off to return to India. I had been away too long and was homesick, but there was a more concrete reason as well, and this helped to convince my tutors to let me go: I wanted to study aspects of politics and economics on the ground –

cattle-development projects, state elections, farming schemes – so as to give some substance to my otherwise theoretical studies. Shanti Uncle and Aunty Henny were sad to see me leave, and Aunty Henny kept up a correspondence throughout the year, almost entirely in German, of gossip and event and comment.

15th January, 1974

. . . P. works in a travel agency (she is *so* thin that one can only see her bones – this remark only for you, please) . . . Uncle is somewhat better, though his blood pressure is still quite high . . . The political and financial conditions here are far from good. Today the railway strike is on for 24 hours. I think we will be having an election at the beginning of the next month . . . Would you please thank your parents for their letters, and your grandmother too. It isn't possible for me to write to each of them individually, as only you can understand because you have lived with us. I am *so* busy – helping Shanti Uncle, cooking, and taking care of many guests – that I really can't get around to anything . . .

We have had new wallpaper put up in the lounge and the dining-room. Unfortunately, the workmen were no good, despite having been recommended to us. At any rate, it looks cleaner. These days, people only want to earn money quickly and take no pride in their work. What can one do?

Vicky, darling, do write again and tell us how you and the family are and what you are doing. Greet everyone warmly from us. Many greetings and kisses to you, from Uncle too.

Your

Aunty Henny

Not long afterwards, while they were away in Mallorca, there was a break-in at 18 Queens Road; the burglars broke open the cupboards and took all the jewellery, cash and dental gold in the house.

We have already got over the shock a bit. What can one do? You simply can't imagine what kind of 'mess' [Aunty Henny uses the English word]

24

they had made in the rooms, and we still haven't sorted everything out. Your room used to be a terrible 'mess' sometimes, but that was, naturally, nothing in comparison. Needless to say, they haven't taken your books, so you can rest assured about that.

For my birthday in June I got a card with a cat playing the flute; I had recently taken up the Indian flute, or *bansuri*. Aunty Henny wrote:

You lazy fellow, why don't you write? Are you working hard and do you find your work useful and interesting? . . . Are you playing the flute a lot? I hope that you are able to play it at least as well as the cat. Then you can give us a performance.

Uncle added about fifteen lines, which must have cost him some effort. He ended with: 'How are your studies going? It will not be long before you are back with us.'

I was indeed soon back with them for one more year, my final year as an undergraduate. But I spent less time with them. As my exams approached I at last began to exercise some self-discipline and addressed myself to my books. Meanwhile, I had applied to the graduate schools of various American universities to continue my studies in Economics. A couple of East Coast schools had accepted me, but my years in England had made me sick of snow and rain. I decided to go to California, to Stanford University, after I graduated, though this meant I would be even further away, both from them and from my parents.

1.10

The Stanford campus was as big as a town – one needed a bicycle and a map to get around it – and was separated from neighbouring Palo Alto by a six-lane road. The pillared quadrangle was massive, and the avenue of palms leading to it endless. All the loud and friendly undergraduates, men and women alike, looked vast and blond, and there were gigantic carparks scattered here and there on campus to accommodate the cars that enabled them to drive at will to nearby San Francisco or wherever they chose around the enormous state of California. Between us and the greatest ocean on earth stood a broad, golden-dry range of almost empty hills, huge tracts of which belonged to the university. Here cattle grazed under a radio telescope, and red foxes and deer cohabited with raccoons and skunks and joggers.

I wrote regularly to Shanti Uncle and Aunty Henny, describing my surroundings, my studies and my state of mind, and they wrote back with news and comfort and responsible advice. Aunty Henny ended her first letter with: 'Keep well, darling, and look after yourself. Your Secretary is too far away to do it.' Uncle wrote: 'Your Aunty has given you all the news. There is not much for me to [add?] except that I miss my "Söhnchen".'

I discovered soon after I had begun my compulsory courses in macroeconomics and microeconomics that I could not get by without wasting a whole lot of time studying. The subject was dry, mathematically unrealistic and intellectually unchallenging. Worst of all were the endless examinations, often two or three a quarter. I felt I was being re-infantalised. There was no time to meander or to think. But I had chosen my bed, and there was no tumbling out of it.

At Christmas I got a card from Uncle and Aunty, and then, presumably in response to my grumbling about my studies, the following advice from Aunty:

9th January, 1976

Dear Vicky,

You are a lovely boy to write to us two letters. Many, many thanks. We were delighted to hear from you, but not so happy to note that you dislike your 'subject' and the way they test you all the time. We only hope with the time you will get more used to it, as there seems no other way out for you, and if one *m u s t* do something, one has to go through it.

In March Aunty Henny wrote:

Now to you, darling. We note from your letter that you are still not
too keen on your subject, and we only hope that after a time you feel
more satisfied and work harder, so that you do well in your exam.
Perhaps it becomes more interesting as time goes on, quite often it is
like that. It is wonderful that you love music which, no doubt,
compensates for unpleasant things and you should certainly continue
with the cello.

The cello, poetry and once again the Chinese language were distracting me from Economics. In poetry in particular I had a
wonderful guide, Timothy Steele, who was teaching at Stanford.
(He is, to my mind, the finest living poet in English.) When,
towards the end of my second year, I won a scholarship to stay at
Stanford and write poetry for a year, my whole family, though
pleased, considered it yet another diversion from my true course.
Aunty Henny wrote to me in cautionary terms:

29th May, 1977

Dear Vicky,

Many thanks for your most welcome letter. First of all
congratulations to your prize. It is absolutely wonderful, and we hope
you will let us read your poetry which has won a fellowship. Well, for
one year you can devote to writing and have not to study Economics.
Though Shanti hated dentistry first, he loves it for a long, long time,
and the same may apply to you with Economics, at least we hope
so . . .

Uncle scrawled a note – quite long for him – which continued
along the side of the page:

My dear Vicky,

I am very proud of your achievement and looking forward to seeing
you soon. We would have lot to talk about. It's a pity that your stay will

27

be so short. Your Auntie and I often think of you and recall the nice time when you were with us.

You are used to taking up challenge and I have no doubt that once again you will prove that you are the master of your destiny. Your hard work and patience will sort out all your problems. A time will come when you will start enjoying the subjects you disliked. You have started the subject and you must finish it in usual Vicky fashion – ahead of every one else.

Good luck. Love. Yours, Uncle Shanti

As it happened, I was unable to visit them in the summer because I had to study third-year intensive Chinese, which was offered only at that time. They, however, visited North America that same summer, though unfortunately only Toronto and New York. Aunty Henny wrote: 'How we would have loved to meet you in San Francisco, but unfortunately it is too far and we have so little time.' Shanti Uncle sent me a cheque for a hundred dollars, and wrote: 'Your Auntie's best friend has been very hospitable and has taken us around as much as she could in this foul weather.' The idea of Aunty Henny having a best friend, and that too in New York, was a surprise to me, but then Aunty Henny and I had hardly spoken of the past – not even when she was helping me learn German. She had never opened the subject, and I had never wished to.

I must have flagged in my correspondence, because Aunty Henny wrote a long letter, mainly about a relative's illness, and ended with: 'Vicky darling, write soon when you find time. We are thinking a lot of you and you know how much you are in our hearts.'

I returned to Economics in 1978, after my year of truancy, and decided on a dissertation subject that would take me to China. It was a combination of demography and economics and involved some research in the countryside. China had begun to open up to the rest of the world: Chinese students came to Stanford to study the sciences, and some Stanford students, mainly in the humanities

28

and social sciences, went to China with the permission of the Chinese Ministry of Education. I hoped to be one of these, indeed had pinned my career on it. The Ford Foundation had promised me a scholarship for my research if I could get to China. But the months passed, and there was no reply from Beijing to my application. After I had pressed my case for a year and a half, I began to despair. My university scholarship had by now run out. A friend managed to find a temporary job for me; this tided me over for a bit. But it was too late to choose a new Ph.D. subject unrelated to China, and to research, write and defend it. I knew that if nothing came through I would have to go back home with my studies incomplete.

Aunty Henny wrote to me at Stanford on 8 January 1979: 'We hope you will be selected to go to China for a year, it would just be most interesting for you. We keep our fingers crossed for you.' She continued with various philosophical exhortations about other family matters.

This letter was followed a few months later by a postcard which, to my astonishment, came from Germany. She and Shanti Uncle had gone over to visit Fred Götte, Shanti Uncle's friend and fellow dentist, who had returned to Germany after a few years in England and had married a Japanese woman. When I asked Uncle about this trip many years later, he said, 'Henny treated it as a visit not to Germany, but to Fred.'

It was Easter 1979 when Aunty Henny went to Germany. She had left as a young woman of thirty, and she was now seventy.

Later that same year, Aunty Henny wrote without further comment that she and Shanti Uncle were planning to visit Berlin, which to me was even more surprising. I do not know if they actually went. For Aunty Henny to return to her hometown could have been an experience of unpredictably profound sorrow and bitterness. Uncle later told me she had never been back, despite various blandishments from the city, but Uncle's memory was not always reliable. (He once told me that Aunty Henny had never returned to Germany at all.) The question of Berlin is still a mystery to me. I have all but one of Aunty Henny's British passports since 1949, when she was naturalised; but the missing passport covers precisely the period in question.

1.11

Early in 1980, at the age of seventy-one, Uncle fell seriously ill. Aunty's letters convey a vivid picture of the course of events through which one can glimpse both their distress and their fortitude.

18 Queens Road,
London, N.W.4 2TL
16th February, 1980

Dear Vicky,

Many thanks for your letter. We were so glad to hear from you though your letter does not sound too cheerful. Unfortunately I have also to give you bad news. Uncle was very, very ill. He had a coronary thrombosis abt. beginning of January. He did not feel well for many months, but our G.P. always said he is fine. He was so breathless, that he could not walk anymore from our house to Hendon-Central. Though Uncle diagnosed himself (his G.P. never) that it was his heart, it was too late, and our local doctor (our G.P.) took it too easy with Uncle, and he must have thought Uncle is a Hypochondric (perhaps I spell it wrong), which of course is wrong, and he should have found it when Uncle complained. As it was not diagnosed earlier, Uncle worked with the Heart infarct which made it so bad. I am glad to say he is a bit better . . .

What a pity you have not heard anything yet about China. We don't know how you will manage to write your thesis in such a short time. I am very optimistic by nature, and it helped me a great deal when Uncle was so ill. I am also optimistic *for you* and keep my fingers crossed . . .

A month later, Aunty Henny wrote that Uncle had had to be taken to hospital with a blood clot in his leg –

which is most dangerous, as it can travel to the heart or the brain or he can lose his leg. Luckily the blood gradually comes back and the leg is getting warmer. It was absolutely cold when we brought him in nearly a fortnight ago. I stayed with Uncle until 3 o'clock in the morning that night in the Hospital (I think I will never forget that night) and came home about 4 in the morning. It was difficult for the hospital to get a cab for me. You know my optimismus helps me, and I was sure he will get over this trouble. For the first time yesterday he was allowed to walk for a few minutes which is a good sign, *before* he was not allowed to move at all . . .

I have not written to anybody in India, first of all I have not the time and secondly not the right relationship (this is only for your consumption) . . .

A month later, a further bulletin:

18 Queens Road,
London, N.W.4 2TL
6th April, 1980

Dear Vicky, Many thanks for your letter. You are really a good boy to care so much for Uncle, which we both appreciate very much. I am glad to say Uncle is better. We went to see the Specialist last Thursday, and he was really pleased with the progress Uncle made. Of course he has to take it still very easy, has to rest a lot, and is not allowed to work until we come back from our Swiss holidays middle of August, and then he has to cut down a lot . . .

We are pleased that you started your part-time job. We wonder whether you find it interesting. Of course you must be busy with your thesis. If you have any financial troubles, do not hesitate to let us know. We certainly help you with pleasure . . .

Uncle was no longer permitted to travel to the altitude of his beloved Pontresina, but his life would have seemed incomplete without the annual Swiss holiday. A month before they set out for the lower altitude of Lenk, Aunty Henny wrote to me to comment on some good news that I had just shared with them.

18 Queens Road,
London, N.W.4 2TL
9th June, 1980

Dear Vicky,

. . . We were more than thrilled to get your letter with the exciting news that you will be going to China. We think it is just phantastic, but you know how optimistic I am, I always told Uncle that you will be accepted, and now your dream has come through. [Uncle had crossed out this last word and written 'true'.] We had in mind to meet you one year in San Francisco, but now in order to meet you we have to come to Peking!!!!

Uncle added:

Dear Vicky,

First of all your Aunty and I wish you a very happy birthday. I was very happy to know that you have not waited in vain for your cherished trip to China. I am a great believer that you will get what you want but you must want it and not just wish it.

I am still not entirely certain what Uncle meant by that last sentence, but I often thought about it in the years that followed.

1.12

I left for China in the summer of 1980 for what turned out to be two years. The Ministry of Education placed me at Nanjing

University. In my second year my brother Shantum and my mother visited me, but no one else in the family did. I kept in touch with Shanti Uncle and Aunty Henny by slow and irregular post.

After months of waiting and applying and struggling against all-pervasive regulations and giving up hope only to have it restored once more, I got to do my economic and demographic research in some villages not far from Nanjing, on the Yangtse.

Because I had so much time on my hands, I saw as much as I could of China. At the end of my first year I travelled, mainly by hitch-hiking on an army truck, from the oases of Sinkiang to the Tibetan plateau; after a week or so in Lhasa, I crossed the Himalayas to Nepal by truck and on foot; and from there flew home to Delhi. When my father suggested I write up my notes on the journey as a travel book, I told him I had no idea how to get it published. In his usual practical manner he suggested I go to a library, take down the addresses of publishers whose books I liked, and write to them, enclosing a map of the journey. One of these publishers, Chatto & Windus, expressed interest in reading a completed manuscript. I wrote the book during my second year in China, and it was published the following year as *From Heaven Lake*.

When, in the late summer of 1982, my stint in China was over, I decided to return to Stanford via England rather than across the Pacific. Uncle wrote, in his increasingly frail hand: 'We have not seen each other for a long time and it will be very nice to see you and hear about all your studies and journeys through Tibet.' Though I had visited England during the earlier part of my studies at Stanford, by now it was four years since I had seen him and Aunty Henny.

My father was in London at the same time as me, and we both stayed at 18 Queens Road. We talked, we walked in Hendon Park, and we helped around the house and garden where we could. Aunty Henny looked much the same as before and was as robust and energetic, but Uncle, despite the fact that he was still working, had aged: his face was tauter and his heart trouble exhausted him towards the end of each day.

Papa returned to Delhi and I left for San Francisco a little later. It was in these last few days when the three of us, Shanti Uncle, Aunty Henny and I, were once again on our own, that something of the rhythm of our earlier years together re-established itself. I would sit and read in the garden or dry the dishes as Aunty Henny and I talked, or parry Uncle's endless attempts to get me to eat more. Once again he talked about the importance of the family and how much my grandfather and grandmother had meant to him. He reminisced about his time in Berlin as a student in the thirties, and about his time in the British army during the Second World War. I enjoyed hearing him talk about the past; his views about the present had grown increasingly censorious.

After returning to Stanford, I continued with my dissertation work, which at this time largely consisted of feeding the village data I had collected into a university computer for months on end. Computer time was cheaper at night, and I often bicycled home under the shiny gaze of raccoons. One morning, after an all-night session, I stumbled into the Stanford Bookstore, thinking to myself that there had to be some sort of life beyond data-entry. I began reading a translation of Pushkin's novel in verse, *Eugene Onegin*. I was caught up in the story – at the same time light and profound, witty and sorrowful – as well as in the astonishing stanzaic form so magically maintained by the translator, Charles Johnston. That evening I finished the book and began reading it again. I was in the grip of an inspiration that would change my life.

From Heaven Lake was published in London in 1983. Apart from my sister Aradhana, who was at college in Delhi and could not get away, the immediate family all gathered for the event. But it didn't seem right to impose ourselves en masse on Shanti Uncle and Aunty Henny. We took a couple of rooms in a small hotel, and visited them almost every day. In the hotel, with no dissertational pressures to distract me, I began writing the first few stanzas of *The Golden Gate*, a novel in verse inspired by Pushkin but set in San Francisco. When my parents returned to India, I remained for a month in England working on the first part of this book, staying with my brother Shantum, who was squatting in an abandoned house in Norwich, and with my friends John and Susan Hughes, both civil servants in London. I did not stay with Shanti Uncle and Aunty Henny because I wanted to work undistracted during the day, but I visited them often.

When I returned to Stanford, my dissertation work fell by the wayside, and I devoted myself to *The Golden Gate*, which was completed in a little over a year. I came to London several times over the course of this year, once to give a lecture about my Tibetan journey at the Royal Geographical Society, once because *From Heaven Lake* had won a travel book award – Shanti Uncle and Aunty Henny were my main guests at the event – and once because Uncle had again fallen seriously ill.

I happened to phone them from Stanford; Aunty Henny picked up the phone. She told me that Uncle had been taken to hospital – he had had another heart attack – and I could tell from her voice that, despite her 'optimismus', she was deeply worried. I had never heard her sound like that – she who of all people didn't want to alarm others or have them fussing over her. I went to the International Center at Stanford to get the papers that would permit me to return to the States, took the bus to San Francisco Airport, managed to get a standby flight, which was all I could afford, and reached London the next morning. After a dreadful interrogation by immigration officials at Heathrow, I was allowed into the country.

Uncle was in Charing Cross Hospital and he looked awful. I stayed with Aunty Henny for a week or so before I had to return. We went to see him together every day. By the time I left he had improved a little. His ward overlooked a large tract of greenery, including a graveyard, and he talked a great deal about how his end was near. 'Nonsense, nonsense, Shanti, why do you always talk nonsense?' was Aunty Henny's irked response in German.

1.13

That year, 1984, was a sad one for the family. My beloved grandmother, Amma, whom Shanti Uncle was so fond of, died late in the year; I never got the chance to say goodbye. On her return from Pune, where Amma lay in hospital, Mama had to be escorted home from Delhi Airport. All around were burned vehicles and buildings – the result of anti-Sikh rioting in the aftermath of Mrs Gandhi's assassination. Many of the instigators of these bloody events were politicians, and though people knew who they were, everything possible was being done to help them avoid prosecution. Things appeared to be unravelling in the country; all our traditions of tolerance and humanity seemed to have dissolved.

Worst of all for the family was my cousin Ira's death at the age of sixteen only a few days before my grandmother's. Ira was the daughter of my maternal uncle and aunt, Sashi Mama and Usha Mami. Three children of theirs had died in infancy from genetic causes, and they had not dared to have any more. Ira was a child whom my parents had borne for them and given to them in adoption within a few days of birth. She had died from a fall from their balcony in Bombay shortly after Sashi Mama had been transferred there from Calcutta by his company. Everyone, particularly the grieving parents, had tried to keep the news from Amma on her deathbed, but once, when Ira's name was mentioned, Amma had said, in Hindi, 'I'll meet her over there.'

Aunty Henny wrote to me a few months later, after some close family friends from India had visited them in London:

18 Queens Road,
London, N.W.4 2TL
16th April, 1985

Dear Vicky,

. . . we got first-class [first-hand?] personal information after the tragic death of Ira. I still cannot get over it. It was the first time I wrote a letter to India (Usha and Sashi) on my own and I must say the most difficult one I have ever written. I understand Usha and Sashi are going on a holiday to Paris, London and Canada and will arrive here on May 9th. I have never met Usha and I am certainly looking forward to seeing her though it may be sad . . .

How is your thesis going? Do you find time to work on it? You must be terribly busy. Hope your work still interests you . . .

Darling, that is all for to-day. Look after yourself.

Uncle and I send you our fondest love.

Yours aff'ly,

Auntie Henny

The reference to my thesis – I was now in my tenth year as a graduate student at Stanford – caused me a little guilt, though no pause. But again I had run out of funds. I now looked for work close at hand, and got a job at Stanford University Press. As for *The Golden Gate*, more than twenty publishers on both sides of the Atlantic rejected it. Then, suddenly, three different publishers wanted it, and it was eventually published in New York by Random House.

Earlier, I had sent Shanti Uncle and Aunty Henny a typescript of the book. Now, as soon as my American edition came out, I sent them a copy. I also mentioned that my British publishers wanted me to visit England to help promote the book. Aunty Henny wrote back:

28th March, 1986

Dear Vicky,

We were delighted to receive your 'GOLDEN GATE' book yesterday. It is beautifully presented, and we love it . . . Though we read the manuscript it will be so much nicer to read your proper book. Your photo is true to life and very expressive. Altogether it is just lovely. We are delighted that you will be coming in June, and we are looking forward so much to seeing you again . . .

We can well imagine how busy you are. Have you any time to attend to your Ph.D.? Are you still working?

Uncle wants to add a few lines. Therefore I stop.

Lots of love and au revoir soon,

Yours aff'ly,

Auntie Henny

Uncle wrote about the book, then added: 'How can you find time to complete your thesis? I only hope that you are not over-taxing yourself.'

Uncle was still clearly far more concerned about my academic career than any literary achievement, but he was right about my overtaxing myself. I was doing far too many things and too many of them superficially. I could no longer juggle my work, my writing, my book promotion, my brutally brief holidays, my academic work, my other interests, my social life and my homesickness. I found myself staring for minutes at a time at my loaded in-tray. I sometimes fell asleep from tiredness at my desk. When I went home, I would turn on the TV and watch American football, a game I barely understood, for hours on end. I slept fitfully at night and walked at all hours through Escondido Village and College Terrace, a familiar figure to all the cats of the neighbourhood, who escorted me from one territory to the next.

Someone had mentioned an analogy that had begun to prey on my mind. Going to California, he had said, was like entering a swimming-pool. It was pleasant, you swam a few laps, and before you knew it, you were fifty years old. I knew of too many Indians who had begun to work there after college, fully intending to go back home after a few years. They had got ahead in their professions, bought a house with a mortgage, and found that their school-age children had become more American than Indian. After a few years they were so embedded in their temporary lives that they only went home for any length of time upon the death or severe illness of a parent. This thought struck an uncomfortable chord. I had been away far too long. I had no 'encumbrances' to hold me back, I had no ambitions in the standard sense, I liked the company of my family and missed them. Everyone was growing older – my father was now sixty-three, my mother fifty-six. Shantum, my brother, was not in India to give them support, and Aradhana, my sister, was growing up without my really getting to know her in the way one does through the humour and abrasion and affection of day-to-day living rather than the intense sociability of sporadic visits.

The $11,000 advance paid to me by my publishers for *The Golden Gate* was enough for me to settle a few debts and to get myself and my possessions of eleven years – more, if one included my time in England – home to Delhi. I made up my mind to return, even with my dissertation unwritten, with the aim of writing a novel set in India. Shanti Uncle and Aunty Henny, who had always inquired so anxiously about my thesis, were not pleased; nor were my parents, who believed in completing what one undertook – as, in general, did I myself.

But my parents did not prevent their son from returning to live under their roof to, in effect, sponge off them. They were happy to see me, and tried to conceal their disquiet.

I thought I would finish my Indian novel in a year or two, and that it might be two or three hundred pages long. In fact, it was to take seven years to complete and would run to over thirteen hundred pages.

Once I got home, all my plans to embark on the novel seemed to disperse into a vague unease. I had a few notes about what I wanted to include in it but I didn't have a story, any characters who gripped me, or even a scene to start things off with. When, in due course, these came to me, I managed to write the first of what would eventually be nineteen parts.

However I soon realised that the novel – which had opened with a grand wedding – now had so many characters whom I was interested in that I needed to take off at least a year simply to understand the varied worlds of law, politics, administration, medicine, farming, manufacture, commerce, education, music, religion, and so on, that these characters came from or worked in. What exactly did one do if one visited a courtesan in 1951, and how would I find someone to tell me? How did the credit market for small shoemakers in Agra work, and what might be the effect of a credit squeeze on people who had little to fall back on? What was it like to be a brown sahib in a white managing agency in Calcutta in the fifties? Were there girls at St Stephen's College in the late forties?

Instead of being constrained by this research, I found that it inspired me with new ideas. It also gave me the confidence to imagine myself into the insubstantial beings I had begun with, to give them shape and personality and vividness – at least enough to make me wish to follow their lives. I wanted, of course, to tell a good story, but I also wanted to get things right. No matter how well a novel is received by readers or critics in general, if it does not ring true with those people who know from the inside the world it describes, it is in the final analysis an artistic failure.

As the novel had begun to expand geographically, I travelled a great deal around northern India by train. In the course of these trips I even visited the small town of Biswan where Shanti Uncle was born. But at the time I had no idea that I might write a book about him, and my notes are somewhat cursory.

I couldn't afford to travel abroad except when invited by literary festivals or conferences. This took me to England a couple of times in the first two years. I visited Shanti Uncle and Aunty Henny as often as I could while I was there.

Both of them were now in their late seventies. Uncle had retired from work at the age of seventy-seven. The surgery had ceased to be a surgery and had become a sort of storage room for old dental equipment, yellowing dental forms, defunct address books and ancient copies of the *Observer*. Shanti Uncle was not in good health. Colin, a cheerful and practical middle-aged man whom Uncle had known since his youth, when he had dated and later married one of Uncle's nurses, helped out in many ways.

Every year brought new crises. Uncle was regularly in hospital with complications arising from his heart condition; on one occasion he had fluid in his lungs. Whenever I said goodbye to him, I had the feeling that it might be the last time I would see him. I did not expect Aunty Henny would die before he did.

1.14

It is something of a tradition in our family that we spend the last evening before anyone goes on a foreign trip at home together, usually seated on and around my parents' bed. On the walls are photographs of the family, on the dressing-table are my mother's perfumes and bangles. We try to ignore the telephone.

I was about to leave for a trip to Los Angeles in April 1989, and we were having our ritual evening at home. But Mama had been trying for some time to get through to Shanti Uncle on the phone. Aunty Henny had not been well; we had been told that she had been in hospital for various tests, but that those for cancer had come out negative. We were therefore concerned rather than seriously worried. When, however, Mama did get through, I could see at once from her dismay that something was very wrong. When she handed the receiver to me, she said, 'Uncle says that Aunty is dying.'

I spoke to Uncle. He was in tears. He did not know if she was going to last even another couple of days. She was very weak; she was hardly eating anything. 'She is skin and bone, she has lost so much weight. You wouldn't recognise her. She refuses to meet her friends, even Mila . . .'

I said what words of comfort I could and begged Uncle to take care of himself. He sounded hopeless and frantic.

I had to get to London at once. I should have been allowed to exchange what was a regular round-the-world ticket, but was forced to buy a new one. By a most lucky chance I had almost exactly the air fare needed in the travellers' cheques that were to provide for my two-month trip. With barely enough left for a taxi at the other end (and none for a hotel), and knowing that I couldn't impose on Uncle at a time like this, I called an Indian friend from my Oxford days who was working in London and told him that, like it or not, I was going to stay with him. I am told that during that week I drank whisky from a teacup at breakfast.

I arrived at 18 Queens Road at about five in the afternoon. After a while, Uncle said it would be all right to see Aunty Henny. I entered the bedroom. She was lying, frail and exhausted, on the bed. She tried to smile, but it cost her both effort and pain; her mouth was bleeding a little, her lips and tongue were dark. 'Vicky, I feel so rotten,' she said. Aunty Henny so rarely complained about physical discomfort that she must have been in agony.

And, as Uncle said when we talked a little later, nature had thrown everything at her. She had myelofibrosis. Her bone marrow had ceased to produce blood cells and her immune system had collapsed. She was prey to a host of opportunistic infections and she had nothing to fight them with. It was too late for a bone marrow transplant or a splenectomy. Transfusions would have been no use; the new blood cells would only have been eaten up by the spleen. She had a stomach ulcer. Her liver and lymph systems were going. A heart valve was not functioning properly. Her kidneys were giving way, and uraemia (with its symptoms of mental confusion) was in danger of setting in; she was not taking in enough water for her kidneys to function properly; each sip of water or soup she drank cost her pain, for her mouth had been taken over by a fungal infection. One of her nurses fed her soup a spoonful at a time, hiding the bowl from view, as that would have seemed too daunting for her to tackle.

She, who was always so active, was bewildered by her weakness: often she could not even rise from her pillow to be sick. Her eyes were gummy and glazed, her breathing difficult, her voice very tired. 'I sleep now, Vicky,' she said.

Even her rest was unrestful; as Uncle told me, she would by turns feel too hot and too cold. She would wish to be covered, then throw off the sheets, exposing her body, and scratch it, though even slight pressure on her skin was painful.

After sleeping at my friend's house, I would come to 18 Queens Road to spend the day. Sometimes I would just sit in her room, or stand by the door. She found the energy to say, 'Vicky, you look so smart. Doesn't he, Shanti? He has had a haircut.' Aunty Henny, a stickler for appearing one's best, was pleased with my blue Tibetan pullover.

Sometimes I sat at the edge of the double bed and held her hand lightly. I looked around at the pink quilt, the small stone owl and hedgehog and frog that I had given them years ago, a photograph of Shanti Uncle as a young captain in the army, the bottles and tubes of medication scattered everywhere. The heart specialist had come in earlier; Aunty Henny had wanted to look good, and the day nurse had applied a bit of make-up and placed a vase of flowers on the shelf. Now Aunty Henny said: 'Vicky, take those flowers away. I cannot sleep in a room with flowers.'

If she had had any objections to my seeing her as she now was – her dentures out, her mouth almost black – she had relinquished them. Once, after about half an hour of silence, she said, 'Vicky, you have come to see your dying aunt all this way.' I protested that she was not dying. She did not deal with my response, but continued, 'Vicky, you are so sweet to come. I never knew you were so sweet. I love you, Vicky. I will never forget it, all my life.' I had never been addressed by Aunty Henny like this. I kissed her grey hair, so thin and brittle. 'Do you think I will get better?' she asked. 'Yes, Aunty Henny,' I replied.

Colin, busy as he was, had taken time off work and was staying in the house to help. Aunty Henny always asked whether he and I had eaten properly. To Cathy, the bright, cheerful daily help, or to Dr Murphy, the young GP who had become devoted to her, she still said, 'You look lovely.' One night she said to Uncle, 'Shanti, pillow.' He could barely make out her words, and asked, 'A pillow for you, Henny?' 'Pillow – nurse,' was her response. It was not for herself but for the night nurse that she had wanted it.

It was clear that any treatment was merely palliative. Dr Murphy spent a good part of her afternoon on the phone to various hospices to find out what they recommended by way of anaesthetic mouthwashes. The day nurse meanwhile advised a glycerine preparation with which to swab her mouth.

As it became evident that Aunty Henny was taking in no food and very little water, the question arose of whether to put her on a drip. But Aunty Henny had a phobia of needles and, besides, this would have involved hospitalisation.

She did not much care for the rather overpowering night nurse who, though she didn't smoke on the job, smelt of tobacco and became more and more edgy as the night went on. The nurse lectured Uncle about his attempt to cling on to Aunty Henny's life: 'If she wants to die, she *must* be allowed to.'

For days, Aunty Henny had asked Shanti Uncle to let her go. He begged her to fight on for his sake. The doctors too had prescribed a dose of morphine to help relieve her pain, but Uncle said to me, 'That would be killing her. I cannot do it. My problem is that I am her husband but I have too much medical knowledge. I know what the morphine will do. Her speech will become slurred; she will go into a coma. I will lose her. But she is in so much pain.'

His distress was painful to see. He halved the tablet, then decided not to give it at all, then said that it was she who wouldn't take it. Once he said she had kept it under her tongue and had spat it out the next day.

He kept associating the five-milligram tablet of morphine sulphate with euthanasia. Though Dr Murphy tried time and again to explain that this was a false connection, Uncle would not listen. He said that he had seen a television programme where a doctor, a renowned specialist, having put on a patient's favourite music and injected her with a large dose of morphine, had held her hand until he had felt an impulse of pressure from her, expressing her thanks.

'I don't think that is necessarily wrong, Uncle,' I said, 'but this is not that.'

'We'll wait till the specialist comes,' said Uncle. 'See, she doesn't want it. See, she's not in pain. Are you, Henny?' Aunty Henny shook her head, knowing that this was what he wanted to hear.

Dr Murphy said, 'Henny, you can't fool me.'

On Tuesday, Aunty Henny raised her voice: 'OK, Shanti, I have that nurse tonight because I've promised, but no more. It is too expensive, it costs a fortune . . . I don't want a night nurse. Never heard such nonsense in my life. I never wake up in the night . . .' She persuaded Shanti Uncle to discontinue the night nurse from Wednesday on.

When I arrived on Thursday morning, I found that the decision had been a disaster. Aunty Henny had been in terrible pain throughout the night, with nausea and vomiting. Colin had had to hold her. She had not been able to get to the bathroom. The sheets had had to be changed. She had nearly fallen over. Colin, with his strained knee and back, had done what he could, but he looked tense and exhausted. For Aunty Henny, who was so fastidious that a single piece of fluff on a carpet disturbed her, it must have been torment.

On Thursday, after that dreadful night, Uncle finally agreed Aunty Henny be given the morphine. On Friday morning, I had to do a couple of errands and got to the house later than usual, at noon. I had called at nine, but had been told there was no cause for alarm. Yet by the time I arrived Aunty Henny was dead.

1.15

Uncle said, 'I don't want to see the body. That is not Henny lying upstairs. That was not even Henny yesterday. Henny left me the night before that. She said, "Shanti, hold my hand." I held it. Then she said, "You have to help me, I am in so much pain." I said I would help her in any way. Her stomach hurt. "Would you like to suck something?" I asked. But her mouth was too sore, too full of pain. After a while she said, "Now you can let go," and I released her hand. That was when she said goodbye to me. The next morning her words were too slurred. It was not Henny any more.'

Aunty Henny died on Friday 7 April, 1989. I had to leave on Sunday, so Shanti Uncle brought the day of the funeral forward by a day, to Saturday. On the day of her death he was much calmer than before, and active with errands. Though I wanted to help him, he insisted, despite what he had earlier said, that I stay behind. 'Someone should be in the house with Aunty Henny.'

When it was beginning to get dark, the undertaker's van drew up. A discreet, pale and plump young man in a dark suit and waistcoat murmured, 'We'll take the lady outside now.'

A little later I went for a walk in the park with Uncle. 'I haven't left the house for weeks,' he said. 'Well, now's the time,' I said.

The weather had been bad; there had even been late snow. But now it was clear, if chilly, again. The garden within the park looked beautiful, with wallflowers and yellow tulips.

At night I returned to where I was staying. Colin kept Uncle up till 1.30 a.m. talking, so that he was so exhausted he went straight to sleep and did not think too long about Aunty Henny not being there next to him.

The following morning, we went to the Golders Green Crematorium. The largest chapel had been booked for the funeral, because at such short notice the others were unavailable. The coffin with its brass name-plaque, 'Henny Gerda Seth', was brought in and placed on a platform. Now Uncle wanted to see the body and asked that the coffin be opened. But the man in charge explained that once it had come in here, it couldn't, by law, be opened. 'All right,' said Uncle calmly.

Colin read the 23rd Psalm. Then Uncle spoke at rambling length. 'We come alone and we die alone . . . She always thought of others . . . "The friendly lady," they used to call her in the shops . . . She worked herself to the bone . . . All my life is here, you were everything to me, but I must go on.'

I said, 'Aunty Henny, I know that if you had allowed us to inform your friends, this chapel would have been full. But you didn't want it, so here are the three of us, Uncle, Colin and I. You used to call me your husband's nephew, but occasionally you slipped up.'

I found it difficult to go on at this point, and Uncle murmured something.

I continued: 'Thank you for giving us so much happiness and for giving Uncle so much happiness for so many years.'

Uncle, weeping, said his life was over.

'And for giving him the courage to go on even without you.'

The man in charge pressed a button, and a little claw emerged from the platform and pushed the coffin through the doors. Beyond that was nothing to be seen but a further set of doors.

1.16

We had always assumed Uncle would die first. When Aunty Henny died, we did not know how long he would be able to carry on. It was not just that, given his arm, he needed help with many things; help he could, after a fashion, obtain. It was that he was shattered and overcome by her loss. He had loved her for over five decades and they had been married for almost four. When he said that he understood her words almost before she said them, he had used the phrase, 'We were so integrated.' Now half of this integral being had been prised away.

People made sure he was not alone. Cathy came every weekday to cook a meal for him. Judy, his physiotherapist, came once a week. His friends in London spoke to him often. His family came over as regularly as they could afford to, knowing that the hardest time would begin a few months after Henny's death, when most people would turn back to their own lives. Colin took over many of the hassles of his life and kept a watchful eye on him, as did his nephew Arun, a doctor who lived in Toronto. Some of his old German and Swiss friends came over to stay each year.

Two months after Aunty Henny died, Mama went to England to be with him. She brought back a card for me from Shanti Uncle. (The references to Leila, Premo and Aradhana are, respectively, to my mother, father and sister.)

Dear Vicky,

First of all I would like to wish you a very happy and above all a healthy birthday. I enjoy the company of Leila but feel guilty to deprive you of her company. It is a great pity that you are not here.

I will be going to Toronto for a fortnight, with some reservation, as I have never gone alone. I hope Aradhana will arrange a nice party for you with all her pretty young friends.

Do let me know if I can be of any help to you. This is my first letter that I have written since Henny's death.

Please convey my love to Premo and Aradhana.

    With fondest love,
      Yours affly,
        Uncle Shanti

P.S. I hope you have settled down to writing.

My brother Shantum was not mentioned in the letter because he was in England at the time. Aradhana was going to get married within a year to Peter Launsky-Tieffenthal, a young Austrian diplomat. When they visited London, Shanti Uncle got on very well with him; they spoke in German together.

Every year after Aunty Henny's death, Mama tried to come to London for a month or so, staying with or as close as possible to Shanti Uncle and spending most of her time with him. So did Michi Mama, my eldest maternal uncle. I, who had been visiting England for longer periods, mainly in connection with my books, often went to see Shanti Uncle, occasionally bringing my own friends to introduce them. Shantum brought over his fiancée Gitu. But though Uncle was happy to see us, and liked company, his loneliness was patent and deep and seemingly incurable.

His vulnerability and nervousness increased. When Mama and Papa stayed with him, they occasionally went to a play or a movie or to visit friends. This upset him greatly. Even when they went out during the day, he would become tremulous if they did not return within minutes of the time agreed. One afternoon, Papa had to go to the shopping centre in Brent Cross to get a glass refill for a thermos flask; he went to six shops before he found one. He had said he would be back by six o'clock, but returned at 6.45. When he rang the doorbell of 18 Queens Road, he found Uncle prostrate with anxiety. He had telephoned the shopping manager of Brent Cross, he had contacted the police, and he had finally become so sick with worry that he was lying on the couch, hyperventilating. When Papa said that he was in his sixties and knew his way about, Uncle said that he could have been mugged. When Papa responded that he had not been on his own and, anyway, could take care of himself, Uncle insisted that he did not know what England was like now.

As time passed, he watched more and more television, saying goodnight to the newsreaders when they signed off. The future held no promise and there was no one whom he could talk to about the past. He was ill and weak and he had no work to do.

All of us in the family were saddened by Aunty Henny's death, but apart from me, who knew and loved her, no one really grieved for her; it was for Uncle that they were so deeply concerned. But I was sad for myself as well. I missed Aunty Henny, particularly whenever I returned to Queens Road – and especially in the kitchen, where, while doing the washing-up, we had held our most companionable conversations. Every time I phoned, I missed her voice, clear and high, announcing, 'Hendon six double three oh.' I missed her friendship and her good sense and 'optimismus'. In the face of her strong reluctance to be inducted into the family, I felt that I had earned the right to see her as part of it.

London for me, throughout my school and even university years, had basically meant 18 Queens Road. After my Indian novel, *A Suitable Boy*, was published, I realised that for a while I could not bring myself to write another book set in India. I began to spend more time in London – staying with friends or in rented flats – and got to know the city in its own right. I had a presentiment that my next book would be set in London. I visited Uncle often, but never thought of asking him to talk at any length about his early life.

1.17

In summer 1994, the family came to England, again to visit Shanti Uncle, but also because an opera commissioned by the English National Opera, *Arion and the Dolphin*, whose composer was Alec Roth and whose libretto I had written, was to be performed in Plymouth. Afterwards, the family drove to Oxford, where we had decided to celebrate my birthday. The weather was glorious, the roads were free, and we were happy to be together. I had invited Uncle to come to see the opera, but Plymouth was too far away from London; he was now eighty-five years old and very frail. We talked about him in the car, and Mama said, turning to me, 'You don't know what exactly to write about next. Why don't you write about him?'

My first reaction was not eager. 'I don't know if I want to write about someone so close to me,' I said. 'And even if I thought it was a good idea, I don't think Uncle would agree to it.'

'Why not ask him?' said Mama. 'You won't know what he thinks unless you do.'

'Well, as I said, I'm not convinced I want to write about him at all,' I replied. 'And I would feel uncomfortable demanding his time for interviews when he's often so tired. Why don't you ask him? It would be less awkward for him to say no to you.'

'I can't ask him if you don't know whether you'll interview him,' replied Mama. 'What if he agreed and then you decided against it? He'd be very disappointed.'

We discussed the subject for a while, and during the next few days I mulled it over. Uncle had had an interesting life, and when he died his story would die with him. If I were to explore it, it would have to be soon, while he still had a little energy and was clear in his mind. I asked Mama to put the question to him. She told me a few days later that she'd spoken to him, and that he had been pleased – in fact, enthusiastic.

I am convinced that one of the reasons Mama suggested I interview Uncle was to give him some project to participate in. I still thought it might be an imposition, but it did not turn out to be so. Sometimes we talked for the whole day. When he spoke of his youth in India or his student days in Germany or about the war, he seemed to be re-energised. But talking about Aunty Henny – which was something I could not avoid, and indeed something that he turned to whenever he could – sank him again into a sense of his own loss.

Any book to emerge from this process was clearly going to centre on Uncle. About Aunty Henny my information would of necessity be second-hand. I could not interview her. Even if she had been alive, the circumstances of her early life would have made me very reluctant to do so. I had no idea that something would happen that would change this balance completely.

1.18

I interviewed Uncle many times, in lengthy sessions that I thought might prove to be exhausting for him. They proved to be more so for me, as I tried to take down at high speed on my laptop the spate of memories, clear for him but confusing for me, that I had released. Uncle's attention span varied, his alertness sometimes dissipated, he often went off into maddening digressions or philosophical disquisitions, he sometimes wept when he remembered Aunty Henny. But he was happy talking about his past life when the present seemed so empty. I was glad that I had undertaken the project.

I carried out eleven longish interviews over five months, between June and October 1994. In retrospect, I wish I had husbanded them out over two years or more, but there was a momentum to them and, besides, I felt that I was competing with time. Even over those few months, I sensed that Uncle had grown physically weaker.

Though I had begun by thinking of the interviews as a duty to be performed by me in my capacity as a sort of family archivist, I soon began to look forward to them. Occasionally, I'd make a note, not just of the interview itself but of the atmosphere surrounding it. My last interview, in late October, for example, had been arranged for about ten in the morning. I went for an early swim in the Serpentine, admired the swans in the drizzle, got to Uncle's by the 113 bus, and rang the bell. There was no response. I noticed the bottle of milk by the door, and the mail protruding from the slot. Had Uncle gone for a walk? – or could he not hear the bell? – or was he, most atypically, not yet awake? – or was he ill? I walked to the phone box a few hundred yards away on the Hendon Park side of the road. The chestnut leaves were wet underfoot.

It took Uncle a little while to get to the phone, and he sounded groggy. He was still upstairs, and hadn't heard the bell. 'Darling, I have had a terrible night,' he said. 'I got to sleep at six o'clock in the morning. You know those Swiss friends of mine were leaving – the Dolders – and I had too much to eat and too much to drink – Bombay mix – and peanuts – and whisky – my legs won't carry me – and I have just come back from the bathroom—'

'Uncle, you should be ashamed of yourself.'

'I am – I am worse than a hooligan.'

When I got back to the house, I noticed his physiotherapist, Judy, getting out of her car, which she had parked next to the red pillar-box. We greeted each other, and I picked up the milk. Uncle opened the door in his pyjamas and frayed, mouse-coloured dressing-gown. He looked rather guilty and pleased with himself.

He leafed through the letters. 'Here, darling, here's a letter for you.'

'But this is addressed to V. K. Seth, to Tuttu Mama.'

'Yes, yes,' said Uncle, looking at it again. 'Why did I give it to you?' He put it in the pocket of his dressing-gown. 'And I had more Bombay mix after they were gone,' he added happily, continuing our earlier conversation.

'That's very bad for you,' said Judy. 'All that fat.'

'But very difficult to stop,' said Uncle. 'Then I came down and gave myself medicines . . . sodium bicarbonate . . . powerful antacids . . . valium . . . Another person wouldn't be alive. Now darling, I forgot Judy was coming today. I'm so sorry. You must eat breakfast with me later. Here is the milk, the—'

'Uncle, there's a smell in the fridge.'

'Yes, they came and brought all sorts of food, my friends . . . they put it anywhere . . .'

'Uncle, go and have your treatment. I'm fine. I'll help myself.'

After his physiotherapy, Uncle had a bath and got ready. We began the interview and I was there the whole day. This was the eleventh and final interview, and the questions covered everything that had gone before – filling up gaps, clearing up zones of uncertainty, trying to resolve contradictory dates, striking out occasionally into new areas. We touched on his grandfather's horoscope and the fruit in the orchard in Bhagwanpur, on his first experience of women, on the syllabus he had had to follow in Berlin, on the difference between a dressing and a filling, on various campaign medals, on the change in the character of Queens Road, on Henny's visit to Germany a decade before her death.

I had visited Uncle regularly before and I would do so again after, but we had now covered all that I thought could be covered in our concentrated interviews, and I was sorry that they were over.

As the years passed, Uncle became physically more incapable; then his mind too began to fail. In 1998, a few months before his ninetieth birthday, he died.

I write about all this later, but now I will start at the other end of his life.

PART
TWO

2.1

Shanti Behari Seth was born on the eighth day of the eighth month of the eighth year of the twentieth century. His birthplace was the small town of Biswan in the United Provinces of Agra and Oudh in northern India.

His mother wanted to name him Vipat Behari, the bringer of misfortune, but her brother prevailed upon her to name him Shanti Behari, the bringer of peace. Shanti's father had died a few months earlier within three days of catching the plague, which was rife in those days. His widow was pregnant with their eighth child, her fourth son.

Since Shanti's mother was a widow before he was born, he never saw her dressed in anything but white. She loved him and spoiled him, but she had an impractical nature, which her grief enhanced. His eldest sister Hirabehn, who was about fifteen years older than him, took him in hand.

So too, from time to time, did his grandfather, a landowner who at one time owned several villages, in one of which, Bhagwanpur, a few miles from Biswan, he lived. He was not a man of great education, but was practical and canny. He protected his house from dacoits by hiring their chief as his watchman. His wife was enraged, but in the perennial raids that took place in the area, their house remained untouched. In the informal settlement of village disputes, especially potentially dangerous communal disputes, he appointed a Muslim and a Hindu assessor, with himself as a sort of chairman. He could not speak a word of English, the language of advancement under the Empire, but he educated his two elder sons to be able to get by in it. One became an accountant, the other a district and sessions judge. The youngest of his three sons was not expected to study but to stay at home to mind his father's estate. This son, Shanti's father, remained in the little town of Biswan and had seven children by the time he died at the age of thirty-four. (An appendix covers the various members of Shanti's family referred to in this book.)

The family house in Biswan seemed large to Shanti when he was a child. It was made of brick and ornamented in front with a cannon. It was a joint-family house, with the downstairs kitchen and store-rooms and bathroom used in common, and the upstairs divided in three among the families of the accountant, the judge and Shanti's late father. But it was mainly lived in by the women of the family, for the judge himself lived in Sitapur and the accountant in Lucknow. It may be that the physical absence of the fathers of his cousins made the death of Shanti's own father less of a burden for him. At any rate, when I talked to him, he did not once say that he wished he had known or seen his father.

Shanti's two eldest brothers, Raj and Achal, were often away from Biswan living with relations and pursuing their studies. Raj was to become an engineer and Achal a doctor. The third brother, Brahma, and Shanti remained in Biswan and had a lively childhood with the standard entertainments.

When I was in Biswan, a snake-charmer came to our house. He showed us the usual tricks, charming the snake while playing the *been*, but there was something hidden in one of his baskets, and he didn't show me what it was. I told him I wanted to see it. He said he had caught a very young cobra, not yet trained and quite dangerous. I wanted to see it fight his mongoose. I remember the fight, a gory affair. The mongoose knew it was serious, he struck just like lightning, you could hardly observe him, he would shake the snake a few times and leave it. In the end, there was a whole lot of blood, but the snake-charmer began to cry, saying that his most precious snake that had not even been trained would die, and even his mongoose was severely hurt. I was young and of course it did not matter to me. But I did notice that mongoose and snake are born enemies. The snake-charmer wanted some more money, I think.

Shanti's eldest sister Hirabehn was, he said, the greatest influence in his life.

Hirabehn had been widowed at an early age, a few years after her marriage to an engineer. She had had a daughter, who died at the age of three. Hirabehn then devoted herself to a girls' school which she, in conjunction with other relatives, had established in Biswan. She loved Shanti but had his measure. When he did something seriously wrong, she knew what hurt him most: she forbade him from playing with his friends. Once when Brahma, who had a stomach ache, was let off school, Shanti feigned one too. Hirabehn showed sympathy and threatened castor oil, and Shanti quickly claimed to have improved.

Hirabehn would give him a little pocket money every day. He was not, however, allowed to buy kites, as that sort of activity was considered vulgar and not to be indulged in by the educated classes. Shanti bought a kite from time to time, tore a bit off the corner, and claimed he'd found it. He would chase away the monkeys from the roof and fly his repaired kite in battles with his friends. The strings were glazed with glass powder to cut the strings of rival kites and bring them down.

On the whole his sister was indulgent, but one day, for unusually unruly misbehaviour (possibly for throwing a stone at a little girl), she locked him up in the store-room. Here were kept the household grain and the delicious pickles his mother made. It was dark and cold, and Shanti hated it. He decided to teach his disciplinarian sister a lesson. There was a hefty stick lying nearby. He smashed one or two large earthenware vats and made a huge commotion, and from that day on, whenever it was necessary, she locked him up in other rooms.

One memory of childhood, Shanti's first experience of death, was vivid to him almost eighty years later.

It was my cousin Omvati's baby. I could see the child was only about six months old; her eyes were turned up; she cried. I had a strange feeling; it was clear that something was badly wrong. Children of that age were not burned, but buried. I will never forget it. I was only about eight or so. Omvati's husband took the corpse and Brahma and I went with him and somebody came with a spade and there was a pond and near the pond she was buried.

2.2

The fact that Shanti's birth came so shortly after his father's death may have been one reason his grandfather loved him so greatly. He let him run about in his treasured orchard, which contained fruit trees from different parts of India: loquats, oranges, bananas, mangoes, lichis, jamuns, phalsas and red plums.

After his wife died, my grandfather kept a mistress. After his first mistress died, he kept another. One day, when I was about eight or nine years old, I climbed up a jamun tree in the orchard. My grandfather's mistress was sitting beneath the tree. A branch broke and fell on her head. Blood poured out of her skull. I thought my grandfather would give me a good hiding. But he just said the equivalent of *sunt pueri pueri* [Boys will be boys] and let me go. I was very ashamed of myself. I can see it all in front of me. They charred some silk over the wound to stop the bleeding.

Needless to say, when my grandpa invited me to visit him, I would take two or three schoolfriends, and we would climb the trees, collect a whole lot of ripe fruit and shake down a whole lot of unripe fruit. 'You go home with your locusts,' my grandfather used to say. He pretended to be annoyed with me and I used to be annoyed with him and say that I would never come back, but the next day he would send his bullock-cart again to fetch me.

Occasionally, Shanti's grandfather would go to a fair to buy cattle, and Shanti was allowed to go on the bullock-cart with him for the journey and sleep in the cart at night.

Once, when Shanti was four or five years old, his grandfather's brother, who had given up the world and become a *sannyasi*, came to the village in a red robe. That was the only time Shanti was to see him. He was old and frail, and two men carried him in a palanquin. He told Shanti that he should discard his family at fifty, so that when he died he would not be attached to anybody.

The shaping of life in anticipation of death also played a part in his grandfather's thoughts.

I remember very well, when I was eleven years old, my grandfather wanted me to be confirmed or undergo the *janeu* ceremony, for which I had to go to Kanauj all on my own. This must have been a *Heimatsort* – how do you say it in Hindi? [Shanti Uncle meant a sort of 'hometown' for members of his sub-caste, to which they would return for certain rituals] – I couldn't understand why my grandpa was so insistent. But when a person dies, the last rites can only be performed by someone who has undergone that ceremony and been invested with the sacred thread. Shortly afterwards, when he died, I had to carry out these rites. My grandfather wanted me to be the sole heir to his fortune. My accountant uncle said that this was not fair, but in his generosity he suggested, 'Don't let your sons inherit if you wish, let your grandsons inherit in equal parts.' Since he and the judge uncle only had one son each, and there were four of us brothers, we got four-sixths of my grandfather's property when he died.

After his grandfather's death, Shanti's eldest brother Raj, now twenty-four years old and working as a railway engineer for the British, took over the role of protector of the family. He decided that Shanti's education was his responsibility, and he supported him with love and money and guidance for as long as he lived. Shanti grew to love his brother as one would love a father; indeed, he hero-worshipped him.

This was my mother's father, my own grandfather, who died ten years before I was born.

2.3

In 1899, Shanti's uncle, the judge Kunj Behari Seth, published a chronicle in Urdu entitled *History of the Seth Family of Biswan.* Seven years later, in March 1906, he published in English a book entitled *Seths of Biswan.* This gives one a lively and somewhat whimsical picture of Shanti's family – that is, my own maternal family – and its background, economic, social and personal. (My surname is Seth because my mother happened to marry another, unrelated, Seth.)

The narrative, which includes hundreds of entries, concentrates almost entirely on the male line of descent. Shanti's great-grandfather was an amiable spendthrift who engaged in the cloth trade and in moneylending. The family archivist records:

> The bad custom of expending beyond one's means on occasions of marriages ruinously exhausted his resources and his purse was almost emptied as he had to marry three daughters.
>
> He was fond of taming birds.
>
> I remember full well of his death-bed. He was not delirious in the least. On the night he was to die he walked on his own legs to sit down at his evening meal. The end came shortly after midnight on Bhadaon Badi 4th, Samvat 1931, corresponding to 31st August 1874. It was very peaceful. He was quite conscious and did speak few moments before the breathing ceased.

This expended purse was to some extent refilled by Shanti's grandfather. Of him his son writes:

> ... During his boyhood he was taught Persian which he did not learn beyond getting by heart some couplets of Sheikh Sadi ... He did not

inherit any large estate of his father; but he was astute enough to manage his affairs in such a way as to turn to profit every business which he started. It may fairly be said that as a businessman he has more blood of his grandfather . . . He has acquired by purchase the entire village Bhagwanpur, which is 1½ miles south-west of Biswan. The revenue of this village, under the current settlement, is Rs. 250 [per annum].

The judge now comes to his own generation and writes in warm terms about his elder brother, the accountant. The entry illustrates both the closeness of family ties and the importance of education among the Seths.

At the age of fifteen he joined the district School at Sitapur where he read up to the Entrance class. In his first attempt he remained unsuccessful at the Entrance examination. He tried a second year but, having been suddenly taken very ill just on the eve of the examination, he could not go up. Thus he gave up his studies and entered the Railway service as a clerk. I must pause here to say, rather remember with gratitude, that his failure was not only something, but a great thing in the accomplishment of a great undertaking. For it impressed on his mind the value of education, and he did not allow the grass to grow under his feet till he gave me a high education, and at his great self-sacrifice, and thus recompensed to a large extent his own failure in the examination. Not only this, the germ of the love of education took a deep root in him, so much so that he has been the pioneer of female education in the Seth family. Notwithstanding all sorts of difficulties in his way he gave creditable Sanskrit education to his eldest daughter. Now his love for reform and female education is centred in his second daughter, Vidyavati, who is yet unmarried and has recently been admitted into the 8th class of the Isabella Thoburn High School, Lucknow. She has already received a fair Sanskrit education by private tuition. His idea is noble, inasmuch as he desires to start a Girls' School through her as soon as she completes her education. His third daughter (Omvati) is reading in the second class of the abovenamed school. . . . He is not only a staunch Arya Samaji [member of the Arya

63

Samaj, a reformed Hindu religious body] in the observance of the Vedic rites, but is a practical reformer to an extent that the family may well take a pride in him. It is unfortunate that most of the well-to-do and educated members of the Seth family have not yet been able to grasp the spirit of his reforms and have consequently failed to hold out the support he deserves. However, the day is not far distant when those who threw obstacles in his way and persecuted him will repent at their action and their posterity will revere him with gratitude.

. . . By his own efforts and private study he rose from a clerk to a third grade accountant.

Twice he underwent operation for the piles and once for hydrocele . . .

The obstructionists referred to were the Seths of Kotra, a much grander branch of the clan, who lived in a vast mansion in a neighbouring village. When Shanti's cousin Vidyavati became the first woman in the community to gain a B.A., the Seths of Kotra decided, in response to such blatant immorality, to boycott the Seths of Biswan and not invite them to their weddings and festivals. This ostracism could not have lasted more than a few years, however, because Shanti recalled sitting on his mother's lap at a huge feast (complete with dancing girls) put on by the Kotra household one summer. He remembered the huge block of ice they bought for the occasion, chunks of which floated in the drinks. Shanti was six years old at the time, and he crunched it and cracked it again and again. It was a fascinating substance, an astonishing novelty.

When the judge turns to the second brother of the three, he writes:

Kunj Behari Seth – It is not without diffidence that I have attempted to write these lines which are rather an autobiography. Insignificant as my life is, I would have never ventured to write it had it not been in fulfilment of the duty as a member of the family whose history I have written.

After detailing his academic progress (including the fact that he came first in the whole of the United Provinces in the B.A. examination in Philosophy set and examined under the aegis of Calcutta University in 1886) and his judicial progress (he was appointed Subordinate Judge, 3rd Grade, in 1903), he describes the education of his children and once again touches on what seems to be a family malady:

> In November 1899 I had to undergo an operation for the piles from which I had suffered long. The operation was so skilfully performed by Doctor H. D. Pant that the success was marvellous.

The entry ends on a wistful note. He lists his living children, then adds:

> Two more children were born to me, to wit, a son who lived for about a fortnight and a girl, Sobhagyavati, who died on 1st July 1903 whilst she was about to complete her fourth year of age. She was a very intelligent child.

The third brother, Shanti's father, gets short shrift:

> Manorath Prasad Seth – Born on Friday, Baisakh Sadi 9th, Samvat 1925, corresponding to 1st May, 1868, he received very little education as our father wanted him to stay at home instead of receiving English education, which was then considered as a mode of earning a living abroad. He entered into the trade of selling metal vessels . . . He is literate in Urdu and Nagri Bhasha [Hindi]. He has got a virtuous and sympathetic heart. He is a follower of the Vedic religion and is ready to aid his brothers in carrying out all reforms. He is joint with his brothers to whom he is always submissive.

The rest of the entry lists Manorath Prasad's children and their dates of birth. Seven are listed; one is not. That child was Shanti, who emerged into the world two years after the book.

2.4

There are no separate entries for women in *Seths of Biswan*, but one of the results of the accountant's bent for reform and his youngest brother's submissiveness was that all Shanti's sisters were well educated, at least in Sanskrit. One sister, Mangla, married an eccentric polymath with degrees in science and literature. On his mother's side too, there was a tradition of learning. Her youngest brother, who had suggested the name Shanti to her, was a scholarly man, well versed in Sanskrit, Prakrit and Pali, and with a deep knowledge of Buddhism. Shanti recalled how, in the archaeological museum at Sarnath near Banaras, he kept him spellbound by explaining the significance of every gesture of the statues of the Buddha. This uncle wrote a number of essays in Sanskrit but never published them. He earned his living by going to various rajas and maharajas and administering their estates, but often, when he went off for a couple of weeks' leave, he didn't return for months.

He once told me, 'If you come first in your class in Biswan, I will give you my watch, which is on a chain in my waistcoat pocket.' Previously, I used to be very playful and passed my exams without difficulty, but this time I made a real effort to study and did come first, not only overall, but in every subject. My poor uncle, at his first step into the house, I said, 'What about my watch?' My mother was very annoyed that instead of greeting him I had asked him for a present. She said that an imitation watch was good enough for me. But I wouldn't let it go at that and worried my poor uncle until he bought me a watch with a chain. I must have been nine or ten years old. You should never make a child a promise that you cannot or don't intend to keep. Needless to say, that watch didn't last very long, as I tried to open it to find out how it ticked.

Curious and intelligent about the working of things, Shanti was nevertheless protected from the effects of the world around. The

Great War of 1914–18 began when he was six years old, and though I asked him about it, he had no memory of it except for some anti-German propaganda and the devastating influenza epidemic that followed the war. Although large numbers of Indian and other non-European troops, including Americans, fought in it, and though it had an influence on the growing strength of nationalist feeling in India and elsewhere, the First World War did not fully deserve this subsequently conferred name, fought as it was mainly in Europe.

After Shanti had studied till the sixth class at the Jai Dayal Seth School in Biswan, which had been founded by a relative in 1895, it was decided to send him elsewhere for a better education, one that gave more weight to English and the sciences. First he was sent to the Jubilee School in Lucknow, which he hated, and where he failed his exams. His brother Raj then sent him to be a boarder at the Theosophical School in Banaras (alternatively spelt Benares or Varanasi). Shanti enjoyed the open atmosphere here and the method of teaching, which emphasised independent thought rather than learning by rote. He was at the school for about five years, leaving at sixteen when he was head boy. Even here, though, he displayed a talent for getting into trouble.

There was a film being shown in instalments at night, *Tarzan of the Apes*, between 10.30 and 4. We decided to leave our bicycles outside the school gates, put pillows in our beds, creep out, see the film and come back. But in the school there was a bedwetting rich boy, who was unhappy because he was not allowed servants and had to have the same pocket money as everyone else. 'You put him right,' a master had said to me. So I would take him in winter, and make him wash his sheet and have a cold shower. It worked. But when we broke bounds he sneaked on us, and when we came back from the film, I was ashamed: the teacher was standing there. The punishment was that I couldn't go to the cinema for three months. Nor to my brother Achal's place, which was just a few steps away from the school.

This was a blow. Though Shanti greatly admired his eldest brother Raj, his greatest love and attachment at the time was to Achal, his second brother, ten years his senior, whom he used to 'more or less shadow about'. When Achal was a student at medical college in Lucknow, Shanti, who knew that expenses were high, would collect all the money he got for Divali, Holi, Dussehra and his birthday and give it to him, and Achal for his part never came empty-handed when he visited Shanti. Achal had wanted to be a doctor from the age of six, and when he qualified, he began to practise in Banaras. He became a very successful doctor, and a caring one. When poor patients came to him, he gave them free treatment, free medicine, and some money to help them keep to the diet he had prescribed.

Shanti passed the school-leaving exam, the Matric, obtaining a first class, for which he was given a scholarship of ten rupees a month. He told his brother Raj, who was supporting him, to deduct this from his stipend, but Raj told him he had deserved it and should use it to give himself a good time.

2.5

When I talked to Shanti Uncle about his eldest brother Raj and his sister-in-law Chanda, what he had to say had a particular resonance for me.

Chanda Seth, my maternal grandmother, whom I used to call Amma, was the only grandparent I have known. Mrs Rupa Mehra, the presiding character in my novel *A Suitable Boy*, is based on her. Published a few years after her death, it is dedicated not only to my parents but also to her memory. As for my mythic grandfather, the very mention of whom would make my grandmother's nose redden and her eyes fill with tears ('turning on the waterworks' in the acerbic view of her eldest son Michi), any information about him would add a few tesserae to the image that I had been piecing together for many years.

The picture that emerges from Shanti Uncle's description of him is of an intelligent, practical, upright, quick-tempered, impatient, affectionate man who was something of a workaholic. He was an executive engineer on the Railways and had a little silver disc which permitted him to board any train and even sit in the engine compartment. He travelled in a special saloon car, complete with lounge, dining-room, bedroom and servants' quarters. His job was to design, build and inspect railway systems, including bridges and viaducts.

One summer, Shanti accompanied Raj to Goona in the Central Provinces where he was going to build a railway – in the wilderness, as Shanti put it.

We were having a siesta. It was dark in the room and the ceiling fan was on. All of a sudden we heard the hiss of a snake. Even in the darkness he got out of his bed and went to the door to get his rifle to kill it. But mind you, snakes don't normally attack people unless they are trodden on or threatened or when they are copulating. They don't want to be disturbed. Or anyone else, for that matter. See, my old memory is good, my new memory – well, I don't even know if I've put my watch on or not.

My brother was a big game hunter. Once, when I was with him, he saw a calf that had been killed by a large animal; it must have been a tiger or panther, though the local people told him it was a lion, a maneless lion. These animals sometimes hide their prey to continue eating it afterwards. When my brother heard this, he had a machan constructed in the nearby trees. He took his guns up, as well as a subordinate, but I persuaded him to take me up as well. He warned me it would be boring: no talking, silent breathing, a fixed position. I was with him for an hour and it felt like eternity. Unfortunately, there was thunder and lightning, and the big cat never came to claim its kill.

He had lots of fads. At one time, when he was ill, our brother Achal came to look after him and travelled with us in a train to Lucknow. Raj wanted to have all the windows closed. Chanda Bhabhi and I used to go into the bathroom to get some fresh air. During his illness, he told Achal Bhaiyya that he wanted to eat sardines, which were not very good for him, very fatty and, in his condition, contraindicated, but he wouldn't listen. Luckily, there were no bad sequelae. In certain things he had his own ideas.

He was very generous, and I was dependent on him. When I was at school I didn't have any money for clothes and my shoes were in poor condition. He took me to a very good shop to buy a new pair of boots. We always used to have breakfast together before he went to work and he used to ask me questions about Geography, History and other subjects. I had to keep myself alert.

Raj's wife, Chanda, was thirteen years younger than her husband, and only two years older than Shanti. They got on tremendously well, and she protected him from his brother's temper. Raj had told Shanti not to use anything belonging to the office, but Shanti borrowed the office bicycle to learn how to ride. After a few falls he thought he had got the hang of it. He even took his seven-year-old nephew, who was staying with them, for a pillion ride. They landed in a ditch, bruised, with the bicycle bent and damaged. Afraid that he was in for a ticking-off and quite possibly a hiding, Shanti told his sister-in-law. She asked the cook to get the cycle repaired, and Shanti pretended they'd injured themselves falling into a ditch while out walking. On another occasion, he sat on the new table that had been made specially for Chanda's sewing-machine, and broke it. She had that repaired as well, and her husband never learned of it.

Chanda was often lonely because Raj was either in the office working or away on assignment somewhere. She suggested that Shanti stay with them permanently and go to a good local school. Shanti tried the local school but didn't like it. Though he felt ungrateful and unhelpful to his sister-in-law, he asked to be sent back to the Theosophical School in Banaras.

Much of the family had moved out of Biswan to Banaras, so Shanti did not often go back to his hometown. During his summer holidays, he accompanied Raj and Chanda to various hill stations such as Darjeeling and Mussourie. For one trip, to Kashmir, when

Shanti was sixteen, they were accompanied by Chanda's father, brother and sister. They stayed on a houseboat on a lake near Srinagar for a while, then trekked to the snows beyond Gulmarg. Two incidents stuck in Shanti's mind from this holiday; one illustrates his persistence or perhaps obstinacy, the other his superstitiousness or perhaps openmindedness.

In Kashmir, we always used to get ponies. Raj told us not to use the pony called Bulbul because he was very wild. After he had left, Chanda's brother Dammu and I thought it would be a good idea to see what Bulbul did. We tossed, and Dammu won, but after a few minutes he returned, saying, 'I don't feel much like carrying on. You go, Shanti.' Hardly was I in the saddle than the pony, who could tell that I was quite small and not a good rider at all, wanted to throw me, as that is what he had done to Dammu. I was determined not to let him, but before I could do anything, he ran off with me clinging to his neck, and after a little distance he sidetracked and went into an ice-cold stream. But I clung on, thinking, If I feel cold, so must he. It was just willpower. On the way back, he was so naughty, I tell you, he wanted to push me into a tree. I am going to beat this pony, I decided. I took a branch from the tree. I beat him good and thorough, I don't know how I got the courage. After that, he was so good you couldn't believe it was the same animal.

What I remember most often now about that holiday is one particular incident in Srinagar. My brother had a friend who was in charge of all the prisons in Kashmir and who had made a study of palmistry. He used to make plaster casts of criminals' hands after getting to know their history. I asked him to look at my hands, and he said: 'You will go abroad, but not by a normal route, and you will not succeed at what you intend to do, and you will go to a war, and you will get an injury in the head, and after the war India will become independent.' Now I had completely forgotten about this incident until twenty years later when I was in hospital in Roehampton, and I thought about how five of his six predictions had already come to pass. The army consultant in Harley Street, Brigadier Bristow, had just said to me about my phantom hand, which I imagined still existed, and which was causing me terrible pain, 'My boy, your injury is not only in the hand but also in the mind.' Curious and amazing. And less than three years after that, in 1947, India did become free.

2.6

Shanti spent the next five years of his life for the most part in Banaras, studying Physics and Chemistry at the Benares Hindu University. The first two years he studied for the Intermediate Examinations, and the last two years for his B.Sc. Honours, but these two periods hardly figured in his memories.

They sandwich, however, an uncertified year that he remembered well and referred to again and again. Raj had had a brilliant career at the Roorkee College of Engineering and had won a gold medal for excellence; and Shanti wanted, like the brother he worshipped, to join the college and qualify and work as an engineer. But though he had won a local painting prize (for his depiction of a blacksmith in a forest – the sort of theme that appealed to the British, according to him), he was hopeless at drawing, one of the compulsory subjects for the entrance examination.

Raj advised him to take a year off from his studies to concentrate on drawing. But after a year, he was still so poor at the subject that when he went to Roorkee to take the exam, he couldn't even complete all the questions. Certain that he had failed in this very competitive examination, he was standing on a bridge over the Roorkee Canal, about to throw himself in, when a man who had been sent all the way to Roorkee by his brother found him and comforted him and brought him home.

Shanti had indeed not passed. Later, Raj told him that if he still wanted to become an engineer, he would get in touch with an acquaintance of his at the Skoda works in Czechoslovakia, who would be able to get him a job there that would allow him to attend engineering classes in the evening. But this did not appeal to Shanti.

In the end, Raj said, 'In our family we have an engineer, an accountant, a judge and a doctor, but no dentist. Why don't you train to do that?' Shanti wasn't at all keen on the profession, but out of desperation about his uncertain future, he agreed. He applied to universities in Paris and Berlin, and since he had by then passed his B.Sc. examinations, was offered places at both. He did not apply to universities in England because dental studies there were too expensive. Raj and Chanda, who had a growing family – they already had three children and were soon to have a fourth – would not have been able to support him in such studies there.

2.7

So in the summer of 1931 Shanti went abroad, but, as the palmist had predicted, not by the normal sea route via Aden and the Suez Canal. Instead, he went from Banaras to Karachi by train, then to Basra by boat, to Baghdad by train, across the desert to Rutba Wells and Haifa in a car escorted by British soldiers to prevent Bedouin attack; to Athens and Marseilles on a heavily over-crowded boat, and thence, by train, with a young American friend he had met on the boat and who claimed to speak French, to Paris, one of Shanti's two possible venues for study.

But his sojourn in France was short. In Marseilles, his friend ordered a meal which turned out to consist of boiled eggs, omelettes and tomatoes and for which they were greatly over-charged. In Paris, they bought tickets for the Folies Bergère but Shanti was pickpocketed and his keys were stolen. By the time he had persuaded the hotel manager to let him into his room and had broken into his trunk with a hammer to get to his clothes – since it was Saturday, no locksmith was available – he had missed the show. He was thoroughly fed up. Out on the street, a girl accosted him and, when he told her to go away, asked him, in a mixture of

English and French, if he was impotent. According to Shanti, 'The whole thing was so disgusting that I decided against France and studying in Paris, and in fact didn't want to stay there another day.'

He caught the boat from Calais to Dover and the train to Victoria, but there was no sign at the station of his sister Mangla, who at the time was living with her husband in London. Shanti had given a porter at Calais some money to send her a telegram; now, given his poor view of the French, he thought the porter had simply pocketed the money. He waited for three-quarters of an hour, then got a taxi to his sister's address, only to be told by the landlady that she had gone to fetch him.

2.8

Shanti's own words best convey the flavour of his next few days in London and the effect of his self-doubt and self-knowledge, vacillation and impetuous resolve.

Mangla's husband was Pran Nath; he was an unusual man with doctorates in Science and Literature from English universities and a Ph.D. in Economics from Vienna. His spoken English, however, was very bad: he called a calf a 'cow's child drinking mother-milk' and ordered 'eggs sitting on the toast'. He'd spend all day in the India Office Library, where he was deciphering hieroglyphs from the Indus Valley civilisation – birds and animals and so on – and for every one he deciphered he'd get thirty or forty guineas from the India Office. He would go on thinking the whole day long, and if you talked to him he wouldn't notice, it didn't register at all, he was thinking of his bloody birds.

In the meantime, I wavered in my decision to study dentistry in Berlin, and wondered whether I couldn't continue to study Physics at either Cambridge or the Imperial College of Science in London. But when I spoke to a cousin of mine – the son of my uncle the judge – who was in

England at the time and had in fact been to Cambridge, he told me what my prospects would be if I studied Physics: if I was very lucky, I might become a demonstrator at a university and help carry out practical experiments, or get a job as a schoolteacher. But there was no possibility of doing independent work. I therefore ruled it out completely. I wanted, more than anything else, to be independent.

But I was still terrified at the thought of Berlin. I couldn't speak a word of German. My brother-in-law, who, having studied in Vienna, had German-speaking friends, invited some of them over for tea so that I could get a sense of what the language was like. When I heard it, I was horrified by its difficulty and incomprehensibility. (At least in French I had understood the word 'impotent'.) I was filled with misgivings and couldn't sleep all night. After seeing my light burning through a second night, my sister said to me, 'Shanti, you can't make up your mind. You are worse than a woman.'

That very morning I went to Thomas Cook's, and asked them for a ticket for Berlin to be made valid for one day only, that same day. They were disgusted, they said their tickets were valid for three months, they thought I was mad, but they did it. I also got myself an English–German and a German–English dictionary from Woolworths for a shilling each, and with these I set out for Germany.

2.9

More than sixty years later, with over twenty thousand evenings in between, Shanti Uncle had an uncannily detailed recollection of his first evening in Berlin. He was not quite twenty-three.

I travelled by ship and train to Berlin. It was July 1931; the day was very warm. I left London at seven or eight in the morning, and arrived at about the same time in the evening.

Now when the train arrived at Charlottenburg [an elegant part of Berlin], some people got out. I asked a gentleman, 'Bitte, Berlin?' He said, 'Ja, ja.' I said, 'Bitte, Charlottenburg?' He said, 'Ja, ja.' I couldn't see how a place could be both Berlin and Charlottenburg, so I thought they were a crazy people. I assumed there was a station somewhere actually labelled Berlin. The next station was Bahnhof Zoo. Some other people got out. Then came Bahnhof Friedrichstrasse. Now most of the people got out. So I got out as well, thinking that this must be it. With so much baggage, my cabin trunk and so on, all I could do was to point with my thumb to the porter. After having deposited my luggage, I didn't know where to go, because I couldn't afford a hotel. I didn't know anyone in Berlin, not a soul, and I was looking for accommodation. By now it was 7.30. Luckily, it was still light.

To my great surprise, a German student came up to me and said in perfect English, 'You look very harassed.' I said, 'You would be harassed as well if you knew my situation, as I don't know any German.' He said, 'The best thing would be for you to go back to Charlottenburg, to an Indian restaurant there. They will probably be able to help you.' He wrote the directions down. At the restaurant, there was a Bengali gentleman who told me that he would arrange for me to go to a *pension* run by a lady from Oxford who spoke perfect English. So the language problem was temporarily solved. By this time I was completely fed up and tired out. I asked him to have my baggage brought from the railway station where I'd deposited it. But his cook was ill and there was nobody there but himself, and he couldn't leave the restaurant.

I took the Friedrichstrasse bus, but in the wrong direction. The conductor indicated by signs that I should go back, and I must say, he was very honest, he gave me my money back as well. When I was on the correct bus I asked my neighbour, 'Bitte, Friedrichstrasse?' He said, 'Ja, ja, ja.' I didn't know that Friedrichstrasse was the name of a road as well as a station, but I realised there was some confusion. I looked up the word 'station' in my dictionary and, absurdly enough, it gave me not *Bahnhof* but *Station* as the German equivalent. I asked four different people, 'Friedrichstrasse Station?' They didn't know what I was talking about. So I got off the bus on to the street, thinking I'd look for the station myself. It didn't get dark till half past ten, but you have no idea how fagged I was.

The problem was that I was carrying on me in English pounds all the money my brother Raj had given me for the whole year. I thought of going into a pub which might be frequented by students who could speak English and would direct me to the station, but I was afraid they might beat me up and take my money. I had the impression from [First World War] propaganda that the Germans, even if they didn't eat children, were very rowdy and hit each other in pubs. So I walked up and down, until finally in desperation I did enter a pub on Friedrichstrasse, and to my pleasant surprise found that its other entrance was the railway station. So instead of having a drink, I got my luggage, took a taxi back to the restaurant and was directed to the *pension* two houses away.

2.10

The woman who ran the *pension* was very pleasant and suggested that he stay there for a few months, since he didn't speak German. But after two nights, Shanti asked the restaurateur how he should set about looking for a room for himself. He was told that if he saw a sign reading *Zimmer zu vermieten*, he should ask the rent and, if he liked the room and the people, take it. He had already made up his mind that he would rent a room only from people who didn't speak any English at all.

He wandered down a few side-streets in Charlottenburg and found a flat where a mother and daughter were letting a room. They spoke only German and indicated to him that the arrangement would therefore be no good for him. He responded that it would indeed be very good for him, and took up his residence there. Every evening, he and his landlady pored over the dictionary to decide what he would have for breakfast the next day. She also recommended a girl who could teach him German, but she was 'too flirtatious', and he decided to go to the university, where there were courses for foreign students. Here they taught foreigners German with the aid of pictures of pigs, geese, grandparents and grandchildren; not a word of any language other than German was permitted. In addition, he forced himself to see as many as three movies a day, incomprehensible though they were.

But the prospect at the age of twenty-three of studying medicine and dentistry at one of the best universities in the world in an impossible language that he would have to learn in a matter of weeks was not comforting. He considered dentistry itself a distasteful profession, and did not relish the thought of spending his life putting his fingers into other people's mouths. He was lonely and miserable in a strange country. Then he got a painful infection in his toes, and this proved too much. He wrote to Raj that he had better return to London, as things were unbearable for him in Berlin. Raj cabled back a single line: 'Shanti, put your backbone where your wishbone is.'

2.11

One day in late September, Shanti came down for breakfast to find his landlady distressed and excited. She said, 'Herr Seth, sehr schlecht, sehr schlecht [very bad, very bad].' At first he thought she was going to have a heart attack, but she pointed at him. He responded that he felt all right. 'Nein, sehr schlecht, sehr schlecht,' she kept repeating, and now pointed at the newspaper. He read that under Sir Stafford Cripps, England had just gone off the gold standard, and that instead of getting 20 marks for a pound, the rate had dropped to 12. He rushed to the bank. By the time he got there the rate had dropped to 11.20 marks, and that was where it remained. Raj had given him £9 a month, which had been sufficient for his needs, but at one stroke his funds had nearly halved.

For a year or so I had a hell of a struggle, I used to eat for only twopence or threepence, and there was no possibility of getting any odd jobs, because of the terrible unemployment. I used to eat at Mensa, a sort of mess run by students. If you had no money, and you were lucky, you could arrange to wash up afterwards. You could eat plenty of rolls there: soup and rolls. That's what I lived on for months. I didn't write to my brother about this, so he never knew I was having a bad time.

But Shanti couldn't cut down on books. Though he still disliked dentistry intensely, he bought his textbooks and began his studies at the Dental Institute of the Friedrich-Wilhelm University. It was a four-year course and the classes were demanding, beginning at eight in the morning and continuing, with a few breaks, until eight in the evening. In addition to having to learn about dental materials and methods, there were all the usual medical classes in anatomy, physiology, histology, pharmacology and surgery. The only parts of the body that the students did not have to study in detail were the limbs and the generative organs, except to the extent that venereal disease, for example, might affect the teeth.

Nor could he do without accommodation. Every few months, he changed his lodgings, trying to find a cheaper place and thus husband his funds. For a while he took a room in the house of a physiotherapist, whose husband, when Shanti had a bad stomach ache and couldn't afford to send for a doctor, suggested he place their large tabby cat on his stomach; this worked remarkably well.

The days followed each other, difficult, unenlivened, lonely. Then he bumped into Arvind, an old friend of his from the Theosophical School in Banaras, and things began to look up. Arvind was studying at the Technische Hochschule; he was a lively young man who spoke both French and German perfectly and had a German girlfriend, Tuti. He introduced Shanti to his circle of friends – Romanians, Hungarians and Germans. They started playing bridge together, something Shanti had learned in India by watching his brother and sister-in-law. Arvind was also a champion boxer in his class at the Hochschule; he persuaded Shanti to take it up. Though Shanti enjoyed this, he could only manage to get to the gym after 8 p.m., which meant that he couldn't eat till 10. One day he made the mistake of challenging Arvind to a fight. Arvind was a weight class above him and beat him so badly that he ceased to get any pleasure from boxing.

After a while, the German government, to counter the fall in the number of foreign students and foreign tourists resulting from the stronger mark, instituted so-called registered marks for foreigners, which would be exchanged for foreign currency at a favourable rate and could be used within Germany but not taken back abroad. Once again, Shanti got twenty marks to the pound and, having got used to scrimping and saving, felt he was living very well. He got a flat at an opera singer's, and she entertained his friends whenever he had them round. Eventually, he saved enough money not only to go back to India for a visit but also to have the luxury of taking presents for the family.

2.12

Sometime in early 1933, the opera singer tired of Shanti having his friends around so often; it was clear the arrangement was not working out. But Shanti didn't want to move out of Charlottenburg, not only because it was one of the best parts of Berlin but also because it was easy for him to get from there to the Dental Institute.

He began to look around. When he heard that there was a room to rent on Mommsenstrasse, he went to enquire. The door was opened by a Mrs Caro, a small, quiet-spoken woman in her early sixties. She lived in the very large flat with her two daughters and her son, all of whom were out at work. The front door opened on to a broad corridor; the room to be let was the first one on the right and separated from all the other bedrooms; it was spacious and full of light, with three double-glazed windows. Shanti noticed that the curtains and furniture were well maintained; it didn't look like a room that had been let before, and it hadn't been. Mrs Caro's husband had died a year or so earlier and the family had decided they needed to rent out the guest-room for the income it could bring. She had an unrealistic idea of what the right rent was, and Shanti had to tell her that what she had suggested was far too low. They then agreed on an acceptable figure.

Shanti discovered more than a year later that when Mrs Caro phoned her younger daughter Henny with the news that they had a lodger, her first reaction had been: 'Nimm den Schwarzen nicht' [Don't take the black man]. This was the beginning of a relationship that was to last five and a half decades.

Shanti's room, the guest-room, was directly connected to the *Herrenzimmer*, which was a large library, complete with grand piano, where the gentlemen could repair to smoke their cigars. This in turn was connected to the spacious dining-room with a table, ordinarily for twelve, which could be extended further, a large sideboard and a tiled hearth; the dining-room could also be entered from the corridor. At right-angles to the first corridor was a second, equally broad, off which were three other bedrooms – 'palatial', in Shanti's word: one room for Mrs Caro, another for the two girls, Lola and Henny, and one for their younger brother Heinz (or Hei, as he was called). At the far end of this corridor was the large kitchen, in effect Mrs Caro's den, where strangers were never allowed.

Mommsenstrasse ran roughly parallel to the Kurfürstendamm, and was located at the centre of Charlottenburg, a fashionable part of Berlin. Trees lined the street and, though it was almost entirely residential, there was also a delicatessen, a grocery, a bakery and a pharmacy, as well as the offices of a solicitor and a doctor. A few minutes' walk away was the open space of Olivaerplatz with its park benches and a famous ice-cream parlour, much frequented during the summer.

At first, Mrs Caro prepared meals separately for Shanti, but since he insisted on sharing his food with whoever was at home, he soon came to eat with the family. Work started at about eight; after an early breakfast, Lola and Henny would prepare their luncheon sandwiches and set out for the office. Heinz was spoiled by his mother; he would wake up after ten and be served breakfast by her. Then, at a leisurely pace, he would make his way to work or to friends' or to the races. His work was a bit vague: he managed the property of his two wealthy aunts, and he was the managing agent of a few other properties. In this, he was carrying on in an incompetent manner what had been done so well by his late father, who had been the managing agent of a large estate.

Mrs Gabriele Caro, or Ella, as she was known, was not rich, and the handsome flat in Mommsenstrasse was not owned but rented by the family. The girls turned over most of their earnings to their mother; this was supplemented by Shanti's rental payments and by some savings. Lola, who was twenty-six, continued to study in the evenings, taking courses at an *Abendgymnasium* (evening school). Henny, who was a year and a half younger than her sister, had wanted to go to university, but, after her father's cardiac illness, had had to do a secretarial course and find work. This she, like Lola, had found at the Mannheimer Life Insurance Company, where she became the private secretary of Herr Mahnert, one of the directors.

Herr Mahnert grew very fond of Henny. So did his son Hans, who began to court her.

2.13

Hans was in and out of the Caros' flat all the time. He was an attractive young man, a student of economics, who spoke excellent French and English. He enjoyed the finer things in life, from pearl tie-pins to ornamental fish, and owned a rowing-boat which he would, on Sunday afternoons in summer, take out on to one of the lakes near Berlin, usually the Sacrower See. In summer, Hans, Henny, Shanti and a few friends would camp beside the lake; in winter they would go skiing in the Riesengebirge near the Czech border.

Hans's mother had died many years earlier. His father Franz, Henny's boss, had indulged his son, and now realised that Hans had become rather soft, weak-willed and dandified. Franz Mahnert himself was something of an outdoors type; though he was in his sixties, he swam in the lake even in winter and sometimes, rather flamboyantly, skied to his office. Meanwhile, for the *mens sana* part of things, he read Seneca in Latin.

Hans liked to combine luxury with camping. He used to share a tent with his father, and while his friends brought sandwiches by way of provisions, he would prepare fresh chicken for himself.

I said to Hans when he went out swimming, 'I'm going to eat your chicken and you can eat my sandwiches.' He said, jokingly, 'Of course.' But I did. I ate his chicken and all I left of it was a few bones. All this was done with the consent of his father, naturally; we had decided we were going to teach Hans a lesson. When he came back, he saw the bones, but looked all over for the chicken because he could not believe I could have done that. Finally, in disgust, he had to eat my sandwiches and see how poor people lived.

For his next birthday I bought him a beautiful tie-pin but hid it under his napkin at dinner. On top of the napkin I wrapped a packet containing a cake of Pears soap. When he opened the packet his face fell. I said, 'But Hans, you've always told me you liked Pears soap from England.' 'Oh, yes, yes,' he insisted, but his face was so transparent you could read it like a book. 'Do you feel I didn't spend enough money?' I asked. 'Oh, no, no,' he protested. Then when he picked up his napkin, he saw the tie-pin. Again, his father was an accomplice, and Henny and Lola were there too, and laughed like anything – yes, even Lola, who was normally so shy.

One birthday present to Hans created some tension between us. He had a wonderful aquarium with all sorts of fish and other creatures in it. This was one of his great delights, and he used to go with me from time to time to a shop in Tauentzienstrasse where there was an aquarium that contained a fish he admired, a particularly beautifully coloured fish, though he thought the price was a bit too high. So I thought that would be a nice present for him and when he invited me over to his house for his birthday party I gave it to him. The next day he phoned me up to say that the fish I had given him had eaten all the other fish. And he got into a row with me! 'It was your choice, not mine,' I said, 'as I'm quite ignorant about fish.' It was a predator, that probably came from the Red Sea. An enchanting, marvellous fish. I had a good laugh.

As Shanti Uncle told me this story, his face lit up at the memory and he laughed out loud. In the wheezy laughter of the eighty-five-year-old I could hear the vigorous laughter of the young man in his twenties he once had been and who in many ways he still was, with his gift for friendship and his penchant for mischief and his great generosity. What happened in the course of the next dozen years to Hans, to his father Franz, to Ella Caro and her three children, Lola, Henny and Heinz, and to Shanti himself, was as strange and unpredictable as what happened in the aquarium that day, an aquarium that I sometimes, perhaps too fancifully, think of as representing the aquarium of history, with its most singular and fascinating denizens being, as often as not, its most dangerous. But it might have been the timing of the gift that created the association. The year was 1933, and Germany had a new Chancellor.

2.14

Living with the Caros, where he neither behaved like a lodger nor was treated as one, Shanti was introduced to Lola and Henny's circle of friends and, like Hans, some of them became his friends as well. The Caros themselves were Jewish. Since the girls had gone to the Fürstin Bismarck Gymnasium, there were more Christians than Jews among their friends and acquaintances. Needless to say, the Caros, in that sad phrase, never thought of themselves as anything other than German.

Lola, the more serious and studious of the two sisters, also had friends from her evening classes at the Abendgymnasium; among these were the Rabaus. Jazko Rabau, a Jew who had converted to Christianity, taught mathematics there; Lola, who was excellent at mathematics, had been one of his students – as had Rose Rabau, Jazko's second wife. Christmas was always celebrated by the circle at their house with carols and *Stollen* and a Christmas tree with all the trimmings.

The friends visited each other and celebrated each other's birthdays. Whenever there was a party in the Mommsenstrasse flat, Ella presided over her kitchen. Shanti was permitted to enter the sanctum, but not Hans, whom she told: 'You've got no business here.' Ella thought Hans had rather a flaccid character, and was not sure he was good for her daughter. It was accepted, however, that he was Henny's unofficial fiancé and that in due course they would get married. Curiously enough, Ella kept a small canary whom she called Hans. Apparently, whenever she said, 'Hänschen, piep mal,' the canary would chirp and kiss her.

Henny was the livelier and more energetic of the two sisters. She dressed well, laughed readily and made friends easily. Shanti liked her a great deal, but he was a good friend of Hans, and left it at that.

2.15

Shanti's studies continued, and slowly he became more interested in them – not only on the dental but also on the medical side. He found it difficult at first to get used to the phlegmatic way in which his fellow students would carve up a cadaver, wash their hands, then eat a sandwich, but after a while he too absorbed their cavalier ethos and no longer thought of dead bodies as something grisly.

He did well. A few examinations in the German system were written, but most of them were oral. Students had to sign up to be examined on one of several dates; the professor would ask some questions, and the grade would be given on the spot. It was the luck of the draw who was on the roster as examiner on a particular day.

For his exam in Histology, there was an outside examiner. Shanti was shown a slide of a few cells. 'What do we have here?' asked the professor. 'Milch,' replied Shanti, at which the professor's face reddened. Only after seeing the diagram that Shanti had drawn did the mollified professor say, 'Oh, I see, you're a foreigner. You meant *Milz*, not *Milch*.' Shanti had mixed up the words for milk and spleen.

For the final exam in Physiology, the six best students in the class were examined together by the top professor in the subject, who asked each question sequentially till someone came up with the right answer. The first question was, 'Why do we give boiled rather than fried food to patients suffering from stomach trouble?' and it floored the first five students, since this was not something that had been taught in class. Shanti, who was last in line, had to think quickly; luckily, his Physics came to his aid. He said: 'If you boil food, the temperature never goes above a hundred degrees, while if you fry it, the temperature goes much higher and the fibres of the meat may get burned, and though it sometimes tastes better, it is not so easily absorbed by the stomach.' He felt embarrassed when the professor told the German students, 'You should be ashamed of yourselves; he comes from an old culture and shows you how stupid you all are. He knows the answer, but you don't – and it is so simple.' He shook Shanti's hand, congratulated him and gave him the highest grade, Very Good. The others were asked other questions and eventually got the passing grade, Satisfactory.

There was one subject, however, in which Shanti performed disastrously and it almost brought his studies to an end. When he went to pay his advance fees for the preliminary examinations, the clerk said, 'Oh, by the way, Herr Seth, we haven't got your Latin certificate yet.' Shanti said, 'You're joking, surely.' But he was not, and the other students confirmed it: Latin was indeed a prerequisite. Needless to say, there had been neither reason nor occasion to study it, either at school or university, in India.

Shanti realised that he would have to squeeze a five- or six-year course into the six months that were left before the preclinicals. (While he was telling me this story, I was so gripped that my own parallel experience, almost forty years later, with German, did not even come to mind.) He hired one of the best professors of Latin at the university at a terrifying eight marks an hour to coach him privately. When he explained to the professor that all he wanted to do was to pass the examinations, he was told to concentrate solely on Caesar's *Gallic Wars*, because for the past five years all the translations had been based on that text. When Shanti went to sit the exam, however, he found to his horror that the text they had set was not from Caesar but from Cicero.

Having no fundamental knowledge of Latin and being utterly unfamiliar with the text, he was certain he had failed so badly that he would not even be considered a borderline case who would be permitted to take a supplementary exam. That night, he could not sleep. Early the next morning he wrote out a petition to Bernhard Rust, the Minister of Education in Hitler's government, and went to the Ministry in the hope of seeing him. He got to see a secretary who informed him that not only could he not meet the minister, he couldn't even meet his assistant's assistant's assistant. Any petition he had should be left at the desk.

Shanti bought a box of chocolates for a young typist in the Ministry and begged her to frame his petition in proper German. He requested that he should be allowed to appear for the supplementary exam (which consisted of an oral and another translation). He stated that when he had started his course nobody had told him he would need Latin in order to sit his preclinicals. He was a posthumous child, his brother was supporting him, and he couldn't ask him to pay for another year just so that he could study Latin.

He heard nothing. On the day the results of the Latin exam came out, after the lists of those who had passed and of those who would be permitted to sit the supplementary exam had been read out, Shanti sat weeping in the hall outside: everyone's name had been called but his own. Finally, after a pause, his name too was announced. It was like a reprieve. In the seven days before the second exam, he ignored dentistry and medicine completely, devoted all his time to Latin, and learned his grammar by heart.

The oral exam was just like a court, with a president and three professors on each side. When I entered the place, the president called out loudly, 'Who is Herr Seth?' I got up with my heart palpitating and said, 'That's me.' He said, 'Herr Seth, you are a very remarkable man. How did you know that you did not pass? You might have done very well.' From his manner, it was clear to me that I had indeed failed and that if the results had come out before I'd taken any action, I would have been finished. Luckily for me, the president asked me several questions on grammar and I rattled off all the answers. He turned to the other professors and said, 'Well, he knows his grammar perfectly. Do you think you want to ask him any further questions?' Naturally, they had to say no.

Unlike the previous time, when foreign students were permitted to use dictionaries for the translation paper, this time they were forbidden, but each student was allowed to ask the meaning of any ten words. As a matter of fact, the translation was again from Cicero. I had to say to myself, 'Keep your mouth shut. If you say anything, you'll be thrown out.' The president came to give me the meaning of my ten words, though actually I wanted to ask for eighteen or twenty.

I did my translation, though I was not very happy. But, to my luck, the president came and stood by my desk. There was one word, a linchpin, the meaning of which made all the difference to the translation: it meant something either positive or negative, but I had made the wrong choice. The professor whispered, 'Surely you don't mean that.' Then I realised he was on my side, and I corrected my mistake. After that I went with some girl students to the pub and I tell you the truth, I don't know how I came home. I drank so much I couldn't remember anything, and I prayed to God to take all the Latin out of my system for ever.

2.16

Among Shanti Uncle's papers is a document issued in June 1933, not by the Ministry of Education but by the Prussian Ministry of the Interior, which presumably dealt with matters concerning foreigners in Berlin. It states, in response to a petition made about two weeks earlier by Shanti Behari Seth, residing in Charlottenburg, born in Biswan, Indian by citizenship, that on the basis of his Physics and Chemistry exams and his Matriculation certificate from the Benares Hindu University and his supplementary exam in Latin certified by the German Institute for Foreigners, he would, exceptionally, be allowed to appear for the preliminary examination in dentistry (*zahnärztliche Vorprüfung*, presumably the preclinicals) at the end of the summer semester 1933 or thereafter. This permission, however, was granted with the express reservation that by passing this examination he would not acquire the right to sit further examinations or to receive a certificate enabling him to practise as a dentist in the territory of the German Reich.

Was all this part of a specific understanding to do with the Latin exam that Shanti had taken in April, a sort of quid pro quo under whose terms he agreed to curtail his further career or at least subject it to review? Or was the petition referred to in the document a more general one, one that would have to be made by any foreign student, or at least any non-white foreign student like Shanti who, however self-contradictory it might seem, considering the Sanskrit origin of the word, might be considered non-Aryan? Less than three months after Hitler became Chancellor, a sheaf of laws aimed mainly at Jews had been passed, but some of these were also intended to act against 'non-Aryans' in general and to some extent against foreigners. One such was the Law against the Overcrowding of German Schools and Universities passed on 25 April.

Hitler had become Chancellor on 30 January 1933. The Reichstag was set on fire less than a month later, on 27 February; the next day Hitler assumed emergency powers. Thousands of Communists were arrested in the weeks that followed and imprisoned in concentration camps. At the parliamentary elections that took place on 5 March, the Nazi Party did not get an absolute majority, but before the month was out, the Reichstag had passed the so-called Enabling Act, which gave dictatorial powers to Hitler both to make laws and to carry them out; from then on, the Reichstag itself was merely a rubber stamp.

Throughout this period, there was an increase in the vehemence of the assaults against Jews which were such a hallmark of the Nazi activists, and in the persecution and indeed murder of Jews in different parts of the country. When the foreign press reported and condemned these events and a boycott of German businesses was suggested, it was decided to retaliate with an official boycott against Jewish businesses on 1 April. That same month saw a new set of laws, decrees and orders: one expelled Jews from the Civil Service, another forbade Jewish lawyers from practising at the bar, another aimed to exclude Jewish doctors from many hospitals and clinics; yet another, the Law against the Overcrowding of German Schools and Universities just mentioned, though aimed at non-Aryans in general, restricted both the enrolment and the overall membership of Jews in educational institutions.

These were the first of many laws passed not with any regularity but in fits and starts over the following years. All this was accompanied by propaganda comparing Jews to germs or vermin, dangerous to the health of a resurgent nation – or indeed any nation. The Nazi Party and those who helped them sought to separate Jews from their fellow Germans in every possible sphere – work, friendship, marriage, cultural life, leisure – in order both to immiserize them financially and to exclude them socially. It was thus hoped to force them to emigrate or to kill themselves: at any rate, to reduce their presence in Germany. The pressure was to be increased until eventually Germany was Jew-free and blood-pure. This rhetoric and these measures were directed against a people who in 1933 numbered half a million out of a population of more than sixty million.

When I asked Shanti Uncle what had happened during his years in Berlin to the circle of friends which included Lola and Henny, he said that some of the Christian Germans had detached themselves from the Caros. Others had been afraid to come to the house on Mommsenstrasse, but kept in touch on the telephone. Yet others visited as usual, ate and sang and celebrated birthdays and Christmas in the usual way, tried to keep up their own spirits and those of their friends, and hoped that in time the madness would pass.

2.17

Whenever Shanti Uncle talked about the historical situation in Germany, he lapsed into generalities.

I was never interested in politics. When I first got to Germany, Hindenburg was in power. It was the Weimar Republic. There was a great deal of unemployment. Hitler became very popular by opening soup kitchens and giving people work making roads, which were to be useful to him in wartime.

On one occasion, out of curiosity, he followed an agitated crowd of students. But there was some shooting going on in a large hall in the university, apparently owing to a fracas between the Communist and the Nazi students, and Shanti quickly left. That was the last political gathering he attended.

When an Indian freedom-fighter – Shanti Uncle was somewhat uncertain about his name, though at first he claimed it was Subhas Chandra Bose – came to Berlin and spoke to the students, Shanti went to hear him. Years later, he was to discover that his movements and those of other Indian students in Germany had been monitored by the British Embassy with the help of informants in order to chart and, if possible, suppress, Indian nationalist currents abroad. In India, meanwhile, though there was no prospect of the complete independence from the British demanded by the Congress Party in 1930, a limited form of provincial government by elected representatives would be instituted after the passage of the Government of India Act of 1935.

As for the larger questions in Germany – unemployment, militarisation, warmongering, anti-Semitism – Shanti Uncle held strong opinions, but they were based more on impression and anecdote than on historical or social analysis. During one of our interviews, à propos of nothing in particular, he said:

To my great surprise, I found that on Ku'Damm, the main street of Charlottenburg, lots of businesses were in the hands of Jewish people, and also that most of the doctors and dentists were Jewish. In Germany, all of them had concentrated in Berlin, especially the professionals. And professors too.

But this remark was quickly followed by other subjects entirely: the sexual peccadilloes of his professor and a visit to the Krupp works. I should perhaps have stopped him and asked him to develop the thought, but this was one of my first interviews with him, and at that time I thought it best to follow, as far as I could, his free association of ideas and memories.

In the interview that followed, between describing the dental use of vitamin K and advising me on my back problems, Shanti Uncle talked about a Jewish friend of his:

One of my friends, Mr Hausdorf, was sent to Buchenwald quite early on. I knew him so well; he used to take me to the best restaurants in Berlin. He was an engineer. In the First World War he made a contraption for both ears so that when one was using the telephone, the message was clearer. The *Wehrmacht* took it over, and so did other countries, and he naturally did very well. Although he fought in the war and got an Iron

Cross for great courage, they sent him to Buchenwald and beat him up. About his Iron Cross, they said: 'You dirty old Jew, you must have stolen it.' He was such a nice man. He said to his wife, she being an Aryan Christian, that she should divorce him so that she could stay in Germany. Unfortunately, I could not help him. But then his daughter got married to the Military Attaché of Santo Domingo, and so he got a visa and got out.

Shanti said that during his years in Berlin he never felt excluded as a foreigner: his teachers treated him well and he was invited to the homes of some of his German fellow students. Quite a few of these students became politicised. The professors were expected to join the Nazi Party and did so, as indeed did many of the petty officials; even the janitor of the Dental Institute was a Party member. People were always being asked to contribute to charities run by the Party, which were usually a front for the Party coffers. Shanti was advised by the student leader, who was friendly towards him, to contribute a bit himself, and he gave them four or five marks. 'Indirectly, it said that I was not against them,' was his explanation.

This same student leader enabled him to get an insight into the vast industrial (and potentially military) power that Germany was building up. A dental clinic had been started up at the huge Krupp steelworks at Essen and a hundred or so students from Berlin were invited to see it. As a foreigner, it was very difficult to get to go on the trip, but Shanti spoke to the Nazi *Studentenführer*, who said, 'Sethy, I'll manage to get you in somehow.' At the last moment he claimed that some German students could not go, and put down Shanti's name.

When we arrived, the man who was running the whole show, Herr von Bohlen, gave us a very big dinner. Krupp didn't have any sons; von Bohlen was married to his daughter. I learned while talking to others at the table that as a foreign student I would not be allowed to go the next day to visit the steelworks, which had a huge and impressive press. Nor would the women students, as their skirts could catch fire if they touched the running stream of steel – so I would have to accompany the girls to a museum. I was not at all happy with this and I approached Herr von Bohlen at his dinner party. I was stopped by his secretary. I gave him to understand that I had come thousands of miles from India and that it would be a shame if I had to go back and say that I was not allowed to see the famous steelworks. And I asked him if I looked like a spy. Herr von Bohlen, who had overheard our conversation, told his secretary that I should be allowed to go. It was a remarkable sight to see – the red stream of steel flowing on and on. And a press that could hammer a huge thick sheet of steel. Naturally, there were drinks afterwards, free drinks, and we students drank so much that some of us got alcohol poisoning. Everything was free there – the best of food, the best of wine – in those very hard times.

2.18

One of Shanti's closest friends in Germany was Philip Zulick, an American medical student who was very tall. Since Shanti was very short, they formed an odd pair, and were called Pat and Patachon after similarly ill-matched comic characters. After Philip failed his preclinical exams in Berlin, he went to Freiburg to continue his studies, and Shanti went to visit him.

We used to go to the market: he was very goodlooking and had great charm and the girls used to fall for him. He suggested that they bring the cakes and that we would take them out for lunch. With the cakes came the cuddling.

Philip and Shanti used to hike together through the Harz mountains; once, they covered 270 kilometres in ten days. They never booked anywhere, depended on luck, and froze when they could not find lodgings. On one occasion, when a farmer put them up in a field, they ended up in a haystack with a girl in the middle.

Shanti's relationships with women during his years in Germany were perfunctory. His brother had said, 'Shanti, enjoy yourself, but not at the expense of your studies.' Shanti said that he never took undue advantage of anyone, and that, though he got excited, he thought that sex was 'not useful'. 'Believe me, it's so difficult when you're young, but you try to suppress yourself.' As for marriage, there was no question of it. 'In Berlin, if there was the slightest talk of marriage, I dropped the girl like a hot brick.'

He made two brief visits to India during the mid-thirties; each time, the question of marriage was brought up by the family. The second time (probably in 1935, though the date is unclear), when he went to visit his mother, who was very ill with diabetes and living with his brother Achal, the doctor, Shanti discovered that Achal had lined up a number of women for him to meet; it was time, he believed, that Shanti settled down. But Shanti would have none of it. He appealed to his brother Raj, who told Achal to leave him alone.

It was Henny whom Shanti liked more than anyone else, though Lola seemed to be the more devoted to him. She corrected the drafts of his papers, she typed any letters necessary. With her gentleness and quickness, her logicality and linguistic sensitivity, she helped him through difficult times in a subject, language and country, all of which were still foreign to him.

Henny, besides, had Hans. But her mother Ella, who was ambivalent about Hans and, it appears, sensed Shanti's unspoken feelings, once said to Henny, in what context it is now too late to learn: 'Even if you marry Hans, as long as Shanti is around, you won't starve.'

2.19

In the summer of 1936, the Olympic Games were held in Berlin. They proved to be a great spectacle and a propaganda coup for Nazi

Germany. The university had asked for volunteers to guide foreigners, mostly Americans, to various attractions around the city for fifty marks a day. Shanti was tempted, especially since the tickets for the Olympics that he had bought for himself could be sold at twenty times their value; but in the event he decided to watch the Games. He remembered in particular the triumphs on the track of Jesse Owens.

During the Olympic Games officials were instructed to be particularly polite to foreigners.

One day my friend Fredy Aufrichtig went for a walk with me in the Grunewald [a large wooded park in Berlin]; he always took his dog. He told me he was going to buy tickets for the *Stadtbahn* for the three of us: dogs, like children, travelled half-price. He gave me a ticket, told me to go upstairs to the platform and said he would join me a few minutes later. When I went up, the ticket-collector looked me up and down with great interest. I thought perhaps he hadn't seen an Indian before. And he let me through without saying anything. Now comes the funny part. A minute later, my friend and his dog arrive and show the collector two adult tickets. And the collector bursts out: 'For goodness sake, I should have seen that coming!' Fredy had given me the ticket for the dog, but the collector, seeing I was a foreigner, had said nothing.

Fredy Aufrichtig was a solicitor, but, being a Jew, he now had to earn his living as a watch-repairer.

Shanti had another curious memory set in almost the same place at almost the same time:

I saw Hitler from very close at the time of the Olympics. I had gone for a walk in the Grunewald, and I saw a few people standing there, with SS men on both sides. No one came to search me or anything. I saw him from so close – not further than that wall there. He had a bridge in his mouth and he was made up with lipstick and all. I thought he might be a homo – but later on I found out that they were going to film him in colour.

Soon after the Olympics, Shanti visited the ancient cultural city of Nuremberg. But it seemed to him that apart from himself, everyone was in jackboots. They did nothing to him, but he didn't feel comfortable. Though he had booked a room for three days, after one day he took the train back to Berlin.

2.20

A few months before the Olympics, in April 1936, Shanti passed the state examination in Medical Dentistry with distinction. Throughout the previous year he had been working on his research for a doctorate, which he obtained just six months later.

His doctoral research dealt with the microscopic changes in tooth enamel and in the dentine inside the tooth that take place when various filling materials are used: silicates, amalgams, gold, inlays, porcelains and oxyphosphates as well as temporary fillings such as zinc oxide with eugenol, the soothing element in oil of cloves. He took cross-sectional samples of teeth with different fillings in them, examined them under the microscope and subjected them to tests. The work fascinated him, and he looked back with amazement to the time when he had hated the thought of studying dentistry.

When he had written out a draft of his dissertation, Lola went over it to correct any infelicities in his German, and typed it out. The first sentence of the final, printed dissertation reads: 'One could describe the filling of carious teeth after the removal of the carious parts as "heteroplastic" in the broader sense.'

Professor Eugen Wannenmacher, under whose guidance Shanti did his doctoral research, was the director of the Conservation Department of the university's Dental Institute. He was delighted with Shanti's work and very keen that, after receiving his doctorate, he should continue to work with him. Shanti had to tell him that unless he earned some money, it would be impossible for him to do

Aus der konservierenden Abteilung des zahnärztlichen Institutes der
Universität Berlin.
Direktor: Prof. Dr. Eugen Wannenmacher.

Die Veränderungen im Schmelz und Dentin unter Füllungen

Inaugural-Dissertation

zur Erlangung der zahnärztlichen Doktorwürde an der

Friedrich Wilhelms-Universität zu Berlin

vorgelegt von

Shanti B. Seth

aus Biswan (Brit.-Indien)

Tag der Promotion: 23. Oktober 1936.

Buchdruckerei Rudolph Pfau, Berlin NW 7, Luisenstraße 21.

Title page of Shanti's Ph.D. dissertation.

so; he couldn't expect his brother to keep supporting him. The professor assured him that from the beginning of the following week he would start on the same salary as the German assistants, two hundred marks a month. But when Shanti arrived for work on Monday, the professor's face was white with shock. He handed him the letter he had received a few minutes earlier from the Ministry of Education, upbraiding him as a Party member for having taken on a foreign student as an assistant when there were so many German students still unemployed.

Shanti had known that he could not practise as a dentist in Germany. But now even academia and research were closed to him. He did not realise at the time how fortunate he was to have to leave the country. He took it hard, regretting that his days in Berlin were over and that he would have to part from his friends and colleagues and make a life for himself somewhere else – perhaps in London, where he had spent just a couple of weeks some five years earlier.

2.21

Shanti describes the next year, 1937, as the most cold and miserable of his life. His German degrees were not recognised in Britain, and he learned that if he wanted to work either there or anywhere in the Empire, he would have to requalify in every subject. He had almost no money – 'enough for bread but not for butter'. Both for studying and for living, Edinburgh was cheaper than London, so that was where he went.

It seemed to him as if he was taking exams every two weeks. So used was he to the experience of Berlin that in his anatomy vivas he blurted out his first answer in German. In another exam, a professor grilled him endlessly about the details of the industrial extraction of nickel and was annoyed that he didn't know the name of the kind of ladle used. But Shanti hadn't attended his classes; indeed, all he was doing in Edinburgh was sitting exams.

What made things even more frustrating was that he was learning nothing new: dentistry in Germany was superior to that in Britain. Before one took one's final exams in Berlin, for example, one had to have performed sixty root-canal procedures compared to just three or four in Edinburgh. The emphasis in Edinburgh was on the extraction, not the conservation, of teeth.

Shanti's one happy memory of Edinburgh was that that was where he met his best friend, Heinrich Etzold – or, as he was later to become, Henry Edwards. Heinrich had qualified in dentistry from Jena a couple of years earlier; he was lucky to do so, for his mother was Jewish. Afterwards, since he was a half-Jew, it was not easy for him to get a job. He went to the Saarland, which in 1935 had been returned by plebiscite to Germany but, since it was in the demilitarised zone to the west of the Rhine, was not occupied by German troops. There he worked as a dental assistant and kept a low profile. But one day in 1936, he noticed that there was a large public gathering in the street; he discovered then that the German army had already marched in. He thought that to stay in Germany would be disastrous, so instead of trying to get out through the regular border, or even waiting to pack a bag, he simply caught a tram to France before the borders could be sealed; everyone else on the tram was French, and it wasn't stopped.

Heinrich's mother (or 'Mum' as she was called by everyone, including, later, by Shanti) had a brother in the bristle business in London. His partner had been the secretary of the Jewish War Veterans' Association; he now arranged with the Home Office for Heinrich's entry into England. For a while Heinrich helped his uncle at the auctions in the docks, sometimes carrying loads of bristles to and from the warehouse. Then, with some support from his uncle, he went to Edinburgh to requalify, like Shanti, in dentistry.

From their first meeting, Shanti and he became friends. As they walked one evening from the Dental School through the Meadows to Heinrich's digs, they began to discuss the future shape of things, particularly about whether war was inevitable.

They talked until four in the morning. It appeared to both of them that there was no avoiding a war, though it was not clear at all how imminent it was.

2.22

After a long year in Edinburgh, homesick for his friends in Germany and worried that, if war were to break out, he would not be able to see them, Shanti went back to Berlin in December 1937. A photograph taken at this time shows him and his friends sitting down to a Christmas dinner. He also paid a surprise visit to Berlin in the summer of the following year, as the earliest of his surviving passports attests.

This passport was issued on 15 July 1938 in London, and as a document reflects the history and style of the time. In those days British passports carried the name of the Foreign Secretary, who was then Lord Halifax, together with an endless list of his honours and appellations, curtailed finally by 'etc, etc, etc'. It was valid for all countries in the British Empire and for Europe (except Spain, where the Civil War was in progress) and Turkey. Under 'National Status' it states: 'British Subject by birth'. Under 'Observations' is the remark: 'Race and Caste: Aryan Hindu (khatri)'. A visa for Germany was issued on 28 July by the German Embassy in London; the embassy stamp incorporates the swastika. An entry stamp at the main station in Aachen is dated the following day. The last foreign exchange transaction in Reichsmarks (from a bank in Charlottenburg) is dated 15 August.

Presumably, the specification 'Aryan' was supplied by the bearer. Given Shanti's family background – many of the Seths of Biswan belonged to the reforming but somewhat anti-Muslim Arya Samaj – it may be thought that this was a sign that Shanti took the attitude, prevalent among some Hindus at the time, that Hindus were somehow allied racially to the dominant Western and

Christian powers and not to 'non-Aryan Semites', whether Muslims or Jews. But throughout his life, Shanti's acts and attitudes implied neither the alliance nor the dissociation. It seems far more likely that since the passport was issued a fortnight before his trip to Germany, the observation was added with the express purpose of avoiding difficulties there, possibly something he may have encountered with officialdom on his earlier visit.

Things had changed greatly since he had been a student in Berlin, especially for his Jewish friends. Three days after German troops marched into Austria in March 1938, Hitler announced to huge, jubilant crowds in Vienna that his homeland had now joined the Reich. After this annexation or absorption of Austria, there took place in Vienna a frenzy, first of Jew-baiting, then of the appropriation of Jewish property. In Germany too the momentum of oppression and vituperation built up. In June, the windows of Jewish shops in Berlin were deliberately defaced with the star of David, the word *Jude* and gross caricatures of Jews. This happened, among other places, on the Kurfürstendamm, a couple of minutes' walk from where the Caros lived. In July it was announced that by the end of the year Jews would have to carry identity cards at all times; in August, that from the beginning of the following year Jews whose first names did not correspond to a bizarre list of Judaic and pseudo-Judaic names would have to insert the name Sara (for women) or Israel (for men) after their first name.

Henny was no longer permitted to work for the Mannheimer Life Insurance Company under Hans's father; she had had to find work with a Jewish solicitor. The family income had dwindled, and the flat in Mommsenstrasse had had to be given up. The Caros now lived round the corner in Bleibtreustrasse in a much smaller apartment. Shanti sensed their growing isolation, as some of their old friends now avoided them.

Unfortunately, most of Henny's friends had been Christian and therefore she was left with a very small circle of true friends . . . She must have been lonely.

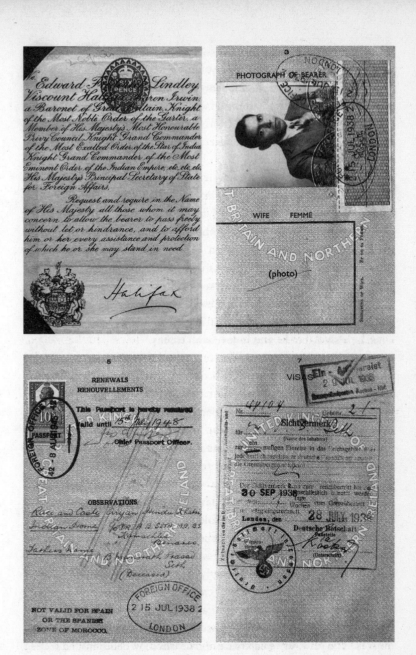

Some pages from Shanti's passport issued in 1938.

Jewish people were also not allowed to go to the cinema or theatre or any other amusement place, and prohibited to go to restaurants. The Jews could only go to a theatre that was organised by the Jewish community and where all the actors and musicians were Jews. I did go to one show, *Fidelio*, with Henny and Lola. I enjoyed it, though the props were not up to standard. The Jews were so segregated that they could only work among themselves.

I stayed with them for a week or two. I personally could go to any place in Berlin, but somehow I didn't feel that I should. Though I was depressed to go out on my own, I did still visit quite a few of my old dental colleagues. Two of them, with whom I was quite friendly, talked about, what do you call the word, the . . . the prospect of war, they thought that the prospect of war was very great, and even told me in great confidence that Hitler was making something special as a weapon.

I still met Hans quite often at Henny's place because he was what was called a *Mischling*: his mother had been Jewish. He was apprehensive when he visited, but he was in love with Henny.

A couple of questions of chronology arise in Shanti Uncle's account of his visit. One is that it might have been too late for *Fidelio*, since performances of Beethoven were (according to Saul Friedländer's *Nazi Germany and the Jews*) already forbidden to Jews in 1937. The second is that it was not until December 1938 that Jews were officially banned from theatres, cinemas and so on. Shanti Uncle's memory could have merged with his knowledge of later events. Or the ban could have been de facto, enhanced by a fear of recognition, insult and violence. When I asked Shanti Uncle more than half a century after these events if he knew about the exclusion as a fact, his response was: 'Yes. I was there.'

He returned to England, deeply worried about the situation of his friends. In November 1938 came Kristallnacht with its widespread and murderous attacks against Jews, including the burning down of most of the synagogues and the desecration of sacred objects. The Jews were further impoverished by being forced to pay a billion-mark fine for the damage inflicted on them. In due course, the Caros were robbed of their jewellery and other valuables by order of the German state: these included the silver dinner service Ella had been given by her parents when she had married. They had to deliver these themselves in two taxi-loads to the appropriate government offices.

Heinz Caro, Henny and Lola's brother, emigrated to South America in 1938, though how he did so is unclear. His mother and sisters were left behind in Berlin. They did not know anyone who could help them outside Germany. Shanti himself wanted to help, but could not: the Home Office required credible sponsorship before it permitted immigration. After qualifying from Edinburgh and moving down to London, Shanti was staying in a boarding-house in Belsize Park and living off very little.

Meanwhile, the window for emigration from Germany was being boarded up. Though the appeasement of Hitler might have bought some time for the British to rearm, war was closer than ever. Czechoslovakia had been invaded in two stages, and it took either too little or too much imagination to believe that that would be Germany's final bite at the map of Europe.

2.23

Qualified now from both Berlin and Edinburgh, and jobless in London, Shanti was in difficult straits. Life in London was expensive. Though he still had a small amount of money from the shares in his grandfather's village that he had sold to his brother Brahma, this was something he had kept aside for an emergency and did not want to exhaust. Job opportunities were rare, but finally he did find one through a dental agency. He was offered a position as an assistant to a Parsi dentist who worked in a street off Ladbroke Grove. Mr Warden was seriously ill with asthma; in fact, he could not even introduce Shanti to his patients. Shanti had to take over the practice on his own, though Mrs Warden was helpful in suggesting what fees he should charge, an important matter in the unstandardised days before the National Health Service. After a while, Shanti suggested that since he was doing all the work, he should be offered a partnership, but Mr Warden refused.

Nevertheless, it was a great pleasure to be practising his profession, and years later Shanti was able to recall some of his first cases.

There was a sixteen-year-old boy, who had a toothache in the upper first incisor, a big tooth. His father asked me to take the tooth out, but after examining it, I said that I could save it by carrying out root-canal treatment. The father got very annoyed and said, 'This is newfangled baloney. I am the father, and I'm paying for the treatment.' I told him it was against my conscience to take out a young boy's tooth when I could save it. This went on for twenty-five minutes. Finally the boy chirped in: 'Daddy, why not give Dr Seth a chance?' I prayed I would succeed, and did everything possible to carry out the treatment in the classical way. I checked it later with an X-ray and it looked perfect. The boy was very happy since he didn't have to have a denture at such a young age.

In another case, a doctor sent a patient to Shanti to have all his teeth removed. When Shanti examined the patient's mouth, he discovered it was in a very bad state, with pus having formed in many of the roots. He told the doctor that he was going to take out only one segment – a quarter of his teeth – in the first session; this turned out to be fortunate.

After taking out the roots and some of the bad teeth, Shanti found that he could not stem the bleeding. After he had spent two hours with the patient and tried everything possible, the bleeding just about stopped.

The next day he sent the nurse at his own expense to go and look up the patient. That afternoon, he appeared at the surgery; the bleeding was continuing. Shanti phoned the doctor and asked him why he hadn't informed him of the man's case history, in particular that his blood did not easily clot, something he would have enquired about himself if the patient had not come to him through a doctor. The doctor was very perturbed. Shanti then wrote a letter to St Mary's Hospital in Paddington, which was not too far, and requested them to attend to his patient's bleeding. A day later the man's wife brought him back to Shanti's surgery. With blood oozing out for more than two days, he was now in shock. The hospital had told him that there was nothing the matter with him, and had painted his wounds with iodine and sent him home. When Shanti heard this, he was furious and wrote a letter to the superintendent of the hospital in which he said that unless they did something positive for this very sick man, if anything should happen to him, he, Shanti, would take further measures. He later heard from the patient that he had been in hospital for six weeks and had had to have transfusions. Shanti said that if he had not taken such forceful action, the patient would have died, and he would have blamed himself for it all his life.

Why did Shanti not return to India to set up practice there? Clearly, the whole clan, particularly his brother Raj, wanted him to; that had been the idea behind his choice of profession. The family story, which I have from my mother, is that at the time of Shanti's second visit to India, he could not find a job because his German qualifications were not recognised, and that he told Raj that he would go back to get a British degree before returning to India. War had then broken out and he could not return.

But this does not appear to be a complete explanation. There was a long gap – more than a year – between Shanti's requalification from Edinburgh and the outbreak of war, during which he could have gone back, but didn't. It may have been that he now saw a better future for himself in England. Or he might have felt, given his urge for independence, that if he settled down in India, he would not be able to tolerate the constant interference in his life that was bound to come from his family. With his mother's death, not long after his visit to her, he probably felt less bound by duty to go back. But as the summer of 1939 approached, there could also have been another reason.

2.24

Henny got out of Germany a month before the war. Hans's mother, who had died long before, had a niece who was married to an Arabic and Persian scholar who lived and taught in London. This was Arthur J. Arberry, whose translation of the Quran, apart from being the most powerfully poetic that I have read, comes with a moving introduction that mentions how his work on the translation helped him at a time of great personal tribulation. Arberry was later to move to Oxford and then to become Professor of Arabic at Cambridge. It was he who was able to offer Henny, his wife's cousin's fiancée, the sponsorship necessary to satisfy the Home Office. Since Henny already knew some English, mainly business English, it was possible to claim she had fluency in the language. She would live with the Arberrys, help with the housework, and take care of their young daughter Anna. In exchange for this, she would get food and lodging.

In late July 1939, Henny travelled by train from Berlin to Hamburg, then by boat to Southampton and by train to London. Shanti, the only person she knew in England, met her at Victoria Station and took her to the Arberrys'.

She came with a trunk containing a few clothes, a few books and a few mementoes of the three decades of her life in Germany. Less than five weeks later, war was declared. Ella and Lola, who had been unable to emigrate, remained within the borders of their own hostile country.

2.25

Among the mementoes Henny brought with her – and which Shanti would not see until more than fifty years later, long after her death – was a leather purse, deep burgundy in colour, embossed in gold. Inside it, next to some poems to her from Hans, was a typed letter from Hans's father, Franz Mahnert, who had arranged for Henny's emigration. It was sent to her on the eve of her departure from Berlin.

Berlin, Steglitz, Kniephofstrasse 59,
23.7.1939

Dear Fräulein Caro,

I feel compelled to say a few words to you before you leave the country. When you were recently at our home, I had the impression that you were taking your departure very hard. I would so like you not to view this parting in such a tragic light.

It is perhaps for you only a very small consolation that thousands would envy you even the possibility that has been offered to you. At any rate, just remember that you will only be leaving your mother and your sister temporarily, and that in all probability you will be reunited with them very soon. (What is one year, what indeed would two be?) So do not shed any tears. The world is beautiful even outside your fatherland; God feels no preference for any of his creatures, has not wished to place borders between them, has given them his entire creation. You will soon find out how wonderfully one can live even in another country, and that there are good people there as well. I believe with certainty that the obstacle that at present still impedes your freedom of action will soon be overcome; so much can happen. And then again – you are so able, and are still young, and the whole of life lies before you, so you are *bound* to be successful.

Our relatives will welcome you with open arms and in the warmest manner, and you can rest assured that they will have a complete understanding of your situation. You will feel quite at home there very soon.

I am glad that you have decided to travel by boat after all. The strong sea breeze and life on board will refresh you wonderfully and change your entire mood for the better. You will reach the hospitable shores of England in a more hopeful mood than would otherwise have been the case. And then you will be in free England and will be envied, ah, by so many.

So travel with inner cheer, not sorrow, to new shores and look confidently into the future. You have every right to do so. And when once again I see you there, which I hope will be very soon, it will give me great pleasure to hear you say that you are happy to be there.

Meanwhile, may I ask you to greet Mr and Mrs Arberry warmly on my behalf, in particular little Anna and her friend and companion Reni and, last but not least [this phrase is written in English], Dr Seth, my dear friend. May I in addition request you to hold good memories of me; I send you my heartiest greetings together with my best wishes for the future. When you were here recently, I wished to speak to you, as indeed I am doing here, but refrained from doing so at the time in order to prevent an elegaic mood from taking over. Once again, be of good heart; often, what is experienced as bitterness proves itself to be a blessing. And how do the French put it? 'Il faut avaler des couleuvres [One must swallow grass snakes, i.e. put up with affronts]' . . .

With warm greetings,
F. Mahnert

2.26

In August 1939, the German and Soviet governments signed a non-aggression pact, to which was attached a secret protocol that included an agreed division of Poland. Hitler saw Eastern Europe as a living space destined for colonisation by Germans; Stalin was keen to expand his communist empire westwards.

Britain and France had earlier in the year given guarantees to Poland that they would intervene if it was attacked. But Hitler, considering the ineffectuality of their response to his actions in Austria and Czechoslovakia, was convinced that they would not risk a general war to prevent his local gains. On 1 September he attacked Poland from three sides with massive force. Britain and France presented him with an ultimatum to withdraw. For them, it was not simply a matter of Poland; the guile, mendacity and aggression that Hitler had consistently displayed made it clear that no guarantee or treaty could be trusted; it was now a question of their own security and their status as Great Powers. Hitler appears to have been shocked by this turn of events, but he did not withdraw. Britain and France, having had no response to their ultimatum, declared war on Germany on 3 September. They could, however, do little to help Poland, which was also attacked, a fortnight later, by the Soviet Union.

Shanti enlisted in February 1940 at the age of thirty-three, five months after war broke out. Mr Warden, whose practice he had been handling, immediately offered him the partnership he had earlier wanted; but by then it was too late.

Though he had never had anything to do with the British Embassy or its functions while he was in Berlin, Shanti found that the officers who interviewed him for the Army Dental Corps knew a great deal about his life there, including the fact that he hadn't taken part in any political meetings.

He joined as a lieutenant. The first thing he did was to go off to Simpson's, the men's outfitters in Piccadilly, to get his uniform made. It was expensive: in addition to his allowance, he had to pay £100 out of his own pocket. He was given a first-class rail ticket and told to go to Chester to join the Western Command. Being a greenhorn, he didn't know when to salute and when to take a salute. Every time soldiers passed him on the street, he pretended to examine the shop windows. At Chester, where he stayed for a couple of weeks, he was given officer's training and taught something of the King's Regulations. Next, he was sent to Cardiff, where, on his first day, a grinning sergeant brought him two large basketfuls of dentures – upper dentures, lower dentures and labels all mixed together – to sort out. A German bomb had hit the dental laboratory, and these had been found in the debris.

Now that the war was on, he had to adopt a more robust attitude towards teeth and their conservation. Soldiers, who might have to fight on the front or be dropped behind enemy lines, had to be dentally fit for at least a year. 'If in doubt, take it out,' was the prevailing philosophy.

The news of the war was not good. By June 1940, the Germans had defeated Denmark, Norway, Holland, Belgium and, most astoundingly, France. They had occupied Paris and the northern and western parts of France, but left an unoccupied zone to be run as an acquiescent ally from Vichy by Marshal Pétain, a hero of the First World War.

Shanti, still in Cardiff, had a curious brush with this earlier war.

There were not enough quarters for officers, so four or five of us were staying with a Norwegian lady who had been vetted for security. I had taken the largest room on the ground floor because I suffered from – still suffer from – claustrophobia. On Sundays in winter it was my habit to have an open fire in my room and to sit in my chair, reading the newspaper and dozing off. But on this particular Sunday I felt like going for a walk after lunch in Roath Park, near where I was living. I walked for an hour and a half. When I returned, I saw that the house was surrounded by military policemen, including a sergeant. I asked him what it was all about. He asked me if I knew Captain Seth. I said, 'That's me.' He took me aside and said, 'I hope you don't mind if I say this, but be careful when you go into your room.' I entered. The chair on which I usually sat was riddled with shrapnel holes and so were the walls. He asked me if I had any enemies, political or otherwise. Clearly, someone must have dropped a bomb through the chimney.

After the MPs had gone, I sat down and started thinking about what could have happened. And I remembered that near the hearth there had stood the shiny brass-plated outer casing of a shell from the 1914–18 war. Obviously everyone had thought it was an empty shell. I asked the landlady whether a different woman had cleaned my room that day, and she said yes. It appeared that by mistake this woman had let the shell slip under the fireplace. Though there was no detonator on the shell, it was probably still full of gunpowder. And with the intense heat of the fire it had exploded.

I was lucky. It was fate. One chance saves your life, one takes off your arm.

2.27

In London, Henny was facing Second World War bombs.

After his successes on the continent, Hitler had turned his attention to the invasion of Britain. From July 1940 onwards, there was an intense and continuous series of attacks by Luftwaffe fighters and bombers on the Royal Air Force and its facilities. Had Hitler succeeded in knocking out the RAF, there would have been no resistance from the air to a German landing; and, since the British army was no match in numbers, training, equipment or combat experience to the German army, Britain would almost certainly have been defeated. When it became clear that the RAF would not be wiped out, Hitler turned, in mid-September, to attacking strategic and economic targets in British cities; any civilian casualties would presumably help to break the morale of the population and force the British government to come to terms. This, the so-called Blitz, was to last till the early spring of 1941.

Shanti kept very few letters in general, and the only two letters Henny sent to him which survive among his papers date from the beginning of the Blitz. They are written in English, which would not have been the language natural to their conversation. Although Henny no longer crosses her sevens, the handwriting is unmistakably German. 'Robert' is certainly a code name for Hans, less German-sounding and therefore presumably less alarming to a possible censor or interceptor. 'Mum', as mentioned earlier, is the mother of Heinrich Etzold, Shanti's friend from his year in Edinburgh, who was now living in London, in Hendon. Henny was working as a child-minder for a Canadian family and earning a small amount by way of pocket money.

Tel: Amb. 1570
88 Seymour Street
W.2.
17.9.40

My dear Sethy,

Again in the shelter since 3/46 p.m. Now it is half past 8 and the air raid is over for a while. The guns are going very hard. I am a little restless to-day, I don't know why, I only hope nothing will happen. – The shelter is overcrowded. Sometimes I think you are perhaps right to go away from London but then on the other hand I don't know where to go. If I go away from here, I would loose [sic] my allowance and this I don't want. Would you perhaps advise me to take a job somewhere out of London? Of course I would feel then very lonely. It is so difficult. – I did not answer the vicar yet, because I have to write such a lot. You have read the letter from Dr Egan. Would you mind to help me to answer him, when I write you what I want to say? Please let me know if you would correct my english. Sethy, I would so much like to see you again. I know you can't come on leave for the moment. If something should happen to me, give my love to Robert, Lola, Ella and Hei. Take all my belongings for you and keep what you like. Give something to Robert, Lola and Ella, so that they all have a remembrance from me. – Tell Robert that I was faithful. He shall be happy because he is such a good lap [lad? chap?]. Give also a remembrance to Mum. – I hope, nothing will happen. But I want to write you this as precaution.

Dear Shanti, I thank you so much for all your friendship. I keep faith in God. – Best of luck for you. With love, Yours aff'ly, Hennerle.

[This last paragraph is squeezed into the margin of the letter.]

The second letter is sent from the same address on 29 September 1940:

My dear Sethy,

It is so nice of you to write me so often in spite of your work. – I hope you have received my last letter. I have deposited the £10/–/– to my Post-Office-Account. You have given me now together £24.–.– and up to now I have not used this amount. I still hope to be able to keep it for you, perhaps I have to take a few pounds because I must admit, it is impossible to live with £1.–.– weekly if one will not remain hungry. And this I will not and you would not like it to know your Kuckuck ['cuckoo' in German] is hungry. Sometimes I have some extra-expenses such as shoe-repairs, tooth-paste etc. and so I can't live with the £1.–.–. In any case, I think hardly anybody has such a friend as you are to me and be convinced, Sethy, you will get your thanks. – I wrote to you that I caught a cold. Thank God, it is a little better and I hope soon to be quite alright. I could not eat for a few days, because I felt a little miserable. Mum has a real flu with fever etc. I nursed her on Friday the whole day long, yesterday I brought her to Hendon where she stays till Monday, to have a rest. – I hope she will be better soon. – Yes, I know Nita, Henry's [Heinrich's] girl friend. I think she is quite nice. Her house is bombed too, she could save some of her furniture and her clothes. She lives now also in Hendon. – I would so much like to go away from London. The sleep in the Underground is horrible. In Amersham we cannot get a room. Everything is full up. So we must see for something else. The other day I got a compliment from the Captain, who sometimes lives in our house and who worked as a doctor in Aldershot. He told me that I speak sometimes like an English girl. Surely he heard me speaking on the phone or to somebody else. I was very glad about that. You also have said I have improved with my english. – I write you soon again, my good friend. I miss you ever so much.

Lots of love and God may protect you.

Yours aff'ly,

Hennerle.

Shanti Uncle did not say much about Aunty Henny's experiences in England during the war. A large number of German

Tel. club. 15 70.   8ᵗʰ Seymour Street
                                            W. 2.
                                                    29.9.40

My dear Lotty,

          It is so nice of you to
write me so often in spite of your
work. — I hope you have received
my last letter. I have deposited
the £ 10/- to my Post-Office-Account.
You have given me now together
£ 24.-. — and up to now I have not
used this amount. I to still hope
to be able to keep it for you,
perhaps I have to take a few
pounds because I must admit, it
is impossible to live with £ 1.-.
weekly if one will not remain
hungry. And this, I will not and
you would not like it. Sometimes
I have some extra-expenses
such as shoe-repairs, tooth-paste
etc. and so I can't live with the
£ 1.-. — In any case, I think hardly anybody
has such a friend as you are to me

A letter from Henny to Shanti, 1940.

refugees – including Jews – were interned on the Isle of Man as potential security risks, and many were sent off to Canada or Australia. Henny was spared this. But London was dangerous enough, and life difficult, and she was beset by anxiety for her mother and sister.

Shanti Uncle told me that, for all her hardships both then and later, she never cried in his presence except twice. Once was in Berlin when in jest he had called her a scorpion; she had gone off sobbing to her mother to complain. The second was when she phoned him to say that the Arberrys had given her Marmite to eat for breakfast. This abomination broke even her resolve.

2.28

After about nine months in Cardiff, in late 1940, Shanti was sent off to the front in Africa. He travelled in one of the first large convoys from Liverpool via the Cape of Good Hope to Suez. The ship was comfortable, and the captain adhered to the high standards of peacetime, even down to the six-course breakfast. But at Durban he had to continue his journey on another ship, which was dirty and overcrowded; when he was the duty officer for the day, he reported that in those conditions everyone would get dysentery or diarrhoea or both. Finally, they disembarked at Suez.

From Suez they went to Cairo; there the major-general in charge of all the dentists asked them where they would like to be posted. Shanti asked to go to Palestine and another officer asked to go to the Sudan. As a result, that officer was sent to Palestine and Shanti to the Sudan.

He was dispatched to Khartoum up the Nile by boat and rail. It was March and already hot, and as the months passed it became worse. The only times he could work were between seven and ten in the morning and between five and seven in the evening. At other times, the dental materials used for making impressions melted and the silicate filling hardened before it could be mixed. As for the effect of the heat on him and his colleagues: 'Between twelve and three you were in a stupor: you were not alive and you were not dead.'

After a few months in Khartoum, he was sent to Gebeit, a hill station not far from the Red Sea. Here the climate was far more pleasant. He joined the 14th Combined General Hospital (of the Middle East Forces), which was half British and half Indian. His dental unit consisted of only three people, but the great advantage of his position was that he was in independent command. He took over from a Scotsman who, in Shanti's words, 'did very little work and multiplied it by six for his reports'. Over the protests of his English assistant, Shanti refused to allow this inflation. Though at the time he was suffering from shingles, which affected his nerves, and had to take morphine injections to ease the pain, he continued to operate.

Shanti was fascinated by the strange fauna around Gebeit. He motored down to the Red Sea and swam among the coral, unaware that sharks had attacked someone there the previous day. Once while he was out walking with a fellow officer in a wadi near Gebeit he saw a lump of earth move; his friend refused to believe it. They waited for twenty minutes and the thing moved again. When Shanti dug it out he found it was a fish covered with clods of mud; he later read that fish such as these survive in dried river beds until the next rain.

One day, the sunlight suddenly disappeared; he thought at first that it was a large rain-cloud, but there was a humming noise that grew louder and louder; millions of locusts were suddenly swarming everywhere and entering everything: his room, the officers' mess, the kitchens. It was far worse for the local farmers, whose crops were devastated. Some of them started roasting and eating the locusts, under whose weight entire branches of now leafless trees were sagging.

Most of the casualties in the hospital in Gebeit were from the Eritrean campaign, the struggle between Italy and Britain (supported by a great many troops from India) for control of East

Africa. Among them were enemy soldiers, mainly Italian but a few Germans too. In an earlier dispensation these might have been Shanti's friends, but he, like many of his countrymen, was ranged against them by historical and personal circumstance in the service of a country that was ruling – and unwilling to relinquish – his own.

In Gebeit in our hospital there were two German prisoners who were badly incapacitated. When I did the rounds and discovered this, I spoke to them in German. Their faces lit up at the sound. One was a blond German and he told me that this defeat was nothing: 'The Führer will come and he will wipe out the whole British army.' I never went to see him again. The other was from Austria. He was shot through the spine and couldn't move. I told him in German that he should try to move his toes. He was very grateful, and the doctors were surprised that after talking to me he was very cooperative. I made a point to visit him every day, and he looked forward to my visits. When I left Gebeit I don't know what happened to him. You have no idea of the difference between the two: a kind man in need of kindness, and an arrogant fool.

2.29

In 1942 Shanti, now a captain, was sent to Egypt, to the Canal Zone. The battle for control of eastern North Africa was being fought in the vast desert to the west of the Nile delta against Rommel and his Afrika Korps. A great deal was at stake: the control of the eastern Mediterranean; access to the Middle East and its oil; the Suez Canal and the link it would provide to the Indian Ocean and the Japanese; and the security of supply routes to the Soviet Union which, since Hitler had attacked it in June 1941, was now an ally of the British.

By June 1942, the Germans had got as far as El Alamein, only about a hundred kilometres from Alexandria. Here, however, their advance was halted.

Shanti saw no action at this stage of the war; he remained in a base hospital and continued with his dental work in his small unit. He was also asked by the colonel, a tall Irishman called Dargan, to do something entirely different: to manage the local medical officers' mess. The food was awful, the sixteen or so officers were unhappy about it, and something had to be done. Shanti agreed; but he took the job with the understanding that he had the colonel's full support.

He got up early to check the rations as they came in. The cook, who could no longer sell them off to the Egyptians, was not pleased, but the quality of the food improved almost immediately. In addition, Shanti would borrow the colonel's jeep to go off and buy whatever was necessary to supplement the rations. The colonel was particularly fond of pink gin – gin with Angostura bitters – and gin was therefore bought by the case, on the black market if necessary. Moreover, as the reputation of the mess grew, officers belonging to other units would come by. Officers got only one bottle of whisky a week, and there was not enough to go round when others dropped in. This too required 'supplementation'.

Every Saturday Shanti would find some excuse or other to borrow the colonel's jeep to get things for the mess, and head off to the pleasant environs of the French Club in Ismailia. There he and his friend Dick Cole, a dental officer attached to the RAF, would order their usual drink, a highball: Canadian rye with ginger ale and a slice of lemon, delightful in a hot climate. They would down quite a few of these, meet officers from other places and return high and happy to their units. On one occasion, Dick and he were travelling by car with a rather erratic driver, who drove off the road at high speed. The car somersaulted four times but luckily did not end up in the Canal. Usually, though, the driver was a man called George Tuck, whom Shanti describes as the soul of reliability and a perfect gentleman. They were to meet again after the war and help each other professionally.

One day the car broke down, and Shanti was obliged to seek

overnight hospitality for himself and Mr Tuck at the nearest place, which happened to be an RAF depot. There was a mess there, and the officers stood him drinks.

All of a sudden, there was a hush, and you could sense everyone's fear. The wing commander had arrived – an unpleasant and aggressive man. After we had been introduced, seeing me in British uniform, he said, 'Come on, Seth, have a drink with me.' I had a whisky. He then got on to the subject of politics and the British Empire and the benefits it had conferred on the natives. 'Look, Seth, you must agree, you're an intelligent man, after all.' I said, 'Look, Sir, I'm not a politician, I'm an army officer, a dentist.' But he went on and on until I said, 'Sir, if you forget that you're a wing commander and I'm a captain, I'll discuss the matter.' With all the other officers standing around, of course he agreed.

'Well, Seth, you must say we did a lot for them out of, well, goodness . . . We educated them, we trained them . . .' So I said, 'Look here, why did you do that? What have we in common? Are we related? Is our language the same? Is our religion? Nothing. So if you say we went into that country because they were stupid and we wanted to subdue them and rule over them, I'll believe you. If you claim goodness of heart, I don't accept it; it makes no sense. As for educating us, Indian culture is far older than British culture. In Roman times, people in the army were sent to Britain as a punishment – it was the most uncivilised country at the time. So why not leave us to ourselves – let us slaughter each other if we wish. None of this is the business of Britain.'

Whether what I said was right or not, I don't know, but he couldn't argue with me. Nor could he pull rank. He just fumed and left. All the other officers hugged me and patted me on the back. They were so pleased that the bully had been defeated. They stood me so many drinks that I don't know how I got back to my camp.

Shanti had little time for bullies, regardless of rank. One evening an Irish officer, the second-in-command of the hospital, who was losing at poker, wanted to continue to play after closing hours in the mess in order to salvage his losses. He ordered a subaltern to tell the wine waiter to tell the engineer to keep the lights on for another half-hour. When the waiter hesitated, he let out a stream of abuse. Shanti, who was sitting at a nearby table, went up to him and told him that he was the secretary of the mess and that any problem should be referred to him. The major promptly turned the torrent of abuse on to him. Shanti told him that he had informed him earlier that the electricity would be switched off at 10 p.m. The major insisted that he hadn't.

He kept saying, you bloody this, you bloody that, you never bloody well said any bloody thing. I said, 'Are you calling an officer a liar? One more bloody from you, and I'll throw you out.' That didn't stop him, and I promptly threw him out.

Oh, my God, I thought. What have I done? I'm for the big jump. The thing is, between a lieutenant and a captain there isn't much of a gap, but between a captain and a major there's a huge difference. I was sitting in my tent when a letter came from the major: 'Captain Seth, report to me at 8 a.m. I will be charging you with insubordination.' I couldn't sleep, I was so worried. At 1 a.m. I was awake, at 2 a.m. At 2.30, my friend, Major Sammy Shone, who was a medical officer in the Indian Medical Service, an officer of many years' standing who could speak better Hindi than you or me, came into the tent.

'What's the matter?' he asked. 'You look like you've been walking on hot coals.'

I told him everything. 'Show me the letter,' he said.

He read it through, then said, 'Take this letter, tear it into twenty pieces, and throw it into the waste-paper basket.' When I stared at him, he went on: 'Either you arrest someone or you don't. But you can't threaten arrest. King's Regulations.'

So I did nothing. I didn't report at eight o'clock the next morning. At nine o'clock I went to see the colonel and explained what had happened in the mess. He said, 'Seth, my boy, should I get rid of him?' 'No, Sir,' I replied.

But the major was ostracised by everyone. No one would talk to him or play poker with him or share a drink with him. It must have been a horrible feeling and a shock. After two days he came up to me without any malice and offered me a drink, and of course I accepted.

Getting to know the regulations was something that Shanti had little time for. He found it hard to cope with army bureaucracy, which dealt with a dental unit consisting of six people just as it dealt with other units. He had to fill in forms that demanded, among other things, how many anti-aircraft guns his unit possessed. Even a 'nil return' had to be submitted in six copies. Others, however, watched out for him.

I lost some equipment – uh, I can't remember the name, see what happens when you get old – a filling instrument with two heads, both ends look exactly the same, a few inches long, it would have cost about a pound. My male nurse told me that if I informed the dental depot that I had lost it, there would have to be a court of inquiry. So in front of me he broke a similar instrument in two, and when I stared at him, he told me that now we had two unserviceable instruments, and that I could sign a form stating as much. I did so and the replacements promptly arrived.

2.30

Among Henny's letters are a few that Shanti sent her during the war; two written while he was in Egypt show something of how their relationship was developing – if at a distance. He continues to refer to her affectionately as 'Kuckuck' or 'cuckoo', and the tone, though a bit lecturing, is intimate. The mention of 'the third person' is puzzling; Shanti does not appear to be referring to Hans but to someone in London. Fredy is Fredy Aufrichtig, Shanti and Henny's friend in Berlin, the practical joker who gave him a dog's train ticket. As for Mizzi and Kizzi, these could be Henny's eyes, or cheeks, or hands, or indeed anything paired.

Shanti's spelling is a bit irregular; but from now on, rather than larding his letters with irksome sics, I shall read them carefully but leave them as they are.

119952 Capt. S. B. Seth, A. D. Corps
14 C.G.H., M.E.F.
27th January '42

My dear Hennerle,

Your loving letter of the 20th Nov, reached me two days ago. The latest news I had from you was your airgraph of the 4th Dec. You haven't written to me as to how you celebrated your birthday, and what present you bought for yourself. I have sent another parcel of sweets to you this morning, which I hope you will get in due time . . .

Now about our quarrell, I again admit that I am to be blamed quite a bit, but that does not mean that you are less to be blamed. After all you used to purposely do things against my wish. You always write to me that everybody thought you were marvelous. I care very little what other people think of you. The main thing is what I think of you. And I don't think any little of you because I some times quarrell with you or give advice which is not always welcome. I also care more what you think of me than what other people think or say about me. The third person in this matter does'nt interest me and should'nt interest you either. We are all human and 'to err is human'. No one of us is perfect. We are bound to do mistakes and we learn quite a bit from our mistakes and faults. The human nature is so complex. Every one thinks in a different way and 'one man's food is another man's poison'. We do not agree even when it comes to grading virtues and vices. I personally despise 'selfishness' and 'conceit'. There may be other people who do not mind them at all. The best and lasting friendship grows out of love, which in itself is stimulated by friendly understanding and bases its foundation on 'give and take'. Friendship and love is the greatest virtue that I worship. I have been at times rather harsh with you. It was more out of love – to make you better than you are and you will agree that no one is perfect, and not due to shear contempt to pull you down. It is true that 'ideal' is very different from 'reality'. I'll be speaking a lie if I did'nt admit that my 'ideal

Kuckuck, the Kuckuck of my dreams' is different from Kuckuck as she is. It is always so. Our dreams and reality are two different things. Though the 'Kuckuck' of flesh gives rise to Kuckuck of the dream. And as no one can get the 'Kuckuck' of his dream but can get or hope to get the Kuckuck of flesh, it is but natural that we all prefer the Kuckuck of flesh though we still dream of Kuckuck of the dream which is our ideal. We try to bring the dream and reality in to one and one can't blame one to try it. Now my darling 'Kuckuck of the flesh', if I do scold you it is just to make you more like the 'Kuckuck of my dreams'. I have gone rather in the abstract, which I hope you will forgive. In short I mean that we have all our short comings and good points, there is no evil in this world and that I love my Kuckuck very much.

I have had a bad cold for last few weeks. I am again down with a severe cold and cough. I could do with a little nursing at my Mizzi's hands. I quite realise how worried you must be about Ella etc. I pray for their safety. You should trust in God and hope for the Best. I really don't know where Fredy is. I wrote twice to his brother in Africa but never received a reply.

Believe me I miss you very much. If you miss me half as much as I miss you, then you must be missing me a lot. I am glad that 'Schwarze punkt' has still place in your heart. Until you erase it out, it will like to remain there.

It is not a lie if I tell you that I dream of you at least twice a week. It is such a torture, this war.

With lots of love to Mizzi and Kizzi. You know what S.L.D. means.

Yours affly,

Shanti.

P.S. I received your Xmas greetings cable which reached me four days ago. It was delayed by the post office.

Schwarze Punkt (black spot) or *Pünktchen* (little spot) were nicknames given to Shanti by Henny on his visit to Germany in 1938. 'S.L.D.' probably stands for 'Shanti liebt dich' (Shanti loves you).

In a later letter to Henny he signs off with 'I.L.D.', which would stand for 'Ich liebe dich' (I love you).

The second letter suggests that Shanti is about to propose to Henny, or that he implicitly already has. It also strongly implies that there has been at least some physical intimacy between them, possibly just an exchange of kisses. The tone of Henny's letters sent in September 1940 does not suggest this or lead one to expect the warmth of Shanti's tone here. It may be that between that September and Shanti's departure from England a couple of months later, he visited London once or more, and that their closeness quickly grew. In the uncertainty of the Blitz, and with the prospect of losing her closest friend in England to the hazards of war, Henny may have melted a little. In the absence of her letters, it is difficult to say if she reciprocated his feelings. To judge from Shanti's words, she was warm but evasive, possibly because, whatever she felt for him, she still loved Hans or felt she should be faithful to him – or possibly for another reason entirely, as the sting in the tail of this letter states when it quotes her mother, the perceptive Ella.

Shanti's language is normally quite pragmatic. Under the pressure of emotion, however, both here and in other letters, it becomes somewhat literary.

119952 Capt. S. B. Seth, A. D. Corps
14 C.G.H., M.E.F.
27th May '42

My sweet Hennerle,

I hope your tooth is alright by now. How I wish I could be near you! I am dying to see you. You have been pretty good in writing to me for the last two months and I do hope its not entirely due to my grumbling but to some extent due to love. You can hardly understand how I miss you. I dream so often of you. I wonder if you ever feel my presence in your sweet slumber. I have received your airgraphs of 17th, 18th, 22nd and 23rd April and your airmail letter of the 16th March. Though the

119952. Capt. S.B. Seth, A.D. corps.
14 C.G.H., M.E.F.
27th May '42.

My sweet Henneli,

I hope your tooth is alright by now.
How I wish I could be near you! I am dying to see
you. You have been pretty good in writing to me
for the last two months & I do hope it's not entirely
due to my grumbling but to some extent due to
love. You can hardly understand how I miss you.
I dream so often of you. I wonder if you ever feel
my presence in your sweet slumber. I have
received your airgraphs of 17th, 18th, 22nd & 23rd April
& your airmail letter of the 16th March. Though the
latter takes longer time but it gives me more
pleasure to read & re-read your so loving letter.
I have this time no words of reproach but
only words of love & friendship. In the last few
times I have been persistantly getting bad cards
but I always thought of you & congratulated
myself on the proverb of "unlucky in cards,
lucky in love". Do you think I am right in
this assumption? I am getting very bad
up these days. How I long to hold my
Kuckuck in my arms & to kiss tenderly
Keizzi & Nizzi! In a few days, the
month of May will pass with all its
romance & sunshine for some but alas!
it has been only a torture to me. Your
presence would have made all the
difference. I know you were always
partial to 'this month'.

A letter from Shanti to Henny, 1942.

latter takes longer time but it gives me more pleasure to read and reread your so loving letter. I have this time no words of reproach but only words of love and friendship. In the last few times that I played bridge I have been persistantly getting bad cards but I always thought of *you* and congratulated myself on the pretence of 'unlucky in cards, lucky in love'. Do you think I am right in this presumption? I am getting very fed up these days. How I long to hold my Kuckuck in my arms and to kiss tenderly both Kizzi and Mizzi! In a few days the month of May will pass with all its romance and sunshine for some but alas, it has been only a torture to me. Your presence would have made all the difference. I know you were always partial to 'this month'.

If it was in my power I would surely fly back to you. But at present or even in near future there is no chance of leave and so there is no sense to indulge in wishful thinking . . .

After mentioning some stockings, shoes and food parcels he has sent to her and a silver bracelet he has bought for her while on a week's leave in Palestine and Syria, he goes on:

I have also been thinking lately that it would be nice to have a house of my own with plenty of children. We both seem to agree on this point, which is very important indeed. Now, *whom* does Kizzi and Mizzi belong to? *Answer this question my schatzle* [darling].

Your letter of the 16th March has made me so Kuckuck sick as I have never been before. I am feeling now so lonely with a feeling of longing and pain. I am glad you have *nice company*. I have to take your word for it, in spite of your past disappointments in friends.

As I wrote to you before I have'nt received any books from you. Unless the publishers are willing to send it free please don't waste any money on it. The name of the book is:— war injuries of the jaw by Warwick James.

I have been seriously thinking of settling down in life after the war. I am sure you will like me to settle down in London? If I want, I guess I might be able to remain in the army. I don't think I'll like to stay after the war. I have saved a little money but apart from this place being expensive the income tax is very high. You will hardly believe me my dear that I paid £120–.–. as income tax last year. This is nearly one third my pay!! . . .

Kuckuck darling, I could go on writing to you for hours. How much would I like to know how you look and feel now after your illness. Tooth trouble can make life miserable. The more I write to you the more I miss you. I am sure you don't miss me so much in spite of your assurance. Ella always used to say Henny has no heart and surely as a mother she ought to know. This is no chiding because it does not originate from me, moreover I do believe that you have a heart. After all it does'nt take much space for 'a tiny black spot'. Kuckuck dear could'nt you for once let me know exactly how you feel towards me.

I really miss my *Kizzi and Mizzi* very much. Whom does Kizzi belong to? Please look after your health. I wish I was there to kiss your pain away from the tooth.

With fondest love, a tender embrace and many kisses to *Kizzi and Mizzi*. I really feel so lonely without you. I wish I could get you out here. Good night and good bye for today my little one.

[unsigned]

2.31

Shanti also corresponded with his brother Raj in India every two or three weeks.

In 1939, war had been declared on behalf of India by the Viceroy, Lord Linlithgow. He had consulted neither the largest Indian nationalist party, the Congress Party, nor the elected members of the central legislature. When he was asked to state Britain's war aims, in particular why Britain, claiming to fight for freedom, continued to make no commitment to Indian freedom and was putting the lives of Indian troops at risk without consulting Indian opinion, the Viceroy made it clear that Britain's war aims concerned resisting aggression rather than promoting freedom, and that its postwar intentions with regard to India consisted of little more than holding a conference after the war on the question of adjustments to the Government of India Act, 1935.

Much of Indian public opinion had been sympathetic to the plight of the British, rulers though they were, in the face of Nazi attack, but this contemptuous disregard for Indian views and rights was, to many, intolerable. A movement of peaceful protest on an individual basis began; the aim was not to disrupt the anti-Fascist war effort so much as to further the aims of Indian nationalism. The protesters were arrested and imprisoned, and freedom of speech and assembly further curbed by laws and decrees.

By early 1942, a series of military defeats had both decreased faith in an eventual British victory and increased concern for Britain, Russia and China should the Germans and Japanese win. The Japanese, who had forced the British into a long retreat through Burma, were now at the eastern borders of India. Sir Stafford Cripps, as a member of Churchill's coalition government, was sent to India to hold talks regarding Indian self-government. It soon became clear, however, that his powers of negotiation had been severely limited by Churchill, who was more interested in allaying American public opinion – and in particular Roosevelt's concerns – with regard to India than in negotiating in good faith. What was on offer was laughable: India would be ruled exactly as it was for the duration; no power would be devolved until after the war, and then too under a formula that virtually guaranteed its disintegration into numerous states.

This insulting offer was rejected by the Congress Party. In August 1942, with Gandhi's acquiescence, the Quit India Movement was launched. Despite the fact that the top leadership of Congress was immediately imprisoned, powerful protests, many of them violent, disrupted large parts of the country. Brutal repression by the British, including the strafing of crowds by planes and the burning down of villages, restored a sort of simmering calm.

It was in this troubled year that Raj became seriously ill with heart disease. At the time of the outbreak of war, he had been travelling with his wife, Chanda, in Tibet; he had overexerted himself at high altitudes, and this had been compounded by his attempt to get back to his post as quickly as possible. There, two and a half years of overwork had caused his condition to worsen. The only surviving letter of his to Shanti is one written in April 1942 from Calcutta, when he was ill but still at his desk.

The eight-anna stamp on the envelope displays the head of the King-Emperor, George VI; an octagonal censor's stamp states, 'Passed'. The writing-paper is plain and blue. The hand is swift and cursive, vigorous rather than elegant, but for the most part quite legible. This is my grandfather's only surviving letter to anyone. Michi, Sashi and Tuttu, referred to in the letter, are his three sons, and Leila his daughter (and my mother).

3 Belvedere Park,
Alipur
4th April '42

My dear Shanti

Received your loving letter after a great expectation. I am glad to know that you are keeping good health. Yours must be an arduous job. It is good that it still keeps cool in the night at your end. Please write to me your welfare every week. We are very anxious as we did not receive your letter so long.

I have not been too well, it is my old heart trouble. I caught it here in the beginning of February and since then I have been in a bad way. If I could get a fortnight or so off I can probably get over it. But the authorities either insist on my going on long leave say 8 months or no leave at all. I cannot afford 8 months leave. However if I am not better soon I shall put in for four months leave and get a refusal in writing. My trouble is I do not know where to spend the leave. If one is ill one does not want to go to new places and wants certain amount of comfort. Brahma and Achal's houses are out of question, though I like Biswan it is dirty and Brahma cannot make better [he crosses out the transliterated Hindi word *bandobast* to use its English equivalent] arrangements, in fact I haven't heard from him since last four months or so. He is too busy with his own affairs and so is Achal. Had you been here I would have had a brother who could have been of some more help.

Michi is at Lucknow and is working hard for his exams. Tuttu and Sashi are doing well at Darjeeling but poor Leila has not been too well. She had an attack of malady called Korea or is it Corea? [chorea: a nervous disease, causing irregular involuntary movements of the limbs] She is better but we are rather anxious about her. Rest is OK. We all feel that Japan will sooner or later get it in the neck but at present she is doing too well. We do hope the barbarians get a good beating.

    With lots of love,
      Yours affly
      [illegible signature]

2.32

A few months after that letter, Raj was dead. Shanti got the news by telegram on 27 September 1942, while he was in Egypt. He later said: 'I went into the desert. I kept myself to myself. Why should I share my sorrow with strangers? You can share it with friends.'

To Henny he wrote:

> 119952 Capt. S. B. Seth, A. D. Corps
> 14 C.G.H., M.E.F.
> 13th Oct '42

My dearest Hennerle,

    You will be perhaps surprised that I have'nt replied to your airgraphs of 7th, 9th and 15th Sept. I was very upset and I still am very depressed, and not quite in a mood to write. Today being 13th your lucky day I am trying to concentrate to write to you. The last sentence will seem rather out of place but believe me dear Kuckuck I am very tired and depressed. I wish you were here to cheer me up. I miss you so much at this hour of need. As an indian proverb goes, 'Religion,

Patience, Friend and Wife are to be tested at the time of adversity.' I have tried the first three but am still very down hearted. My eldest brother about whom I wrote to you in my last letter expired on the 27th Sept. night. I can hardly believe that he has left us for ever. You can't imagine how upset I am at this great calamity, which has befallen our family. I have not only lost a very dear brother but also my foster-father in him. He was my favourite brother for the last ten years. I know he loved me very much and I feel so miserable that I could not even pay my last homage to him. When I left him in 1936 he was hail and hearty and I can hardly imagine that he is dead. He was a very good brother to all of us; no he was the best brother one could wish. I have'nt even one thousandth his generosity, his uprightness and his kindness. For two days I was crying most of the time my heart out and I felt so lonely. At times I wished to be dead. After my mothers death he represented everything. He was my India, my home. As long as he was alive I was sure of a hearty welcome and felt quite secure. How could God be so cruel as to take my dearest brother from me. He has gone away but his memory will remain fresh for ever. How can I forget all his kindness and help! When my dear mother died I was very sad but then she had lived nearly full span of life. My brother was hardly 47 and we were not prepared for this mortal blow over night, his two letters which have escaped destruction have become most cherished. In his letters he proposed a world tour with me. When he was'nt keeping well he wrote to me that it's a pity I was not there to cheer him up. My poor sister-in-law she must have undergone a hell. He has left behind his wife, three sons and a daughter. You have seen the photo of the eldest as a little boy. He is now 16. He wrote to me only few days ago. He is such a sweet boy. He had cabled to me about my brothers death. My brothers illness must have costed a lot of money, I do not know the exact financial position. The least I can do is to help in their education. I am sorry to bother you with all this. But I need consolation. I wish you were here. I feel so lonely. Time is a great healer but my dear brothers death will leave for ever a gap which can never be filled. I wish you had met him. He was a great man in true sense. I wish every one had a brother like him. Michi – my brothers eldest son wrote to

133

me that few minutes before his death my brother had a strange smile. I wonder what that mysterious smile meant. Was he content to die when the end came? Was death better than life to him? These days I have no interest in life. I hope you can understand my feelings. The irony of fate is that I sent £10–.–. to my sister-in-law as a present to buy a dress which I least expected would be a mourning dress. I do not know why we are here and why we die and where we go. I do not know whether there is heaven and hell. But I do know that if there is heaven then my brother must be there. I miss him terribly. I have now to see him through Michi his eldest son. From now on Michi's achievement will be my brothers achievement.

I am sorry my darling that this letter is sad but I did not wish it to be. It was forced on me by cruel fate.

With love,
Your very unfortunate
Shanti.
I.L.D.

2.33

Fifty years after Raj's death, Michi, then sixty-six years old, wrote a moving and in some ways curious letter to his two brothers Sashi and Tuttu and his sister Leila in which he mentioned another expression on his father's face that day. Their mother Chanda ('Ma' in the letter) had died some years before, in 1984. (Michi himself died in 1999.) Michi's letter is typed, which is a blessing, since his handwriting was atrocious. The errors of spelling and grammar are almost certainly those of the transcriber or more probably amanuensis, as Michi's written and spoken English were excellent. He has gone over the typescript and corrected the more obvious errors, for example the misspelling of his sister's name as 'Leela'.

Dear ____,

    As you know I write to the three of you about this time and previously to Ma. This year it will be 50 years since Daddy's death and I will probably not write again. Chapters have to be closed but the memories will linger. I have never told any of you of the actual details. We had no reason to believe that his condition had deteriorated very badly. It was a Sunday like it is this year. The Quit India movement was on, but was generally fizzling out except in parts of Bihar. Stalingrad was besieged but there was talk that this was a trap into which the Germans ultimately fell. We were staying at the B. R. Singh hospital and one of Daddy's colleagues had asked me out to lunch with his family. When I got back later in the afternoon, there also did not seem to be any particular deterioration but he had been ill and struggling for several months. I remember it was just getting dark when the doctor took me aside and told me that if you want to say a few last words to your father you better go in now. I was completely baffled and stunned that I said what is wrong. He said – 'Well, he is already started turning blue at his feet and it is just a matter of a little while.' I do not think Ma had been told. I have never asked her and she has never told me, but when I went into his room, the nurses were fussing around and Ma seemed to have some strange foreknowledge because she was hyperactive and busying herself with things. You have to remember that he was lying in bed for so long that he had bed sores, continuous drip, so very frail and obviously breathing was not easy but we had been through crises like this before. However this time when I went up to him he had a strange look in his eyes part beseeching, part affectionate, part expectant and maybe a little frightened. He could not speak. He just lifted his hand and put it on my head. Sounds a bit like a movie script but it is not quite that bad. It took him another hour and I do remember that when he did speak he asked for the time and strangely enough it seemed to be his main concern. What is the time? I think that as he died he probably soiled himself (sordid, but this is the way we go) and Ma had no idea she was cleaning a dead body. Luckily by that time Kewal uncle and a few others maybe Miradi, Sir L.P. and Lady Mishra had arrived. They took her away. It was about 8:15. We had been given a small room in the hospital and I think we lay awake most of the night. I was too young to understand the finality. I do not think I was scared but I was apprehensive of the future. I did not realise then that Ma was only 36 and I was only 16½. It would be nice and dramatic to say that I swore that I would look after the family but I did not even know that I had to do it. The pleading, beseeching look has stayed with me. It was only last year for the first time I told Shanti Uncle about it – and now all of you.

I do not think that Ma or I or together took any vows and I still remember that when I was to get married, Uncle Dutt who had done more than anybody else to keep the family going, objected. Aunty Dutt who is not sufficiently appreciated by us said what nonsense, after all he is now providing a home for Chanda and the children. Of course I became very anglicised but that was the flavour of the period and I think because of it [we] were all able to get a start in life. We have come a long long way in these 50 years. We three brothers have retired and Leila you will retire in a few weeks.

Perhaps only I knew him as a father and a human being. Leila got a lot of fatherly affection in 1941 when she stayed back in Calcutta. For Sashi perhaps some memories, but he was too young to know him as a person but only as a father. For Tut[t]u he was a myth. At eight he could only have been in awe and in affection. I still remember the letter he wrote when he got the news in school, 'Pa [the headmaster] told me daddy had died, I did not know what to do so I cried.' Well shall we leave it there as I think that beseeching pleading last look has been answered and we now approach the winter of our years.

With much love as always,
    Yours,
        Michi

There are many more details and when we meet you can ask me. There are many explanations and many questions – not easy.

Since I first came across this letter, I have read it again and again. I have often wished that I had known my grandfather, but I wonder

Henny's mother, Gabriele Caro, known to everyone as Ella. Her father was the manager of a newspaper in Prague.

Ella and Isaac Caro at about the time of their wedding in Dresden in 1906.

A family photograph of the Seths taken at Banaras by the Chakraverty Studio in 1930 or 1931, shortly before Shanti's departure for Germany. Shanti (in the back row) is holding his nephew Sashi in his arms. To the right are his three brothers: Raj (the eldest, my grandfather, with a flower in his buttonhole), Achal (a doctor) and Brahma (an agriculturist).

In front of Raj sits their mother (holding baby Leila – my mother). On either side of her sit her brother (a Sanskrit scholar) and Raj's wife, Chanda (my grandmother, leaning on her arm). Directly below her arm is her eldest son, Michi. Shanti's eldest sister, the disciplinarian Hirabehn, who was a great influence in his life, is third from the left in the middle row.

Shanti's mother, Mohini Devi, shortly before her death. He visited her twice from Germany, but she died while he was abroad.

Henny with her father, Isaac Caro, shortly before his death. About a year after he died, the Caros took in a lodger in their large apartment in Berlin: Shanti.

Clockwise from the right:
Lola and Henny. Their rather feckless younger brother Heinz. Ella with her canary. Henny and Heinz. Ella and her two daughters.

Henny and Hans were always elegantly turned out,
whatever the degree of casualness or formality.

Henny at the top left of a water-polo pyramid.

On the Hafelekar, a peak near Innsbruck: the 'three-girl family' Lili Würth, Lola and Henny on a walking holiday in Austria in 1932.

Henny with the Mahnerts on an outing by the Sakrower See near Berlin. Hans's father, Franz Mahnert, is holding Hans's wire-haired terrier, Whisky (or Whisky's predecessor), on a leash. Hans sits in the tree, with one young woman on either side. Henny is holding the legs of Miss Garrasch (later, Gerda von Gliszczynski), Franz Mahnert's longtime companion, who, in the hard times that followed the war, kept him from starving and freezing.

Henny, as naiad or dryad, about to go for a swim in the Sacrower See.

if I – whatever that 'I' means – would then have known my father. I should explain what I mean by this.

After my grandfather died, my grandmother and her children were supported not by any pension but by a few meagre savings and in particular by the generosity of the Dutts, an older couple from Darjeeling who had befriended them earlier and in whose house they were now invited to stay. (Mrs Dutt was something of a tartar, but as strict with herself as with the children.) Even after they had begun to make their way in life, the four children were not well off. Had their father been alive, he would probably have become a member of the Railway Board and moved in elevated social circles; that, together with Michi's advanced anglophilia, would almost certainly have put paid to any attempt by my father to woo my mother. My father was working in shoe manufacture as a supervisor at Bata rather than in the Civil Service or one of the professions, or as a covenanted assistant in a British managing agency. He spoke Hindi well, but his spoken English was not polished. He dressed rather too well and his shoes were somewhat flashy. He chewed paan. He had been rusticated from college and in effect debarred from education for five years for hauling down the British flag and hoisting up the Congress one. It is most unlikely that he would have been considered by my mother's family – perhaps not even by my mother – to be the suitable boy he more than proved to be.

2.34

We do not have Henny's response to Shanti's letter regarding the death of his brother in Calcutta. What has survived from about this time is a series of messages regarding the situation of her sister and her mother in Berlin.

In 1942 Henny managed to communicate a few times with them through the British and German Red Cross. The messages were sent on a standard Red Cross form, on the back of which the response of the recipients was recorded. Both message and response were confined to twenty-five words and had to be passed by the British and German censors. Henny sent the first message on 5 January 1942. On its outward journey, the Swiss Red Cross stamp in Geneva says, '20 Jan. 1942'. The German Red Cross stamp says, '6 Mrz 1942'. On its return journey, the Swiss Red Cross stamp says, '21 Avr 1942'. It would probably have arrived in London in another two to three weeks.

DEAREST MUTTI AND LOLA
   I AM WELL ALSO AS REGARDS WORK. LIVING
COMFORTABLY. PLEASE WRITE IMMEDIATELY. EMBRACE YOU
WARMLY AND KISS YOU LOVE YOUR
   [signed] Hennerle

On the back of the form is the typed response:

Dearest Hennerle
Overjoyed about your news think lots about you we are healthy
write again soon greet Hei Littlespot [their nicknames for Heinz and
Shanti] Warmest greetings and kisses
   [signed] Mutti   Lola

Henny's second message, dated 26.5.42, reads:

DEAREST MUTTI AND LOLA OVERJOYED ABOUT YOUR NEWS.
I AM WELL. LITTLESPOT ROSEL AND FAMILY ALSO WELL.
LILLI HAPPY MOTHER HEARTFELT [the untranslatable German
word *innig*] KISSES EVER YOUR
   [signed] Hennerle

The response reads:

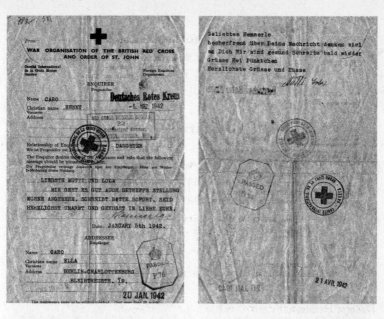

Two Red Cross messages.

Dearest Hennerle
Always happy about news from you. Write more often. We are healthy.
How is Heichen [Heinz]? Greet all. Warm greetings kisses yours
    [signed] Mutti, Lola
20.7.42

Henny's last message is dated 5.10.42:

DEAREST MUTTI AND LOLA HAPPY ABOUT YOUR NEWS ALL
WELL WITH ME. WARMEST BIRTHDAY WISHES. HEARTFELT
[*innig*] GREETINGS KISSES ALSO OLGA FLORA [Henny's aunts]
    WITH LOVE YOUR
        [signed] Hennerle

The last response from her mother and sister reads:

Dearest Hennerle
News from you at last, was growing worried. Nothing new with us.
Take care of Heinz. Warmest birthday wishes. Greetings kisses
    Mutti, Lola
26.11.42

In each case it would have been at least four months from the time
Henny sent out her twenty-five words to the time she received
twenty-five words in response.

But even as the first of these messages was making its way to
Berlin, a meeting was taking place there of which only the
euphemistic minutes survived after the war, and these too in a
single copy. It had been planned for the end of 1941 and had been
delayed by the American entry into the war following the Japanese
attack on Pearl Harbor. It took place on 20 January 1942 in a villa
on the Wannsee, a lake close to the Sacrower See where Henny
used to spend her Sundays with Hans and Shanti and other
friends.

The subject of the conference was how to deal in a final manner with the Jewish question in Europe, and the conferees, who represented various branches of the Nazi Party and departments of the German government, agreed as follows:

> In the course of the final solution, the Jews are to be taken under appropriate direction and in a suitable manner to the east for labour utilisation. Separated by sex, the Jews capable of work will be led into these areas in large labour columns to build roads, whereby doubtless a large part will fall away through natural attrition. The inevitable remnant, which doubtless constitutes the most resistant element, will have to be dealt with appropriately, since it represents a natural selection which, were it to be released, would have to be regarded as the germ cell of a new Jewish revival.
>
> In the course of the practical implementation of the final solution, Europe will be combed from west to east, with priority given to the territory of the Reich including Bohemia and Moravia.

This policy was secret, though in Germany at least it became for many people something of an open (if still furtive) secret. Whatever she knew or hoped or feared or expected, Henny could not have imagined anything so pragmatic, evil and bizarre. The consequences of this policy for her family were not to reach her until after the war.

2.35

119952 Capt. S. B. Seth, A. D. Corps
14 C.G.H., M.E.F.
17th Nov '42

My dear Hennerle,

. . . This airgraph is intended to bring you my heartiest good wishes on your happy birthday. I have already sent you an airmail letter with a cheque for a modest present and I hope you have received it. This is the second occasion that I have to depend on a [illegible word: punched out in the file] piece of paper and pen to reveal to you my love and confidence at the happy occasion. I trust it will not be very long when I can celebrate [illegible word] and the last two birthdays with you. This does not seem wishful thinking any more after the recent good tidings of war. I hope it finds you in sound health with tooth and all.

    With fondest love and kisses,
      Yours affly,
      Shanti

Though it would be a while before he could celebrate Henny's birthday with her, the tidings of war were indeed good. In October 1942 the Germans, who, under Rommel, had got to El Alamein more than a year before and had stabilised their position there, were driven back by Montgomery; they were soon in full retreat.

About a week before Shanti's letter, in order to airlift and convoy reinforcements to French North Africa, where the Allies had gathered strength, the Germans had felt compelled to occupy Vichy France.

Two days after the date of Shanti's letter came the great tank attack by the Russians that was the first major step towards the encirclement and eventual destruction of the German Sixth Army at Stalingrad.

In the Atlantic, the loss of life and shipping caused by U-boats was being countered more effectively, partly owing to codebreaking intelligence.

On the borders of India, the Japanese were overextended. In China and elsewhere, too, they were beset.

In the Pacific, after the loss of the main Japanese aircraft carriers at the Battle of Midway, a battle in which the cracking of the Japanese naval code was vital, the Americans saw their way open to an eventual advance towards Japan.

In terms of *matériel*, America's industrial power was increasingly being harnessed to the war effort.

Shanti's next posting was in Syria, in Trablous (or Tripoli, as it was confusingly called; it is now in Lebanon). He had no idea why he was sent there, and had almost nothing to say about his time there except that he found scorpions in his boots. According to *Fight No More*, the memoir of a friend of his, Anup Dutt (no relation to the Dutts mentioned earlier), who was an officer with the Indian Medical Service, 'Shanti joined No. 17 Field Ambulance while we were in Syria, and it was later found that his was an incorrect posting. However, he remained and came to Italy with his Unit.' Shanti Uncle merely said about this posting, which was to have such a profound effect on his life, that the army 'sometimes made silly decisions'.

When I talked to Dr Dutt about his wartime memories of Shanti Uncle, he recalled Shanti's pet rabbit, Chuk-chuk. I mentioned this later to Uncle, and he was delighted to be reminded of him.

I called him Chuk-chuk to copy his snorting sound. He was a completely white rabbit; he must have been a girl's pet rabbit. I got him in Tripoli. He ran into my tent. And when he saw me and I put my hand forward, he jumped into my lap. I was the mess secretary, and so I made him the mess mascot. I never put him into a cage or anything. He used to sleep in the tent and run around, and we – the cook and I – used to make sure that he always had something to eat that he liked. He was a real white VIP. You have no idea how much of a pet he was. Wherever we went, with the field ambulance or on the ship to Bari, he went.

After spending most of 1943 in Syria, that winter Shanti went to Italy. He accompanied the invading troops to a country that had been an enemy but which, after Mussolini's downfall, had thrown in its lot with the Allies. The fact that it had taken some months to negotiate and sign the treaty gave the Germans the opportunity to disarm the Italian forces and occupy the country themselves. Italy would thus have to be fought for, and the campaign, despite an encouraging start from Sicily up to Naples, would now prove to be slow, gruelling and costly.

2.36

We were among the first troops in a convoy of ten or eleven ships going to Bari. The ships were lying offshore, and the German planes came and bombed them. Luckily, we had disembarked. We were in an olive grove, full of scorpions.

It rained all night – there was water in my tent. I slept through it all. In the morning I found that my slippers were doing the tango, and my boots were floating beyond them.

The idea was that the Germans should think that we were going to attack on the eastern side of Italy. But the same night or the next night we crossed half the width of Italy and got to a place called Potenza, high up in the mountains.

It was so cold that one driver, awake when everyone else had gone to sleep, tried to keep warm by using petrol to light a fire. But the can, which was in his hand, caught fire. In order to save the others, he jumped from the first floor with the can, and the next day he was found dead down below in the grass. He must have been concussed, but that wasn't how he died. Nor was he burned. He had frozen to death.

The rain and cold were part of the reason why the Italian campaign was so difficult. The other reason lay in the nature of the terrain. The Apennines run like a spine down the length of Italy – a spine with spurs running off it. Between these spurs, short, often rapid, rivers flow down to the sea. Working their way up the west coast of Italy in order to get from Naples to Rome and beyond, the Allied armies thus faced a series of obstacles that acted as effective lines of defence for the Germans.

Churchill was keen on an Italian campaign. Success in North Africa had to some extent cleared the way for an attack across the Mediterranean, either in Italy or in the Balkans. Though he and the Americans had agreed that the planned D-Day landings in Normandy would be the main vehicle for the invasion of Europe,

Churchill still believed that an earlier, strategic thrust in Italy would tie up German troops, provide quick morale-boosting victories through rapid advance and the likely capture of Rome, and, if all went well, bring the Allies to the borders of Austria, now a part of Greater Germany. The Americans, who feared an Italian campaign might disperse their strength, were less enthusiastic, and hedged their acquiescence with conditions.

Churchill, who had talked of attacking the 'soft underbelly of the Axis', was frustrated by the fact that it had proved to be anything but soft. The land, criss-crossed by rivers and steep ridges, was no good for tanks. Indeed, in the rain-pelted, muddy mountains, only mules would do for transport.

The German troops in Italy included some of their finest; they were led by Field-Marshal Kesselring, an excellent professional soldier. The Allies under General Alexander – British, Americans, Indians, Canadians, New Zealanders, French, Poles – moved slowly up the west coast, taking the obstacles one by one. The most difficult of these was Monte Cassino. The Allies arrived here in early 1944, and got bogged down for many months, unable to advance. In some respects, the battles fought here recalled the gruelling warfare of the First World War.

It was at Monte Cassino that Shanti lost his arm.

Two major roads lead northwards from Naples to Rome: one along the coast, the other – separated from it by mountains – some miles inland. This latter road skirts the towering mountain of Monte Cassino and then moves towards Rome along the Liri valley. But advancing towards the Liri valley was the problem. From Monte Cassino – and the massive, thick-walled fortress-like Benedictine monastery resting on its peak – everything in the valley below was visible to the Germans, and artillery could be directed accurately at it from there or elsewhere. The valley, almost throughout the rainy winter, was a muddy swamp, with the Rapido, into which the Liri flowed, rushing swiftly across it. At the foot of the mountain lay the town of Cassino, which was in German hands and heavily fortified.

Four attempts were made between January and May 1944 to advance past Cassino into the Liri valley. The first battle was a hurriedly conceived affair in support of a landing by American and British troops at Anzio, further up the coast, closer to Rome. The landing was successful and took the Germans by surprise. At Cassino, however, the attempted night crossing of the Rapido by the main American force, preparations for which were made in daylight in full view of the enemy, was a disaster. So were attempts later made, after crossing further upstream, to attack the Germans in their well fortified positions, many of which had been blasted out of solid rock during the previous months. Despite this, the Americans managed, against great odds, to survive in a few pockets in the mountains north of Monte Cassino.

Meanwhile, at Anzio, the Germans quickly brought in reinforcements from north of Rome, not from the Cassino sector, to contain the beachhead. They then made preparations for a massive counter-attack. With the Allied troops at Anzio now under great threat, a second – almost diversionary – battle, at even shorter notice, had to be launched at Cassino. It was at this time that Shanti and his unit moved into the battle zone.

In *Cassino*, a fascinating account of the battles that is both detailed and wide-ranging, Fred Majdalany writes of the task force assembled for the second battle:

> This brought into the arena two of the greatest fighting divisions of the war, the 2nd New Zealand and the 4th Indian. They were utterly dissimilar in personality and method but alike in being able to claim a long record of success dating back to the earliest days of the war. Both brought to Cassino and the badly shaken [American] Fifth Army an almost arrogant conviction of invincibility born of their great victories in the Western Desert. An aura of glamour invested these two divisions.

After a difficult relief by the Indians of the remnants of American troops, who had held out against starvation and exposure and enemy fire in their mountain pockets, an advance was attempted along a bare ridge near the monastery. But every move along 'Snakeshead Ridge', as the Americans dubbed it, could be viewed and countered from the surrounding heights, all of which were in German hands. It was now decided to bomb the monastery from the air in order to knock the peak out as an observation post and because it was felt, on balance, that the vast building was more useful to the Germans as fortification than as rubble. The ground and air forces, however, did not coordinate their plans.

The ground troops were not fully informed when, owing to good weather, the bombing was brought forward to the morning of 15 February. But once it had taken place, there was no time to waste; in the mountains, the 4th Indian Division were told to attack that night. Undersupplied and with insufficient time to prepare for the battle, they suffered appalling losses. Two nights later, down in the valley, the New Zealanders at great cost captured the railway station at Cassino – a position that would have helped the army make a break past Cassino into the Liri valley. But this Maori battalion was forced by German tanks to relinquish their gains the following day. The road across flooded ground that the sappers had tried to build by night in order to allow Allied tanks to support them could not be completed quite in time.

It was an expensive price to pay for lack of communication. For all the loss of life and the destruction of a great monastery, one of the springs of Western civilisation, nothing was achieved.

2.37

Shanti was in the Cassino area for several months. It was the first time he had seen sustained warfare at close hand. He learned when a major attack was to take place by noticing when the hygiene department, which had to estimate how many men were going to die, began to dig trenches in the rocky soil as a provisional resting-place for bodies before burial later, possibly much later, in a cemetery. The presence of clergymen was also a good indicator of when battle was about to begin.

It was difficult, often impossible, to get the wounded out during the Cassino battles, particularly in the mountains. Stretcher-bearers had to carry them down steep and slippery paths, often in snow or freezing rain and under mortar fire, for miles; many of the wounded died on the way. By the time the survivors among them reached a road, they would have had no treatment for several hours. To move them in the normal way to an advanced dressing-station and thence to a casualty clearing station (where surgery might be carried out) and thence to a base hospital far from the battle, would be too time-consuming and traumatic. Besides, serious head wounds were far commoner here than elsewhere. Both shrapnel and the little *schuh* antipersonnel mines became particularly dangerous on the rocky ground, splinters of which compounded the damage by flying upwards and outwards. It was on this front that field surgical units in tents or under canvas flaps attached to lorries were used for the first time; the doctors were brought forward towards their patients rather than the other way around.

It was in such an advanced field ambulance that Shanti's dental unit was placed. When I asked Shanti Uncle whether his unit was in the mountains or the valley, he said: 'We were on the hill, we could see the Germans with binoculars. You couldn't have seen them from the town or from below the hill.'

He described the conditions under which he worked and lived in the battle zone:

The surgery tent was about twelve feet by nine. The tent I used to sleep in was a bivvy, a bivouac tent; you had to crawl in like a blooming dog. Shells went over your head like express trains. After a while I ceased to notice them. Some of the boys who were killed were so young. I never wrote to their parents. I thought, let them think they died in action. But many of them were killed in the shelling.

148

In this multinational force, there was no uniformity when it came to eating habits or food supplies.

An American field ambulance that departed in a hurry left an excellent supply of provisions, including tinned chicken. (They also left their dead to be buried.)

The Cypriot muleteers took good care of their mules, who were calm under mortar fire but bolted if they heard a whisper. When, directly in front of Shanti's surgery tent, a mule was hit by shrapnel, it did three or four somersaults into the air. But even before it had gasped its last breath, he said, the muleteers had begun to carve it up.

Another culinary casualty was Chuk-chuk, the mess mascot, the well travelled rabbit from Syria. He was carried up to Monte Cassino, remained in the front line, and was allowed to run about freely. One day he disappeared. A search party was sent out, but found nothing.

'Somebody must have eaten him up,' said Shanti Uncle.

'Who would have done that?' I asked.

'I can tell you. There were Poles, there were Cypriots.'

'The French?' I suggested.

'I don't think so,' replied Uncle meditatively.

2.38

Some of Shanti's reminiscences have the surreal and disturbing quality of dreams.

I climbed a mountain and I found someone there with binoculars, uniform and pistol. I spoke loudly in English; he didn't reply. I wanted to approach him so that I could borrow his binocs and see the Germans more closely. The more I followed him, the more he ran. For some reason I wasn't afraid. I thought, I'll just get closer and then he'll understand that I just want to borrow his binoculars. I was unarmed. I don't know what

149

happened; he disappeared. He was not wearing a British or Polish or French or German uniform. To this day I don't know what he was. It was similar to a khaki British uniform, but in a different cut and with different markings, but I couldn't see him closely. He was a white man.

Another time, I climbed a little hill near Monte Cassino, and that's where I saw the children's toys. There had been shelling. I went to a house. The children's toys had been left behind, the bread not completely baked. It broke my heart. I couldn't even eat. What happened to the blooming children, I don't know.

2.39

After the bombing of the monastery and the unsuccessful battle in February, it was decided to attack Monte Cassino a third time, and quickly. Again, the New Zealand and Indian divisions were to be used, but this time on a narrow front, in tandem. The idea was not, as before, to make a flanking movement, but to go straight up the mountain to the monastery.

This was to be achieved by carrying out a series of objectives in order. First, the town of Cassino was to be obliterated by intense aerial bombing in order to crush any German resistance there. The infantry were to move in immediately; behind them would come tanks to provide support. Next, Castle Hill, behind the town, was to be taken. Since this led, by a rocky saddle, to the main mountain of Monte Cassino, it provided a route to the next two objectives, a couple of bends on the tortuous road that led to the summit. Then came Hangman's Hill, so named after a gallows-like pylon it supported. The next step was the summit of Monte Cassino with its persistently deadly observation posts.

Because of the need for tanks, it was necessary to wait till the ground had dried out somewhat. But the skies broke in late February and it rained every day for three weeks. Finally the attack was launched on 15 March, the inauspicious Ides.

The bombing was effective, but insufficient infantry followed it to take over the rubble that was all that remained of the town before the Germans could recover. When they did recover and began to defend the ground, it had to be fought for yard by yard. Craters made it difficult for tanks to support the New Zealanders, but that had been anticipated, and a few tanks managed to manoeuvre into the ruined town while the engineers repaired the road behind them. That night, however, rain fell heavily. The craters filled with water and the ground turned to slush. No further tanks could make it through.

Castle Hill and the first bend were taken by the New Zealanders, and that night, while the Rajputana Rifles were battling for the second bend, the Gurkhas took Hangman's Hill. By doing so, they got to the penultimate objective even before the bends in the road were secured. Though this was excellent news, it created severe problems of supply from Castle Hill. On the fifth day of the battle, one of the best German divisions, the First Parachute Division, attacked Castle Hill, the key link to the forces on the main mountain. After a bitter fight, they took it back. The forces on Hangman's Hill were cut off, and there was now no question of an attempt on the summit.

Over the next few days the Gurkhas, exhausted, starving and freezing, were with great difficulty taken off the mountain. The Indian and New Zealand divisions were finished as a fighting force. What physical gains had been made were consolidated, but the Allies had to accept that they still could not get past Monte Cassino to the Liri valley and the road northwards to Rome.

2.40

On the first day of this third battle, the following signal was sent out by the colonel in charge of the medical staff:

Copy of FLAMBO signal SD219/23159 dated 15 Mar '44.

Arrange move D British Dental Surgery Unit 1 BO 1 BOR 4 IORs 3/4 ton stores from 4 Ind Div to CANCELLO soonest (.) on arrival under comd 3 Dist rep to 16 combined general hospital

---

Subject: – <u>Moves – Dental Units.</u>

<u>Very Urgent.</u>
<u>Secret.</u>
Main HQ 4 Ind Div.
No. 034 / M.
16 Mar '44.

<u>C.C. D Br. Dental Surg. Unit.</u>
   Forwarded for necessary action.

P.S.   [signed] J G St . . . man [illegible]
16.3   Major
DLP / –   f Colonel,
                          A.D.M.S.

This signal, typed in blue on flimsy and crumpled white paper, and signed in faded sepia ink, was among the documents Shanti kept all his life. It was sent under the authority of FLAMBO (the administrative advanced Allied Forces Headquarters in Italy, which combined logistics in forward areas for both American and British forces) and it required him and the small dental unit he ran to move back from his front-line position with the advanced field ambulance to a base hospital in or near the town of Cancello, not far from Naples. (He was the BO, or British officer, referred to in the first line of the order; the other personnel referred to are British and Indian other ranks.) It was received by him on the second day of the battle with mortar and artillery fire stuttering sporadically around him. He decided not to act on it immediately but to wait for a day because his friends wanted to have a small farewell celebration for him that evening.

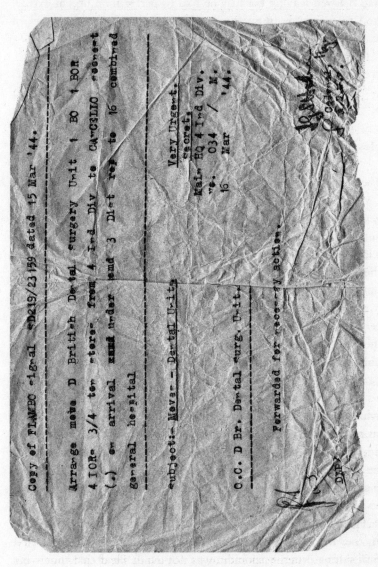

The FLAMBO signal.

The myth prevalent in our family had been that Shanti Uncle had delayed leaving because he had to perform an urgent extraction for someone in great pain. When I mentioned this story of sacrifice to Uncle, he shook his head impatiently.

2.41

He described how his arm was blown off:

There were no trenches near my dental tent. It was a hilly and rocky area. I was sitting behind my panniers – the boxes in which I kept my dental gear – and my hand was outside. All of a sudden, there was a big bang, and my hand was off and hanging by my skin. There was terrific pain and a lot of blood. I waited for twenty minutes. The shelling went on. Then I thought, nobody would know I was here. More bleeding. Best to run through the shelling to the tent where the medical officers were attending to the wounded patients. There were quite a few there; I knew all the officers by their Christian names, and they insisted they would do it themselves for me. But even after an injection of morphine, the pain was unbearable. I got another but then I don't remember anything.

The doctors staunched the bleeding and amputated his forearm while the shelling was still going on. He was quickly sent away from the front to the casualty clearing station. The road was bumpy, and the jolting of the ambulance caused him a lot more pain. When he reached the clearing-station, he was given painkillers and sleeping tablets, but to little effect. Early the next morning he was moved to a general hospital in Caserta, not far from Naples.

He had no appetite at all, but the staff insisted he eat something. As they knew he liked whisky, they gave him some. They also gave him sulpha drugs – penicillin was not available at that time – but he said that these, besides causing him sleeplessness and diarrhoea, did a lot of long-term damage to his liver.

His friends and fellow officers came to see him. General Alexander, when he visited the hospital, happened as a result to see him as well, and assured him, 'Everyone will look after you.'

'What will I do? What will I do?' – the thought came to me again and again.

Mount Vesuvius, I believe, erupted at that time, and they showed it to me. I was not interested in a volcano or anything, but they tried to take my mind off my problems, and they were really good to me. They gave me whisky, they gave me eggs, and what more could they do?

That morning I'd operated on a few patients. Now I was useless for anything.

I still can't work out why the Germans shelled us. True, they were above us, they had the advantage. But there was a sort of understanding that neither side would shell the medical people on the other side. I very much doubt they wanted to shell us, because when our ambulance travelled at night, they didn't shell it. They could easily have killed us. Maybe they shelled us that afternoon because there was artillery nearby – or maybe the mules that were used for transport. Who knows?

From the Caserta hospital the first letter I wrote was to Henny. I wrote in capital letters, like a child writes, and it took me four hours just to write six lines or so. I was also very ill from liver and drugs – more even than because of my hand. It was an air-mail letter. I have thrown all that away. I don't have anything to do with the army, all that rubbish. I can't even find my army cap or uniform. The Eritrean war, the Italian campaign . . . medals, they just come with the rations.

2.42

But Shanti's letter, written with a shaking left hand in pencil, was among Henny's papers, not his own, and therefore had not been destroyed.

DEAR HENNERLE,

MOST AWEFUL THING HAS HAPPENED TO ME, MY RIGHT FOREARM WAS COMPLETELY SEVERED BY A SHELL. THIS HAPPENED ON THE AFTERNOON OF THE 16th INSTANT. SOME OTHERS WHERE KILLED, BUT FROM MY UNIT I AM THE ONLY ONE INJURED. WHEN I SAY MY UNIT I MEAN THE FIELD AMBULANCE AS WELL. IS IT NOT IRONY OF FATE, THAT THE VERY DAY I WAS HURT, THE POSTING ORDERS FOR A BASE HOSPITAL HAD COME FOR ME. I HAVE BEEN HAVING VERY SEVERE PAIN IN MY STUMP. I AM SIMPLY GOING THROUGH HELL. WHY MY LIFE HAS BEEN SPARED I DO NOT KNOW. THEY ARE TALKING ABOUT PUTTING AN ARTIFICIAL LIMB LATER ON BUT AT PRESENT I AM SO FED UP THAT I WOULD RATHER DIE. AS YOU NOTICE I AM WRITING WITH LEFT HAND AND IT IS'NT VERY EASY EITHER. THIS IS THE FIRST LETTER I AM WRITITING TO ANYONE.

I DREAD TO THINK OF THE FUTURE. THE PRESENT IS BAD ENOUGH.

I HAVE RECEIVED YOUR LETTER OF 6th INS. PLEASE REMEMBER ME TO KHANNAS [distant relations of Shanti living in London] & HENDON FRIENDS.

WITH LOVE

YOUR MOST UNFORTUNATE

Shanti

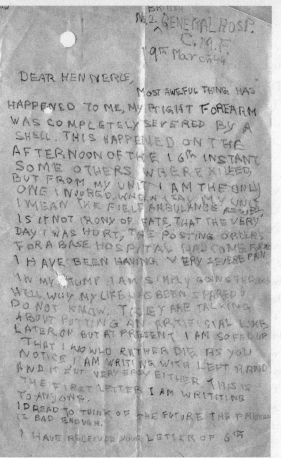

BRITISH
No. 2. GENERAL HOSP.
C.M.F
19th March 44

DEAR HEN NERG, MOST AWEFUL THING HAS
HAPPENED TO ME, MY RIGHT FOREARM
WAS COMPLETELY SEVERED BY A
SHELL. THIS HAPPENED ON THE
AFTERNOON OF THE 16th INSTANT
SOME OTHERS WHERE KILLED,
BUT FROM MY UNIT I AM THE ONLY
ONE INJURED, WHEN I SAY MY UNIT
I MEAN THE FIELD AMBULANCE AS WELL
IS IT NOT IRONY OF FATE, THAT THE VERY
DAY I WAS HURT, THE POSTING ORDERS
FOR A BASE HOSPITAL HAD COME FROM
I HAVE BEEN HAVING VERY SEVERE PAIN

IN MY STUMP I AM SIMPLY GOING THROUGH
HELL, WHY MY LIFE HAS BEEN SPARED I
DO NOT KNOW, THEY ARE TALKING
ABOUT PUTTING AN ARTIFICIAL LIMB
LATER ON BUT AT PRESENT I AM SO FED UP
THAT I WOULD RATHER DIE. AS YOU
NOTICE I AM WRITING WITH LEFT HAND
AND IT ISN'T VERY EASY EITHER. THIS IS
THE FIRST LETTER I AM WRITTING
TO ANYONE.
I DREAD TO THINK OF THE FUTURE. THE PRESENT
IS BAD ENOUGH.

I HAVE RECEIVED YOUR LETTER OF 6th

INS. PLEASE REMEMBER ME TO
KHAWNS' HENDON FRIENDS,
WITH LOVE
YOUR MOST UNFORTUNATE
Shanti

Shanti's first letter to Henny after he lost his right arm.

2.43

A fortnight after this first letter, he wrote another, also in pencil, Once again, he tried to write his name not in block capitals, but as a proper signature:

67 BRITISH GENERAL HOSP.
C.M.F.
2nd APRIL 1944

My DEAR HENNERLE,

I HAVE ALREADY WRITTEN TO YOU ABOUT 10 DAYS AGO FROM NO. 2 GENERAL HOSPITAL. AS I WROTE TO YOU BEFORE I HAVE LOST MY RIGHT FORE-ARM FOUR INCHES BELOW THE ELBOW BY A SHELL. I WAS TRANSFERRED TO THE ABOVE HOSPITAL & AM AWAITING EVACUATION ON A HOSPITAL-SHIP TO ENGLAND. THE CHANCES OF MY BEING IN LONDON ARE PRETTY GOOD. I THINK THEY PUT ARTIFICIAL LIMB AT ROHAMPDEN. I AM STILL SUFFERING FROM GREAT PAIN IN MY ARM. TO MAKE THE THINGS WORSE I HAD A SEVERE ATTACK OF DIARRHOEA FOR 18 HOURS AS SOON AS I CAME TO THIS HOSPITAL. THANK GOD IT IS ALRIGHT NOW. DARLING KUCKUCK I HAVE BEEN UNDERGOING A TERRIBLE MENTAL AND BODILY TORTURE. I WISH YOU WERE HERE TO GIVE ME HOPE, AND COMFORT, AND COURAGE. FOR DAYS I HAD NO HOPE TO LIVE BUT SOME HOW I LINGERED ON. MY COLONEL AND OTHER OFFICERS HAVE BEEN COMING TO VISIT ME NOW AND THEN. THEY HAVE BEEN ALL VERY KIND. I HOWEVER MISS YOU & HENDON FRIENDS AND KHANNAS. YESTERDAY THE COLONEL SENT TO ME YOUR LETTER OF 28th MARCH. IT BROUGHT ME A RAY OF HOPE BUT MADE ME VERY HOME SICK.

I AM VERY SORRY TO LEARN THAT MUM [Heinrich Etzold's (Henry Edwards') mother] IS NOT KEEPING GOOD HEALTH. I HOPE SHE IS BETTER NOW. IT IS NOT POSSIBLE FOR ME TO WRITE MANY LETTERS SO PLEASE INFORM HENDON AND

OTHER FRIENDS ABOUT MY CONDITION. I DO NOT KNOW
HOW LONG I WILL HAVE TO WAIT FOR THE SHIP. I MIGHT
HAVE TO FORWARD MY THINGS ON TO YOU WHEN I REACH
ENGLAND, OR DO YOU THINK I SHOULD SEND IT ON TO
HENDON FRIENDS OR KHANNAS.

MY HAND IS HURTING BADLY BUT I MUST NOT STOP. I
MUST TELL YOU HOW MUCH I LOVE YOU. I HAD PLANNED
TO MAKE YOU HAPPY. BUT WHERE IS THE SENSE. I HARDLY
KNOW WHAT MORE MISFORTUNES ARE IN STORE FOR ME.
THAT VERY HARD STRUGGLE LIES IN FRONT OF ME, OF THAT
I HAVE NO ILLUSION. I AM VERY GLAD THAT GOD
PROTECTED YOU. YOU ARE MY ONLY HOPE, I AM MISSING
YOU AS I NEVER MISSED YOU. IS IT LOVE OR IS IT PASSION?
THE OTHER DAY I DREAMT THAT I AM WITH YOU ALONE ON
THE TOP OF A CLIFF, WHICH IS HIGH UP IN THE CLOUDS.
THERE WAS NO ONE TO DISTURB OUR HAPPYNESS – OUR
ECSTASY. ALAS! IT WAS ONLY A DREAM. ONE KISS AND A
LOVING EMBRACE FROM YOU WOULD HEAL MY WOUNDS
MORE THAN ALL THE TREATMENT I AM RECEIVING HERE.

MY LOVE TO ALL MY FRIENDS.

WITH FONDEST LOVE AND UNSATIABLE DESIRE TO HOLD
YOU IN MY ARM & NEVER LET YOU GO. WITH MILLIONS OF
KISSES TO MIZZI AND KIZZI.

YOURS IN PAIN BUT IN LOVE

Shanti

2.44

Shanti's arm was examined by a doctor at the hospital in Caserta.
When Shanti asserted that it was fractured above the point of
amputation and asked that the bones be reset properly, the doctor
disagreed; he insisted the arm was not fractured and refused to take
an X-ray.

Shanti returned to England in a hospital ship that was leaving from Naples. Because it was crowded, he was at first told he would have to sleep on the floor. The matron, however, seeing that his plight was worse than that of many others, changed his place with that of an English officer. She was kind to Shanti; she tried to keep up his spirits by pausing to talk to him in the middle of her busy rounds and to induce his appetite back with a grapefruit every morning.

When he got to England, he was sent to City Hospital in Nottingham. Here again a consultant did not believe him when he said he had a fracture. Finally, he persuaded the radiologist to take an X-ray. It was a classic fracture, as he had said all along, an oblique angulated fracture of the radius. But by now it was too late; his bones had set in the wrong position, and the surgeons would have had to operate above the elbow. This entailed its own risks, including the possible loss, if anything went wrong, of the elbow itself. In the event, Shanti decided against it.

After a month or so in Nottingham, he was sent to London, to Queen Mary's Hospital in Roehampton, which had a limb-fitting centre. Here they made him a false arm from metal and leather into which he could fit his stump; it had a mechanism for turning the hand on its axis, and another for releasing it to allow one of a range of contraptions to be fixed on instead. But because his bones were badly joined, he could not use these other contraptions or indeed carry anything heavier than a glove in his hand. From the very beginning, he experienced a feeling of great pain and tension in the amputated limb – a sense that his hand still existed as a phantom hand, but that someone was twisting it and turning it. The slightest pressure made the agony worse. At night he could not sleep and had to take a heavy dose of sleeping pills.

At Roehampton, they gave him a Nelson knife, which curved at the end to become a fork. He would now be able to eat most food with his left hand without having to have it cut up for him. He was also provided with stump gloves and a glove for his artificial hand. He carried a companion glove in this hand until someone told him it looked as if he was carrying flowers. At the end of May 1944, he was discharged from Queen Mary's, but continued to attended their limb-fitting centre as an outpatient.

Henry Edwards was the first person to come to see Shanti; he visited him in Nottingham. He told him he should stay with him and Nita and 'Mum' in Hendon, or else with Mum's sister Rosie, who lived not far from them; there was room in her home because her husband, the bristle merchant, had gone to America for the duration of the war. Rosie was a flamboyant and expansive character but a recklessly cautious driver; she was regularly stopped by the police for going too slowly. Shanti stayed with her, but it was Mum who really looked after him – 'just like a mother', as he would later say. She nursed him and dressed his wounds and encouraged him. But he did not know what to do with himself. He had lost his hand and his profession and he had no hope, no confidence in the future.

From the hospital in Nottingham, Shanti had written to Henny in an almost feverish manner about his phantom hand.

Capt. S. B. Seth,
A. D. Corps
City Hospital,
Hucknall Rd.,
Nottingham.
21.4.44

Dear Hennerle,

yours and Khannas telegram reached me the same day. I have also received your very loving and encouraging letter . . .

Darling you seem to have too high opinion of my ability. But don't you know there is a lot of difference in what I am today and what I was at 3 P.M. on 16.3.44 when I carried 'him' – that was my best comrade – my pride – my defender – my £.sh.d., mortally wounded by a cruel shell. I carried him with my left, to Resucitation tent while the shells were still falling around me. Why I betrayed him, that was my 'Might', I do not know. If I had stayed in my tent I would have followed him unto death as I was already bleeding profusely. But No, I let my right

161

hand die and be thrown into the heap of rubbish to be later on eaten by worms and insects! You won't call it a brave deed? My remaining right arm [the remaining part of the right arm], who served the 'bread winner' has been more faithful and yearns for the departed 'master' and just refuses to believe that 'he' is not there and in his wishful thinking produces the 'phantom hand'.

I have slight fever and some thirst . . .

> With fondest love and kisses
>> Yours affly
>>> Shanti

Shanti also told Henny not to visit him. He longed to meet his 'little Kuckuck', but he would soon be in London. He did not want her to make the journey to Nottingham, very likely in pouring rain, on an overcrowded train on Sunday, the only day she was not working. Besides, the hospital might be a 'protected area' and this could entail obtaining permits and dealing with the authorities.

They met when he got to London. Henny had been living in a boarding-house in Bayswater and working for a small pharmaceutical export company. Daily life for her, as for most people in Britain, had been hard, with long hours, shortages and rationing. Apart from those few Red Cross messages from 1942, she had had no word from Lola or her mother, and was filled with anxiety. However, given the character of the Aunty Henny I knew, she would have stifled her dread and just got on with things. Nothing could be changed from a distance and, as she often said to me while teaching me German:

> Happy he
> Who forgets
> What no longer can be changed.

2.45

What, meanwhile, of that different world, the Battle of Cassino, where Shanti's arm had been blown off? What happened there, and to what end?

After three failed attempts, at great cost, to take Monte Cassino and move northwards, it became apparent that only overwhelming numbers combined with surprise would succeed. General Alexander now waited for the winter rains to cease, the river levels to fall and the ground to harden with the spring. He deceived Kesselring with the impression that he would launch an amphibious landing north of Rome, thus tying up some German divisions at a safe distance. He reinforced his forces near Cassino till he had a three to one superiority over the Germans. This build-up, as well as improvements in roads and the placement of ammunition dumps and stores, was carefully camouflaged from the enemy.

In order not merely to advance but also to draw in and destroy the maximum number of German divisions, Alexander had decided for this fourth battle to attack on a far broader front than before, along both the roads to Rome, the coastal highway as well as the highway through the Liri valley below Monte Cassino. The former would be the job of the American and French divisions of the Fifth Army, the latter of the British and Polish divisions of the Eighth (the British being supported by Indians and Canadians). The crucial attack on Monte Cassino itself, the most difficult task of all, would be the job of the Poles.

At eleven at night on 11 May, half an hour before moonrise, sixteen hundred guns roared into action along the whole front. It was the prelude to an extensive multifaceted action. Monte Cassino was attacked from the back, along Snakeshead Ridge; the Poles, unlike the Americans and Indians before them, had sufficient numbers and supplies to be able simultaneously to attack all the surrounding heights and thus reduce German fire support against Polish troops on the ridge. Even so, and especially during the day when they were totally exposed, casualties were very heavy, and the Poles were driven back. They had, however, inflicted equally serious casualties on the Germans and reduced the pressure on the British and Indians in the valley beyond.

The British and Indians, having crossed the Rapido River, were able to consolidate their positions. The French were pushing ahead with great success. The Americans on the coast were temporarily held in check.

In the course of the next few days, the Allies, though taking greater losses than the defending Germans, reduced enemy numbers to the point where the front began to give way. Most remarkable and fearsome of all the Allied troops were the twelve thousand Moroccan *goums* attached to the French divisions, who, clad in Arab garb and equipped with knives, moved silently and without formation in the zone between the two highways through mountains that the Germans had thought militarily impenetrable.

The British broke through the defences to the Liri valley and moved towards the highway north. The Poles attacked the mountain heights again; and finally met up with the British. The months-long deadlock had been broken, and the march north begun. The Germans on Monte Cassino itself, unable any longer to utilise its excellence as an observation point to help other units direct their fire, and unable to hold on to it themselves, withdrew except for their wounded. The Poles hoisted their flag on the ruins of the abbey a week after the battle started.

Over the next week a second defensive line was broken, and German troops were now in full retreat along the Liri valley. Alexander's plan was that the part of the American Fifth Army that was in the Anzio beachhead close to Rome should now break out and cut the Germans off at Valmontane, inland from Anzio, where there was a gap in the mountains. It was the perfect trap. The German Tenth Army could be completely destroyed, and the Italian campaign could in effect end immediately, and south of Rome.

The American divisions under General Truscott broke out and advanced to fulfil this plan.

But now a blunder occurred that almost all military historians find difficult to explain except as a compound of vanity, idiocy and insubordination on the part of General Mark Clark, the commander of the Fifth Army. He knew the critical importance of the plan, he knew that the cost of not carrying it through was that the tens of thousands of Germans who extricated themselves from the trap would be able to regroup and fight on. He ignored his superior, Alexander, and ordered his subordinate, Truscott, to curtail the forces he sent to Valmontane and to concentrate the larger part on a drive through the Alban Hills towards Rome. Clark wanted to ensure that his army would be the first to enter Rome – though this had in fact already been agreed upon – and that his name would be associated with this achievement, glorious in appearance if vacuous in military consequence.

General Clark did not give his order directly to General Truscott but passed it through a subordinate. Frustrated and bewildered, Truscott insisted on speaking to Clark, but Clark was not available. Truscott was thus compelled to obey the order. Rome was taken, to the clicking of many cameras. But large numbers of Germans escaped to fight further north through another winter at the cost of the lives of yet more Allied soldiers and Italian civilians.

Clark had entered Rome on 4 June. On the 6th the Allies landed in Normandy. The centre of gravity of the war in Europe shifted. The American high command, which had never been keen on what they saw as the diversion of Italy, now insisted, as had been agreed the previous year, that the South of France be invaded; American and French divisions were withdrawn from the Italian campaign to this end. This was deeply unfortunate: the German forces, even if they had not been captured at Valmontane, were still in headlong retreat, and could well have been driven back to the Alps and the borders of Greater Germany. As it was, in the face of a greatly weakened opposition, they now established themselves along another defensive line in the mountains south of the

Po. For all the effort expended and suffering undergone, Italy became and remained a sideshow.

<h1 style="text-align:center">2.46</h1>

In April 1945, Shanti received a letter from the War Office which began:

> Sir,
>   I am directed to refer to War Office letter P/119952/2 (A.M.D.6) dated 2nd June, 1944, and to state that, since it has not proved possible to find you suitable employment in the Army Dental Corps within your medical category, it is regretted that there is now no alternative but to relegate you to unemployment with effect from 1st June, 1945, i.e. 56 days from the date of this letter.

He was granted a disability pension as well as, later on, an allowance for 'lowered standard of occupation'. But though he could no longer practise as a dentist, he refused to be 'relegated to unemployment'. As he often – perhaps too often – used to tell me, 'I'd rather have sold matches on a street corner than go on the dole.' He was thirty-six years old.

Even before the army relinquished him, Shanti had started looking for work.

When he had been barred from paid employment in Germany nine years earlier, Professor Wannenmacher had given him an introduction to a friend and colleague of his in Britain. This colleague, Alfred E. Rowlett, had been Chairman of the British Dental Association and was now Treasurer of the Fédération Dentaire Internationale, whose motto, incorporated in their letter-head, was 'Dens sanus in corpore sano'. Shanti was invited by Mr Rowlett, who lived on London Road, Leicester, to visit him. Shanti confused this with Leicester Square, London. When he recounted this error to me, he embarrassedly covered his mouth with his hand.

Mr Rowlett had helped Shanti with advice and, when war broke out, had encouraged him to sign up. They had kept in touch during the war. In one letter, Mr Rowlett, with a fine disregard for the censors, had even quoted an adage in German, 'One enemy is too many, a hundred friends too few.'

When he heard of Shanti being wounded at Monte Cassino, he wrote to sympathise, and added:

We have faced difficulties before together, as you will remember on your return from Berlin and I hope you will let me share your troubles and contribute in any way in which I can to the solution of the difficult problem which lies before you now . . . I hope you will not think it improper if I quote a proverb – of which Dr Stuck was very fond – 'Mit gutem Willen kann man alles machen [With good will, one can do anything]' . . .

P.S. I think the skill you have already acquired in calligraphy augurs well for the future.

Now, through his widespread contacts, Mr Rowlett helped Shanti apply for positions at various universities – for instance, as a demonstrator – but without any success. He then encouraged him to apply to dental firms, and as a result of his recommendation Shanti got a job with the Amalgamated Dental Company, which at the time was the largest dental firm in England. With his background in research, he became a professional adviser. He read up on innovative techniques in dentistry and on new materials that were being invented, and travelled around postwar Europe giving lectures and liaising with branches and outlets of the company and with prominent figures and organisations in the dental world.

He continued to correspond with Mr Rowlett. Most of their letters deal with mundane affairs. By now Hitler was dead and

Churchill had been defeated by Attlee at the polls. Neither of these momentous events enters the correspondence. But on 1 September 1945, Mr Rowlett, who had been deeply agitated by what had happened the previous month in Japan, wrote him a letter in which personal, professional, political and philosophical matters were curiously juxtaposed and merged. Some phrases in the letter are typed in red; these are here printed in italic.

Dear Capt. Seth,

Thank you for your letter of August 24th. Owing to excess of work and paucity of secretarial help I was not able to reply before your departure for Zürich where you will meet delightful people, and where your knowledge of German will stand you in good stead. It is some years since I had any close contact with the staff at the Zürich house of the Amalgamated and I do not know what changes may have occurred in the personnel since my visit. I should be glad if you will mention to the director that you have received a letter from me and that I send my warmest greetings to those who received me so kindly and generously before the war.

The *atomic bomb* is indeed a fearful weapon, one can only hope that its effect will be to shock the world into Reality, and make the human race understand that economics and politics are means and not an end. All – or nearly all – the people who demand a clear statement of the Allies' peace aims call out for some arrangement that shall secure *abiding peace and a lasting settlement*. There is no such thing as abiding peace and a lasting settlement in this world. Peace is not a static thing; it is the supreme example of balance in movement.

If we deprive ourselves of the eternal Absolute, we shall inevitably deify and make an absolute of some temporal thing or other – be it Liberty, Equality or Progress in any of their possible forms; be it Race or Reason, or even Unreason, or the perpetual flux of Relativity. If we make Peace an absolute, it will inevitably plunge us into the tyranny of war . . .

Our duty is to face the future with restrained optimism and, each one of us according to our capacity, bear in mind that our goal is Creative

Peace, and that the text in the Gospels is not 'Blessed be the *peaceable*' but 'Blessed are the *peace-makers*' . . .

What Shanti made of this, or how far the contents of his own letter triggered it, cannot be known, since he rarely kept copies of his letters. But he was in later years much given to philosophising about the Absolute and Eternal, and about Atman and Brahman, quite often over the cornflakes. This letter from Mr Rowlett, though entirely anomalous, is possibly less surprising than it at first appears. Perhaps, in his own extreme agitation, he felt it natural to express his thoughts thus to a colleague who would be a sympathetic listener, not only because he was of a philosophical bent, but because he himself was, in a way, *in extremis*.

2.47

Shanti got on with his work at the Amalgamated Dental Company. Because of his artificial arm, he was unable to demonstrate anything physically, so he learned to make documentary films, at first to supplement his lectures and later, as his technique and ability improved, for independent use elsewhere. He tried to do everything himself, from the script to the photography (often with telephoto lenses or photo floodlights) to the splicing and editing. When taking photographs, he would hold the camera against his chest with the side of his artificial arm in such a way that there was no pressure on the stump. He attended the classes of well known documentary film-makers and was elected an Associate of the British Kinematograph Society.

He wrote reports of all kinds for circulation among the various departments of the company: 'Dr Seth's interview with Mr Everett, Director of the Prosthetic Department of the National Dental Hospital'; 'Dr Seth's visit to King's College Hospital to discuss matters with Mr Trotter in connection with Gingivectomy instruments';

'Report on Standardisation of Dental Materials'; 'Dr Seth's Report on his lecture on Full Denture Construction and demonstration of colour film "Rational Technique for the Edentulous Case" to the Students of the National Dental Hospital'; 'Professional Trends'; 'Dr Seth's report on the lecture on "Local Anaesthesia in the Practice of Dental Surgery" by Dr J. J. Posner (U.S.A.)'; 'Dr Seth's trip to Zurich to study the Zurich Products and to film "Syntrex"'; 'Dr Seth's report on the Annual General Meeting of the British Dental Association'; and so, prolifically, on.

When he lectured abroad, he promoted his company's products; one of the most important of these was 'Zelex', a material used in making impressions. The Norwegian dental profession, for example, was treated to Dr Seth's lecture on 'The Chemistry of Alginates in Relation to Impression Technique', which was delivered with a view to introducing Zelex plus the 'unit pack'. The sales possibilities of Oral Zelex were introduced later during the same trip to that receptive country.

Nor were the Danes to suffer unmerited deprivation. As Dr Seth reported when he appeared before their Association of Younger Dentists: 'Many questions appertaining to the Company's products were asked and answered. The lecture was very well received and appreciation shown in the usual manner.'

For the *Dental Magazine and Oral Hygiene* he wrote an article, 'Evaluation of Porcelain and Acrylic as a Replacement of Natural Teeth', but this was a summarising article; at the ADC he got little opportunity for independent research. On one occasion, however, he was asked to test an adhesive invented by a Swiss scientist, Oskar Haggar, who became a close friend. It was he who, years later, welcomed me, a weary hitch-hiker, into his home in Zurich. On another occasion, Shanti met Professor Dolder, the Dean of the Zurich Dental School, who immediately said, 'Ah, but I know you.' When Shanti demurred, Professor Dolder said that he had come across his doctoral dissertation in a technical bookshop and had read it with avidity; he too had been working on the effects of different filling materials on the tooth.

In the course of his work at the company, Shanti met the foremost academics and practitioners in his profession; this would have been impossible had he either remained in the army or practised dentistry in his own or someone else's surgery. Besides, at the Amalgamated Dental Company he had professional security. But he was not truly happy in his work. He longed to practise dentistry 'hands on', so to speak; and he found it hard to relinquish his dream of independence, of working for no master but himself.

2.48

It was Henry Edwards who, from the moment he saw Shanti in the hospital in Nottingham, helped keep this dream alive. He had heard of a dentist up north who had lost his arm in the First World War and who carried out extractions and made dentures (though he did not do fillings). Henry put Shanti in touch with him. In response to Shanti's letters, Mr Beaton wrote:

G. M. Beaton   153B High Street
Dentist   Stockton-on-Tees

Hours of Attendance
9 a.m. to 12 noon.   8/7/1944
2 p.m. to 6 p.m.
Thursdays 9 to 12

Tel No. 66568

Dear Mr Seth,
    There is nothing to prevent you carrying on in your profession successfully if your health is OK & you adopt the right temperament.— Do not be self conscious or sorry for yourself in any way. Be proud to know that you have had the *Guts* to do a dangerous job & won through.

An artificial arm will help you in many ways with practice – get a light dress arm with first two fingers close enough to hold a '*Mouth Mirror*' so that you can pull the lips apart when injecting for upper or lower. For lower left extractions tip chair back & steady Patient's chin with artificial right arm. Lower right is easy with Patient in upright position & operator front right. Most upper extractions are easy & the difficult ones would still be difficult if you had as many Arms as an Octopus.

Lower Impression taking is easy, insert tray sideways in right of Patient's mouth. Straighten & press home. Sideways left for upper & press home. The same routine applies to multiple extractions under N_2O [nitrous oxide or laughing gas] & with a good throat Pack in the correct position there is very little danger of teeth slipping down throat.

Filling & Sealing can be taken in your stride, starting with easy jobs first.

If your arm is amputated below elbow & you have full use of same, you are lucky. All I am left with is barely two inches of stump measuring from right shoulder but this is enough to enable me to manipulate Artificial Arm. I got my Packet in a Tank Aug 8, 1918. A shattered right arm with multiple wounds on back & right leg but consider myself 100% fit now. Have kept up the hobbies of my youth, Dancing, Fishing, Shooting & Motoring & have driven a car through the Principal Capitals of Europe – the longest run being through France Switzerland Italy Jugoslavia Hungary Austro Germany & the Old Germany with Holland & Belgium thrown in.— a very nice holiday without trouble or exertion. Your Future is what you decide to make of it & your Pension will always give that feeling of independence.

If you were in this area you could practice taking a few imps [impressions] etc but your Dental Friends in your district should give you these Facilities. If not Practice on your relations at home.

Hope to hear of your early success & never mind the snags.

Conclude with kindest regards

from

G. Beaton

On this generous and rather frighteningly gung-ho letter, written in a careful and fairly legible hand, Shanti has scrawled '19/12/44', which must be the date of his reply – more than five months later. It is comforting to realise that Shanti Uncle was almost as poor a respondent to letters as am I.

Beaton's next letter is dated 28 December 1944; he lists a few Stockton hotels and says he will be delighted to pass on any tips when Shanti comes to visit. He adds that he will be away for a few days but should start again 'full blast' by the second week of January.

Some of Beaton's tips proved useful, but not those involving the use of the stump or artificial hand. Though Shanti had lost less of his arm than Beaton, what remained was almost unusable; he found that he could not tolerate the weight even of a mouth mirror.

No further record of Beaton exists among Shanti's papers, but it is pleasant to imagine this meeting of these two unusual men, professional colleagues, each with similar injuries, each with aspirations to independence, one English, one Indian, veterans of the two great wars of the century.

2.49

After Rosie's husband came back from America, Shanti went to live in a nearby boarding-house, but he continued to meet Henry, Nita and Mum every couple of days. Henry was doing well. He had a weekday practice at the Angel, another on Saturdays at his house in Hendon, and yet another for a short while in Harley Street.

Shanti had been practising using dental tools on plaster casts with his left hand; but he had neither the occasion nor the courage to practise on a patient. Less than a year after he had joined the Amalgamated, Henry suggested that he treat one of his patients. Shanti recoiled at the thought.

One Saturday evening, Henry phoned and asked him to come over immediately. He was apparently in very great pain.

He said, 'Oh, Shanti, this tooth is hurting me.' It was a lower premolar. I said, 'Why tell me? I can't use my left hand, I don't feel I can do anything.' He put up an act, saying it was too late, it was after 5 o'clock, and he couldn't get another dentist. 'How can you let your friend suffer like this?' he kept asking me. I told him I would never do a filling. 'At least put in a dressing, then,' he said. 'Go on, drill it.' I had never handled a drill with my left hand, but now I thought I had no choice. Poor fellow, I must have tortured him. There was a little cavity, but the decay had not gone very deep and I'm sure it had not been hurting him as much as he said. He just wanted to give me confidence. What a friend he was.

Henry praised Shanti's skill and told him he had handled things very well. He emphasised the fact that a dentist for the most part uses only one hand; the other hand holds the mirror. 'You have proved you *can* work as a dentist,' he said. 'Why don't you use my surgery in the Angel on Saturdays, when I'm not there. If it's a difficult case, make an appointment for when I can be there.' Shanti agreed, and began with a few dressings and fillings. Nita, now Henry's wife, was an experienced dental nurse; she helped out where necessary. When a patient came in, he or she was seated in the dental chair before Shanti entered in his white coat. By the time they saw he had only one hand, they could do nothing. But after he had operated on them, they regularly recommended him to friends.

After this trial had proved successful, Henry suggested that Shanti work in the surgery at Henry's home in the evenings after he himself had stopped work for the day; a nurse who lived nearby would come in from six to eight o'clock. Shanti was happy to agree. The pace of his work was slow, but he was thorough and exacting. When he needed to use his left arm for other things, the nurse would hold the dental mirror. As before, if there was an extraction to be done, Shanti would fix it for a time when Henry could handle it.

Shanti's pleasure in recovering and using some of his old skills now led him further:

By now I had gained confidence, and wanted to do extractions myself. I told Henry, 'I'm itching to take a tooth out.' Some time later, he took me to his practice in the Angel, where one of his patients needed a tooth extracted. He gave the patient an injection, and just at that moment, as he had previously arranged with his nurse, she came in and said that she had had a call about a patient who was bleeding all over the floor. Henry then said, 'This is an emergency. I am afraid I have to go and make a home visit, otherwise this other patient will bleed to death. Captain Seth is a very good dentist; he will take over.' The patient could say nothing. As it happened, his tooth was very loose, and it was not difficult for me to take it out. He was very happy and said, 'It's the best extraction I've ever had.'

Henry now told Shanti: 'Take up dentistry again as your full-time profession.' But the fear of trying to build up a practice by himself at a time when equipment was almost impossible to obtain, when he had few patients and owned neither a house nor a surgery of his own, was too daunting. Most of all, Shanti was convinced that patients would not voluntarily come to a one-armed dentist. He continued to work at Henry's practice, but could not strike out on his own.

He fell into a routine. He would do a full day's work in the technical division of the Amalgamated in Swallow Street in the heart of town. He would then take the tube to get to Henry and Nita's house in Hendon by 5.30. He would work at the surgery that was part of their home from 5.45 till 11 p.m. with a break for dinner, usually with them. On Saturday mornings, and sometimes afternoons, he would again work in the surgery. This gruelling regimen – combined with travelling and lecturing for the ADC – continued for three years. Though he loved his dental work and practised it with scrupulous care, he had to carry it out in the evenings when he was already tired. His patients liked him and Henry appreciated him, but he was in danger of burning himself out.

Through all this, his arm continued to give him trouble. For a year after his amputation, painful little pieces of bone – sequesters – kept coming out of his stump. Over the next few years he underwent various forms of treatment. In 1948, in a letter to the Ministry of Pensions he wrote:

Since I received my injury I have been suffering from constant pain in my amputated limb . . . I underwent a course of electrical treatment at the hands of a private practitioner in 1945 and 1946 but this failed to improve my condition. I also consulted the late Brigadier Bristow who was the Chief Consulting Surgeon to the Army, and visited Queen Mary's Hospital in Roehampton at various times for advice and inspection. As the pain in my arm grew worse it was decided by the Orthopaedic Surgeons in the Limb Fitting Centre that I should undergo an operation, and I was operated on by a Mr. Perkins, the chief Surgeon in Charge of Queen Mary's Hospital, in October 1946. I remained in the hospital for 3 weeks. In spite of this operation I am still getting constant pain, tenderness and feeling of tension which often keeps me awake and I have to resort to sleeping tablets.

Later in 1948, Shanti was surprised and moved when Henry, Nita and Mum told him what they had discussed for some time among themselves – that he should join Henry's practice as a partner. But his decision was almost immediate.

Without thinking, I turned it down on the spot. I told him, 'Henry, I cherish our friendship more. Our partnership will not work out. You are a very quick worker and I am a very slow worker and I have a very independent mind and my own ideas about dental practice.' They all said, 'Shanti is too selfish. Now that Henry has so many patients, he could

176

really do with a partner.' But refusing it was the best thing I ever did. Partnership is the worst ship that has ever been built. Our friendship would have been destroyed.

After a pause he added: 'God has been kind to me; he has given me answers.'

2.50

Shanti had been living in lodgings at 19 Queens Road, Hendon, a large semidetached Edwardian house that faced Hendon Park. In late 1948, a similar house next door, number 18, came up for sale. It too had a small front garden; in the long back garden stood two apple trees. Shanti liked the light and greenery. He bought the house for about £5000 from Sir Cornelius Gregg, a civil servant who had helped devise the Pay As You Earn system of taxation and who was retiring to Ireland.

Shanti's bank gave him a mortgage on the usual terms. But the first company he went to for home insurance told him they would impose an extra premium of ten per cent on him because he had been born in India and they doubted his creditworthiness. He asked them whether they would have imposed a similar premium on an Englishman who had been born in England but lived in India. When they could not reply, he told them that he would have nothing to do with them, and obtained insurance elsewhere.

He lived on his own. At first, there was not even a carpet in the house. With the help of a friend, he carried his bedstead, mattress and bedclothes from his old room next door to his new home. Nita lent him a bridge table and four chairs, and bought him a kettle, four cups, four saucers and four side-plates.

Working the way he did, he had no time to cook. For breakfast he ate Ryvita and tomatoes, toast and marmalade, and occasionally cornflakes. In the evening he had ham, cheese, salad and fruit:

again all cold. But since he was working with the Amalgamated, he had a hot lunch in town during the day, and at least twice a week he ate a decent dinner at Henry and Nita's.

Henry's charlady, Miss Paris – who actually did speak French – spent a couple of hours a day cleaning. The previous owner had wanted him to buy the stove in the hall, which used anthracite, but Shanti had decided that getting out the ashes using only one hand would be too much for him. He decided on gas heating, though there was a long waiting list for this. But when the gas company learned that he had lost his hand in the war and that he was living alone, they quickly installed a gas fire in his bedroom and one in the lounge.

Despite his handicap, he liked to garden at the weekends. To dig, he would rest the head of the spade on the ground, and lean his weight against the top of the handle. He loved being out in the fresh air. Whenever he could snatch the time, he would cross the road and take a walk in the park.

This was to be Shanti's home and workplace for the rest of his life. Here he established himself in his profession, from here he got married, here he lived with Henny, here I lived with them for a few short years, here Aunty Henny died, here he spent his last few years, here he too died. When I spoke to him during the time when, once again, he was living alone, he said:

So much has changed on this road. Almost all the front gardens have been paved over. And so many of the houses have been converted: the developers buy four or six semidetached houses, and build a big block of flats. They tried to buy this house from me, and offered me hundreds of thousands of pounds. I told them, 'You can give me a million pounds. This is my home, I won't move.'

A year or so after Shanti bought his house, he decided to put up his own plate and practise from there. He chose the large, sunny room on the ground floor for his surgery; it faced the roses in his garden as well as the trees in the park beyond. But he could see these only on Saturday mornings or during the long summer evenings, since on weekdays he operated from 6 to 10 p.m. after his day's work at the Amalgamated.

The difficulty of getting dental equipment owing to the acute postwar shortage was overcome by Henry, who was an excellent customer of the suppliers. He ordered all the equipment in his own name, claiming that he wanted to start another practice at 18 Queens Road. Everything, including the plumbing and flooring, was completed in short order.

On Shanti Uncle's professional cards his name and credentials read: 'Dr. S. B. Seth, L.D.S., R.C.S. (Edin.), B.Sc., D.M.D. (Berlin)' but on his burnished plate he added the words 'Dental Surgeon' and removed the appellation 'Dr'. Like surgeons, dentists in Britain were normally plain 'Mr'; and Shanti was concerned that his academic doctorate might make people consult him about an appendix.

He got himself an evening nurse, and waited for patients.

There already was a dentist just a few houses away on Queens Road; he had recently bought the practice of an established dentist of forty years' standing, and everyone told Shanti he would have stiff competition and find it difficult to succeed. But this did not deter him; his practice gradually increased. His first patient didn't know in advance that his dentist would have only one arm; he had simply had toothache, noticed the sign and come to him off the street. Others came by word of mouth once there was a core of satisfied patients. Yet others were recommended by friends, including a university friend of Shanti's from India who was living in London at the time. A large number of patients were sent to him by George Tuck, the colonel's jeep-driver in Egypt. Mr Tuck and his wife lived in Hendon, and both of them became his patients too. But Shanti very rarely had any referred to him by doctors because, as he said, he didn't hobnob with them and in particular because he refused to give his patients a general anaesthetic, when a doctor would be paid to attend. If a patient insisted on having a general anaesthetic, he would send him or her to the Eastman Dental Clinic, a postgraduate institution in Gray's Inn Road, where there were facilities for coping with every emergency. Shanti preferred a local anaesthetic, which was safer – or if, for example, all the lower teeth needed to be taken out, a block injection on each side.

As time went on, he expanded his repertoire of techniques, adapting the standard methods to the use of only one hand. He operated on the gums; he extracted wisdom teeth. The one thing that was impossible for him was suturing. It had to be done with both hands by a single person; a nurse could not assist with this. So if, for example, a patient had a large cyst and, after draining, the gap was wide and needed suturing, Shanti would send him to the Eastman Dental Clinic.

There was one particular problem that Shanti faced, and that had more to do with his mind than his arm.

Every right-handed dentist works from the right-hand side of the chair from the patient's point of view. Now that I was left-handed, I had my surgery arranged in such a way that I could work from the left-hand side of the chair. But, and I don't know exactly why, this turned out to be prac-tically impossible for me because I was psychologically so right-handed. Even with my left hand, I would work from the right-hand side of the chair and therefore I had to bend a lot and this caused my back a lot of trouble. Eventually I had to have physiotherapy and even manipulation under general anaesthetic, and I was confined to bed for three weeks. I was told that for three weeks I wouldn't be able to move at all and would go through hell, and I did.

I've had back problems and elbow problems most of my life. There was even a time when I lost the full use of my left hand. I used to get some-body to treat me at lunchtime. I was afraid the patients would find out and I'd lose my practice. It was also always in my mind that I dared not make a mistake, otherwise people would say, 'He's only got one hand. No wonder he isn't any good.'

2.52

Henny and Shanti had been brought closer by the war. He had been the one to meet her when she arrived from Germany. It was to him that she turned for advice when she wanted to do something other than domestic work at the Arberrys. It was to him she wrote from the bomb-shelters during the Blitz. Her mother, her sister, and all her friends in Germany were in a separate, incommunicable universe. So too was Hans. Her brother Heinz, whom she had little respect for, was somewhere in South America, and rarely got in touch.

Even when Shanti was far away in the Sudan or Egypt or Syria or Italy, their letters reflect their concern for each other and, in Shanti's case certainly, love. After he lost his arm, she comforted and encouraged him. But during the month that he was in the hos-pital in Nottingham, she did not visit him. Had she been passionately in love with him, it seems unlikely, despite the diffi-culties of travel, the pressures of time and his own insistence, that she would have waited till he was in London to see him. Yet Shanti was the sole link to her old world, and she admired him and cared for him. When he was back in England, there seemed to be an understanding among their friends that they were a couple. It is dif-ficult to know how things really stood. Almost no correspondence between them exists for the years immediately following the war.

The one birthday card which survives from those years says much in little. It depicts a snowy scene in a village, and contains a humdrum printed aspiration which Shanti feelingly incorporates into his written message. (By now he writes with his left hand almost as well as he used to with his right.)

19 Queens Road
London N.W.4
13th Dec '46

My dearest Hennerle,

How the time flies! When I think of how I met you first in 1933 just *13* years ago in Berlin and celebrated your birthday in Mommsen Str 60, then all the happenings of the past come in front of my cerebral vision in quick succession.

I know how you have suffered and how at times your mind was overcast with clouds of dismay and desperation but like a brave girl you have managed to keep your chin up.

I hope and pray that

> May the hours be sunny ones
> Throughout the joyous day
> And in the future best of luck
> Keep all dark clouds away

with fondest love   From
Shanti

P.S. I hope to receive my birthday kiss when I see you at 6 P.M.

The cause of this dismay and desperation was the news she received after the war from Germany about her mother, her sister, many of her friends and, in a way, also about Hans.

PART
THREE

PART
THREE

3.1

Both Henny and Shanti were born in 1908. The passage of the years from then until after the Second World War has been recounted for the most part in Shanti's voice. Henny has been silent, or almost silent, throughout.

By the summer of 1994, when I realised I wanted to write this book, she had been dead five years. I could not ask her about her family, her childhood, her schooldays, her work, her friends, the changing atmosphere in Germany during the thirties, her flight to England, her experiences as an immigrant, the war and, in its aftermath, her search for her family. I could not ask her about Hans, about Shanti Uncle, about her mother and sister and brother. But even if she had been alive, it would have been difficult, in both senses of the word, to get her to talk about these things.

Aunty Henny was an outgoing but reticent person. Even Shanti did not know what she thought of Hans. Even he did not know how she felt when she heard of the fate of her family. When he was in Berlin in the thirties, she and her family had had too much pride to talk at length about any sense of injury they felt about being excluded, gradually or suddenly, from the world they had grown up in and the country they had believed was theirs. Would I have succeeded in understanding something of what she felt? Would she have divulged anything? Would she have wanted me to write about it at all? Would I, in the interests of my book, have been able to discount or excuse the pain to her of probing these wounds? Would I deliberately have put our own relationship in jeopardy?

I think it unlikely. And, as a result, this book would have been mainly about Shanti Uncle. I could not justly have called it *Two Lives* unless her voice played a role as strong as Uncle's. And, had it not been for a fortuitous discovery long after her death in the attic of their house, hers would have been a supporting role.

When Aunty Henny died in 1989, Shanti Uncle, in his grief, and reminded at every turn of his loss, destroyed any pictures of her he could find, and indeed anything that reminded him of her. When, some five years later, I asked him whether any letters sent to her had survived, any photographs from her youth, any mementoes of her past, anything at all that would help me understand her times through her eyes, he said that there was nothing. Remembering Aunty Henny's own brusque attitude towards superfluous objects and papers, I did not doubt that he was right.

I interviewed Shanti Uncle at length in order to preserve his memories and follow his life. During the next summer, my parents came to England on a visit and stayed at 18 Queens Road. They came at least once every year or so, mainly to help Uncle cope with his besetting loneliness. Papa, with his practical bent, enjoyed helping with odd jobs around the house. Mama just enjoyed spending time talking to Uncle or cooking him an Indian meal from time to time, happy in the knowledge that their visit was doing him good.

One afternoon, hoping to help Uncle clear out the attic, which was still a crammed and confused mess, Papa noticed a small cobweb-covered tan-coloured cabin trunk with wooden ribs and dull brass studs. There were labels on the side and on the top; it had belonged to Aunty Henny. The attic sloped down from the centre, and the trunk was lying in a far recess. It had clearly lain untouched for decades. Owing to its position, it had escaped the destruction of Henny's things that had followed her death. It contained a trove.

For some unaccountable reason, I never asked to see the trunk itself, but, judging from Papa's description and the fact that Henny travelled by sea only once, it could well have been the one with which she left Berlin for Hamburg, Southampton and London in the late summer of 1939. She must have brought it when she left her boarding-house in Kendal Street, Bayswater, in the summer of 1951 and came to live with her husband in Queens Road. Its contents were added to over the next decade.

A few files dated from slightly later, but not many. There were some books in German, a few photograph albums, some financial files relating to Germany in the fifties. There was a small morocco-and-gilt leather purse containing handwritten poems. Most important of all, there was a file of letters sent to her – and even the occasional carbon copy of a letter sent by her – covering almost exactly the decade of the forties.

When my father brought these objects into the garden, where Uncle and I were sitting in the sun, we were both amazed, I at the possibilities they implied, he by the fact that so much had not been known to him, even about the person he understood best and who had best understood him. He looked at the photographs, some of them of Henny in her teens, and several times he remarked, not in sadness but almost in wonderment, how 'pretty' she had been. It was a euphemism: Henny always looked attractive, but she had in her youth been enchantingly beautiful.

As for the contents of the morocco purse, the poems written by Hans to Henny, Uncle only said, in response to my questioning, 'I swear to you, on Henny's soul, I have never seen these before. I never knew all this existed.'

Uncle told me to keep the things; he did not want them, and he knew they would be of use to me for the book. But neither he nor I could have anticipated just how rich the material was, so rich in fact that it provided me with an image of Aunty Henny at least as acute as that of Shanti Uncle. Her friends write to her and through the tone of their words create a sense both of their personality and of hers. She writes to them, speaking in a voice that recreates her presence, and she says things she never said to Uncle. She talks with pain and clarity about the very matters I would have found it impossible, had she been alive, to broach.

Indeed, considering the private person she was, I have sometimes wondered whether I should, even with Uncle's blessing, and even after her death, have ranged freely over her correspondence, some of which was intended for no eyes other than those of the recipient. But these letters deal with a period of great historical consequence in Germany and may help to enrich, through their intimacy, our understanding of the lives of ordinary people caught up in the events of those times. Some of these – for example, the letter from Hans's father to Henny just before she left Germany in 1939, or the Red Cross messages Henny exchanged with her mother and sister in 1942, or Shanti's letters to her from his hospital bed in Italy in 1944 – have been introduced already.

These examples bring me to a second reason for overriding my initial uncertainty about mining the contents of the trunk. Every even-handed biography of a completed life has to deal with private matters and to present its subject as fully as possible, even if the subject, when alive, might have preferred to keep these matters obscured – or at least not open to the world. It is to help bring Henny to life that I am flouting what I feel would have been her wishes. But perhaps I am wrong; perhaps, in retrospect, judging the intention of this book as a whole, she might have approved, or at least not disapproved. This whole matter is vexed, and even more so because I loved her and value her memory.

It was from this collection of paper – printed paper, typed paper, handwritten paper, photographic paper – found by my father that day that I began to create for myself an image of Aunty Henny as she had been, only partly as I might have envisaged her, but to a great extent as neither I, nor even Shanti Uncle, could have imagined her to be.

3.2

Henny's earliest correspondence dates from 1939, but other items go back further. The photographs in the albums tell of a time when her father was alive; there is also a cache of unmounted photographs from the time of his wedding in 1906; some are earlier still. One afternoon, again in the garden, I asked Shanti Uncle to identify them one by one; but many of the earlier identifications are based on surmise.

The few books in German that Henny must have brought with her as an exile to England are a small atlas, a couple of textbooks for learning English, a small volume of folksongs set to music for the lute, and three large, slim paperbacks illustrated with full-page black-and-white photographs: on modern German sculpture, on German baroque architecture and on the German countryside in the spring.

Five other books were in the trunk, but they have different provenances. One of them (in English) was published by Chatto & Windus in 1941: *The Rubaiyat of Omar Khayyam* translated by Edward FitzGerald. Two of them appear to be gifts given after the war: the poems of Michelangelo translated into German by Rilke, and a book on Dürer. The final two, and for me the puzzling ones, are two hardbound books in black: a Jewish bible in German and a Jewish prayer-book, in German and Hebrew.

Aunty Henny was not religious, and these two books are heavy. It is unlikely she would have brought them to England with her. Her sister Lola gradually became more conscious of her Jewishness and more religious in practice. Could this be one of the books that Lola asked non-Jewish friends of hers to keep in safe custody and to give to Henny after the war? If so, would it not have been a great risk for them to keep such obviously Jewish possessions? At first I had thought these books were family heirlooms; but nowhere in them is the surname Caro (her father's side of the family) or

Schmelkes (her mother's). The prayer-book has no sign of owner-ship; the bible has the notation 'Adolf Berliner 1912' handwritten on it. After Lola, like Henny, was sacked from the Mannheimer Life Insurance Company for being a Jew, she worked for a while for a Mr Berliner. He later emigrated to the United States; could these be things he gave her or possibly left behind for her to take care of? There is a long and fascinating correspondence between Henny and him after the war, by which time he had assumed a different name, A. G. Belvin. Henny was both scrupulous and efficient in the matter of possessions. But there is no mention on either side of these two books.

I treat them as talismans; I often dip into them. If only they could speak and tell me where they have been, what hands have held them, what insight or faith or peace they have brought and to whom, how they survived a bitter and desecrating time and by what circuitous means and ways they have come down to me, a quasi-agnostic Hindu.

The more frayed of the two was published in Berlin in 1893; it is the fourth edition of the second part of the prayer-book for the new synagogue in Berlin: it deals with the service for New Year and for the *Versöhnungstag* – the Day of Atonement, Yom Kippur. It is for the most part in Hebrew with German translation, and opens on the right. The psalms and prayers are, however, interspersed with rhymed hymns in German on the Christian model, untranslated into Hebrew, such as this one which forms part of the Yom Kippur service:

> Lord, my God, my light and staff and shield,
> My true guide upon this earth's dark face,
> Judge me not by what my deeds should yield.
> Judge me, Lord, according to thy grace.

At the end of the book is a brief appendix on the fundamentals of Jewish morality in fifteen points, as perceived by the unnamed author: perhaps it acts as a recitable credo. (Each point is followed by a paragraph or two of explanation.)

Judaism teaches: 1. the unity of mankind.

It commands us therefore 2. to love our neighbour, 3. to protect our neighbour and his rights, 4. to be aware of his honour, 5. to honour his beliefs, 6. and to assuage his sorrows.

Judaism calls upon us 7. through work, 8. through the love of truth, 9. through modesty, 10. through amicability, 11. through moral rectitude, 12. and through obedience to authority, 13. to further the wellbeing of our neighbours, 14. to seek the good of our fatherland, 15. and to bring about the loving fellowship of all mankind.

Points 12 and 14 find themselves embodied in a prayer that is included in both the services:

Prayer for the Rulers

Lord of the World, Father of Mankind! You have set authority over the earth, that it might be a defence for right and a protector of order. Preserve and bless our King

Wilhelm II,

the Kaiser of the German Reich, that under his sceptre truth and righteousness may blossom. Bless the Empress and Queen

Augusta Victoria,

his consort. Bless the Dowager Empress Friedrich. Bless the crown prince and the whole royal house. Bless the entire German fatherland, that righteousness and fidelity, peace and wellbeing may prevail therein and all its children be united and made happy. Bless our hometown; may it bloom and flourish. Bless Israel in all places and in all lands . . .

The prayer-book was published at about the midpoint of a period of peace, lasting almost half a century, between the Prussian victory over the French in 1870 (followed in 1871 by the unification of Germany under the Prussian king, now Kaiser, and his Chancellor, Otto von Bismarck) and the beginning of the First World War. But early in this period there were reminders of the vulnerability of a minority viewed by some with suspicion or resentment whenever the population at large – or an influential

Das Schofarblasen.
(Fällt am Sabbath aus.)

בָּרוּךְ אַתָּה יְיָ אֱלֹהֵינוּ מֶלֶךְ הָעוֹלָם אֲשֶׁר
קִדְּשָׁנוּ בְּמִצְוֹתָיו וְצִוָּנוּ לִשְׁמוֹעַ קוֹל שׁוֹפָר:
בָּרוּךְ אַתָּה יְיָ אֱלֹהֵינוּ מֶלֶךְ הָעוֹלָם שֶׁהֶחֱיָנוּ
וְקִיְּמָנוּ וְהִגִּיעָנוּ לַזְּמַן הַזֶּה:

תְּקִיעָה. שְׁבָרִים. תְּרוּעָה. תְּקִיעָה:
תְּקִיעָה. שְׁבָרִים. תְּקִיעָה:
תְּקִיעָה. תְּרוּעָה. תְּקִיעָה גְדוֹלָה:

(Vorbeter und Gemeinde.)

אַשְׁרֵי הָעָם יֹדְעֵי תְרוּעָה יְיָ בְּאוֹר פָּנֶיךָ יְהַלֵּכוּן:

(Vorbeter.)

אַשְׁרֵי יוֹשְׁבֵי בֵיתֶךָ עוֹד יְהַלְלוּךָ סֶּלָה:

אַשְׁרֵי הָעָם שֶׁכָּכָה לּוֹ אַשְׁרֵי הָעָם שֶׁיְיָ אֱלֹהָיו:

(קמה) תְּהִלָּה לְדָוִד אֲרוֹמִמְךָ אֱלוֹהַי הַמֶּלֶךְ וַאֲבָרְכָה שִׁמְךָ
לְעוֹלָם וָעֶד: בְּכָל־יוֹם אֲבָרְכֶךָּ וַאֲהַלְלָה שִׁמְךָ לְעוֹלָם וָעֶד:
גָּדוֹל יְיָ וּמְהֻלָּל מְאֹד וְלִגְדֻלָּתוֹ אֵין חֵקֶר: דּוֹר לְדוֹר יְשַׁבַּח

(Vorbeter und Gemeinde.)

אשרי Heil dem Volke, das auf den Posaunenschall achtet,
das im Lichte Deines Antlitzes, o Herr, wandelt.

(Vorbeter.)

אשרי Heil denen, die in Deinem Hause weilen, Dich
preisen immerdar. Heil dem Volke, dem also beschieden. Heil
dem Volke, dessen Gott der Ewige ist.

תהלה (Pf. 145.) Loblied von David. Ich will Dich erheben,
mein Gott und Herr, Deinen Namen preisen immer und ewig.
An jedem Tage will ich Dich preisen und rühmen Deinen Namen
immer und ewig. Groß ist der Ewige und hochgepriesen und

Pages from the 1893 prayer-book.

Gebet für den Landesherrn.

Herr der Welt, Vater aller Menschen! Du hast die Obrigkeit eingesetzt auf Erden, daß sie ein Schirm des Rechts und ein Schutz der Ordnung sei! Erhalte und segne unseren König

Wilhelm II.,

den Kaiser des Deutschen Reiches, daß unter seinem Scepter Wahrheit und Gerechtigkeit immer mehr erblühen! Segne die Kaiserin und Königin

Augusta Victoria,

seine Gemahlin. Segne die **Kaiserin-Mutter Friedrich.** Segne den Kronprinzen und das ganze Königliche Haus! Segne das gesammte deutsche Vaterland, daß Gerechtigkeit und Treue, Friede und Wohlfahrt in ihm walten und alle seine Kinder einen und beglücken mögen. Segne unsere Vaterstadt, gieb ihr Blüthe und Gedeihen! Segne Israel an allen Orten und in allen Landen. Segne unsere Gemeinde, segne ihre Vorsteher und Vertreter, ihre Schulen und wohlthätigen Anstalten sammt Allen, die in Treue an ihnen wirksam sind. Segne ein jedes Haus unserer Gemeinde, Männer und Frauen, Eltern und Kinder, das Alter und die Jugend. Stärke die Schwachen, heile die Kranken, richte auf die Gebeugten, schenke Trost den Trauernden, ewiges Heil den Dahingeschiedenen. Gieb, o himmlischer Vater, daß Dein Reich, das Reich der Wahrheit und des Friedens, immer mehr und mehr sich ausbreite und laß die Tage nahen, in welchen Du als Herr der Welt erkannt sein wirst, Du als der Eine und Dein Name der Einzige, auf daß alle Menschen Dich anbeten und aus jedem Munde Dein Lob erschalle. Amen!

part of it – suffers or panics. In 1873 there was a stock-market crash across Europe, which in Germany affected many members of the aristocracy and the middle class. There was a virulent out-pouring of hatred against the Jews during the long recession that followed. It was at the end of this decade that the greatly respected Prussian historian Heinrich von Treitschke published an anti-Semitic essay that included the words to be so prominently displayed generations later in the huge banners of the Nazi rallies: 'The Jews are our misfortune.' In this he followed a long tradition of the excoriation of Jews, some of the most poisonous of which stemmed from Martin Luther.

By the time the prayer-book was published, things appeared to have quietened down; there was an atmosphere of order, assimilation and increasing prosperity. Around the turn of the century, grand synagogues were built in the main cities of Germany. The bible that I have is a version 'for school and home', newly translated by Dr S. Bernfeld and published in Frankfurt at about this time, in 1906, two years before Henny was born.

3.3

Henny's birthday was the thirteenth day of the twelfth month, and as I browsed through the bible, I experienced an eerie jolt when I came up short against this same date, though from a calendar far removed from the Gregorian:

[Esther 3.12–14]

Then were the king's scribes called on the thirteenth day of the first month, and there was written, according to all that Haman had commanded, unto the king's lieutenants, and to the governors that were over every province, and to the rulers of every people of every province according to the writing thereof, and to every people after their language; in the name of king Ahasuerus was it written, and sealed with the king's ring.

And the letters were sent by posts into all the king's provinces, to destroy, to kill, and to cause to perish, all Jews, both young and old, little children and women, in one day, even upon the thirteenth day of the twelfth month, which is the month Adar, and to take the spoil of them for a prey.

The copy of the writing, for a commandment to be given in every province, was published unto all people, that they should be ready against that day.

Haman's murderous intentions towards the Jews are bluntly recorded in the Book of Esther, as is their deliverance, celebrated on Purim; but in Germany, millennia later, the murderous trail of paper was couched in ellipsis and euphemism, there was no seal, there was no clear warning of exact intent, and there was to be no deliverance till half the Jews of Europe had been killed.

3.4

During the course of 1942, the three Red Cross messages mentioned earlier came through from the enemy country Henny had once called home. Now, towards the end of the year, she got a postcard from a neutral country which told her a little more about her mother and her sister than they had been able to convey in the measured words they were permitted in those messages.

The postcard is from the Pawels, Frejgatan 47, Stockholm. It is written by Henny's aunt Malchen in the old German script in a somewhat spidery hand with a strong forward slant, a hand that looks as if it might enjoy occasional flourishes but eschews them, trying to squeeze as many words as possible on to a small surface.

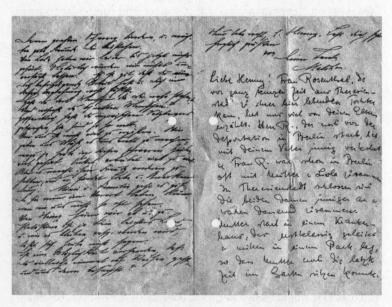

Malchen and Siegfried Pawel's letter from Sweden.

My dear Henny,

We were very happy to hear from you after such a long time, and particularly to hear that things are going well for you. Naturally, we very shortly afterwards passed on your news to your mother and Lola. I received a letter from Lola recently. Lola is still busy at her old job [at the Jewish community organisation, or *Gemeinde*], but unfortunately your mother's health is not too good. First she suffered greatly from rheumatism, which she has apparently overcome, but now her heart appears to be under strain and she has to take things easy. Lola is of course a very caring daughter, so you can be sure that simply everything possible will be done for your mother . . .

This was the last communication sent during the war that gave Henny a clue of what had become of Lola and her mother. The next letter from the Pawels is dated three years later, more than five months after the surrender of Germany. Auntie Malchen writes first.

There is little comfort in what she has to say.

20.10.45

My dear Henny,

Only today have I had the chance to reply to your kind card; partly the pressing demands of house and office – Emigration Assistance, Refugee Welfare Office – and earning a living, partly the fact that I haven't always been in good health, have not let me do so earlier. Besides, I unfortunately hadn't heard anything about your mother and Lola. Now who should come over to my place just a short while ago but a Frau Rosenthal, who used to live in Berlin, and who told me that she and your mother, whom she knew from Berlin, had been in Theresienstadt together. Your mother went on this journey to some extent more calmly because she went with the Glasers [Henny's two old aunts]. Lola was deported later. It must have been bad for your mother in Th; the pain in her legs alone must have given her a lot of trouble. She spent her 70th birthday in Berlin, and got good news of Heinz from

Hans Altmann there. Unfortunately, she died in Th. My dear Henny, this news will strike you hard. May time assuage your deep pain and may good friends stand by you.

We have heard nothing about Lola so far. Naturally, we will try in every way to find out what has happened. It is good that you have work that satisfies you and that you feel happy in this respect.

Are there people there who are close to you? And do you live with good people? We hope that you have spoken meanwhile to the Salzburgers; they are such nice people.

There isn't much to tell from our side. We take pains to keep things up in the house, which in these difficult times really takes some effort. Uncle works far too much. But it gives him great pleasure to help others, and he finds love and recognition in that. Mimi and her family are well; because they now live in the suburbs, we can't see each other all that often. We hear about Heinz [a different Heinz, not Henny's brother] now and then. Palestine is really not an easy country to live in, and how things will remain or develop there is difficult to say at present.

Is there any possibility that you might perhaps travel and could then visit us?

Now farewell, dear Henny, let me send you my warmest good wishes.

Your Aunt

Malchen.

Her husband, who writes in the modern script, adds a few details:

. . . Your mother died in a hospital that was excellently run and was situated in the middle of a park, so that even in her last days she was able to sit in the garden. She did not suffer any want; at the time, the standard of care was still basically satisfactory. Of Lola unfortunately there is no news; she stayed on in Berlin because of her work, so that Frau R. doesn't know anything at all about where she went. Because we are constantly getting news indirectly that people managed to live 'underground' in Germany and are only now making themselves known, one shouldn't give up all hope.

Goodbye, dear Henny,
　　With warmest greetings,
　　　　Your
　　　　　Uncle Siegfried

Uncle Siegfried's advice is as kind as the emollient details he gives. The facts of the concentration camp of Theresienstadt were very different, however, from the picture he paints here.

3.5

Allan George Belvin or 'A.G.', probably the Adolf Berliner whose name was inscribed in the bible, now lived in Atlanta and worked as a certified public accountant. It was he who gave Henny an idea of what might have happened to her sister. His letter is dated just a few days before the Pawels' regarding her mother.

　　　　　　　　　　　　　　　　　7th October, 1945

Dear Hennichen:

(I find it so laughable that we say 'Sie' to each other, and so today without further ado I shall say 'Du' [the more intimate form of German address]; I will claim my brotherly kiss some other time), therefore, dear Hennichen:

I am writing to you today for personal reasons, as also with regard to Lola. Here is an excerpt from the *Aufbau* [a German-Jewish newspaper published in New York] of 21 Sept., in which it is mentioned that Cora Berliner and 50 employees of the [Jewish] Representation in Berlin were deported, so that I have the hollow feeling that Lola's fate is described here. There is a second matter besides. I wrote to you that Frau Schalow was very friendly with Lola, that both of them regularly visited my mother, and that you should try, if possible, to find out her present address. Now a miracle has occurred; she has herself made contact – in fact, via a British soldier – and the letter reached me. Sadly, it contains news that is not so good for you, my dear Hennichen, because she asks in her letter whether I have heard anything about Lola. With that, my last hope has vanished, for Lotte [Schalow] was the one person who could have reported any news of Lola . . .

And that brings up something else. I have already told you that I had good friends in Holland. All, except for Frau von Sassen (mixed marriage, herself Jewish), are dead. Frau v. S. only managed to save herself because she let herself (at the age of perhaps 60) be sterilised – 'destarred', as the dogs in their base fashion called it. From all the details she gave me, I have lost all hope that any full Jew could have saved himself. So I now hold out the most slender of hopes for my brother Ernst and for Lola. Perhaps we should be glad that we do not know anything more exact about the way their lives ended. I almost hope that your mother – as indeed my own – died before the worst actions began . . .

Henny did not give up her last hope. She placed a *Suchannonce* – a missing-persons advertisement – in the *Aufbau* in New York, and tried to trace Lola through various Jewish agencies in Britain too, but though a few former colleagues and acquaintances responded, none of them had any news of Lola.

Possibly because of the slow re-establishment of postal links with a devastated Germany, it was a whole year after the war ended that Henny finally made contact with her friends in Berlin.

Some of her Jewish friends had been deported and methodically murdered by order of their fellow citizens; some had committed suicide; some, who were in mixed marriages to Aryans, had managed to remain in Berlin; some had 'gone underground', but been discovered and killed; one or two of these so-called U-boats had survived. Any survivors, without exception – as also all Henny's Christian friends – had been bombed from the air by the Americans and the British or from the ground by the advancing Russians and reduced to a state of wretchedness, with almost no shelter or clothing, heating or food or medicine or possessions – ill or injured, weakened by hunger, and stricken with grief for relatives and

200

friends who had died. Few if any of them lived at their former
addresses, which in most cases were heaps of rubble.

One of those who first contacted Henny was Lola's friend Alice
Fröschke, who was not Jewish. Everyone in the circle of friends
called her Fröschlein – little frog – though her photographs belie
the nickname: she was about ten years older than Lola and looks
lean, bespectacled and even somewhat prim. She was unmarried
and lived with her old and ailing mother.

From Fröschlein Henny received, if in one respect at third
remove, some specific news about Lola.

Alice Fröschke
Berlin W 15
Uhlandstr. 175   6 May 1946

My dear Henny,

I have trembled about this possibility all these years – that you would
one day write and ask about Lola . . . This evening I found your kind
letter at home. I am replying immediately.

I was with Lola and your mother right until the end. Both were taken
away in May 1943. Once before, when Lola was not at home, they had
come for your mother, who was very weak and wretched, and had taken
her away, though Lola, who was employed by the Gemeinde, was able as
a result to protect her. She was even successful in getting her set free. I
remember as if it were today that one evening, as we had arranged, I
went over to your place, that no one was at home, and that a neighbour
told me that Lola was on her way to look for her mother and to get her
set free again. Herr Wolfsky [a common misspelling of Wolffsky], Lola's
boss at the Gemeinde, helped her a great deal in this. On the next
evening, we had arranged with Lola that we would come again. My
sister and I met her. Your mother was back again, but very downcast.
From then on, we arranged on each occasion the exact time when I
would next come, so that in the evening Lola could let me in. I was there
around the middle of the week and wanted to come again the next

Tuesday to visit Lola. But my mother said to me one day, when I came home, that Lola had phoned to say that I couldn't come any more; and from that – which she very carefully said on the telephone – my mother understood that both Lola and your mother had been taken away.

Lola had promised to call me once again. Every evening I sat by the telephone; she didn't call. Finally, on Sunday – I was just about to leave the house, because Alice [Pasch, whose sister Else is mentioned later in this letter] had telephoned me – in order to avoid deportation [a so-called *Transport*], she had left her home and was hiding in a suburb somewhere – when Lola's call came. Lola said, shaking off all my pleading and questioning, that I couldn't see her any more. I begged her to come to the window so that I could at least wave to her from the street one more time. She was, in fact, allowed as an employee of the Gemeinde to come out of the collection camp every day to go to the Gemeinde and could telephone from there. As I repeated my request again and again, she finally asked me if I could come to her. Often non-Jews – married partners – would come to the Gemeinde in order to make inquiries. So I saw her and spoke to her on that Sunday before the 17th May 1943 – the day she was sent away – for the last time. She was so sad. Your mother was only taken away after her. Thus they were to be parted at the end.

Lola went with a charming young colleague of hers, a young woman. I asked whether I could inquire after her and after your mother from Herr Wolfsky. And I was often at the Wolfskys' after that. Lola was sent to Birkenau, which was part of the frightful camp of Auschwitz. Oh, Hennerle, when I write this, all the old sorrow wells up once again; no, it is as if one can never conceive again of ever being at peace. Lola wrote again; it was a postcard in block letters, but [it ended with] her small, unmistakable, delicate and graceful signature, which I used to say as a joke looked as if it had been made by a fly. The Wolfskys and I sent her a parcel, but no further news came from her.

In October of last year (1945) a [female] doctor, whom the Wolfskys know, gave them the news that the young woman who had been deported together with Lola had died of dysentery and in her feverish state had requested the doctor again and again, that if she herself survived, she should tell the Wolfskys about her death, so that they could pass on the news to the young woman's daughter, who lives in America. So then the Wolfskys naturally also asked about Lola. The doctor had also seen Lola; she too had been in a bad way already from the terrible Transport, but she was not actually ill and therefore didn't enter the 'hospital' barracks, like Frau Michaelsohn, Lola's colleague. The doctor had then seen Lola for a little while longer, and then no more. And because she didn't pass through the hospital barracks, in which the poor people died of their illnesses, there remains only the other way. Ah, Hennerle, I am crying bitterly as I write all this to you. If only I could, when you receive this letter, sit beside you and hold you tightly in my arms and weep with you. Do you know, your mother was to the very end so courageous, she was just as she always was, I so greatly admired her. And Lola, our Lola, who had such a fine soul, who was so noble in her character and way of thinking, whom no one could ever say anything against – and could only say that she was a distinguished person, full of goodness for all those she loved, self-sacrificing, unchangeable. I always thought she would return. In all those long months since she went away, I dreamed of her and spoke to her so vividly in my dreams, and then one hears, two and a half years later, that she is no longer there, simply gone.—

What have you heard about your brother? Do you have news of him? Alice, Else Pasch and Lonni are, the Wolfskys tell me, almost certainly not alive any more – one has to take it that they too are dead. This sorrow will never let us be fully happy again.—

We are still alive. Almost all the houses in Uhlandstrasse are destroyed or burned out; ours too is in a dreadful condition. Fearful years lie behind us. My father died on the 10th of August last year. My mother has had severe dysentery. In addition, though she will soon be 80, she was operated on this year. I too am soon going to be 50, am feeling really old, and have also been very ill. It would give me great pleasure to hear from you and Shantilein. I have often thought, if I met him here on the street, what a joy it would be . . .

My mother greets you warmly; and just as warmly and lovingly – in remembrance of Lola – both you and Shanti are greeted by

Your

Fröschlein

3.6

After Fröschlein's letter, to which no reply is on file, Henny could not have entertained any hope of her sister's survival. The next month came a letter, typed on rough, brownish paper, from Herr Wolffsky, under whom Lola worked at the Gemeinde. The letter gives an insight into Lola's character and what happened to her. That Wolffsky himself was not killed was due to the fact that his wife was not Jewish, though in the last phase of the war and the extermination programme, even this would not have assured him protection.

6.7.46

Dear Fräulein Caro,

. . . Your sister requested me, should the opportunity present itself, to convey to you her farewell greeting, which I now willingly do.

As you are no doubt aware, at the outbreak of the war your sister worked in the local Organisation for Assistance in Emigration. When, in November 1941, this work had to cease, your sister joined a department that was run by me as part of the then Jewish community organisation [Gemeinde], and I had the good fortune to work with her until her deportation. This criminal and senseless destruction of human life, by striking your sister struck a person who, through her exceptional capabilities, especially where she could apply them, was of truly indispensable use. With her knowledge of the field of statistics, her articulateness, her skills in typewriting and stenography, she was the most able of our female colleagues. That led at least to the fact that it was comparatively late, as one of the last, that she had to meet the dreadful fate that awaited her, and that she was thereby also able to protect your mother until that point in time.

When the terrible date arrived, and your mother and sister had to enter the collection camp, from which the deportation followed, I was able to speak to your relations right up to the point of departure, and somewhat help them get over the moment when they were torn from each other. This I did, having promised your sister that I would take care of your mother, who was left behind. I managed to do this, in that, on the day after the departure of your sister, I spoke to your mother and sought to console her. But on this very day your mother left for Theresienstadt.—

I received a sign of life from your sister, probably the only one that exists after her deportation. I am sending you this sad farewell greeting, which would have been addressed to you, had conditions permitted. From your mother too I received the enclosed card, to which we responded with a Care parcel. Unfortunately, no further news was received.

Your deeply sensitive sister must – it is barely imaginable how – have suffered fearfully under the barbaric conditions in such a camp. There was no possibility of her surviving such torment of body and soul. I would wish that she did not have to suffer such torture long. Your mother's constitution too was not in such a state that one could assume one would see her again.

Today we are faced with the sorrowful certainty that these two people are part of the millions of innocents who have fallen victim to wanton murder such as has never before been seen, and which one hopes will never be forgotten . . .

I hope that my lines find you in good health and I remain, with many friendly greetings,

    Yours sincerely,
    Adolf Wolffsky

Enclosed are two plain postcards, written in pencil, addressed to Herr Wolffsky. This was the last writing Henny would see from her mother's and sister's hands.

The individual letters of the name and address on Lola's postcard, as indeed of the message itself, are not connected but separate, which might have been a requirement. They are unformed and weak, like those of a child or someone so desperately ill she can hardly hold a pencil. Only the signature itself is cursive. The postcard is dated about two months after Lola was deported from Berlin.

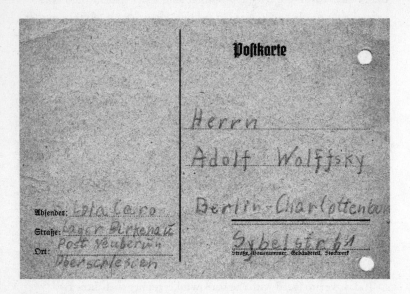

Lola's postcard from Auschwitz-Birkenau.

Ella's postcard from Theresienstadt.

Herr Adolf Wolffsky Sender: Lola Caro
61 Sybelstrasse Birkenau Camp
Charlottenburg Post Neuberun
Berlin Upper Silesia
15. 7. 1943

Dear Herr Wolffsky,

am here in the camp, am working and am healthy. I hope you and
your family are well. With many kind greetings to you, your wife and
Jonny, as also to my remaining Berlin friends

I remain

Yours sincerely   Lola Caro

The other postcard is numbered 42930 in pencil and the sender is
indicated as 'Caro Gabriele, Theresienstadt Qu 808'. The handwriting is cursive.

Theresienstadt 26/7.43

Respected Sir,

Only today have I been able to get around to sending a sign of life.
After an illness, I am, thank God, better. I would be very happy to know
if Lola has been in touch; I hope to have news from you very soon. All
parcels and packages arrive daily. With best wishes to all and to you,

Yours sincerely,

Gabriele Caro

Henny wrote back to Mr Wolffsky a few days later. When talking
of Lola and her mother, she echoes Fröschlein's words.

Henny Caro 27, Kendal Street,
London W. 2,
26.7.46

Dear Herr Wolffsky,

Thank you for your letter, even though its contents were infinitely
painful for me. I simply cannot grasp that my dear mother and sister
have fallen victim to this ruthless murder, and the thought of it lets me

find no peace. It is just unimaginable how my loved ones, who had such fine souls and who were so noble in their character and way of thinking, must have suffered. The 'thousand year Reich' will not last, but even after 1000 years Germany's shame will not be forgotten . . .

In the hope that my lines find you in good health, I remain, with good wishes for you and your family,

Yours sincerely,

[unsigned, since this is a carbon copy]

3.7

What happened to Henny's mother and sister after she left for England?

Many of the measures of exclusion and isolation have already been touched on. By the time Henny left Germany, she, like all Jews, would have had to carry an identity card at all times. Her passport would have been recalled and a new one issued with the large red letter J stamped on it – an innovation instituted at the instigation of the Swiss, who were keen to stem Jewish immigration without jeopardising the free cross-border movement of other Germans. The new middle name Sara, which would have been forced on her, as on all female Jews, would have had to be included in all official communications, from sending a postal order to applying for emigration papers. In any face-to-face dealings with officials she would immediately have had to announce that she was a Jew and to produce her identity document.

At the beginning of 1939, Hitler announced to the Reichstag:

Today I will once more be a prophet. If the international Jewish financiers inside and outside Europe should again succeed in plunging the nations into a world war, the result will be not the bolshevisation of the earth and thus the victory of Jewry, but the annihilation of the Jewish race throughout Europe.

The process of systematic and official robbery was also well under way. Jewish businesses had been 'Aryanised' (sold to non-Jews) for a ridiculous price. The property of emigrants was confiscated by the state. In February 1939, it was announced that Jews were not allowed to keep any silver. Any valuables they owned had to be delivered to the municipal 'Pawn Institution' for the greater good of the German treasury. By late July 1939, when Henny left Berlin for Hamburg and took the steamer to England, she would have known that those whom the Nazis had dubbed subhuman would not find the cruelty now visited on them alleviated by the impending war.

In the course of six years, since the coming to power of Hitler, the Caros had descended into a deepening well of dismay. Now, for four years of the coming six-year war, Henny's mother and sister were to survive in conditions of increasing misery and oppression. Then they would be done away with.

As the war progressed, more and more deprivations were imposed upon them. Within a month of the war starting, their radio would have been taken away. In due course, their telephone would have been ripped out. They would have been permitted to use public telephones, but only for speaking to Aryans. Later, the use of even public telephones would be prohibited.

Their ration books and coupons would have been distinctively marked, first with a J, then with the word 'Jew'. Their rations would have been drastically cut. There would be no meat for them, no eggs, no white bread. Even the meagre food they were permitted could be bought only between the hours of four and five in the afternoon, so that they would not inconvenience or associate with the rest of the population.

Shortly after the beginning of the war, they would not have been allowed to leave the house after 8 p.m. Later they would not have been allowed to leave their residential district without written police authority. They would not have been allowed to use a subway train, bus or tram during the rush hour, and at all other

210

times would have to give up their seat to a 'German'. Later, public transport would be denied them altogether, except to go to work, and then only if the distance was seven kilometres or more.

From September 1941 they would have had to wear a large black star on a yellow background with the word 'Jew' inscribed, in the middle of the left front of their clothing, whenever they appeared in public. In October, the Gestapo was told by the Reich Security Main Office that any friendly contact in public between an Aryan and a Jew was to be discouraged:

> I order that in such cases the Aryan party is to be taken into protective custody temporarily for educational purposes, and that in serious cases they be put into a concentration camp, grade I, for a period of up to three months. The Jewish party is in any case to be taken into protective custody until further notice and to be sent to a concentration camp.

Reinhard Heydrich, the head of the Reich Security Main Office, wanted to concentrate the Jews in particular places, but he did not want a ghetto in Berlin; he was worried about the danger of disease, the possibility of resistance, and the reaction of the rest of the population. Instead, Jews were compelled to live in specific apartment houses throughout the city, and one of these seems to have been the house in which the Caros had rented an apartment from 1938 onwards, Bleibtreustrasse 19. From 1942, a Jewish star in black on white paper would have been posted on the front of this house to mark it out and to discourage potential non-Jewish visitors.

But by then, the transports from Berlin had begun, both to Theresienstadt and to 'the East' – whether to concentration camps or to the intermediate stage of a ghetto. Berlin was being emptied of its Jews, and, though there was always scope for refinement, the policy and practice regarding their disposal were working well.

In his letter to Henny, Adolf Wolffsky mentions that Lola worked at the Gemeinde (*Jüdische Kultusgemeinde zu Berlin*) or Jewish community organisation, at first in the emigration office and then, when emigration was forbidden in 1941, in another office, though he does not specify which. As a result of her work in the Gemeinde, Lola was not conscripted for forced labour like other Jews. She was also one of the last Jews to be 'transported'. The Gemeinde of Berlin, as well as the national Jewish organisation, the Reich Association of Jews in Germany, whose headquarters were also in Berlin, were far too useful to the Nazis to be dispensed with too early in the process.

The Reich Representation of German Jews (*Reichsvertretung der deutschen Juden*) was founded in 1933 under the leadership of the well respected liberal Rabbi Leo Baeck but encompassed a wide range of German-Jewish opinion. It was not permitted to use its impudent title for long; in 1935, it was forced to change its name to the Reich Representation of Jews in Germany (*Reichsvertretung der Juden in Deutschland*). In 1939 it was once more renamed, this time the Reich Association of Jews in Germany (*Reichsvereinigung der Juden in Deutschland*). It had been a voluntary associative body for promoting Jewish welfare as well as representing the views and the plight of Jews to the wider public and to the authorities. But in July 1939 it became by decree a compulsory association under the direct command of the Gestapo ('the supervisory authority') for all those defined as Jews by the Nazis under the Nuremberg laws, regardless of how they saw themselves. As refugees poured into Berlin from the countryside and smaller towns, as Jewish children were ejected from state schools, as Jews were thrown out of their jobs and robbed of their property and savings, the Association did what it could to alleviate their poverty or distress and to help equip them for the future: to provide shelter, food, winter relief, schooling, training, emigration assistance, and so on. But at the same time, unwittingly – or perhaps helplessly – it assisted in the undermining of this future.

Much of the preceding recital of anti-Jewish measures has been summarised from Raul Hilberg's magisterial and insightful book *The Destruction of the European Jews*. But the paragraph in which he comments about the ambivalent role of the transformed Reichsvereinigung is worth quoting in full:

> Significantly, this transformation was being accomplished without any change of personnel or designation. The Germans had not created the Reichsvereinigung and they had not appointed its leaders. Rabbi Leo Baeck, Dr Otto Hirsch, Direktor Heinrich Stahl, and all the others *were* the Jewish leaders. Because these men were not puppets, they retained their status and identity in the Jewish community throughout their participation in the process of destruction, and because they did not lessen their diligence, they contributed the same ability that they had once marshalled for Jewish well-being to assist their German supervisors in operations that had become lethal. They began the pattern of compliance by reporting deaths, births and other demographic data to the Reich Security Main Office and by transmitting German regulations in the publication *Jüdisches Nachrichtenblatt* to the Jewish population. They went on to establish special bank accounts accessible to the Gestapo and to concentrate Jews in designated apartment houses. Toward the end, they prepared charts, maps, and lists and provided space, supplies, and personnel in preparations for deportation. The Reichsvereinigung and its counterparts in Vienna and Prague were the prototype of an institution – the Jewish Council – that was to appear in Poland and other occupied territories and that was to be employed in activities resulting in disaster. It was a system that enabled the Germans to save their manpower and funds while increasing their stranglehold on the victims. Once they dominated the Jewish leadership, they were in a position to control the entire community.

Wolffsky states that Lola's many skills – linguistic, stenographic, statistical – made her 'of truly indispensable use'. Alas, one wonders to what use these skills were eventually put.

3.9

The rounding-up of the Jews was the job of the Gestapo (the Secret State Police), helped by whoever they needed: the SS (the Nazi elite corps), the SA (the storm troopers, or Nazi militia) or the regular police force. Once a train with a certain number of wagons had been reserved with the Transport Ministry to travel at a certain time on a certain date along a certain route to a certain destination, it became necessary, as far as possible, both to keep to the timetable and to utilise the space on the train. (Such efficient bureaucratic arrangements were among Adolf Eichmann's particular skills.)

The Gestapo required the Gemeinde to provide it with lists of Jews who were not exempt from deportation (by reason, for example, of marriage to an Aryan). The Gestapo selected from these lists names up to the requisite number, and informed the Gemeinde. The Gemeinde informed the people selected. They were told to stand by at a certain hour in their houses. The Gestapo then came and picked them up – after making sure that their furniture and other household property were correctly accounted for and listed so that they could be confiscated once they had 'emigrated'. It was difficult for people to avoid arrest by going underground without means or help or papers, but some did. Others committed suicide. In such cases, the property was meticulously listed, as if the person was going to be transported anyway.

At first, when the Gemeinde requested that certain people not be sent off, their names were replaced with those of others. Later, as Berlin became increasingly depleted of Jews, it became more difficult to find 'material' to fill a particular train, to quote one memo written by a member of the Reichsvereinigung after a conversation with the Gestapo. Exemptions became rarer.

As their prey became scarcer, the Gestapo began rounding up people without warning at their workplaces or in the streets or – often at night or early in the morning – in their houses. This may well have been the explanation for the fact that Ella was hauled away and had to be traced, probably to a collection camp, by Lola. At this stage, those employees of the Gemeinde who remained could plead for their immediate relatives.

On one occasion, the Gestapo rounded up a number of Jews married to Aryans. But the Aryan spouses demonstrated in the street near the building where they were interned pending deportation, and made such a noise and fuss that it was decided, for the moment, to let these spouses go. At a certain level, the Nazis were wary of public opinion and did not want to arouse sympathy for Jews.

To this end, and also to save their own manpower, the Gestapo introduced an innovation in late 1942: the use of Jewish orderlies to help them in their actual work of arresting, listing, tallying and removing. A Jewish Order Service was set up; any orderly who refused to do his duty properly or who warned anyone of what was to come would be shot and his family transported to the East. Leo Baeck, the President of the Reichsvereinigung, later explained that he was powerless to prevent this, and that he had hoped that the Jewish orderlies would be gentler and more helpful than the Gestapo, thus making the ordeal easier.

The arrestees were confined to a *Sammellager* or collection camp, sometimes for a day or two, sometimes for weeks on end, depending on many factors, such as the numbers needed to make up a particular train-load. The collection camps included one of the three (out of forty) synagogues in Berlin not destroyed during Kristallnacht and the large premises of the old people's home on Grosse Hamburger Strasse. These had to be made ready by the Gemeinde, who would also have to supply provisions for the people and guard them. For every escapee, two guards would be 'sent East'. Late in 1942, the Gestapo ordered that, in the interest of space, the kitchen be torn out and all furniture removed from the Grosse Hamburger Strasse collection camp. This may have been why Fröschlein was so distressed, in a letter to Henny, that she had not been able to get any hot food to Lola the last time she saw her. (They had met in the Gemeinde, to which Lola was paroled from the collection camp for work during the day.)

But Henny's mother and sister did not remain in Berlin for long after their initial arrest. On 17 May 1943, a transport of four hundred people set out from Berlin for the East. Lola was on it. On 18 May, a transport of one hundred people (an 'old people's transport') set out from Berlin for Theresienstadt. Ella was on it. On the 19th, though there were still a few Jews scattered here and there in the city and though sporadic transports would continue right until the last year of the war, Berlin was officially declared Jew-free.

3.10

Theresienstadt or Terezín, to which Ella Caro was sent, was a large and forbidding fortress set in the pleasant plain of the River Ohre, a tributary of the Elbe. It was located in the German-controlled Protectorate of Bohemia and Moravia, which before the war had been part of Czechoslovakia.

The fortress had been built by the Austro-Hungarians against the Prussians at the end of the eighteenth century. Later it became a garrison town. In 1941 the Germans made it a ghetto for Jews, mainly from Czechoslovakia and Greater Germany. It was to be a place for older Jews, and for those who were to get some sort of preferential treatment by not being sent directly to a killing-camp. Though Theresienstadt was a place of brutality, desperate overcrowding, deprivation, slave labour, disease and high mortality, it also maintained a sort of cultural life and some small elements of Jewish decision-making. Many aspects of life in Theresienstadt were organised by a Jewish camp administration under the control of the SS. The Germans even managed from time to time to provide bizarrely stage-managed spectacles of quasi-normality for observers from the outside world who made short visits.

A transport of about a hundred people left Berlin on each of three successive days; Ella's was the second of these. She would probably have travelled in a passenger car, to conform to the impression that the Nazis sought to give – that the whole process was a humane resettlement in fairly idyllic surroundings.

Zdenek Lederer's book *Ghetto Theresienstadt*, translated from the Czech and published in English in 1953, describes the structures, conditions and history of the camp with a calmness and analytical distance remarkable in one who was confined there for several years. From it one gets a clear sense of what life and death there were like. Survival – what one's rations were, what one could somehow procure by way of additional nourishment, and in what degree of crowdedness and squalor one was forced to live – depended crucially on where one was on the social ladder. Ella, being old and not in good health even when she arrived, was at the bottom of the scale. Prisoners had on average two square metres of living space; there was one insanitary bathroom for every fifty. Twenty to forty women lived in each small barracks. Old people, who had been told that Theresienstadt was 'a sort of spa where the aged and infirm would be given every possible care and consideration . . . soon learnt that they had been deceived. They were . . . stripped of their belongings, and housed in lofts or small cubbyholes where they had to sleep on the bare floor.' The rations of the aged and infirm had been reduced the previous year in order to help the heavy workers. They even received fewer laundry vouchers.

By the time Ella got to the hospital in Theresienstadt, she would have been sick and malnourished and prone to any kind of infection. Conditions there were not like those described in the Pawels' letter to Henny. Medical equipment and supplies were completely inadequate.

With the exception of the general hospital, all hospitals lacked the facilities and the staff for anything more than the most perfunctory treatment. The homes for the aged were overcrowded, and the wards for chronic diseases were filthy hovels. The patients starved, and their diseases were usually aggravated by incurable diarrhoea. Many of the patients died in hospital; their beds were hurriedly and inadequately disinfected and taken by newcomers. The air in the wards was stuffy and death was considered a trivial occurrence.

Infectious diseases such as gastroenteritis, pneumonia and tuberculosis were rife in Theresienstadt. Owing to the efforts of the Health Department, however, there were no serious epidemics of, say, scarlet fever or typhoid; these were kept in check by delousing and inoculation upon arrival.

In the course of research I found a document entitled 'Inoculation list of the Berlin Transport I/93, 18th May, 1943'. I/93 was the Theresienstadt administration's equivalent of the old people's transport number 88 from Berlin. On this typed list is the number 12609 and the name Gabriele S. Carow (corrected manually by the removal of the w). The year of her birth, 1871, appears in the appropriate column. Against her name is the handwritten notation, 'died 16/10/43'.

On another printed list, the typed surname 'Carow' is crossed out and replaced with 'Caro' in what looks like her own hand, and her maiden name, typed 'Schmeltes', is replaced with 'Schmelkes'. She was meticulous to the last. On a list of names compiled years later by researchers trying to collate dates, her birthdate is marked '???' but her death date is marked 'k 18.10.43' (where the 'k' might represent *Krankenhaus*, or hospital). The two dates are close enough. Suffice it to say that she died almost exactly five months after she was transported from the city where she had lived all her married life.

Had she not died there, she would very likely have been shipped off on one of the transports to the East so dreaded by the prisoners, which were the SS's response to the necessity of creating enough space in the camp for new arrivals – and later, to the policy of liquidating the inmates and emptying the camp. The most common destination of transports from Theresienstadt was Auschwitz.

In the midst of all this crowding, she died alone, far from her scattered family, of whom she had no news. If she did hear about Heinz, it would have been months earlier. Of Henny she would have known nothing. Nor could she have had any exact idea where Lola had been taken – except that it was to the East, probably somewhere in what had once been Poland. In the one postcard she managed to write, in late July, to Mr Wolffsky, she asked for news of her. But by that time, Lola, who had in fact been sent to Auschwitz, was almost certainly already dead.

3.11

Lola would have been taken from the collection camp in the heart of Berlin to the train bound for Auschwitz. She would probably have travelled in a crowded cattle car bolted from the outside. She would have had no food, little if any water and no toilet facilities throughout this journey in the heat of mid-May. Many people died in the course of such journeys.

This particular transport appears to have taken not the usual eighteen hours, but two days. While it left Berlin on the 17th, there is no record in the *Auschwitz Chronicle* – a day-by-day compilation of events at the camp drawn from various documentary sources and memoirs and published in 1990 – of the arrival of a train on that day or the next. On the following day, 19 May 1943, an entry states:

Approximately 1000 Jewish men, women and children arrive with an RSHA [Reich Security Main Office] transport. After the selection, 80 men, given Nos. 122476–122555, and 115 women, given Nos. 45168–45282, are admitted to the camp. The other more than 800 people are killed in the gas chambers.

There is an inconsistency between the number of people who set out from Berlin – four hundred in all – and the number who arrived at Auschwitz. But this may help to explain the unwonted length of the journey. As was often the case, by arrangement between the Reich Security Main Office and the Transport Ministry, the train could have travelled via some point or points where additional numbers of wagons, already laden with their quota of Jews, would have been waiting to be added to the train.

Selection from among the deportees took place on a long railway ramp as soon as the train arrived at the part of the Auschwitz complex known as Birkenau. SS officers with guns, whips and guard dogs and Jewish inmates assigned for the purpose would have supervised the unloading. Clutching their hand luggage, but forced to leave everything else on the train, the exhausted, hungry, thirsty and filthy deportees would have been divided into two groups, with men on one side and women and children on the other. This ripping apart of families would have been followed by the selection: SS officers and SS doctors would make instant decisions as to who were and who were not capable of work. The latter were taken straight to the gas chambers. The former were absorbed, for a while, in the camp.

Lola was not old, nor was she accompanied by a child; either condition would have doomed her instantly. From Fröschlein's letter, it appears that Lola was among those absorbed rather than immediately gassed. The postcard she sent Herr Wolffsky giving her address as Birkenau also suggests that she wrote it from within the camp.

The vast Auschwitz complex, of which Auschwitz II, or Birkenau, formed a part, was located in a closed forty-square-kilometre SS 'zone of interest' in the partially drained swamplands between the Vistula and its tributary the Sola, in what had once been Poland. (The translation of the name Birkenau – Birchmead – is as charming as the translation of the name Buchenwald – Beechwood.) Birkenau had vast sub-camps for men and women and an area within easy walking distance where most of the gas chambers and crematoria were located. Unlike parts of the complex, such as Buna, also known as Auschwitz III, which were mainly slave-based and industrial in purpose, the purpose of Birkenau was chiefly exterminatory.

Most of the camps whose principal or exclusive purpose was extermination – Belzec, Majdanek, Sobibor, Chelmno, Treblinka – lay in the German-ruled and German-named General Government, that part of Poland that had not been swallowed up in 1939 into Germany or the Soviet Union. But Auschwitz – which, owing to its nodal position on the Central European rail network, had once been a labour exchange where German industrial employers had picked up cheap Polish labour and which for the same reason was now so useful for the purposes of accumulation and extermination – had been so swallowed, and now lay in Germany proper in the province of Upper Silesia.

The extermination of Reich Jews on what was now Reich soil and the appropriation of their property aroused legalistic qualms in the souls of certain bureaucrats and Nazi officials, including the timid but murderous Heinrich Himmler. The cover letters sent by the Gestapo to the Finance Ministry compassing the appropriation of the property of Jews who had emigrated or been deported from the Reich were not, strictly speaking, accurate if they were still in Germany. These qualms were stilled in due course. In September 1942, Dr Otto Thierack, the Minister of Justice, agreed with Himmler that Jews, Gypsies, Russians and other 'asocials' could be delivered to concentration camps without a specific charge. A month later, he suggested that the incarceration in prisons (within his ambit) of such people was not a useful step towards their extermination. He stated therefore that he had no interest in them and authorised that they be delivered to the police, whether the Gestapo or others, who could do with them whatever they wished, 'unhindered by the laws of criminal evidence'. This statement from him was enough. No law needed to be passed for this relinquishing of vast numbers of people to outlawry. No longer were they protected by the criminal code. Reich Jews could legitimately be exterminated on Reich soil.

After selection, Lola would have entered the electrified barbed-wire precincts of the women's camp. Her head would have been shorn, she would have been made to strip, she would have been disinfected, and a number would have been tattooed on her forearm. Any property she had brought from Berlin would by now have been taken off the train to 'Canada', the centre for the sorting, listing and official theft of the property of inmates for the benefit of the German Reich. Now the clothes she had worn would be taken away and she would be given striped clothing and clogs. This is what she would wear for the rest of her life – a few more weeks.

The Death Factory, written in 1945 by Ota Kraus and Erich Kulka, two former inmates of Auschwitz, and published in English in 1966, describes and analyses existence in Auschwitz. The chapters relating to Birkenau, and the women's camp in particular, give one a sense of what Lola would have experienced.

> Birkenau was situated in a swamp. The climate was murderous; death lay in wait in the air, on the land and in the water. Undernourished bodies fell easy victims to malaria, typhus, dysentery and other illnesses.
>
> Persons suffering from fever are tormented by insatiable thirst. But at Birkenau there was no drinking water, only warning notices: *Kein Trinkwasser!* ('Not drinking water'). Healthy and sick alike drank poisoned water.
>
> During the drought and heat the prisoners were at the mercy of clouds of mosquitoes. It was noticeable that the birds seemed to avoid the whole area, as though they were aware of the terrible things going on there.
>
> In the mornings and evenings the region was veiled in the camp mist of the marshland, and this unhealthy atmosphere was further contaminated by the smoke and stench from the nearby crematoria. The wretched prisoners felt their last strength ebbing from them as they dragged their wooden shoes through the thick slime of the surrounding swamps.

The dreadful and scarce food, mainly thin soup, the lengthy marches to and from sites of brutal overwork, the lengthy roll-calls in searing heat, the filth and overcrowding of the sheds in which the prisoners lived, destroyed what residual strength or spirit they may have had.

A woman prisoner testified in 1946 as follows:

We received our food in large red enamel dishes which were merely rinsed in cold water after each meal. This was a direct cause of mortality and epidemics, for as all the women were ill and could not go out at night to the indescribably filthy trench to perform their natural functions, they used their dishes for this purpose. The next day they collected up the dishes and emptied their contents into the washing-up tubs. During the day another batch of women used the same dishes for food.

The cruelty of the guards was inventive.

SS wardress Volkenrath, for instance, would pour cold water on Jewish women as they stood naked for hours outside the blocks in the winter during 'selection'; then, screaming abuse, she would set the dogs on them . . . The SS wardresses often punished women by making them stand at attention without shoes at the entrance to the camp where they were watched from the SS guard-room. If they moved at all, the punishment was increased; they had to kneel on the gravel with bare knees and outstretched hands. Stones were then placed on their hands, and if a single one fell to the ground, the prisoner was beaten.

Miserable and filthy, hungry and weak, far from help or hope and deprived of any news of any loved one, Lola might well have felt alone in a universe created by the most bestial of humans and presided over by a pitiless power.

The selection referred to above would have been one of those that took place periodically, whenever the Auschwitz camps became too crowded. An SS doctor would examine the naked prisoners on parade and determine who was to be condemned to die. One assumes that this is what happened to Lola. To quote Fröschlein again:

The doctor had then seen Lola for a little while longer, and then no more. And because she didn't pass through the hospital barracks, in which the poor people died of their illnesses, there remains only the other way.

After this internal selection, Lola would have been taken to Block 25, where she and many other women would have waited for death – for hours, possibly for days – without food or water. Unlike some of those who had just arrived on transports, they would not have had much doubt about what was going to happen to them.

Some hours before their arrival was expected at their final destination, the engines there, if not running already, would have been started, so as to feed air to the furnaces.

Lola and the other women, and possibly men, women and children from other blocks would have been herded out and made to march, five abreast, to the gates of the crematorium yard – probably Crematorium 1 or 2 of the four crematoria that served Birkenau.

Along a grey path amid green grass she would have walked to the grey railings that led down a dozen steps to an underground undressing-room, a vast space with supporting pillars and benches and pegs. Here she would have been ordered to take off her clothes and shoes and to remember the number of her peg so that she could retrieve what was hers after the so-called disinfection and bath. The oak doors beyond would have been opened, and the SS personnel would have urged, and finally forced, the people to enter the huge underground 'disinfection room', in fact the gas chamber. Here too there were pillars from concrete floor to ceiling, but these pillars were hollow and perforated. Lola would have been crammed in with the others, up to two thousand or more. The oak doors would have been closed and secured, and the lights dimmed or turned off. What thoughts went through her head in these last few minutes of her life it is presumptuous to imagine, but it is difficult to doubt that among them must have been thoughts of Henny, Heinz and her mother.

Arriving in a Red Cross ambulance with large green tins in their hands, an SS officer and a non-commissioned officer – after donning gas masks – would have walked to the grassy mound above the chamber, unscrewed the covers to the pillars, and poured in the mauve-coloured, bean-sized crystals of Zyklon-B. These would, upon contact with air, have produced a lethal gas. When this poured out of the perforations in the pillars, Lola would have begun to die in agony and terror, gasping for breath.

Within between five and twenty minutes she and everyone else would have been dead. The peephole in the oak door would have helped those in charge to ascertain the situation. In half an hour, the suction pumps would have been turned on. In due course, the oak doors would have been reopened and the lights turned full on. What would have greeted the eyes of the special group of prisoners – the *Sonderkommando* – detailed for the next stage of the process would not have been corpses scattered evenly across the floor, but a huge pile or piles of corpses. Since the effect of the gas would have been most apparent close to the floor at first, then higher up, everyone would have been struggling in desperation for air, clawing at, trampling down and climbing upon the bodies of their fellows in order to gain a few extra moments of breath and life. Babies and children, like the weakest and oldest, would have been crushed at the bottom of the pile.

Lola's naked body, grotesquely contorted, possibly broken-boned, her face blue and unrecognisable and bleeding from mouth and nose, her legs streaked with shit and blood, would, after a hosing-down, have been dragged out of the room, possibly with a noose and grappling-hook, to a large lift that would have taken her together with the many others up to the ground floor of the building. Here, in the furnace room, a trolley would have moved her body along to continue the procedure. Any gold teeth she might have had would have been broken out of her mouth with pliers, and she would have been tipped out of the trolley into one of fifteen large cast-iron ovens. She would have been disposed of in about twenty minutes, her own residual fat helping to sustain the heat of the oven, thus saving fuel.

Her hair, shorn off earlier, would have had various uses, from the manufacture of felt to insulation to submariners' socks. Her bones, if any fragments remained, would later have been ground to powder. This, together with any ashes that had not been dispersed through the chimney as smoke, would eventually have been dumped into the River Sola.

3.12

After a couple of my books were translated into Hebrew, I was invited to a writers' conference in Israel. I requested that the Israeli Embassy in Delhi issue my visa on a separate sheet of paper so as not to jeopardise my chances of travelling to any Arab country. When they issued it on the passport itself and I protested, a large 'cancelled' was stamped across it and the separate sheet made out. Now, when I travel to a Western country, particularly in the current nervous climate, I am occasionally questioned about why my Israeli visa was cancelled.

Each participant to the conference was invited to bring a companion. I asked Yasmeen, an old friend of mine from Delhi, to come along. Yasmeen, an architect, was very interested in seeing Jerusalem and Tel Aviv but, being Muslim, felt she would have little chance of doing so under other circumstances. Friends of mine in London had told me to get in touch with friends of theirs in Jerusalem. I did this, and Yasmeen and I were invited to their house the same day for the customary pre-Sabbath meal to which they had invited several of their friends. The Zamirs' warmth, openness and hospitality overwhelmed us; and Yasmeen, who, apart from everything else, is very beautiful, was something of a hit.

The delicious meal and the sense of welcome aside, there was among the company the sort of considered decency that is hard to maintain in difficult times. Itzhak Zamir, our host, had been Attorney-General in an earlier government, but had resigned over the suppression of due legal process in a case involving the death or maltreatment of Arab prisoners in the custody of the Secret Service. A guest, Amnon Rubinstein, who was a member of parliament from one of the more liberal parties, had been Minister for Education, with a particular enthusiasm for education for the Bedouin. Another guest, Aharon Barak, the Chief Justice, who had taken decisions and delivered judgements in the teeth of organised ultra-religious protest, invited us to see the Supreme Court. Yasmeen got into conversation with a woman who turned out to be an architect as well; she lived in the old part of Jerusalem, and asked her to visit her. Everyone was as loquacious and as reluctant to say goodbye as anyone in Delhi; it took at least forty minutes to get to the door.

The literary conference continued; my evenings were fairly flexible. One evening, Yasmeen and I went to visit her architect colleague in the old city. We got lost. There were few people around, and they were nervous when we approached them. A boy, about twelve or so, who appeared to be mentally disturbed, attached himself to us, and gestured for us to follow him. We found ourselves no longer in the Jewish but in the Muslim part of the city. Here there were more people out in the narrow streets, but they seemed to be hostile and we were a little afraid. A group of young men asked us – challenged us, rather – to state who we were and where we were going. When they discovered that we were Indian, and that Yasmeen was Muslim, the sense of threat dissolved into friendliness, and we were guided on our way.

I did not think of Aunty Henny during my first few days in Jerusalem. But talking to Aharon Barak in his room in the Supreme Court brought back thoughts of her. Aharon came originally from Lithuania; most of his family had been murdered by the Germans when he was a small child; he and his parents alone had escaped. (It was in Italy, where they finally arrived, that for the first time he saw adults smile.) His chambers in the court faced a rose garden and a cemetery. He said that not a day went by when he did not think of death, and that it gave shape to his life.

A few days after I arrived in Jerusalem I went to Yad Vashem, the memorial, spread out over many acres, to those who had suffered in the Holocaust. I had a free morning, and planned to spend a few hours walking around and thinking about things. But I got talking to a woman at the entrance and she mentioned that, apart from the memorial, there was an archive at the site that documented many of the events of the times. I thought I would defer my visit to the memorial for an hour or so; I went to the archive, sought out material, and began to read. One trail led to another; almost before I knew it, it was evening. I cancelled my appointments for the next day, and again came to the archive in the morning. Just half an hour before it was due to close, I realised that if I didn't see the memorial right away, I would miss my chance. I visited it, indeed rushed through what should not have been rushed through. But, moving though it was, and even as my immediate surroundings pressed in on me, my mind kept returning to the pages that I had pored over for the last two days, and certain documents in particular.

The names and birthdates of Gabriele and Lola Caro had led me from one source to another, and finally to two rolls of microfilm. Mother and daughter had indeed been transported from Berlin within a day of each other. Gabriele Caro was taken to Theresienstadt on the 88th *Alterstransport* (old people's transport) of 18 May 1943. Her number on the transport list of two hundred people is 195, and the entry reads as follows:

Serial no.	Surname	Name	Date of Birth	Place
195	Carow, née Schmeltes	Gabriele Sara	11.11.71	Prague
Address	Registration no.	Remarks		
Charl., Bleibtreustr. 19	0 195	——		

There are no remarks following her name. Why would there be? She was a woman in her seventies, a widow. Even had her husband been alive, since he was not Aryan, his existence would not have reprieved her. The remarks by the names of other people on that list and similar lists I studied showed a methodical categorisation of special circumstances: Jakob Adler, born 1890, 'Certificate of having been wounded in battle; iron cross class II; long-term public employee', together with his wife and twelve-year-old son; or Joel Singer, born 1892, 'Long-term employee of the Jewish Cultural Association; Medal for Valour from Hesse'. From the Theresienstadt transport no. 104 of 19 April 1944, almost a year later, many cases such as the following appear: Grubert née Meyer, born in 1873, 'nicht mehr best. priv. Mischehe' (further abbreviated later in the list to 'n.m.best.pr.Mi.E'). Her husband had possibly divorced her or, more probably, had died, and she, at the age of seventy, alone and no longer in a 'privileged mixed marriage', was now eligible to be killed at the pleasure of the German state.

Who knows what fine distinctions of treatment would be accorded those with remarks beside their names while they were in Theresienstadt before they succumbed there to hunger or disease or were shipped off to an extermination camp.

As for Lola, no. 171 on *Osttransport* no. 38 of 17 May 1943, her entry on the manifest reads as follows:

Serial no.	Surname	Name	Date of Birth	Place
171	Caro	Lola Sara	23.7.07	Berlin
Address	Registration no.	Remarks		
Charl., Bleibtreustr. 19	176	——		

I scrolled the microfilm up and down to see if there were any remarks at all for anyone on Lola's list of four hundred people. There were none. The final column was completely blank. There was no need even for the pretence of distinctions here. This was an *Osttransport*, an 'East-transport', and led straight to Auschwitz-Birkenau.

Handwritten ticks and notations in the old German script adorned these lists. But whose were these, and how had the lists survived at all

176	Spanier	Benni Israel	4.10.87
177	Spanier geb.Schotten-fels	Bella Sara	30.9.99
178	Scheurenberg	Paul Israel	10.10.92
179	Scheurenberg geb. Löwenthal	Lucie Sara	20.12.88
180	Scheurenberg	Klaus Israel	20.9.25
181	Wedel	Rosa Sara	26.1.??
182	Wieluner	Fritz Israel	2?.?.90
183	Wieluner geb.Müller	Ilse Sara	15.5.94
184	Zwirn	Alfred Israel	15.4.9?
185	Neumann	Peter Israel	27.?.??
186	Abraham	Alfred Israel	?.??.0?
187	Abraham	Bruno Israel	??.?.??
188	Abraham geb.Putziger	Ilse Sara	8.?.00
189	Braun	David Israel	?.?.??
190	Braun geb. Jaffe	Frieda Sara	??.??.?0
191	Braun	Marianne Sara	??.?.??
192	Jaffe geb. Hirsch	Sophie Sara	??.?.??
193	Jaffe	Bertha Sara	??.?.??
194	Bern geb. Hein	Franzicka Sara	3.4.71
195	Carow geb.Schmeltes	Gabriela Sara	11.11.71
196	Brasch	Alexander Israel	26.1.??
197	Danziger geb. Crohn	Kathi Sara	27.10.9?
198	Cohn	Karl Israel	16.1.67
199	Cohn geb. Schlesinger	Anna Sara	26.3.78
200	Cohn	Ilse Sara	?7.8.31

Gestapo transport list, 88th Old People's Transport (Ella is no. 195).

	Berlin,Trautenaustr.20	O 176	EK II,langj.Angeste..
..tenburg	dto.	O 177	Ehepaar
	N. 4, Kladncrstr.5.	O 178	EK II,Kriegsverdiens..
	dto.	O 179	kreuz,Sturmordner,An..
	dto.	O 180	Familie
..riedland	N. 4, dto. b.Goldstein	O 181	
..tz	.., Landshuter..r..5	O 182	EK II,Ver.Abz.,langj.
			Angestellter
	dto.	O 183	Ehepaar
	Charl., ..belstr.1..	O 184	
	..nd., Gieselerstr..	O 185	
..o	.. 50, Marburgerstr.1.	O 186	langj.Angestellter
	.. 50, ...	O 187	Grund.G.Milit...ped..
..e	dto.	O 188	Ehepaar
	Schb.,Speyererstr.10	O 189	Ver.Abz.,EK II,langj.
			Angestellter
	dto.	O 190	
	dto.	O 191	Familie
..que	dto.	O 192	
	dto. b.Br.un	O 193	
..enbu..	Charl.,Kantstr. 78	O 194	
	Charl., Kleibtreustr. 19	O 195	
	..nd., ..tgolderstr. 55	O 196	
	Charl., Waitzstr. 9	O 197	
	.. 54, Cor..hstr. 5	O 198	
	dto.	O 199	Ehepaar
..hof	W. 15,Kaiser-llee 20	O 200	langj.Angestellte

when the Gestapo had done its best to destroy its records? The answer is probably that they were found not with the Secret State Police, but with some branch of the Finance Ministry. The note that accompanies each of the lists is addressed to the Finance Administration, Berlin-Brandenburg, for the next step in the process was for the German Reich to absorb the property of its victims in accordance with law. The letter that accompanied Lola's transport reads as follows:

Secret State Police
State Police Office, Berlin
Berlin C2, Grunerstrasse 12, at the corner of Dircksenstrasse

To the Finance Administration
Berlin-Brandenburg
– Office for the Disposal of Property

Berlin NW 40	IV C 3 – J.E. –
Alt Moabit 143	Berlin, 22. May 1943

Re: Evacuated Jews

Please find enclosed a Transport List of those Jews whose property has devolved upon the Reich through confiscation within the frame of reference of their deportation [*Abschiebung*: literally, 'shoving off'].

The property has not been forfeited, but through confiscation has passed into the ownership of the German Reich. This is with reference to the 38th East-Transport.

The assets of those Jews marked in the Transport List as foreigners have not been confiscated for the time being. The property statements remain at the present office. The administration of these assets will until further notice be carried out from here.

The property statements for numbers 61, 124, 141, 241, 297 and 383 are not available.

pp: [signed: illegible; a series of zigzags,
with no attempt to represent letters of any kind]

Form No. 3

As I was staring at this letter, something happened that has never happened to me before or since. My right knee began trembling rapidly and violently. There was nothing I could do to stop it. Suddenly I heard a voice behind me address me in English with a very strong German accent: 'If you would like, I can help you with the German.'

The very accent embodied sickness and evil, and I turned round in a fury to face – just an alarmed young man, a German schoolboy, about seventeen years old, on a study trip with his classmates, some of whom were also in the room. Perhaps seeing me stare at the screen in apparent incomprehension had made him try to help, even in this particular place to imply regret for what he was in no way guilty of. If these thoughts flashed through my mind, I could still barely master my anger. 'I don't need any help,' I said with no attempt at politeness. I turned back to the microfilm machine to print out the letter; and after a few minutes my knee became still.

3.13

One of the casualties of the process of exploring the material for this book was my pleasure in the German language.

Hindi and English were languages I had grown up with. At school in India, since one had to take up a third language, I had also studied a bit of Sanskrit, though, as with most schoolboy study of classical languages, little residue remains. German, however, was different: it was an adventure, a love affair under pressure, a concentrated incursion into another world, tied closely to my memories of my first year in England, to reading Kafka's *Letter to My Father*, to singing 'Heidenröslein' with Aunty Henny in the kitchen, to hitch-hiking across Europe at seventeen, to the landscape of the Danube and the Rhine and the Vierwaldstätter See, to the friendliness of strangers, to references (which I often heard in Germany) to the so-called *Indogermanische Verbindung* or connection.

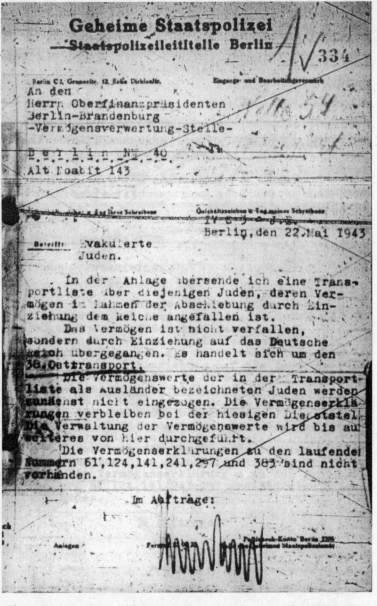

Gestapo cover letter to the Finance Administration, Berlin-Brandenburg, regarding the 38th Transport to the East (on which Lola was sent).

I had grown to love German poetry: Goethe's short poems and bits of his *Faust*, the dark melancholy of Trakl, the eccentricity of Christian Morgenstern, an occasional poem by Hölderlin or a couple of lines from Gryphius or Silesius.

But my favourite German poet from the moment I first read him was and still is Heine, clear and deep and unpompous, full of longing and sardonic tenderness and sudden twists of mood. Almost any of a hundred poems bears his unforgettable touch, but some of those that recur to me again and again are 'Als ich, auf der Reise, zufällig' (When on my journey I by chance), with its heartbreak at the core of a humdrum conversation; 'Morphine', with its profound, almost languid resignation to illness and death; and poems of exile such as those that begin with

> *Denk' ich an Deutschland in der Nacht,*
> *Dann bin ich um den Schlaf gebracht;*
> (When at night I think of Germany
> I am deprived of sleep;)

or

> *O Deutschland, meine ferne Liebe,*
> *Gedenk' ich deiner, wein' ich fast!*
> (O Germany, my distant love,
> When I think of you, I almost weep.)

or

> *Ich hatte einst ein schönes Vaterland.*
> (I once had a beautiful fatherland.)

Even Heine I could no longer read. It did not help, strangely enough, that Heine was, partly in his own eyes and certainly by the Nazi definition of things, as much of a Jew as Christ was, and would, like Christ, have been exterminated as vermin. The stench of the language in which I had read the phrases from the Gestapo letter clung to his words as well. Indeed, the consciousness of what the country he yearned for would have done to him made it even more unbearable to read his work. Heine himself was too long dead to become another entry on a transport list; but his books and poems were burned and proscribed. 'Die Lorelei', which was so well loved as to have become virtually a folksong, was 'anonymised' and, stripped of its author, allowed to continue in anthologies. Yet how could the following lines have been rescued, embedded as they were in a poem contrasting urbane and witty Paris, the city of his exile, with his longed-for homeland, ruder yet tenderer? –

> *Mir ist, als hört' ich fern erklingen*
> *Nachtwächterhörner, sanft und traut;*
> *Nachtwächterlieder hör' ich singen,*
> *Dazwischen Nachtigallenlaut.*

> (It seems to me, as if I heard from afar
> Nightwatchmen's horns sound, soft and familiar;
> As if I heard nightwatchmen's songs,
> And between them the sounds of nightingales.)

I had grown to love Lieder too. When I was working on *A Suitable Boy*, which took me several years to complete, Schubert saved my soul. I loved singing Indian classical music, but strumming the *tanpura* to sing a raga dragged me straight back into my book, some of whose characters were Indian musicians. It gave me no respite from work; and yet, without singing, my life was barren. It was then that an English friend, Jackie Shipster, who was living in Delhi at the time, encouraged me to sing a few songs from Schubert's *Winterreise* with her at the piano. Later, an Austrian friend, Christoph Cornaro, also a pianist, tempted me into *Die Schöne Müllerin*, which for some reason I had resisted. I became completely addicted to both works, and to many other songs besides. But it was the six songs that Schubert set to poems by Heine that haunted me then and haunt me now, from the ironic charm of 'Das Fischermädchen' to the simplicity and sorrow of 'Ihr Bild', to the bizarre horror, close to madness, of 'Der Doppelgänger'.

These songs, which are some of the last works Schubert wrote, form part of the posthumously compiled song cycle *Schwanengesang*. Had he, before his death at thirty-one, known more of Heine's poems, what further marvels would we have had? My musical friends rebuke me for not appreciating fully Schumann's settings of vast swathes of Heine; but I would exchange all the songs and all the garrulous postludes of *Dichterliebe* and *Liederkreis* for one more setting by Schubert of a poem by Heine.

One day, I was looking through an edition of Schubert's song cycles when I noticed that the introduction had been written by Max Müller, the great nineteenth-century scholar of Sanskrit. This was because his father, who had died as young as Schubert and whom the young Max could hardly have known, was the poet Wilhelm Müller, who wrote the words of both *Winterreise* and *Die Schöne Müllerin*. Though this was merely coincidental, and though the introduction itself was not all that interesting, the link, at one remove, between Sanskrit and Schubert gave me a quirky kind of pleasure.

Christoph, my pianist friend, was the Austrian ambassador to India, and the first time we met properly was after a blessing in the Vatican Chapel in Delhi for my sister Aradhana's wedding. The civil service by the registrar and the Hindu ceremony in our garden were to take place the next day. The reason for the Catholic service was that the groom, Peter Launsky-Tieffenthal, was a young Austrian diplomat and, like most Austrians, Catholic.

Here again was a link, close to home, that connected me to the German-speaking world. But even my ties to a beloved brother-in-law could not, after those two days in the archive at Yad Vashem, reconcile me to the language. The very verbs stank. I could not listen to Bach's *Matthew Passion*, the piece of Western music I most love. I could not even listen to Lieder. Peter's English is as good as mine, but occasionally, however falteringly, I used to exchange a word or two in German with him. Now I couldn't bring myself to. Logic and justice told me that this was absurd, but it was as if the language itself forced images upon me that I could neither dissolve nor resist. Over a poem in which wild roses and golden pears leaned out over a swan-frequented lake, I would hear, '... *Das Vermögen ist nicht verfallen, sondern durch Einziehung auf das Deutsche Reich übergegangen ...* [The property has not been forfeited, but through confiscation has passed into the ownership of the German Reich ...].'

After some months I forced myself to read the letters that Aunty Henny's friends had written to her after the war, together with her own replies of which she had kept copies. Slowly, through the humanity and the decency and, yes, the friendly but slightly catty gossip of these letters, a sense of ordinary life led by ordinary people displaced, or perhaps overlaid, my previous revulsion. My ability to read the language recovered; my blind distaste was stilled; and in time even my old love, now both deeper and more troubled, revived.

3.14

One such friend was Ilse Schmidt (not her real name), who wrote the following letter just before Henny left Germany. Henny and she had been schoolfriends and confidantes. Some members of the circle, including, to some extent, Fröschlein, disapproved of Ilse, thinking of her as flighty and trivial – far too romantic, not earnest enough, and greatly enamoured of fine clothes and fancy footwear. Henny's mother, though, liked Ilse.

Ilse's writing is attractive: curly and quite feminine, but unfussy.

My dear, dear Henny,

   Today, on the day of your departure, everything appears truly melancholy to me. I ache to take you in my arms and I wish that the sun may shine for you there, as you deserve. My lines should make you happy and show you that I am more devoted to you than you give this so-called faithless girl credit for. But you know all too well, Hennerle, that such a true friendship and bond spans even distances, borders and time.

     I think of you with devotion and warmly press your hand.

      Your

      Ilse

Seven years later, Ilse Heydt, as she now was, wrote her first letter to Henny after the war.

It is through letters such as these that Ilse and others from Henny's circle provide us with a picture both of themselves (thus letting us see the kinds of friendships Henny formed) and of Henny and the other members of her family. Through them we see from diverse perspectives the prelude to the deportation of Ella and Lola, and what the news and continual consciousness of their death meant. The writers refer with longing to happier times – of festivities and sailing, of skiing and music-making, of the intimacy and boisterousness of friendship, of idealism and hope – and conjure them up in a way that even Shanti, in his interviews, was unable to do. Moreover, through a description of their circumstances, they bring to life the situation in Germany, and particularly Berlin, in the aftermath of the war – and reflect upon the war itself, so recently over: not only upon the acts of courage or moral support by which they sought to comfort each other during that harsh time, but also upon the conflicts, weaknesses and fears that strained, sometimes beyond any future repair, the ties that bound them together.

The murder of her mother and sister had fallen like a thunderbolt on Henny, but no less difficult and vexed in its own way was the effort she felt obliged to make to sort out her relations with friends who had shared or been implicated in the sufferings she had undergone. The social fabric of her life was not entirely destroyed by political events, but these had deeply shaken her faith in, or altered her views of, the people she had known and the community in which she had grown up.

Ilse writes:

Frohnau, 9. 7. 1946

My dear Hennerle,

How happy I was to get your letter! Fröschlein had already written to me that you had finally got in touch. We had waited so long for that. How often during the dreadful years of the war were our thoughts with you, who were now there, far from everybody who knew you so well and loved you so much, having to spend those difficult times in uncertainty and anxiety, and how ardently we hoped that you had been spared from the terrible bombs. You are so tender and lovable, and you had to go through such desperately harsh times, dear Henny, and we could do nothing to make things easier for you. In every respect our hands were tied; you will know that all too well. If only we could sit down together sometime and show you all our love and devotion! Perhaps you can return here once again, even if only for a visit. I can imagine that it would be very hard for you to see once more all the familiar places of your childhood and youth, those wonderful years of carefree happiness, and all in a condition that arouses horror. Your beautiful ideals of magnanimity and helpfulness, how cruelly have they been dealt with after all that you have experienced, after all that has been done to you. It is so terrible for us to have to tell you about it.

If anyone deserves your love and gratitude, it is Fröschlein, who with great love and quite fearlessly helped and supported your loved ones to the end. She was the tireless intermediary when I sent her food coupons from Frohnau, with which to buy something for Lola and your mother and then bring it to them. I was at that time prevented from doing much because of the baby (my son was born on 21 February 1942). He was in hospital for three months after the birth, and because I breast-fed him

240

for a whole year, I had to go to the hospital daily for that purpose. But I was happy to be able to help in some small way. Lola knitted a little cardigan for my boy and made a stuffed animal for his first birthday, which we hold in high esteem. And your mother gave me such beautiful green wineglasses for my wedding, which are undamaged to this day. If they remain with me despite the requisitioning, I will give them to you as a beautiful souvenir, so that you at least have something from your mother's home.

My dear Hennerle, how often has my heart bled when I think of our lovely familiar boating trips and see what is left to us of all that. The Castell boathouse has been razed to the ground, the villas on the Lesser Wannsee are in ruins; my boathouse is still standing, but my boat has been taken away – by whom, it isn't possible to ascertain. But one could get over all that, if the people we loved were still there. Just the matter of Hans (may I speak of it without giving you pain, my dear Hennerle?) quite shook me. At the time, he wrote me a personal letter clarifying things and told me the reasons for the step he had taken. I told him honestly and sincerely what I thought of it: that I didn't share his point of view but that ultimately it was he who had to decide. We met each other only once after that, by chance on the Pohle See; I felt bitter when I saw an unfamiliar girl in the old familiar boat, 'Sunshine'.

At that time my husband was sitting in my boat with me; I had met him by chance at a seminar for interpreters and within a very short time we had got married. I have never regretted this swift decision; it was a leap into a happiness I had never before known, into a magic land of love – of the sort one only otherwise finds in fairy-tales. We are so very happy. In our five years of marriage there hasn't been a single discordant note, not a single angry word. We are in soul and spirit and also body so close and so in tune with each other that I wouldn't want to change my state with anyone on earth. The war has thrown a shadow over our marriage – we have only rarely been together. I've followed my husband each time as soon as it's been possible, with or without my child, if he's been anywhere that I could get to – at the end, even after the [Allied] invasion, to Lorraine, which was very unpleasant, but we have tried, as frequently and as much as possible, to be together.

Then came the Catastrophe [the collapse of Germany], which wiped out all our property and savings, and even my health. Through the strain of the flight and the months-long hunger in the refugee camp I was reduced to 39 kg (with clothes) and contracted hunger-typhus, which I have only got over after a great deal of care, and still have heart trouble, which, however, what with peace and better food, is gradually improving. I also underwent terrible months of uncertainty, so long as I didn't know whether or not my husband was alive, and only when, in January of this year, I got the first sign from him that he was alive, did my health improve. During my absence from Berlin (August 1943 to August 1945) I have been through all sorts of sorrows and difficulties; it was no easy life for the evacuees. Empty rooms were allotted to us – no lamps, no ovens – and we had to get used to the most primitive, most hateful life. And at the same time I had to raise a child, to keep him clean, to bring him up properly, to take good care of him, to take care of his emotional needs!

Ilse describes how she had almost nothing to wear, and how her friends managed to get together for her a few items of clothing and some clogs, a curtain that she used to make bed linen, and so on. She remarks plaintively: 'Can you imagine how I feel when I am so dependent on gifts [cast-offs]?' She describes how she worked on a building site, and then knitted and sewed for a living. 'What I earned served for rent, food, etc. and also enabled me to obtain by barter an old woollen dress and all sorts of small necessities, for example a pair of shoes for the child. I hope I don't sound too wretched to you now, Hennerle?'

Ilse's father's house was reduced to rubble. The nightly bombing also resulted in his sustaining a left-sided paralysis of the nervous system, which she can still notice in his eyes.

Do you remember how we cut out paper dolls throughout one Sunday because you wanted to prepare yourself for a job as a children's teacher in England? At that time I could hardly have dreamed that I would soon use this very art for the sake of my own little son. It is so wonderful to have a child, despite the many worries and responsibilities of these difficult times. He is a bit delicate, which is no wonder considering the privations: children get only a minimum of milk (50 grams daily of dried milk) and have had no fruit at all for the last two years. And there is always the worry that he will contract tuberculosis, though the last two tests, thank God, were negative.

Quite suddenly last week I was assigned a job via the Employment Office to a French office in Tegel as secretary and book-keeper. It is certainly a difficult adjustment, to be out of the house by a quarter to seven in the morning, and to return home at half past seven at night, with only four slices of dried bread, and then in the evening to do all the housework and take care of the child. The little one is taken to the kindergarten daily by my mother and brought back in the evening, and then I fetch him from her place. I have, after all, got to earn some money; I've already sold all my cutlery and vases and that sort of stuff in order to keep the wolf from the door.

Ilse now tells Henny a little more about her husband, Dieter Heydt (not his real name), who has been interned or imprisoned by the French. While he does not appear in person in these pages, Ilse's husband and the uncertainties about him give rise to a great deal of tension and perplexity, particularly for Henny.

I have often enthused about you to my husband; he knows you well and now also knows that you have got in touch again. He also got to know Lola and to value her, and felt comfortable in the old circle of friends from earlier days, for example, he played chess with [Jazko] Rabau and had discussions with him. You will certainly like him. In his imprisonment he has the post of interpreter and librarian (his previous profession was librarian in the State Library in Berlin) and adjutant to the camp leadership, and is getting on very well. But for the moment there is no possibility of his returning home, because he will be the last to be released. He has also lost his job as a civil servant, because he, like all officials, was a [Nazi] Party member, not from the heart, as everyone knows, even the Rabaus, and can attest. (I would never have married

243

such a man, you know that best of all. Nor would I have let myself, like your friend Irmchen, be dictated to with regard to whom I could or could not associate with.) So our future doesn't look too rosy. He will have to work on a building site at 0.72 Reichmarks an hour unless things change. But I love my husband, and will bear every care and difficulty with him, because I know how good and noble he is and that he has never done anything wrong, and particularly not against you hunted and tormented people. I can vouch for all that.

That's why it is doubly necessary that I earn something now. Since August 1940 I have had a tiny flat, a room and a half in a basement, but cosy, with a little garden plot. The central heating has not been on, I have frozen terribly and the skin on my hands has cracked open with the frost; I have sewed for weeks on end with bandaged hands. But perhaps this time we will get a little coal. Certainly, the flat, especially with our little fellow, is a bit small, but at least it has so far not been taken from us, as has been the case with so many others, who lived in such large and splendid dwellings. That is certainly just.

So, dear Hennerle, I have now poured out my heart to you. Write to me in detail, I have a thousand questions for you . . .

Write really soon; ask me whatever interests you; I look forward so much to your next letter.

Fondest greetings and hugs,

Ilse

Many many thanks for the stamps on the envelope, which delighted my collector's heart!

Henny's reply is far longer than her usual, fairly clipped, letters. She talks about the loss of her beloved mother ('Mutti') and sister – and about Hans Mahnert's marriage, subjects she never discussed with Shanti.

Henny Caro   27, Kendal Street
                                              London, W. 2,
                                              12th August, 1946

My dear Ilse,

I was so happy to get your kind letter, especially because warm and sincere friendship spoke out of it. Yes, Ilselein, I have suffered unending torment over the fate of my loved ones, and will never get over it. That you were so devoted to Mutti and Lola till the end shows how strong in character you are, but I knew that some of my old friends had remained strong, particularly you and Fröschlein.— Since you have mentioned the matter of Hans, I should say a few words about it, and this is certainly the first and the last time that I shall speak about it. I request you, dear Ilse, naturally to exercise the strictest discretion. I know that political and religious views definitely played a part with him, which even your lines confirm. It is a purely academic discussion, but I would be interested to know what explanations in this regard he gave in his letter to you. You can rest assured that this will remain between the two of us. I request you again, never to let any of this be passed on to anyone else; I know we are friends, you can count on me and I on you, for it has been proved by events that we are true friends. In my heart, I have completely finished with the matter of Hans, and bear him no resentment at all. Everyone is the architect of his own future and must build his life to the best of his own knowledge.

Ilselein, that you have found a suitable life-companion and also have a little child has made me very happy. What is your little son's name? So your life surely has meaning for you, even if at present it is certainly hard and full of privations. I will do whatever I can to make it a little easier. These are not empty words; I mean them sincerely. Let me assure you that I understand you, value you and want to do good by you. Unfortunately, I didn't send anything for you in my first parcel to the Rabaus, because I didn't know at the time if you were in contact with everyone. This parcel has meanwhile arrived, as I heard yesterday from Hans's father, with whom I am in contact by letter. I will very, very soon send another parcel to Rabau and include some things for you. This is the only way I can send a parcel to Berlin, and I hope that things will soon change, because it is of course much more personal when one can send something directly.

Henny goes on to describe her work – that she has a responsible position in a firm that produces pharmaceutical preparations and exports them all over the world – and to tell Ilse in fairly brisk terms about the loss of Shanti's right hand.

Thank God, he has got over it completely both physically and mentally, and has a very good position in the largest dental firm in England. He works more or less in the scientific field, makes technical films (at the moment, he is working on a colour film) and writes articles, and you would be astonished to see how skilled he is with his left hand. He can actually drive a car with his one hand, and has even got his driving licence. So there is really no reason to pity him. I would tell you as a friend if it was otherwise. He is very fond of all of you, particularly those who were good to Mutti and Lola to the end, for, as you know, our home for him was a second home. [Henny uses the word *Heimat*, which almost carries the implication of a second hometown for an exile.]

By the way, Ilselein, could you possibly make things for your little boy out of Shanti's old suits? The material is good, but the suits are too small for Shanti (yes, even for Shanti). So please let me know – just as in general I ask you to write completely openly to say if you need anything in particular. I do all this willingly from the bottom of my heart, and I know that if the circumstances were reversed you too would willingly do the same. We are, after all, FRIENDS! Only very few people understand what friendship means, but surely I can say that we belong to these few.— Ilselein, when sometimes I read old letters, I feel as if I am burrowing into a grave, and so you will, I am sure, understand that I can't visit you there anytime in the near future. Yes, willingly, all too willingly, would I chat intimately with you once again, but perhaps there will be another opportunity later.

With regard to Ilse's husband, Henny writes just two lines: 'I hope that you are very, very soon reunited with your dear husband. I think very highly of you that you have told me everything about him so honestly.'

After some talk of scattered acquaintances and friends, she draws to a close:

I get so many foreign stamps from my export firm, and I will now collect them all for you until I can send them on.

Farewell for now, my dear, good Ilselein. Greet all your loved ones warmly from me. A kiss to your little son. To you, fondest greetings and heartfelt hugs.

> In true friendship,
> Always yours,
> [unsigned: carbon copy]

3.15

The matter of Hans, which Ilse touched on, and which Henny responded to, is something that she brought up with no one else in the circle of friends who remained in Berlin. In the leather purse found in the attic of 18 Queens Road are about twenty-five hand-written poems from and by Hans, each folded twice; two small photographs of a sort of altar constructed on Hans's table (comprising a photograph of Henny, a poem in his own thin, self-consciously ornamented script, and a few flowers); and the typed letter from Franz Mahnert, his father, that he sent Henny shortly before her departure from Berlin.

This noble and straightforward letter, quoted earlier, from the man who made Henny's escape possible, sits uncomfortably next to the poems by his son, her erstwhile fiancé. The poems are models of vacuously affected doggerel. Here is one, which in the original is rhymed in irregularly scanned couplets in the manner of William McGonagall:

To my beloved, my Hennerle!

In my heart's dearest depths you live, O my beloved,
By every one of love's ways you return to me.
I feel you always standing by my side.
I feel your spirit go with mine.

In life's huge-paced haste and hurry,
I always find time to spend with you.
And it is just this that gives me courage, joy and strength.—
You serve me a goblet full of the juice of life.

Even if I were far from here in the most distant land,
I would never despair.
A firm bond ties us together,
A bond of friendship and love!

Even if Death came to fetch me,
You should not be sad,
For with my last thought of you, dearest Hennerle,
                I will sleep in peace.—

            From your
            Hans

Another poem, addressed to 'My Henny, whom I will love until my death!', describes his heart's yearning for her rosy lips and continues:

        I belong to you and you to me.
        Can the world then lovelier be?

The theme of undying fidelity continues in 'To my dear, sweet and cute Hennerle, whom nothing in the world can substitute for me', which ends in a little climax of callow rhyme:

248

> So let me serve you for eternity,
> I am your servant, your slave on bended knee
> And always for you will ready be.

In another poem, 'To dear Henny!', he promises:

> Then I am prepared to take this oath before you:
> 'You will I love, just you alone.
> You should be the quiet happiness of my love!'

This poem is flecked with water or tears. It appears to have been crushed or crumpled, then smoothed out and folded away like the rest.

If it is self-dramatisation that rules in Hans Mahnert's verse, it is self-justification that rules in his prose. The following letter was the first Henny received from him after the war, around the time that she first made contact with her other friends in Berlin – including Hans's father. It appears to have been unfolded and refolded many times. It is handwritten, and not in German but in English. (A few minor spelling errors have been corrected.) In it, Hans refers to a letter from Lola to Henny, which, unfortunately, is not in her correspondence file.

Dr Hans Mahnert   Berlin, Neukölln, 13 July 1946.—
                                                Siegfriedstr. 43

Dear Henny,

I wonder what you said when recognising the sender of this letter! You would be mistaken in case you solely expect an attempt of defending myself – these lines are addressed to you as a former good friend of mine whose friendship I would like to be assured of also for the future. This makes it so much easier to me to give you – I will try so at least – a report of facts and events, a report founded on true life.

Before my going into details I want to tell you that I was more than glad to hear of your professional success and of your good post. I am

249

An die liebe Henny!

Da meine Liebe Dir nicht viel wert
Möcht' ich Dir lästig nicht sein
Stoße mich von Dir und laß mich allein
                    Deinen Sklaven, –
Der Dich immerfort liebt und verehrt!

Willst Du den Schmerz mir ersparen,
So sag's mir nur grad' ins Gesicht:
    Dich liebe ich nicht!
Dann will ich gern von Dir scheiden
Um für Dich zu leiden,
Dann bin ich bereit Dir zu leisten den
                    Eid:
„Dich will ich lieben, nur Dich allein,"
„Du sollst mein stilles Lebensglück sein"

Einmal nach Jahren wirst Du's erfahren,
Ward einer zu Grabe getragen, –
Nicht sollst Du fragen wer es war
Der in Deinem Glück das seinige sah..

One of Hans's poems.

glad also to know that you are – as it seems – in good health. Your surely numerous friendships in England (rather sad for me that I am altogether lacking good friendship), your more or less interesting professional work and above all the special milieu you live in will certainly make life worth living and will give you a steadily new impulse. It is of course a great tragedy that your mother and Lola are probably no more alive. This is a very painful and bitter event especially for those who knew your mother. The cruelty of those events can hardly be described. Unfortunately thousands of people were taken away from their homes and vanished for ever. I shall always think of your mother as some sort of 'super-woman' always prepared to make sacrifices for her children and friends to an extent so far unknown. Your mother – in my opinion – certainly belonged to the real and better heroes of civilian life. I also admired Lola whose perseverance, energy and unafraid attitude in those dangerous times were simply astounding. May the time help you to get over those dark events.— Did you – by the way – receive any news from Heinz and do you know which job he actually has? May be he will visit you one day!

Now, as for ourselves: I believe you received the news of my engagement as Lola to whose letter I added some lines (Lola's letter to Heinz in South America) told me later on that you had received that letter. I guess what you must have thought and what you are perhaps still thinking of me. But don't you think after all that natural facts of life are at the end stronger than all human being's intentions? I hope you will not object to my being frank to you by mentioning that at the time I got married I felt and I was convinced to have found the wife best for me. May be I did the right thing, may be I was mistaken (time ~~will~~ can only prove whether right or not) – anyhow I would have felt a hypocrite would I have pretended love which surely wasn't the love which one generally expects between married people. In my opinion it would have been highly immoral in case I would have acted differently.— Considering the circumstances I was also convinced that this decision of mine was taken in our mutual interest! I wouldn't say I am unconscious of guilt, knowing also that you had sacrificed me many years. Still, I hope you wouldn't remember those years only from standpoint of sacrifice. In spite of the things that happened later on –

251

didn't that time give us much light and joy? Apart from my believing in fate, things couldn't perhaps turn out differently, considering the separating differences, war and other general circumstances. And what do we know after all of 'fate', the secrets and mysteries of life. Only by our feeling we can judge that such things exist. Reflecting upon things that way you will arrive at conclusions which in my opinion contain more truth than all the other more or less abstract statements.

After all that happened I would be lucky to know if you don't reject my wish for further good friendship, main condition of it being that all obstacles which might have been in our way are removed. Therefore we must assure ourselves of mutual frankness!

I hope I am not ennoying you [Hans probably means 'boring you', a carry-over from his French] by giving you a brief summary of what I was doing last time although I believe that my cousin [Mrs Arberry] has already given you some news. Not long after the Russians had occupied Berlin I got a job at the Magistracy of Berlin – Central Labour Office – as 'Referent für den Landeinsatz in Berlin und Brandenburg' (Principal in charge of Mobilization of Work for Agricultural Purposes). I kept this job which I left more or less of political reasons until May 1946. Since that time I am working or employed in Finance Division of the American Military Government where I am doing translation work. This last job of mine generally gives me much satisfaction.

Before closing I wish you all good luck and send you my kindest regards. I would be very glad if you would occasionally find the time to drop a few lines.

Yours,
Hans

This strange letter, larded with mock-punctilious, frigid qualifications and bristling with a dozen different kinds of psychological obtuseness, could almost be analysed line by line for its unfailing wrong-footedness. But clearly Hans expected the letter to go further, probably to his relations, the Arberrys, for it is difficult to see why he would otherwise have bothered to translate his position as *Referent* into English.

3.16

Henny did not know how, if at all, to reply to Hans's letter. She could not turn to anyone in her circle of friends in Berlin for advice in case things should get out; and talking to Shanti was out of the question, since he was both Hans's friend and in love with her. She finally sought advice from A. G. Belvin (né Adolf Berliner), her accountant friend in Atlanta. There was some precedent for these confidences; for A.G. had earlier turned to her in deep depression, almost desperation, about his marital troubles, and had greatly valued her sincere, humane and responsible advice. Besides, there was a bond of common sorrow between A.G. and Henny: each had lost a mother and a sibling – in A.G.'s case, one of his brothers – to the Nazis. They correspond in German.

In a letter dated 31 July 1946, two and a half weeks after the date of Hans's letter, which she may or may not by then have received, Henny first touches on her mother's and sister's post-cards:

A few days ago I had a letter from Herr Wolffsky, who worked together with Lola in the Jewish Gemeinde, and he gave me Mutti's and Lola's farewell greetings. I am enclosing a copy of his letter. In his letter he included two cards, one from Mutti from Theresienstadt, the other from Lola from Birkenau, and you can imagine how sad, how unendingly sorrowful I am, and I will never get over it. Sometimes I am so overcome that I don't think I can go on.

She then talks about Hans's father and elides into the question of Hans, but does not mention his letter:

From Hans's father, old Mr Mahnert, I received the enclosed letters. (You can destroy them once you have read them.) Old Herr Mahnert is now 76; he has lost everything, and I would like to help him. I have sent him some cigarettes through other people, but I can't send food from here. I have indicated to him that I would ask you to send him a few food parcels, and I would be grateful if you could fulfil this request of mine. He was always a very decent sort of man, and I value him for his character. Perhaps you could write him a couple of lines as well, if you are so inclined; but please don't mention anything about a possible marriage between Shanti and me. Hans has married a Polish Christian girl. I am very friendly with the relatives of old Mr Mahnert who live over here; his niece is Jewish, her husband Christian, he is a Professor at London University. They cannot forgive Hans for having changed so much, as apparently he has, so I hear. I'm sending you part of my answer to old Mr Mahnert, and I am certain he'll understand my letter. Although I despise Hans's action (not because he married another woman but because, as a half-Jew, he changed himself – please understand me correctly), I have forgiven him in my heart and hope that he has found a suitable life-companion.

The next letter in the file was written by A.G. just a few days later, on 9 August, but there has clearly been a letter from Henny to him in the interim, in which she has enclosed a copy of Hans's long letter to her. A.G. addresses Henny as 'My dear Hennychild' (Mein liebes Hennykind). After describing a difficult sacrifice he has decided to make for the sake of his marriage, giving up what he sees as his rights in order to maintain his obligations, A.G. goes on to say:

Now let's see how it is with Hans. He certainly has no rights and obligations in the 'abstract'. He has given you up (and himself as well), because he looked upon Hitler as a future leader of the world, and he would have given you up in exactly the same way if you had remained there and been deported and gassed. That sounds hard, but it is probably true. Naturally, one can explain that by referring to the compulsions of real life, and I have absolutely nothing against that – but in that case one shouldn't try to get in touch again, but let matters rest with those realities, or what one saw as realities.

Hans has behaved feebly, and his letter too is weak. He has disgraced himself in his own eyes, and is trying to make good through artificial heroism . . . You should write to him 'occasionally' (oh, how strong he is: he writes to you, and has to wait so long for your answer) and so on and so forth.

What does he want? Either his marriage is not successful and he wants to weep on your shoulder and find understanding, or else he wants to establish new relationships with the now all-powerful Allies (or goodness knows what), but nothing productive, i.e. productive for you, can come out of this . . .

No, don't reply at all. Your memories are worth more than what has come out of them, and these memories are true and not liable to fade. If you simply can't bring yourself not to reply, write him a coldly indifferent letter to the effect that you are pleased that he is so happily married and has obtained such a good post, and that he is a man who will always land on his feet . . .

Henny responded:

19/8/46

My dear A.G.,

It was really sweet of you to reply to me so promptly. I fully agree with you as far as Hans is concerned, and I believe, you know, that I have entirely finished with this matter in my mind. In my view, the main reason for his letter was that he feared that I would cast him in an unfavourable light with his relatives here, who really like me – which obviously would not occur to me even in my dreams. I intend to reply to him as follows:

Dear Hans

'I have rec

. . .

This part of the letter to A.G. is a blank; the letter provisionally written to Hans does not exist even in the form of a draft. Henny continues:

255

I assume that you find this all right. In any case, I won't reply for a long time because I really don't want to have a correspondence with him. Please, dear A.G., write and tell me with complete honesty whether I can always turn to you if I need advice. It is so good to know that one has a friend whom one can turn to for advice in every situation in life.

As for your personal affairs, I am really happy that you have finally come to a decision. It must certainly have been difficult for you, but I believe that through this decision you have found inner peace.

A.G. replies ten days later, at first describing fall in Atlanta:

Autumn is magically beautiful here, and lasts from about the middle of August till the end of November, with very gradually yellowing trees and a wonderful and pleasant warmth.

He continues:

Now to your letter, and whether you can always turn to me. What sort of question is that? I am simply not going to favour it with an answer!— I don't agree with you about Hans. I believe, as I wrote to you before, that not to reply is by far the best course. If you don't reply, he can think whatever he likes, and it doesn't provide him with a link for further communication.

After giving a couple of examples of people with whom he's had to use this method, he writes:

On the other hand, the wife of an earlier client of mine wrote to me from Kaulsdorf that her husband had been shot by the Russians etc., and to these people, who had backed out of our professional relationship and never contacted me again, I have written a letter of rejection, rather like the one you once sent me.

The implications of this last sentence are puzzling – perhaps it relates to a rejection in Berlin – but it appears that A.G. tried his luck with Henny once again a little later; though the letter in which he did so is not extant, it seems that he asked her to become his life-companion. The last letter of 1946 between them was written by Henny and refers, among other things, to this matter – as gently and tactfully (and finally) as she can.

Henny Caro

27 Kendal Street,
London, W. 2.
31st December, 1946

My dear A.G.,

I was very happy to get your birthday greetings, and it didn't matter in the least that you got the date wrong by 10 days. I am the unlucky child of the 13th! I could certainly sense your birthday kiss . . .

You are absolutely right in what you have written about the Germans. For most of them, the war was only a misfortune because they lost it and as a result don't have anything to eat. That there are now people who wish to dissociate themselves from them, seems incomprehensible to them. I myself have written without mincing my words to a girl who wished to have the question of what I think of her clarified, that I want to have nothing to do with her any more . . .

I am so happy that you have finally made up your mind about things, for in my opinion too this was the only right decision in an unbearable situation, which you had suffered under for so many years. I am also happy about this solution for the sake of Rosel [A.G.'s wife] and, naturally, particularly because of your children.

Yes, my dear A.G., I too have the feeling that through the exchange of our thoughts in these letters, we have grown very close, and I could certainly think of a man such as you as a life-companion: a man who is, no doubt, complicated (which I like), but nevertheless clearly and purposefully makes his way forward in life and asserts himself, but who also lets himself be guided unconsciously. But, my dear friend, I am so happy that you have got yourself out of one mess [Henny uses the English word] and I value you far too much to wish to lead you into another one. And so it is my sincere wish for the New Year and for all future years that we should continue our good friendship and that we should remain good comrades who will stand by each other mutually in every situation in life . . .

I got a letter from my brother Heinz yesterday, saying that he is now living in Buenos Aires. He again asks me to support him. I know that you are against it, and I will probably not do it. I hear from friends of mine, whose parents are in Argentina, that they cannot get permission to send money there from here . . .

And now, my dear A.G., goodbye for today. I wish you everything beautiful and good in *1947*!

I embrace you warmly and shout out a 'HAPPY NEW YEAR' to you, Rosel and the children.

    Many warm wishes,

      Yours ever,

        [unsigned: carbon copy]

Though Henny let A.G. down gently, she did not offer Hans the comfort of a correspondence. His letter remained unanswered.

Hans sent one poem to Henny after the war; it is typed. At first I thought that Henny might have typed it out herself in order to keep the original safe elsewhere; but it bears the characteristic marks of the typewriter on which Hans's father, Franz, typed his letter to Henny in 1939: the thickened e, the incomplete capital S, the m lower than the t in words like *bestimmt*. Clearly Hans had deliberately chosen – but why? – to eschew calligraphy.

The poem is undated, but was probably sent at about this time. It implies that Hans knows that Henny is attached to Shanti, and is hurt by her deliberate silence.

MY DEAR, GOOD HENNERLE!

I know, you may not be able to stand me any more.
Nevertheless, I will love you for evermore.
Your *whole* heart is given to another,
Who, you may think,

258

Can love you much more.
Why do you not tell me,
That you can not ~~any longer~~ bear me?—
That with all the faults and defects
That you see in me
You do not love me any more.
My love is worth nothing to you,
It has only taught you so far
That I am not worthy of you
With all my faults and complicated feelings!
And if you wish to say farewell to me, do not hesitate long,
And let me not the torments of love
Suffer so long!
I wanted to weave a band of friendship,
My whole life was and is for you alone!
But if it is your unshakeable will
Never to hear from me again or to see me,
Then will I come one last time to you to implore you:
You should never take my name again,
You should never recognise
Him who in silence loves you still,
Who gives you his heart and soul!—

Still, if someone ever asks you,
Who it is who has just been carried to the grave,
Whom this cool earth buries,
You can say with certainty:
'He was eternally faithful to me,
He loved me greatly,
And even before his death
He swore it anew.'

Shanti kept up contact with his old friend for a few years; he
suggested Hans meet them in Switzerland. When Shanti brought up
the matter with Henny, she said that he could do as he pleased; it

was a matter of indifference to her. Hans, not having heard a word from Henny, did not, in the event, risk the journey.

3.17

One other fractured relationship, and in this case explicitly so, is touched upon in some words from Henny in a letter to A.G. quoted earlier:

I myself have written without mincing my words to a girl who wished to have the question of what I think of her clarified, that I want to have nothing to do with her any more.

This statement shows a side of Henny that I had not come across in her letters until I arrived at the end of her correspondence file, at the letter W.

Lili Würth (not her real name) was one of Lola and Henny's oldest friends. One of Henny's four photograph albums consists entirely of pictures of the three of them on a climbing trip in Austria. It is a small album, with one picture on each page. In white ink on the grey background are various notations in Lola's clear and classic hand. The very first picture, captioned 'The "three-girl family" in the mountains', shows the three of them standing together by a path through a valley with the mountains rising steeply behind them. Lili's right hand rests on a stick; Lola stands diagonally behind her, her hands on Lili's shoulders; Henny stands behind Lili in a similar stance. Lili looks determinedly at the camera, and Lola meditatively, but Henny has a gentle smile.

There are pictures of the three young women, singly or together, on their own or posing with alpine babies, alpine dogs and alpine guides – against waterfalls, log cabins, glaciers and high alpine peaks. There is a picture of Henny, looking extremely chic, sitting on a hillside with a young man from the Tyrol. Another shows Lili 'the intrepid mountaineer', resting in a heroic stance halfway up a steep, rock-strewn slope. The album ends with another copy of the picture with which it began. This time it reads: 'The "three-girl family" before the return journey to Mittenwald – the end of a dream!'

There is a date on this last picture, but all one can see is '16'. The month and year have deliberately been scraped away, possibly as a safeguard in case the album fell into the hands of anyone who might accuse those pictured within of consorting with each other across the 'racial' divide. The faint residue of the very last digit, however, is more compatible with a 2 or 3 than anything else, and if indeed these pictures were taken in 1932 or 1933, that would mean that Henny was twenty-three or twenty-four at the time.

I have included a brief description of Henny's circle of family and friends in Berlin in an appendix to this book. Lili was part of this circle. But after the war, Henny got the sense from other friends that Lili's attitudes and views on the events of the time had greatly changed. One such comment came from Rose, the Christian wife of Jazko Rabau, who, as mentioned earlier, was a Christian convert but Jewish by birth – and therefore classified as such by the Nazis. He had been Rose's teacher at the Abendgymnasium; they had fallen in love and married. Jazko had a daughter, Inge, by his previous marriage, whom he had managed to get to America before the war, but who now rarely wrote to him. He was older than the rest of the circle of friends and they called him 'Uncle Jazko'. Henny and Shanti sent their parcels of food and other gifts to him and Rose for distribution; they sometimes had to do this clandestinely or indirectly (for instance, via Mr Wolffsky's daughter, who was working with the British authorities), since packages were not always easy to get into Berlin.

Rose begins by writing about Henny's gift, which has been sent but has not yet arrived, of a hot-water bottle for Fröschlein and her mother. She talks about the impending horror of another winter without heating, then says:

In addition, Fröschke's mother has become very weak through an operation and bloodletting and must lie down a great deal. When one looks at her, one can readily believe that she will soon follow her husband to the cemetery. At any rate, those who are left behind will know how and where their parents left this life, which we can't say about our own loved ones. And that is one of the most dreadful things about this, now, after we have got to know all the details, to forever be imagining one's dear ones and how they must have suffered through it all. I am totally sick at heart because of all this, and will never get over it.

One wonders whether the originators of all this grief even feel a fraction of this? My Jazko had to go to the Jewish Gemeinde on the day when all the employees, including Lola, were deported by the Gestapo. My existence alone saved him from the same fate. Sometimes I was afraid that I would not be able to bear the constant anxiety, for there were so many daily oppressions. And finally, I would also have been carried off, if the end of the war had been postponed by just two weeks. As one now reads from accounts, the law was about to be presented.

And nevertheless one is astonished when Lili and her sister assert that all that was mere propaganda. I have the feeling that she would rather live under the previous dispensation, because things went so well for her then, and she could gorge on roast goose while the Jews were forbidden even to eat meat etc. Lili's brother-in-law was in Poland at the time as the manager of a Polish factory, living like a little king while others had to go to the front, and Lili's sister and mother kept going to and fro by turns (by 1st-class sleeper, naturally) in order to fetch geese, meat, butter, eggs, etc. from there. Not once, however, have I heard a single word of abhorrence for all the monstrous atrocities. Perhaps they are inwardly ashamed? ?

Still, we keep up friendly relations with Lili, for she herself has remained faithful to us, though we couldn't go to her (for fear that her sister would denounce her to the Gestapo). But she kept up with us in secret. For Lola and Jazko were simply the 'exceptions'. Because of that, Jazko has expressed his thanks to her by giving her character references (which former Nazis very gladly accept from Jews). We hope to be able to make music again with Lili and the Dietrichs; that should then bridge the times.—

At almost the same time – September 1946 – Fröschlein apologises to Henny for a lapse: Lili had given her a letter to post on to
Henny, but the letter had 'slipped into something else' and now,
during her holidays, while clearing her desk, she had found it and
was sending it on immediately.

Henny replies:

I have got Lili's letter, and I must tell you in all honesty, I wish it had
'slipped into something else' at your place for ever. I don't yet know
whether I will reply to her, and if I do, she will be disappointed. But I
can't do anything else. I have the definite feeling with this sort of person
that they have no revulsion for all that has happened, and that they
would happily wish the old times back, because things were so much
better for them then. These people, and I know Lili very well, have only
made 'EXCEPTIONS' – I mean, in Lili's case, the 'exceptions' of Lola
and Uncle Jazko, and – as you will certainly understand – I am inwardly
far too embittered to swallow that. Perhaps you understand, and
perhaps not, but I will not force myself into friendship or fine words.

The letter from Lili that Fröschlein forwarded to Henny covers
two sheets of foolscap in a script that is beautiful and fluid and
forward-slanting, somewhat delicate, somewhat strong. It is a
strange, cold, defensive-aggressive letter.

> Berlin, 12th June 1946
> [but sent on to Henny much later]

Dear Henny,

How many years have passed since we last saw each other?! At last
the opportunity presents itself to bring ourselves in communication with
each other, at least by letter. But – I almost have the impression that this
doesn't matter to you at all. For us it was an experience when the first
news from you came and Fröschlein reported it and read it out. In the
first moment, I wanted to get your address immediately so I could write
to you. But immediately afterwards, it struck me that you had not
mentioned a word about the Dietrichs or me – and then I became

suspicious. And this uncertain feeling was strengthened when I recently heard of your reply to Fröschlein [in which Henny may have spoken or enquired warmly, as she did elsewhere, about the upright Dietrichs, both of whom forbore from associating themselves with the Nazis, even during the war]. So, in order to clear up the matter, I am now putting the question to you quite openly: is it pressure of time or forgetfulness on your part; or is it rather that you now count me as one of those 'bad Germans' or even as one of those 'bad Nazis', and therefore want to have nothing more to do with me? Kindly be so good as to give me a straight and honest answer, all right?

Although we here believed, throughout the years, that the friendly relationships that existed in our circle would persist despite anything that happened, and took it for granted that we would renew the connection once again as soon as it became technically possible – it is certainly possible for it to be otherwise, i.e. *this* thought occurs to me now for the first time! In our circle of friends, despite everything, the connection has remained possible and has continued to exist.— But you are far further from us in everything in both space and time – and between us lie not only sector- and zone-borders, – but the Channel. You have lived for years in a different world, – who knows how this world has reshaped you in these years or what different kind of outlook you have meanwhile absorbed there? That is why I am framing this very precise question and hope for an equally clear and honest reply. Though certainly a negative answer would be painful for me, I would still prefer clarity. And if it has to be, I will come to terms with that as well. I have anyway lost many people through the war, who were close, and (comparatively speaking) even *very* close – and have had to come to terms with this. And life continues – as chance or fate willed it, one *oneself* somehow *remained* alive.

Fröschlein has already told you of Lola's sad fate, – that even she, who never did anything wrong and was so noble and selfless, fell a victim to this terrible course of events is infinitely sad and tragic. But of what use are words? And right until the end she remained so unchangeably herself – and so courageous and submissive to her fate.

Have you heard anything about Hei?

Hans Mahnert, paddling his boat 'Sunshine' – so called because of Henny's father's nickname for her – on the Sacrower See.

Shanti and Hans on a picnic.

Hans, Henny and Shanti on a
skiing trip in the Riesengebirge
on the Czech border.

Shanti at his studies.

Lola correcting and typing
Shanti's dissertation.

The circle of friends: Jewish, Christian and Hindu. On the back of the photograph is written: 'to our dear Shanti as a memento of Christmas 1937 in the company of his friends'. From left to right: Hans Mahnert; unidentified woman; Henny; Shanti; Lili Würth; Jazko Rabau (at whose house Christmas dinners were traditionally held); Annerose Dietrich; Lola; Alice Fröschke (or Fröschlein); Rose Rabau. The photographer (whose signature is among those on the obverse) was probably Hans Dietrich.

The friends posing outdoors: Lili, Hans Dietrich, Fröschlein, Lola, Annerose, Shanti, Henny, Hans Mahnert.

Above left: Fröschlein, who, with great courage, supported Ella and Lola until their deportation from Berlin in 1943.

Above right: Ilse Heydt (née Schmidt), considered somewhat flighty by others in the circle, but who, like Fröschlein, proved her constancy by helping Henny's mother and sister at considerable risk to herself and her family.

Right: Ilse's eighteen-month-old son, listening to his father's watch. Dieter Heydt, a librarian, was (as he had to be in order to keep his job) a member of the Nazi Party.

Below left: Lili Würth, who, though she made exceptions of the Jewish members of her circle, was seen as an apologist for the Nazis. Henny, generous to her other friends, broke off relations with Lili after the war.

Below right: Ursel Alexander, who, though Jewish, survived the war by going underground, at one time living in a hostel run by the SS; she claimed that her husband had fallen on the Russian front.

Clockwise from top left:
Shanti at a German war memorial:
'To our heroes 1914–1918'.

Stormtroopers in jackboots.

The crowds at the Berlin Olympics in
1936, arms raised in the Hitlerian
salute. The board displays the results
of the Men's 100-metre finals won by
Jesse Owens.

The movie *Stormtrooper Brand*
showing at the Palace cinema.

Shanti in Egypt with his fellow officers,
British and Indian.

Captain S. B. Seth, 119952, Army Dental Corps, Middle East Forces.

Berlin – Friedenau
Kirchstrasse 29
9 Dec. 1946

My dear Henny,

We got a card from Lili Würth yesterday, in which she mentioned that you had told her in a letter that you didn't want to have anything to do with her. Clearly this attitude surprised her. I must say that I fully understand your feelings. It is now the case in Germany that the very people whose fault alone it was to have caused the great misfortune that has struck the world now make out that they have always been 'against' it. All those who earlier were the most assiduous supporters of Hitler, who denounced everybody, and who were against Hitler only in their dreams, are today completely harmless fellows. One asks oneself today where all the Nazis actually were and how Hitler could ever have become powerful at all, when no one ever voted for him. But one thing is absolutely certain: if Hitler had been victorious, then all those who (supposedly!) want to have nothing to do with him today would once again immediately become the most convinced Nazis and anti-Semites that they used to be. They have not undergone any transformation. Lili belongs to this sort of person. She is indeed not a bad sort, but she followed the terrible criminal just as thoughtlessly and willingly as the other Germans. She too complained about the British and the Americans when they bombed Berlin and she had to sit in the cellar. But she didn't complain when the Germans destroyed Coventry and everyone rejoiced when Hitler said, 'I will erase their cities!' They found that quite in order. They only regretted that Churchill took away Mr Hitler's eraser.

Lili oughtn't to wonder that she's now paying the price for her behaviour. In my opinion, as soon as postal communications were re-established, she should have written a letter to you with the following content:

Dear Henny, The most unfortunate war in the history of the world is at an end. I feel a compelling need to tell you how tormented I have felt that it is we Germans who brought so much sorrow and

misfortune on the world. Day and nig[ht] all of us have brought a heavy burden [...] sinned. When we chose Hitler to be ou[r ...] think that he would develop into a scou[...] passed, we slowly recognised that we had [...] terrible criminal. Our enthusiasm for him [...] hatred and disgust. We were ashamed to b[e ...] choice but to watch his shameful deeds wit[h ...] not speak out, for that would have meant ou[r ...] having changed the course of events at all. N[...] in the history of the world has been brought [...] can express what until now I have had to stifle[...] that you were made to suffer so much pain an[d ...] loved ones and many friends. I reproach mysel[f ...] because I feel I too am to blame for it. I only hav[e ...] help, for my own part, to make up for what Ger[...] committed. Rest assured that I share in your pain [...] prepared to make the greatest sacrifices if only I c[...] tragedy that has been visited upon you.

She has never written a letter like this. But by silence o[ne ...] rest a wrong that has been committed. Lili has very hap[...] advantages that the Third Reich gave her in good measu[re ...] every right to dissociate yourself from her.

With fondest greetings,

Yours

Jazko

The first letter to Henny from the Rabaus, sent just a [...] earlier, had been written by Rose on two large sheets o[f ...] first of which was headed with an impression of the fa[...] Parliament building in Berlin. It was a strangely tact[...] since the building, dedicated in the words inscribed on [...] its pediment 'to the German people', was the represe[nt ...] much that was shameful in recent German history:

presentatives who, abdicating their own responsibility,
Enabling Act that let Hitler rule by decree.

may just have been the postwar shortage of paper; cer-
contents of the letter were stark enough. Rose states that
's relatives except for two sisters – one married to an
ne who hid herself 'underground' – had been killed.

riends, acquaintances, teachers and students, if they were 'non-
have gone the same way, with the exception of very few
s; and these are almost all (in so far as they live in the American
n their way to the U.S.A. in order to turn their back on
ny, which has treated them so badly.

goes on directly to make a point which, however true,
cruelly blunt:

ere certainly extremely fortunate to have left in good time, and
at, if for nothing else, need not be angry with Hans for having
ed someone else. For basically you owe him your life through
he did then. Though, of course, it turned out otherwise than
nally planned.

ndeed, had Hans married Henny before the war, it would likely
e been fatal for both, and there may have been an elliptical allu-
n to this in Hans's letter to her. As already mentioned, Hans's
ther had died many years earlier, and not many people knew
at her religious or racial background had been; but she was a
w and this made Hans, in the taxonomy of the Reich, a
schling (half-breed) of the first degree (one with half-Jewish
od). Under the Law for the Protection of German Blood and
onour, signed by Hitler and others in September 1935, he was
rmitted to marry only another Mischling of the first degree, in
hich case his status would have remained unchanged, or a Jew, in
hich case he would have been reclassified as a Jew. Had he done
, and had he and Henny remained in Germany until emigration

I will close for today. Before I tell you about myself and my present life, I will wait for your answer.

Meanwhile, fond greetings from me in the spirit of our friendship of old.

Your Lilikind

Henny replies hard but straight:

Henny Caro   27, Kendal Street,
                                                      London W. 2,
                                                      22nd November, 1946

Dear Lili,

I have received your letter. – You demand an honest answer, and I must tell you that the events of these many years have fundamentally reshaped my view of the world. Those people in Germany with whom I remain in contact belong to the category of those who I am 100% convinced worked against the Nazi system, and not those, like you, who only made 'EXCEPTIONS' of those in our circle. I must be convinced that those with whom I remain in a relationship of friendship today share my view of the world.

I have gone through too much to be able to think differently.

I wish you all good luck for the future.

With best wishes,

Your

[unsigned: carbon copy]

3.18

Jazko Rabau wrote to Henny a few days later in a clear, correct and very vertical script, well suited to a school inspector and erstwhile teacher of mathematics:

became impossible, they would, barring a miracle, have been murdered by the German state.

A Mischling of the second degree (one with a quarter Jewish blood – one Jewish grandparent) was not even allowed to marry another Mischling of the second degree, but only a full-blooded 'Aryan', in order to breed out any residue of Jewish blood. But a Mischling of the first degree, like Hans, could marry a full-blooded Aryan only with special permission. That is what he must have done when he married a non-Jew in 1941 or 1942.

Jews were not allowed to marry Mischlings of the second degree or 'Germans'. Those, such as Jazko, who were already married to Germans like Rose when the law came into force, and who were neither divorced by their partners under encouragement from the Nazis nor unfortunate enough to see their partners die, thus themselves reverting to the status of unprotected Jew, had their mixed marriages classified as 'privileged' or 'not privileged' under a directive issued by Göring at the end of 1938, after Kristallnacht. If the man was German, the marriage, childless or otherwise, was privileged, unless any children were being brought up as Jews. If, as in Rose's case, the woman was German, the marriage was privileged only if there were children born of it and any such children were not being brought up as Jews. Inge, who had been sent to America when she was barely ten years old, was a child from Jazko's first marriage, and Rose and Jazko had no children of their own. Their marriage was therefore not privileged, and they were, step by step, excluded from the 'German community', and forced to live in so-called Jewish houses.

Jazko had written to Henny about a month after Rose. In this letter he had described conditions in their circle and in Berlin. He asks:

What have the Nazi criminals made of Germany? A heap of rubble, ruins and ashes. Destitution everywhere and indescribable hunger and misery . . . A frequently occurring case: two schoolchildren (brothers) have between them only one pair of shoes (torn, naturally). In the summer, they go barefoot. In the winter they take it in turns to go to school; only one can go, the other must remain at home . . . There is a shortage of teachers. There are districts in which there is only one teacher for 140 to 160 children! But we're working at it; one hopes that the children will some day build a better, peaceful Germany . . .

It's certainly better for the two of us in that we are human beings again and not free game to be hunted. And no more bombs are falling. We can go to bed at night and know that the Secret State Police will not suddenly ring the doorbell to take me away, that there will be no nightly air-raid alarm and that the next morning our home will not be in ruins or in flames.

Jazko writes movingly about what he and Rose felt when they learned that a parcel was on its way from Henny and Shanti:

We very much look forward to the parcel mentioned, and not only because of its contents. We were even more moved by the spirit of true friendship and warm humanity that it betokens. When, like us, one has experienced nothing but hatred, threats and insults even from the circle of one's former 'friends', then such tones sound like the music of angels. So there are people outside who understand us, who value us and who wish to do good by us! That in itself consoles us and gives us new courage to look into the future, however harsh and full of privation it may be. We two live in a harmonious marriage which has enabled us to bear a great deal. But nevertheless we need other people; we are, after all, social beings. During these long years, we were shut out, pushed away and ostracised by these other people. We feel rather as a dog would feel, who, after having been beaten and pelted with stones by everyone, is now suddenly stroked.

Henny writes back about a month later; she has moved, without realising it, because she does not ask for permission, from the more formal *Sie* mode into the more intimate *Du* (or rather, since she is writing to both of them jointly, *Ihr*) mode. In her letter she unconsciously quotes Ilse's of 1939 about the tenacity of true friendship. After expending her personal grief on the page, she suggests that a great memorial to the dead be built; she could not have known that in Berlin, the heart of the extermination machine, it would be more than half a century before such a memorial would be brought into existence.

7th August, 1946

My dear friends,

Thank you for your kind letters. I would have replied earlier if I had not been so deeply depressed by the many sad reports that I have received from Berlin about the fate of my loved ones . . . Among the worst is that Mutti and Lola were separated at the end, an almost unimaginable torment. We will never get over the fate of those we loved – that these poor people had to remain behind in the slaughterhouse. The tortures that were inflicted on them are impossible to get out of one's mind. When one reads how these Nazi gangsters, who themselves drove thousands and millions to their deaths, now beg for their lives, one really sees the hollowness of these mock-heroes . . . But none of this can bring back our dead. Somewhere one must create a huge memorial to them that will make a deep impression for ever on everyone who sees it, even on those who have never known these experiences or do not wish to believe them.

It seems that the Rabaus must have talked about reciprocating her generosity in the future, because Henny writes:

I do all this most willingly, from the bottom of my heart, but when you talk to me about 'equivalent value', you really make me very annoyed. I am certain that you would do the same just as willingly if the circumstances were reversed, since we are friends in the truest and best sense of the word, for only a true friendship such as ours can span distances, borders and time . . .

Please be convinced, my dear friends, that I will do everything I can to make your lives a little more pleasant, and that this is a special joy for me. How happy I would have been, had I been able to do this for my mother and sister, but since this has unfortunately not been granted to me, I do it for you, my 'chosen relations' [*Wahlverwandten*], with all my heart; you are a piece of my 'HOME'. Rest assured that you have friends who think of you and are with you.

3.19

Both Jazko and Rose were saddened by the fact that they heard very rarely from Inge, who was now married and had small children. They had just received her second letter in nine months. Nor did she send Care parcels. 'Presumably, the situation with regard to need in Germany is not known in that part of America,' wrote Jazko, 'and besides, it might be financially difficult for her.'

Inge had admired Henny when she was a child: to be 'slim like Henny' had been her ideal. Now Henny decided to write to her (in English), telling her how happy she was about her father's survival.

As I have heard from some friends of mine in Berlin, he has suffered a lot, both bodily and mentally, under the hardships and malnutrition. He lost practically all his belongings during the bombing attacks and it was lucky for him that his wife belonged to a different faith, otherwise it would have been impossible for him to escape the Concentration Camp. Your father and Mrs. Rabau are extremely modest and seldom complain about the hardships which they are undergoing even at the present moment.

Henny emphasises the fact that she is writing on her own behalf and suggests with great tact that more frequent letters and a Care parcel or two would not come amiss.

When he heard what Henny had done, Jazko wrote:

Dear Henny,

You know the old proverb: in times of need, one knows one's friends. In the 12 years under the Nazis we have often had the opportunity to measure our so-called 'friends' by this saying. Many were weighed in the balance and found wanting. Few passed the test. You, however, surpass them considerably. Your last letter, with the copy of a letter to Inge, has shown us your greatness of spirit. We were deeply moved. We have certainly believed you were a good and true friend, but now you surpass yourself. If I were not married to the splendid Rose, to whom I literally owe my life, I would propose to you despite our difference in age. Only now do we recognise clearly how much Hans Mahnert lost in you and how little he has gained in Wanda . . .

Ilse had mentioned earlier that in discussions within their circle, the Rabaus had consistently taken Hans's side in the matter of his decision to marry Wanda. But one of the arguments that the Rabaus used was similar to the one that Henny herself used with Inge – probably in order to reconcile her to her father's second wife – namely, that Hans's marriage to a Gentile had the indirect effect of increasing his chances of survival.

Rose adds a few lines to Jazko's letter. She demurs from the description of 'splendid Rose', and continues:

With regard to the good things that the gracious Christmas fairies have sent us, and that have called forth great joy in everyone, it is worth noting that they have been chosen with great empathy. Jazko claims that these were only the second pair of shoes in his life that fitted him as soon as he put them on and that gave him a pleasant, comfortable feeling the very first time he wore them. The chocolate, starved of it as we were, we immediately gobbled up. With the other good things we will brighten up our Sundays. But with the cigarettes we have been able to pay for Jazko's dental treatment. (He had to have the root of a tooth removed.) Consequently, one might speak of Shanti's tele-dental treatment.

She describes with some sadness how, though the tradition of birthday coffees among the friends is still kept up, the music-making and Christmas celebrations of the past have fallen away: sorrow and privation and distance and the pressure of time each play their part. Lili is still in mourning for a married man whom she loved and who died in a car accident two years earlier 'and doesn't want to have anything more to do with Christmas'. As for music-making:

the trains are packed, so that one can't take an instrument with one; and besides, no one ever has any time. The Dietrichs [Hans Dietrich liked singing and playing the violin] live in the back of beyond [literally: where the foxes say goodnight] in Wilhelmshagen, which takes between four and five hours to travel to and from. The old times have therefore gone, and we live on our memories.

Now I have become quite melancholy. And yet I wanted in this letter to tell you about my complete joy over the Christmas surprise. Thank you very much!

Warm greetings from your Rose

Henny scrupulously specified what each person was to get when she sent these parcels to the Rabaus' address. In Lili's case (twenty cigarettes, one chocolate, two packets of Oxo cubes), she added two words in parentheses, distancing herself from the gift. The list of recipients reads: 'Uncle Jazko (Father Christmas), Rose, Froeschlein, Ilse, Mr. Mahnert senior, Hans Dietrich (director of music), Annerose Dietrich, Lili (from Shanti).' Even though Shanti Uncle told me, almost forty years later, that he did not particularly like Lili, he presumably did not wish to hurt her unnecessarily by excluding her from those he wished well.

Over the course of the next few years, Shanti and Henny sent many scores of parcels to their friends in Berlin. When they could send food, they did; when they couldn't, they sent anything else that was needed, from stockings to darning-wool to cigarettes to combs to scarves to shoes, anything they thought might be needed in the desperate conditions that reigned in postwar Germany. These were times of shortages in Britain too, with dozens of items, from clothing to meat to tea to sugar, rationed. Indeed, things became worse in the years immediately following the war; the meat ration was reduced and even bread and potatoes were rationed at one stage. Besides, the regulations about what could be sent abroad kept changing – at one time one was forbidden from sending rationed goods; at another, that was all one was permitted to send.

At every turn, Henny reassured her friends, for whom the position of perpetual recipient must have been difficult, that she knew that, had their positions been reversed, they would have done the same.

But what was to come out of Berlin for Henny was not merely gratitude and friendship.

A couple of letters from Rose followed in early 1947, which present a complex, resentful side of her character. In the first, while acknowledging that Inge has sent her and Jazko a Care parcel, she points out that Fröschlein gets many more from her friends in New York. She adds that Lili's job with American radio entitles her to a card which lets her get

1,200 calories every day in highly nutritious food (unusual things and things that have become virtually unknown in Germany among them), while there are other poor devils who earlier had less than the normal consumer and even today don't have any more.

The other letter contains some strangely catty remarks about Ilse, who came to see them on Jazko's birthday in mid-March:

Of course, things are financially and in terms of sustenance quite good for her, because she works with the French occupation forces in the distribution office for food etc. But of course she has to do something for that. However, she seems to be fortunate, for when her little boy was sick, she got oranges and fruit juice and butter etc. from the firm, all luxuries that Germans can't get, and that certainly show how much she must be loved by her boss. What's more, her mother sews for Madame. And in addition, her boss is supporting her in trying to get her husband released from prison, which requires several recommendations, since Ilse's Dieter was a Party member and an S.A. man [a Nazi storm trooper]. However, because his involvement didn't go any further, Ilse hopes that he will not have any further difficulties. As far as we could, we have also made efforts on her behalf.

This last letter and the disturbing phrase that Rose Rabau slipped in about Ilse's husband's credentials, agitated Henny greatly, and she did her best to find out whether it was true. But at about the same time, she became aware of some troubling actions, during the war, of others in their close circle of friends.

3.20

Fröschlein was Lola's closest friend and a person of uncompromising decency and courage. It was she whom Henny was to turn to in the matter of Ilse's husband. But, as it happened, in late February 1947, more than a month before Henny read Rose's almost parenthetical remark about Dieter Heydt, Fröschlein wrote a letter to her in which (in response to an earlier question by Henny) she talked about Ilse:

Ilse has recently been ill, but she is better again; the little boy too is in good health once more. Dear Hennerle, you write about her husband, and I understand just what you mean by your question. I got to know him when Ilse introduced him to our circle; it was just after her wedding; I keep getting mixed up as to whether it was 1940 or 1941. [It would have been 1941.] He got to know Ilse when she was with Rose. The Rabaus were there for my birthday; it was celebrated belatedly because Ilse had got married on the very day of my birthday and had

blizzards, and now the thaw with such widespread flooding. And you had as little coal as us . . . and frequent power cuts, as I've just learned from the newspapers. I find this dreadful, particularly when one has no electricity the whole evening. One falls behind so in one's work, since one can't, because of the cold, sit up till 10 o'clock to wait for electricity. Mostly one creeps despairingly into bed . . . You suffer just as much as us, and the war began because of our country, but I wonder if you would understand that I have wished a thousand times that the situation was reversed and that I would much rather innocently suffer all this than know how defamed we are throughout the world.

The second letter, headed '*Only for you!*', gives Henny the background to a quarrel at present raging between Fröschlein and Lili; its immediate cause was the question of the storage of Lili's goods, during the course of which Lili apparently accused Fröschlein of a lack of sympathy for others. Again and again in the letters of Fröschlein and others, one finds Henny taking on the role of confidante, for which she is suited not only because of her sympathy but also because of her distance.

In the crucial third letter, to which it would have been superfluous to add a 'for your eyes only' admonition, Fröschlein pours out the murky matter that has been dammed up in her memory for years. She tells Henny that she has written and torn up one letter already. She then mentions Henny's last letter, in which she refers very warmly to the Rabaus, saying that it now seems to be 'too terrible of me to write to you what you will now come to know'.

As I wrote to you once before, when Lola and your mother were taken away, Lola phoned me and spoke with my mother, who gathered from her careful words that this was to be her farewell. I did not know where Lola was or from where she had called me; at that time I did not yet know the Wolfskys [Lola worked under him in the Gemeinde] and didn't know where they lived; I just waited for Lola to perhaps call me a second time, as she had implied she would, and every evening that week didn't move from the telephone.

At this time Frau R[abau] came to us once in order to tell us what we already knew from the telephone call. I was at the office; she spoke to my mother, and because she said that it was possible that her husband might once again see Lola and that she might possibly bake a small cake for her, my mother, who had to assume that we wouldn't be able to see Lola again before her departure from Berlin, gave her a few ingredients for this cake; it was probably flour and fat – that sort of thing. When Lola did, after all, get in touch again and I was, upon my insistent request, able to call on her, I found out that she was in her office. That Sunday she parted from me in tears . . . But she also, and in tears, complained bitterly about the Rs. They knew, because he [they?] lived in the same house as Lola, but one storey lower, that Lola still went to her office every day, an exception that was made for the employees of the Gemeinde, who were allowed to leave the collection camp every day to go to their offices as long as they were still in Berlin. R did not once go to visit Lola, he didn't ask after her even once, he did not once take her anything to eat – which, as I found out, they had so much need for even here. Nor did she ever see anything of the cake. Lola told me bitterly that the Wolfskys brought her soup every day, while R didn't tell us anything and didn't take any care of Lola at all.

She also told me that day, full of bitterness, that those people who were in the same situation as the Rabaus [i.e., in mixed marriages] were already waiting to take their places [presumably, in the apartment at 19 Bleibtreustrasse] . . . Wolfsky, who behaved towards her so very movingly, was an exception . . . From that time onwards, I often went there; they were such charming people. But then he too wanted to get out: he had lost all his relations here, except for his brother in Australia. Frau Wolfsky said to me on the last day that, despite everything, it would be hard for her; for that I was deeply grateful to her. Can you understand that?

Dear Hennerle, how can I explain to you now why I didn't go there and simply break off relations with R? Today I don't understand it myself, but I have to imagine myself back into those times. I told everyone about all this, because I was so outraged . . . I held back from the Rs; but after a long while, somehow or other, we got back together again.

When they heard that I had been with Lola at the Gemeinde at the end, Rose – after months – sent back some of the ingredients. Earlier, too, when I was travelling somewhere and had asked her to do it, she had had to take the coupons from Ilse to buy something for Lola and take it to her, as I otherwise always did. She used the white bread coupons for herself, and gave Lola black bread.

Later in the letter, Fröschlein berates herself on two counts, very different in their magnitude and implications; the second of these brings forth a deeply emotional response from Henny.

Fröschlein writes:

Röschen apparently told Ilse once that we had all been frightened at the time, including me. Yes, that was indeed true of everyone, of them as well, and that was certainly understandable. One gave a start whenever the doorbell rang. You must know from the newspapers how things were here, but it is still very different when one lives through it. I was so anxious about Lola and Mutti, and although I myself was worried, mainly because of my parents, I overcame that and went to Lola in the Gemeinde – though Wolfsky told me later that it had been very dangerous, for there were often surprise raids. And yet, I would never again have found peace if I hadn't done it. On that day, I had no fear, Hennerle, you can believe me, but only the greatest pain for Lola, who had no hope and wept so and whom I have indeed never seen again. I often wonder whether I did everything I could have; I cudgel my brains and ask myself why on that Sunday I didn't take Lola some warm food. But when she phoned, I rushed out immediately to see her. I took something with me for her, but if I had known everything beforehand, I would perhaps have quickly made something warm. Why did we not persuade her to hide? She didn't do so because of her mother. And would she have succeeded anyway? Alice and Else [Pasch] were discovered as well. Rebuke me if you think it right, Hennerle.

Please let this letter, I beg you once again, remain between us two . . . Please reply soon; I am waiting anxiously for your letter. Fondest greetings from your
   Fröschlein

3.21

Henny's reply carries traces of Jazko Rabau's own remarks about friendship.

Henny Caro

27, Kendal Street
London, W. 2,
18th April, 1947

My dear Fröschlein,

I got one of your letters of the 23rd March five days ago, and then waited for the other, which arrived only today, though you posted both of them together.

Yes, my dear Fröschlein, I was so very melancholy at heart when I read all that you wrote to me, and it shows me what people who call themselves your friends are like. In times of danger one sees who one's friends are, and this is proven time and again. I can well imagine how bitter an experience R's behaviour was for Lola, and that causes me great pain. But for your sake alone I will not break with them completely; I promised you that, and I will keep my word under all circumstances, so long as you are in Germany – and then we can speak about these things again. In any case, I thank you for your openness. All that great sorrow arose in me again, and I feel so dejected. I haven't said a word about this to Shanti; I want to keep it from him. But when I tell you that Shanti, without having the least idea about all this, doesn't think much of R and that he has often said that to me and still says it, it is truly astonishing and shows his great inner sensitivity. According to him, the Dietrichs are people of real worth, and I value them too.

It shows me your greatness of spirit, Fröschlein, that you can't get it out of your head that you were not able to persuade Mutti and Lola to hide. Because you mention this to me now for the first time, I will honestly give you my opinion about it, naturally without implying the slightest reproof towards you. Since 1943, when I hadn't heard any more from Mutti and Lola, I secretly hoped so deeply and prayed each night that you or some of our other Christian friends would keep Mutti and Lola hidden. Fröschlein, please take this in the right spirit, and don't take it in any way as a reproof, but you can naturally understand my thoughts and hopes. I know how very much you have done, which very few others did, and that you remained a staunch and faithful friend to Lola till the end, and I will never forget that. Sadly, it was probably fate that she didn't come through. Some, who were kept hidden, managed to survive. Some not, and because I am a fatalist, I believe in destiny, even though that is not always a consolation. Fröschlein, hopefully you understand me, but I am telling you just what I think, because we are friends after all, and I hope that the feelings of friendship which you had for my sister will also to some extent be carried over to me.

I heard in the meanwhile from Rose Rabau, and also learned from her that you had had a falling-out with Lili. Lili appears to be one of those people who are of the view that they have gone through the most and lost the most, and it is good that you have spoken your mind to her. Rose R. also mentioned something to which I am not indifferent, and that is why I am writing about it to you. With reference to Ilse, she wrote to me that her husband was a Party member *and* in the S.A. That he as a state official belonged to the Party, I can understand (though Hans D[ietrich] didn't), and you had written about that to me. But that he was in the S.A. was by no means compulsory for him and makes me very suspicious. Fröschlein, when I think that my own mother and sister were taken away by the S.A. people and were driven to their deaths in the most murderous way, I am gripped by such horror, and I beg you to give me your thoughts on this matter. You haven't so far mentioned anything at all about this to me. I request you to keep the matter between us for the moment, but I must have clarity, and only you can help me. I know that Ilse is a decent person, and always was, but I couldn't square it with my conscience perhaps at some later date to have contact with her husband if I knew all this to be true, and I would never force myself into a friendship, for this must always be unforced and natural and founded on trust.

283

Henny now tells Fröschlein that she, Shanti and Margot intend to invite her to London. (Margot Weissberg, née Berlowitz, whom Fröschlein knew from Berlin, had left Germany for England several years before Henny. She was the owner and manager of the pharmaceutical firm where Henny worked.) Because Margot's husband is not too well, and because Shanti plans to buy a house soon, he insists that Fröschlein stay with him. Henny writes: 'It would really be marvellous to see each other again. What do you think of our idea????'

She goes on, in response to Fröschlein's request for advice on the improvement of her English, to recommend several writers – J. B. Priestley, Aldous Huxley, Hugh Walpole, A. J. Cronin, W. Somerset Maugham, H. G. Wells, Rudyard Kipling, George Bernard Shaw, Arnold Bennett and Warwick Deeping – adding: 'I read them with pleasure and they are certainly worth reading.' She ends:

Shanti and I will very soon be sending you a small book. I naturally only read English books. It would seem quite strange to me to read German; I have, in any case, not done so for years.

And now, my dear Fröschlein, that's it for today. Greet your dear mother warmly from me. I hope she is better now. With a big hug for you and many warm greetings.

Ever your

[unsigned: carbon copy]

3.22

Fröschlein waited a few days before replying to Henny's letter.

Berlin, 6. May, 1947

My dear Hennerle,

Your letter of 18 April, which reached me on Saturday the 26th, has shattered me, just as mine shattered you. Everything comes alive again, everything that one thought about and considered in those terrible months. Not only now, no, even then I continually thought that one had to persuade Lola to do what so many others were doing. Whether she would actually have managed it, who can say? In all the nights that followed that dreadful evening when I went to Lola's and heard that a woman (whom I also knew through Lola and Mutti) had been taken from that house, I lived in anticipation of what then became terrible reality, and I thought all the time about what one could do. At the time, your mother was often very ill and horribly weak and wretched. I don't know if you can understand it, but often in my innermost heart I prayed that it might be granted to her to pass away quietly in her bed, so that everything else would be spared her. I thought this only out of love for your mother. It was actually not possible to keep two people hidden so that no one would have any idea of their existence . . . Your mother would certainly have given herself away. Perhaps one might have been able to persuade Lola on her own, but she naturally didn't want to leave your mother alone, and definitely didn't want to take this path. But what torments me is this: couldn't one at least have tried? Might one perhaps have succeeded? . . . I know you don't want to reproach me, but I torture myself enough about it. Some people did survive; why not a person like Lola? Feeding her would have been the least of it; in times of hardship, one can be hungry together.

Fröschlein describes, however, the virtual impossibility, even for those who were young and resourceful, of keeping themselves hidden for long. By 1944, because there were so many bombed-out people everywhere without homes and often without papers, it became easier to 'remain underground'. But this was not the case in 1942 and 1943. Their friends the sisters Else and Alice Pasch, who had left their home in September 1942 to avoid deportation, had managed to obtain identity cards and ration coupons under new names. They had settled down in a small place not far from Berlin, had shown themselves everywhere, had merged into the fabric of local life with skill and assurance and not stood out in any way. They had managed to hold out till May 1943. But they were then discovered and deported and killed.

Fröschlein also mentions an article that she read on the day Henny's letter arrived, about their old English teacher at the Abendgymnasium, Mrs Harnack, an American by birth, who had married a German, Arvid Harnack, from a famous scholarly family. Her husband was hanged by the Nazis in 1942, and she herself the following year.

The night after your letter came, bringing everything to life again, and as I also read about this terrible business, I was unable to sleep. But I thank you for your letter nevertheless, and ask you always to write to me about what you think and feel. I have felt exactly the same, and I trouble my head endlessly about what I have left undone.

I believe that to tell you about that matter regarding R was the right thing to do, because Lola, in those last hours that I spent with her, turned away from them so completely, and I wouldn't have been able to bear it if you had asked me once again who had looked after Lola and I for my part had remained silent about it. I cannot grasp what could have moved him to show so little love and friendship to someone who had once admired him, though Lola at the end changed her opinion greatly.— I often went to visit your aunts Olga and Flora [Glaser], and Flora said to me very often – which is something that now somewhat consoles me – that the friendship between Lola and me that lasted till the moment when she had to go, had meant so much to Lola. And it also consoles me a little that I was with her till the end, but it is, for all the bitterness, so very little. I grieve over all this deep in my heart, and I will grieve over it as long as I live.

I am writing you another letter, which I will ~~enclose~~ send separately.

Ever your

Fröschlein

In this second letter of the same date, Fröschlein – in rapturous terms – thanks Henny (as she has already thanked Shanti and Margot) for their invitation to London:

Oh, the mere thought has made me quite crazy! I have already been picturing Shanti and how I'll live in his little house, and you'll come around all the time and we can chat to our hearts' content and talk about everything that moves and has moved our hearts in these long years of separation. I can imagine how you will come and fetch me, how we will fall into each other's arms and probably not even be able to speak for a long while . . . but then, so much the more. Oh, if only that could happen. But the plan and the idea are already so beautiful that they give me pleasure all the time. But it can't happen. How can you burden yourselves like this????

She talks a little about her misunderstanding with Lili, at the same time giving one a picture of Lola – and also of Hans Dietrich, who has been referred to by members of the circle, but has not yet appeared in his own right in these pages:

On the 1st of June we will all be together in order to celebrate Hans Dietrich's birthday belatedly. I had told him that, owing to Lili's letter, I wouldn't come, and he wrote to me very kindly saying that I had to be there. They would invite Lili at Whitsun if she could make it then. I like Hans Dietrich and Annerose very much; I can still hear Hans teasing Lola (he always said that if he were allowed two wives, she would be the second). Even at school, whenever she had to give a reading, he would tease her by saying that she shouldn't shout so loudly! (And that too of our little Lola who, out of modesty, spoke so softly.)

In the same letter, Fröschlein touches on the question of Ilse's husband. She says that Henny's enquiry has greatly astonished her. She had no idea that Dieter Heydt might have been in the SA; had she known, she would have told Henny about it. It was certainly possible, since Rose Rabau was with Ilse when she first met her husband, that Rose knew something that she, Fröschlein, didn't. On a recent visit by Fröschlein to Ilse, there had been other company present, and it had not been possible to pose such a question. But later, since Fröschlein in any case wanted to know how matters stood with respect to Dieter Heydt's release and return, she had asked Ilse directly.

And now I am no wiser than before. She said that she didn't know anything about it, or something similar; she only got to know her husband afterwards. What did Rose write to you, and from where did she get her information? I will, if the opportunity presents itself, ask Rose in a subtle way about this. I was not quite comfortable with Ilse's answer. I will write to you if I get to know anything more precise, but at the moment I don't.

3.23

Henny replies to Fröschlein – in English, for the first time – in a joint letter with Shanti. In it she quotes in German Rose Rabau's exact remark about Ilse's husband. She also says that rather than sending food packages via the Rabaus for distribution, they are now going to send them directly to the intended recipients.

The Rabaus, unaware of Fröschlein's revelations to Henny, continue their correspondence. Henny's first letter to them in April is somewhat cool and entirely newsless. The next letter from Berlin, signed '2 Rabaus' but typed, and therefore composed by Rose, tells one something of the situation in Germany almost two years after the war.

This morning once again I had cause to be quite unhappy. A very clean little old woman, her face full of wrinkles, came to the door. She could have been your mother or mine. I gave her a small coin and a slice of bread, which one has to do many times a day, because there is great hardship, especially among the old. They don't throw themselves into the whirlpool of the black market, like young people and even children do. This old woman wanted to kiss my hands; I only just managed to stop her. This is not the first time either. Even men thank one for a slice of dried bread in this humiliating way – a sign that they must very, very often have to knock on doors in vain. What really shocks me is the fact that old people, grown helpless, have to suffer for the guilt of ambitious creatures, while in some newspaper or other one reads that the first Care parcel sent by Germans abroad (certainly former Nazis) came to Frau Bormann [whose husband, Martin Bormann, had been head of the Nazi Party Secretariat and one of Hitler's closest collaborators]! I was very sad about this modest, moving old woman.

And yet the sun laughs outside, as if there were nothing but happiness in the world. At least these helpless people no longer have to freeze, as happened to many hundreds this winter.

Early in June 1947, Henny sent the Rabaus a packet containing flour, tea, and a tin each of egg powder, crayfish and sardines. Ten days later, the Rabaus sent a letter which was a compound of wise philosophising and unusually sharp gossip. They discuss the quarrel between Fröschlein and Lili; claim that they have heard from Hans Mahnert's wife Wanda that his father's longtime companion, Gerda von Gliszczynski, has got not only the Mahnert family jewels but also those belonging to Fredy Aufrichtig, which had been stored at the Mahnert house for safekeeping; and go on to talk of the paucity of the Care parcels sent by Inge from America:

We would be happy enough if she sent us a really nice letter more frequently. That would give us a lift again. One would know how things are in other parts of the world. And that would make the burden of everyday life lighter. Most people still think that only in Germany is there hardship, and that only in Germany is this or that not available. But there are poor people and misery everywhere. And one's own need makes one envious and resentful. One can see this even with otherwise really good-natured people. Egoism and the instinct of self-preservation seem to be the strongest elements in this world. Happy the land that is rich enough not to recognise its most hateful aspect, as one does nowadays in impoverished Germany.

A joint letter from Shanti and Henny, once again in English and typed by Henny, follows. Despite the ending – 'Now, dear friends, we send you our kindest regards and our love. A kiss to Uncle

289

Jazko from Henny. A kiss to Roeslein from Shanti' – Henny, who so far has kept her promise to Fröschlein not to give her away by behaving differently towards the Rabaus, cannot quite disguise her impatience and criticism. Perhaps she was particularly irked by the comments from on high on the subject of human selfishness:

Yes, we have heard already about the misunderstanding between Froeschlein and Lili. We can hardly believe that anyone could quarrel with our dear little Frosch . . . We are very glad to learn that Inge writes to you more often. We are sure she is a very nice girl, judging from the letter she has written to Henny. She must be very busy with her two children and the household work . . . It is quite a news to us that Mrs. von Gl. has the family jewels from Fredy Aufrichtig. This cannot be true, because we are often in contact with Fredy who is now in Shanghai and who has not even once mentioned a word about it. Moreover Frau Aufrichtig with her other Son has also written to us from South-Africa without saying anything about it. It seems some people have nothing better to do than to spread *Greuelmaerchen* [horror stories]. Still, it is not our business to take part in their quarrels.

As for the horror stories that the Rabaus by implication stood accused of spreading, Henny might well have included among these the indication from Rose that Ilse's husband had been in the SA. At any rate, in their next few letters the Rabaus are more circumspect about spreading gossip about individuals, confining their critical observations to the psychology of the Germans, or human beings in general; and indeed, these observations are acute.

I am certain that if I go out in my new coat, people will say: 'Yes, well, the victims of Fascism, they've got something now, while we just have to go around looking like this.' (One hears something of this sort in every queue that forms somewhere for something.) Instead of being ashamed of wrongs committed and suffered, one's own needs make one unjust and envious. But people are probably like this all over the earth, with the exception perhaps of so-called primitive people. Nevertheless, I am already looking forward to my new coat which, thanks to the art of tailoring, will improve my appearance.

That 'one's own needs make one unjust and envious' or that 'egoism and the instinct of self-preservation seem to be the strongest elements in this world' does to some extent explain the Rabaus' behaviour towards Lola. They lived in constant terror and uncertainty and hunger, the life of the one preserved only by the existence of the other. They did not dare to step out of line in any way; it would have provided the authorities with an immediate excuse for doing away with them. Perhaps they had even more cause for fear than Fröschlein if they had been discovered taking food to Lola during her last few days in Berlin, when she had to shuttle between the collection camp and the Gemeinde; then felt ashamed that they had not delivered the cake or anything else to her; and later delayed returning the ingredients because they felt uncomfortable about the whole matter. On another occasion, when Annerose Dietrich was bombed out of her home, the Rabaus behaved generously towards her, but in that case, since she was not Jewish, they had somewhat less to fear, and would not have been so crippled in their ability to act.

With the terrors of war over, even the morality of the war itself is a vexed question. The Rabaus describe what happens when they invite a couple whom they are fond of to meet a colleague who has just returned from a visit to England.

Unfortunately, this led to a difference of opinion when Dr Panzer said that she felt a deep sense of guilt, and that every German had to feel the same. The Ullrichs took a different view. They were of the opinion that Chamberlain and all the other politicians had made a deal with Hitler, so that one couldn't throw any blame on the Germans. And we count the Ullrichs among our most valued friends! Yes, indeed, the Germans are a very unusual people.—

3.24

It is through the intimate and confiding letters that pass between Henny and Ilse Heydt that one gets the most lively sense of Henny's earlier life in Germany, including insights into the other members of the Caro family: Ella, Lola and Heinz. They also most tellingly reveal her feelings about Hans Mahnert's marriage – and even hint at what she may think about love in general.

At the end of August 1946, still a few months before the question of Dieter Heydt comes up, Ilse talks about the explanation that Hans Mahnert gave her when he married Wanda in 1941. Henny had asserted some weeks earlier:

I know that political and religious views definitely played a part with him, which even your lines confirm. It is a purely academic discussion, but I would be interested to know what explanations in this regard he gave in his letter to you.

Ilse's reply is surprising:

I cannot remember the exact words of his explanation; at any rate, I remember that he talked not about religion or his world-view, but only of general personal grounds – more or less, that you were not suited to each other. I felt that he had discovered this at a rather unfortunate time, just when you were away. Judging the matter quite neutrally, it can certainly be the case that people drift apart from each other or very suddenly decide that they aren't suited to each other, when 'Mr Right' or 'Miss Right' comes along. But when one considers for what purpose and from what cause you went to England, one must find Hans's attitude quite remarkable. You had yourself sometimes felt – and told me this in confidence – that it was not a grand passion that tied the two of you together. But I nevertheless took Hans for a decent person, who would never leave you, particularly when you were dependent on him.

It wasn't the fact so much as the manner of it that I didn't find fair [Ilse uses the English word]. If you had been able to talk things out face to face, everything would have been fine; you would certainly not have stood in his way. But to do things in this manner behind your back was not nice. He could have waited till the two of you had come to an understanding. That's what I think about it . . .

Ilse mentions that when their friends met up and 'the case of Hans and Henny was discussed in a lively manner', all of them other than herself and Fröschlein were 'on Hans's side', though perhaps they would no longer acknowledge it. She adds:

The most painful of my experiences of the last years is in fact not the loss of my belongings but the changeability of opinions and judgements in the general and the particular . . . Now, as is probably best, the matter is closed once and for all, but I wish you better luck – to compensate you for all your sorrow and to bathe your future life in warmth and sunlight.

Lola is mentioned in a surprising context in the same letter.

I will naturally also write to our dear Shanti. Did you know that actually he was Lola's secret and only love? It is so sad to think about it. Perhaps he doesn't know it himself. I rejoice in my heart that he remains so courageous in life and that he has had so much success. How wonderful it would be to see you two beloved friends once again, despite all disappointments, in the old homeland (that is what it should remain for you *despite* everything that has happened, at least in our hearts).

Heinz too comes in for an unexpected mention.

The news about Hans came to your mother . . . on the day that she found out that the money from your relations for her and Lola's affidavits had already been spent by Heinz. I only heard about this matter later from Fröschlein; and your brave and gracious mother kept all that locked in her heart and continued to show dignity and kindness. I don't know to what extent you are in touch with Heinz and how much you know about this matter, and I don't want to tell you what I still only know in part. Unfortunately, it is all now unalterable.

That her brother Heinz, before leaving for South America, had run through the funds that were intended to help his sister and mother get out of Germany must have been bitter news for Henny. Even in early 1941 before the Soviet Union closed its borders, it was possible, if difficult, to get out, though, with increasing restrictiveness, age limits were being placed on potential emigrants by the German government. Fredy Aufrichtig, however, emigrated, possibly via the trans-Siberian railway, to Shanghai, as did A. G. Belvin's brother Luther. Even if Ella or Lola had not been able to get out, the money would still have helped make their life a little easier.

In her reply, dated 4 October 1946, Henny does not talk about her brother at all. She tells Ilse how happy she is to read her 'words of sincere and heartfelt friendship. Old love never dies, Ilselein, and we two were always attached to each other.' Talking of the mutability of people in general and of Hans in particular, she echoes not only an earlier comment she made to Ilse but also Ilse's own recent words to her:

I am very happy to hear from you that Hans has not changed his world-view; I must have misunderstood both a report from an old friend in Berlin and also your first letter. This is worth more to me than anything else, because nothing disappoints and embitters me so much as when *people* change as suddenly as the weather. I do not resent Hans at all. Everyone is the master of his own fate, and must know what is best for him, and I only hope that he has found a suitable life-companion. Ilselein, all this is absolutely *only for you*, and I would be grateful if you would confirm that to me, and then we will never speak of it again.

About Shanti, Henny writes:

Shanti is fine; in fact, in the next few days he is due to have a small operation on his amputated arm (the shortening of three nerves) because he still continues to suffer pain, but I hope that after this, everything will be all right. Yes, I knew that Lola liked Shanti very much; in general, Lola sought out as friends only those people who were particularly worthy or estimable, such as Fröschlein, Shanti, you, etc. Shanti really has a wonderful heart and such a truly fine character.

Seeking out someone as a friend is clearly not the same as nurturing a secret love for that person. Henny is not normally so evasive, or perhaps elusive. But her comment may not be merely deflective; it could be that deep-seated and intense love was not in her nature, and therefore not something she could particularly empathise with. She may have felt happiest in a strong and sincere friendship with someone whose character she admired; perhaps this was her very interpretation of love. If Henny and Hans were indeed not attached by any grand passion – and Henny does not contradict Ilse on this point – she may well not have felt crushed and heartbroken at Hans's 'faithlessness' so much as disappointed and disillusioned by it. When Ilse later writes to say that it seems that Hans is not happy in his marriage, and that she can't help feeling a bit glad about it, Henny replies:

Although he has, as you can well understand, disappointed me a little, I feel a bit sorry for him because he is a good fellow, though very weak in character. Despite everything, I would have wished to hear that he was happy.—

Yet against these speculations of a passionless relationship, at least on Henny's part, stands the mute evidence of the crumpled and possibly tear-stained poem to her from Hans, so carefully smoothed out again and replaced with its fellows:

Then I am prepared to take this oath before you:
'You will I love, just you alone.
You should be the quiet happiness of my love!'

In the winter of 1946–7, Ilse apologises for not writing more often. She had to nurse her son, who fell ill with 'a heavy, feverish cold'. As for celebrations, she was almost glad that she had to go to work on Christmas Eve, Christmas Day and New Year's Eve, 'for it is exactly on such festive occasions that one is most aware of how alone one is, that even the most beloved ones are absent'. She is trying her best to get her husband released, but it may be a long while yet. 'All the necessary applications are going ahead, but the paper war is so extensive and the instructions so complicated that one person on her own can't begin to attack it. But I am not giving up hope, and am fighting like a lion!'

In one letter she describes her daily march to work, five kilometres each way:

I put on old trousers (that I used for exercise), then an old skirt, and only then a dress, a jacket, a coat, and assorted scarves over my head, for the wind blows hard and I have to tramp over the fields between Waidmannslust and Tegel. Public transport is so bad that I'd rather walk through ice and snow than wait for hours at the shelterless stations. As a result, I've already frozen my toes, despite wearing men's shoes padded with socks. Thank God it is dark in the mornings and evenings and my French colleagues are used to my finery and glad that I always make my long trek and come to work despite everything.

In another, she remembers happier times she shared with Henny:

You would be terribly ashamed if you were to bump into me, with twine instead of laces in my shoes, like an old tramp! That makes me yearn for the summer all the more, when I won't need to put on so much and can look a little more civilised. For as a woman it is in one's nature to be a little vain and concerned with appearances. How happily

296

I would go to the Kadewe [Kaufhaus des Westens: a large department store] with Hennerle once again and buy material and stockings and a thousand pretty little things, as we often used to. Since I don't have all those pretty little things any more (*all* my handbags, *all* my scarves and mufflers, *every one of* my pullovers, everything of fur has been carried off), I feel I look really wretched, and the worst of it is that then some people (those who have never suffered any loss) feel that they can treat us accordingly. This has made me very bitter . . .

In February 1947, Ilse herself falls ill and is confined to bed for some days, but pulls herself together, 'for I am after all the bread-winner of the whole family and can't allow myself to fall seriously ill and lose my job as a result'. She thinks back to Sundays long past, when she and Henny, even in wind and rain, would wander out into the countryside – 'how open you were to everything beau-tiful and could never get enough of the beauties of nature'. Now her Sundays consist of nothing but chores – cleaning out the flat, washing and mending her son's torn socks and dirty, ragged under-wear made out of old clothes, and attending to a thousand small matters that need dealing with.

And on Sunday afternoons my little lad waits for me to take him on my lap and to play songs for him on the piano, all the lovely songs that he so likes to sing: 'Sah ein Knab ein Röslein stehn [A boy saw a little rose]' and 'Komm lieber Mai und mache [Come, lovely May]' or 'Schlafe mein Prinzlein schlaf ein [Sleep, my little prince]'. And then, when I have written another letter to my husband, this day too is over, and I haven't managed to tackle even a thousandth part of the work that awaits me. How I long for a time to come when I can stay at home and get my household going again and when my husband lightens a little for me the difficult struggle for existence.

A month later, when both she and her son fall ill, she writes to Henny:

You can imagine my cares and worries, how often I lie sleepless and find this little scrap of life quite hopeless and not worth the bother. Only then can you truly get a sense of how much good your words and deeds do me, how much they affect me and how they give back to me my trust and belief in humanity.

Ilse's friendship means a great deal to Henny too. In one letter, in which she sends birthday greetings and 'a kiss from Aunty Henny' to Ilse's son, she adds, 'Goodbye, my dear friend, and let me hear from you again soon. I am enormously happy whenever a letter comes from you'; and indeed, all her letters to Ilse, more than to anyone else in the circle, brim with warmth and affection.

Over all this, casting a sort of benison on their friendship, is the presence of Henny's mother, who always stood up for Ilse when the others found fault with her, and to whom Ilse, despite the risks involved, was loving and supportive till the end:

On the birthday of your dear, respected mother, I thought about her with love and painful memory. There is no place where I can lay flowers for her, but she will sense my love across the grave, and there is still someone to whom I can show this love, namely you, my Hennerle. You know that I have forgotten nothing of all that we have shared together of the Good and the Beautiful.

3.25

It was at about this time that Rose Rabau dropped the damning phrase 'since Ilse's Dieter was a Party member and an S.A. man'. There is no mention in Henny's next letter to Ilse of her suspicions or any hint that she has asked Fröschlein to inquire about the matter. It is a brief letter, warm without being intimate.

Since Ilse loved her husband passionately, it is difficult to see how her friendship with Henny would not have been damaged if

Henny had shunned him. But, pending the resolution of the question, it is apparent that Henny does not wish to extend her love for Ilse and her affection for her son to any feeling for her husband. Nor is she willing to feign regard for him or to be obliging to him in any way. In an earlier letter, Ilse had written that her husband, who was a librarian and a bibliophile, had sent a trunk containing his best books – including rare works and first editions – to his parents in Pomerania for safekeeping. In the postwar dispensation, Pomerania had become part of Poland and it was now – owing to politics, bureaucracy and the severance of transport links – almost impossible to get the books back. Ilse wrote, 'My husband is so miserable about his beloved books', and puts forward a proposition to Henny, which is clearly intended as a ploy for getting the books out of Poland and eventually back to the Heydts.

What do you think: is there any sense in making over to you the books that, as I wrote to you, are with my parents-in-law? Would you be able to get them over to yourself by some means, perhaps through the authorities, if they were dealt with as your property? Or would it be impossible, even for you, to get them from there?

Henny's response is not very forthcoming; in fact, she seems almost deliberately to get the wrong end of the stick:

It is really terribly kind of you to think of sending me your books, but I must confess quite openly that I haven't read books in German for years. But I will take the thought for the deed, and thank you warmly for it.

In the course of a discussion on stamps, Ilse veers into a paean to her husband:

Please, please, attach different stamps (i.e. of different values) on the envelope; I collect them eagerly; my husband is very keen on them. I am so proud of him and wish you could get to know each other; you would get along well. You think in the same idealistic way and put great value on a noble character and a good heart, and that's what my husband has. You can well imagine how lonely I have been all these years and how much I have missed him.

Henny is absolutely unresponsive with regard to this prospective meeting. Her only mention of Ilse's husband is to ask if he has been set free.

Finally, in early 1947, Dieter Heydt was set free. He managed to get a post as a librarian at the University of Marburg, far to the west of Berlin. (The town of Marburg, surrounded by hills, stands on the River Lahn, a tributary of the Rhine.) Ilse and her son, now five years old, followed.

Dieter Heydt, a tall and once strong man, had greatly changed during the previous two years. Ilse wrote: 'I am very happy I will be seeing my husband soon; only, he has become quite different through his imprisonment: so shy, uncertain, ill at ease in the world; and it is bound to take a long time before he can get used to the new and totally different conditions of life.'

For her too the change was to prove hard. She would have to abandon the city she had known all her life, and leave her father, her mother and her sister, not knowing when she would see them again. 'But one belongs, after all, with one's husband; we were separated for long enough, and here in Berlin there is no possibility of work for him. Thus, through the economic conditions of the post-war period we have all of us in some way lost our home.'

Being uprooted and transplanted into a less devastated part of the country was not an undiluted advantage, especially since her husband's salary was half what she had earned with the French military administration in Berlin:

Here in the western part of Germany, people have not suffered such loss; they go about in neat and tidy shoes and stockings, in fur coats and nice modern clothes, so that one gets very depressed when one goes

300

around looking like a scarecrow. They don't know much here about Russian atrocities, about plundered houses and homes, and all their cupboards are full of linen and underwear. I feel bitter pain when I see that. And those who have the most are the most hard-hearted.

Worse was to follow. Many of their things, which they had stored under lock and key in the State Archives of the University Library in Marburg, were stolen – presumably by her husband's colleagues.

A basket with all my bed-linen, that I had rescued by pram and rucksack under Russian bombardment at the risk of being killed during our flight, all my towels, kitchen towels, table-cloths, embroidered bed-covers, my vests, my knickers, my petticoats, in brief, everything that is necessary for a housewife has so completely disappeared that I couldn't even change the beds for Christmas, because I now no longer have anything other than what was actually in use . . . We have been badly hit, and I have wept day and night that there are so many bad people in the world, who, after we have suffered so many losses, have now taken our last remaining possessions . . . Even the police will hardly find anything, for in the present conditions of need the things have probably long since been taken to the countryside and exchanged there for meat and fat. For the child's sake, we tried nevertheless to organise our Christmas as beautifully as possible, and we succeeded. For the first time in four years we were all together; we even decorated a tiny Christmas tree.

Dieter Heydt continues to work in the library and to pursue his private research in Etruscan studies. In 1948, however, his qualifications and promotions are de-recognised because they were obtained during the 'Nazi period'. Although eight years previously he was already a graduate civil servant, he has to start again as a trainee. The post he had been promised when he went to Marburg was filled by someone else. Nor did he any longer receive even his meagre salary but only a subsidy, a sort of family support. And, as

Ilse writes: 'because he is only in the preparatory service, he also doesn't have any claim on housing! (We must therefore learn to move like angels in the heavenly spheres.)'

These were hard times for Ilse, compounded by poor health: at one time she suffered from severe anaemia and collapsed in the street from sudden weakness. But throughout all this, she drew strength from the love of her 'two men' and her friendship with Henny, who continued to shower her with affection and whatever gifts she could manage to send.

I myself have resorted to magic in order to provide both my beloved men with a filling meal every day. My little boy is forever calling me 'my little wife' or 'you delicate little thing', and is as tender as a little lover. Early in the New Year he'll be going to school, and we're now trying hard (so far in vain, of course) to get hold of a schoolbag and a slate. We still haven't even managed to get winter shoes for him, and now don't let him out of the room in the cold and damp weather; this, however, doesn't seem to dampen his exuberance and cheerful nature. He also wants to marry me soon, and his daddy is already quite jealous . . .

(Despite my grey hair and the forty years I'll clock up next month, I clearly still stand a chance with young men!)

Though Henny almost never mentions Ilse's husband, she tries to put attractive stamps on her parcels, if not for his sake, then for the boy's; and Ilse appreciates it.

They are, you see, quite crazy about all foreign letters and judge each stamp with the eyes of connoisseurs, to see whether they have it 'already' or 'not yet'. Our boy is not yet six years old, but he can read quite well already, and is an eager stamp-collector. You would be amused by the little lad. Father Christmas brought him an album and a pair of tweezers for his stamps, and now he talks of 'Guatemala' and 'the Dutch Indies' and 'Costa Rica' just like an old salt, and provides his father with serious competition.

These chatty letters are something of a contrast to Henny's own, which, though warm, are brief; and at times Ilse pleads for more. 'I know so little about your present life, little Henny,' she writes in one letter. In another, she says, 'I would so love to hear from you in detail about how and where you live. Do you live in a furnished room, do you cook for yourself, do you have a lot of free time, can you spend a lot of time with Shanti, do you two ever get the chance to get away for a bit?'

In fact, not only Ilse but several of Henny's other friends complain that she doesn't write much about herself. About the present, she is very factual; what she says is almost in the nature of a report to the board. But with no husband and no child, working hard at the pharmaceutical company and living in furnished rooms in a boarding-house in Bayswater, Henny probably had neither much news to give nor the time to give it if she had. As for the past, she never reminisced about it as her friends did. It is quite natural for Ilse to say, 'I still laugh when I recall the stern woman from the Emigration Office who examined you, asking you how one prepared pike interlarded with bacon . . . ah, our present worries are very far from those . . .' Or, 'You have taken so many wonderful walks with me in wind, rain and mist, do you remember? I miss that so much now!' Henny had an abstract and evaluative bent and was less inclined to savour specifics, especially if they were in the past. Nor, unlike Ilse, whose remarks, such as the two above, carried the coda of a sigh, was Henny given to 'if onlys' or 'alases'. She was a realist, an accepter of fate as something lived through and done with. What was the point, she would have said, of trying, through memory, to redeem the unredeemable, if all it left one with was emptiness and unbearable pain?

Worrying about Dieter Heydt's past may also have brought up terrible images, but, as Henny implies in her letters to Fröschlein, she was compelled to do this in justice to her mother and sister, and because she set high standards for character and did not take friendship lightly.

When Ilse asks her for a photograph, Henny promises to have a few taken as soon as the sun comes out, and adds that she thinks she has become more 'English' in her appearance – a remark that Ilse asks her (in vain) to explain, since the photographs themselves are a long time coming. When finally they do arrive, Ilse shelves the discussion of Englishness for questions of greater immediacy:

Which of us is really the slimmer? I am no match for your petite figure; you still have such a delicate waist, whereas I on the whole am somewhat more broadly built, especially in the hips and around the tummy – not even the last few years have altered that, because it's the shape of my frame. Only, now I am very lean about the shoulders and there, where I once used to have a bosom. But I get liver injections for my anaemia now, and feel appreciably better . . .

Through all the hardships of Ilse's life, nature provides a comforting and sustaining strand – sometimes literally so, as when she gathers the first nettles in spring for food; they 'provide us,' she says, 'with such good vegetables (the only ones that we have)'.

But more often there is no need for a practical purpose:

Our joy, as always, is the beauty of Nature; and now the first birds are emerging, the first buds, the first snowdrops, and we go out for walks once again with our little son and enjoy the mild breeze, the first beautiful rays of sunshine.

In April, a month further into the year:

Spring here in this marvellous hilly region is truly beautiful, and the sun shines without the need for coupons, and gives us new strength. We spend our Sundays from quite early on (we bring sandwiches and coffee with us) in a secluded clearing in the woods, far from the frequented paths – above us the sky, around us the chirruping of the birds – and let ourselves be bathed in the radiance of the kind sun. There we hear nothing of politics, of hate, of embitterment, or the usual talk of food and rationing, but feel happy and relaxed. You, dear Henny, know this wonderful feeling for Nature from earlier days, and we want to bring up our son in just this way, not as a dancing boy or in a party tavern or political association.

3.26

Henny's silence regarding Ilse's husband would not have been lost on Ilse; nor, when Fröschlein asked her the question point-blank, would she have been unaware that the answer would probably have been passed on to Henny. The fact that it was Dieter's own political associations that were in question may have been behind Ilse's determination that her son not be brought up in the world of power and demagoguery and ready-made comradeship. But Ilse was keen to emphasise the good in those she liked; the times had been complex and most people had had divided loyalties and purposes. Early in their correspondence, she reminded Henny of how she had tried in the old days to bring peace between herself and others in the circle.

I have thought so often about you and about your idealistic approach, always and despite all differences of opinion to live at peace with all your friends. So it will certainly make you happy to know that I enjoy a friendly relationship with Lili, that she has also already visited me a couple of times, and that I have a warm relationship with the Dietrichs as well.

Henny had replied:

I am glad that you are again on good and friendly terms with the Dietrichs. I am convinced that not only Hans [Dietrich] but also Annerose are fine, sincere people, and I remember only too well how they always expressed themselves against the Nazi system . . .

Lili Würth has also written to me, but my pen rebels when I think of replying to her. Have you ever heard a single word of abhorrence from her for all the monstrous things that happened? . . . Ilselein, I know I can write my views openly to you, because you are, after all, my friend, and I hate insincerity. I also know that you are completely frank with me. If you, like me, had lost your dearest ones through these crazy criminals, you would certainly think exactly the same.

Ilse, out of fairness to Lili and perhaps also because of the implications of Henny's last sentence – for the 'crazy criminals' would certainly have included the Nazi storm troopers – wrote back:

What you write about Lili may be correct, but somehow she was not the worst, and, despite her infected family background, remained true to Lola till the end.

Henny did not ask Ilse directly whether her husband Dieter had been with the SA. Nor did Ilse admit anything further. Nor did Henny question Rose Rabau directly about the remark she had let drop.

When, in the course of a letter in English to Fröschlein – presumably to give her practice in the language – Henny quoted Rose's remark in German, she added: 'Although we would like to know about this matter, we do not want that Ilse or Rabaus should know that we have written to you in this connection.'

Fröschlein, referring to the vague and inconclusive answer she had previously got from Ilse, and to the fact that Dieter had by now been set free, wrote back in June 1947:

[Ilse] was not at Rose Rabau's on the 1st of June, since she had gone with her son to Marburg to see her husband. Hopefully, she will sort things out, but when will she actually be able to make the move? Since I recently had to pass on her regards and to say that she had gone to see her husband, I brought the subject around to him and to the question about him. Rose said that Ilse herself had told her about the matter. But to me Ilse had said, 'No', not as far as she knew. I now also recall that Rose made some sort of remark once that could perhaps have had a connection with this. But I didn't know about it. If I find anything out, I'll write to you, I promise. I helped Ilse too, and she should have told me something of that nature. But she was, as I wrote to you, kind and helpful [to Lola and Ella] and completely irreproachable in her attitude; and she has really won me over as a result.

Henny's side of the correspondence is very incomplete, since she did not carbon-copy everything she typed. But Fröschlein's letters carry no implication that Henny tried in subsequent letters to press the point. Fröschlein, for her part, did not mention anything. She only wrote, about Ilse's prospective move:

She is supposed to be going to Marburg, and despite all her love for her husband, that will be hard for her. Here she has – even if it is tiny – her *own* home; there she will have to live in a furnished room, and what's more in the home of the mother of her husband's first wife, who died. It throws a favourable light on him that he is on good terms with the mother of his late wife, and also with Ilse's parents.

There the matter rested and, short of research by me or by someone else, rests. Part of the reason for Henny's lack of insistence was that she did not want a breach with Ilse, whom she loved. Another was that Fröschlein was beset with worry and grief for her mother, who was incurably ill with cancer.

That last paragraph was from an earlier draft of this book. An exacting friend, who looked over the draft, underlined the words 'research by me', and added above: 'Why not? The plot is unfinished.' His remark was just. Even if Henny herself never did find out the truth of the matter, there had to be an answer one way or another.

Making the final revisions to the book while trying to ascertain facts germane to the story was rather like tying one's shoe-laces while sprinting for the finish. My German publishers were very helpful in suggesting and following up various leads. From an obituary published by a learned society, of which Dr Dieter Heydt was one of the founders, it was possible to trace his career forwards and backwards from the period covered by Ilse's letters. It appears that he went from the University Library in Marburg to another library, where he retired as director in the mid-seventies. They tried to find his files, but the library had recently moved and no one knew in which cellar the documents were buried.

Another promising source was the large centre in Berlin founded by the Americans after the Second World War to document the crimes of the Nazi period. This is now part of the Federal Archive. But detailed information from this institution is protected by law from all but close relatives for a period of thirty years after the subject's death. Since Dieter Heydt died in the early eighties, it will be some years before the archive can be further explored.

What the Federal Archive was able to reveal was limited to his party number and the date, in 1937, when he joined. Since 1933 was when Hitler came to power, 1937 is not a particularly early date for joining the Party. Heydt was therefore probably not motivated by ideological enthusiasm; he would have joined out of ambition, anxiety or blindness, or because it was the line of least resistance. (As he was born in late 1910, he would have been twenty-six at the time.)

Whether he ever joined the SA, that institution so resonant with horror for Henny, we do not yet know. It is true that if he did, the fact that he associated with his wife's circle of friends, several of whom were Jewish, would, had it been discovered, have put both him and Ilse in a difficult, possibly even dangerous, position. But whereas joining the Party might have been necessary for him to maintain his job, joining the SA, as Henny pointed out, was by no means incumbent on him; and it is difficult to see what could explain or justify it.

But these speculations revolve in a vacuum. For the moment, pending the crucial question of his membership of the SA,

Fröschlein's is the only judgement that we have, and it appears to be a heartfelt and balanced one: that Dieter Heydt was probably 'as we would wish him to be'.

3.27

Fröschlein's mother's cancer was inoperable. It swelled her left arm and extended visibly towards her back and in the direction of her heart. She suffered agonising pain and moaned day and night. In June 1947, in despair at having to stand by without being able to help, Fröschlein wrote to Shanti asking him if he could obtain for her some strong painkilling medication such as morphine. Shanti immediately got in touch with friends of his who were doctors. But strict rules governed the use of dangerous drugs such as these, and they could only prescribe it for their own patients. Besides, as Henny discovered, it was forbidden to send morphine from England to Germany.

Fröschlein wished to keep her mother at home, not send her to a hospital. 'If she were taken away now, she would know that she would never return. Why should she suffer that grief? So she will have her old surroundings till the end.— '

Throughout this period, and indeed even earlier, Fröschlein, who was not the most boisterous member of the circle, referred repeatedly to events in the past that had made her laugh. She recalls

all the wonderful hours that I spent at your home – when Shanti was there and Hans [Mahnert] always visited and we always formed such a large company at table, which pleased little Ella. I recalled what silly things Hans and Shanti always did, and as a result came to the story about the film, 'It Happened One Night', and laughed so much, thinking of how Hans lost his jacket and then left his replacement jacket on the train. And do you remember how we sometimes used to laugh about Marga? And your nose always became quite white and tears rolled down your cheeks for laughing and we laughed more and more when we looked at you! Even the memory of it made me laugh! But when it then occurs to one, that all that has gone and will not come again, can never come again, then one is even more saddened afterwards.

She recalls the first time she visited the Caros; Lili brought her along. At first, Fröschlein had been reluctant, not having been invited, but Lili had reassured her that the Caros kept open house.

So I dared to, and how often I came after that! Lola invited me that first time so sincerely to the ceremonial opening of your new room; it was so pretty. We still addressed each other with the polite 'Sie', but all that soon changed. And how Fredy Aufrichtig later always came with his dog, and the young fellows always had great fun with Ella!

At the last Christmas the two of them were to spend together, that of 1946, Fröschlein and her mother send Henny their greetings, and Fröschlein reminds Henny of Christmases past that they spent at the Rabaus'.

Once you came on later with Shanti and, together with Lola, presented me with a little canary. You brought it with you, and while we were sitting in the next room it began to sing and you began to laugh, and I heard nothing!!!! And then Rose lit the Christmas tree, we sang Christmas carols, and afterwards at dinner the presents were joyfully opened! How often during these last years have I looked at the photograph of one of our last Christmas Eves, which Shanti also took part in. But even then Lola already looked so serious. The last few years were already very oppressive, but the worst was still to come. Once, I recall, it was 1942/43, Lola spent her Christmas with us, and I took her home at night. Because of the blackout everything was deserted. Today once again I read the word 'Birkenau' in the newspaper – that was where Lola was; it must have belonged to Auschwitz – and it was as if I had been stabbed.

Music was as double-edged as memory.

On the Day of Repentance [the Wednesday before *Totensonntag*, the last Sunday before Advent] I went with Ilse, who had phoned me shortly before, to a beautiful chamber music concert. There one forgets for once – unless everything is stirred up afresh through the music.

A few months after Fröschlein's letter about her mother's illness, she wrote:

Berlin, 18.10.47

My dear Hennerle,

now I too have no mother any more. On the night of the 9th/10th October, after endless suffering, she went home for ever. Grete [Fröschlein's sister] and I were by her side.

Fröschlein goes on to describe the manner of her mother's death, which was peaceful, and her burial beside her husband 'in the Heerstrasse cemetery, the most beautiful that I know'.

I tell myself again and again that no pain and cold can harm her any more and that she now sees what she has believed in her whole life long; but it is bitter to be left here on one's own. At dusk particularly I feel quite heart-sick. We had often spoken of this parting beforehand. Mother knew how ill she was, and I asked her to greet for me those whom I loved in the land on the other side: my father, Lola, Alice . . .

Two days after Mother's death, I found two letters from her to Grete and to me. She had written them with a trembling hand on the 15th of September; they are her blessings and farewell. My sister said that Mother had almost died as a result; one can see from her handwriting the strain it cost her.— . . .

Many loving greetings from your
deeply sorrowing
Fröschlein

Henny Caro   Dr. S.B. Seth,
27, Kendal St.   19, Queens Road,
London, W. 2   London, N.W. 4   9/11/1947

Dear Froeschlein,

We express our deepest sympathy for your heavy loss. We know how attached you were to your mother and how much you will miss her. But perhaps it can be a small consolation to you that your dear mother has been released from her unending pain. How much we wish we were together with you in these difficult days, and we only hope that you have the strength to get over these painful hours. Because we hadn't heard from you for so long, we already suspected the worst, and unfortunately we were right. Fröschlein, we feel sincerely for you, you can rest assured of that. Sadly, our words cannot be much consolation for you but be convinced that you are not alone and that you have true friends who are always with you, – though so very far away! It is often the case in life that one is parted from those who are the most dear to us; we know that, sadly, from our own deepest experience.

Keep your spirits up and have courage! With heartfelt greetings and embraces,

     Your devoted friends
      [unsigned: carbon copy]

Two months later, since she has still not heard from Fröschlein, Henny shoots off an almost military letter, demanding a reply. The second of two short paragraphs reads:

Please write immediately upon receiving these lines, even if briefly, so that I know how you are. Shanti is also very concerned about you and sends his warmest greetings.

More than a month passes before Fröschlein's reply.

My dear Hennerle,

You had good reason to be angry with me, though I beg you: please don't be! I hope so much that you understand me and that you can imagine how I feel. I have had the constant feeling that I couldn't go on, and when this got worse, I even went to the doctor. It is, as I suspected, my heart. I couldn't get any air, the least action exhausted me, I was always tired and incapable of doing anything . . . Something is not right with the heart muscle and there is also a defect in a valve. In addition to all these things I have been suffering from deep depression. I'm not able to cope with things any more ever since Mother died. I lived for so many years with her, and now I am suddenly alone, and missing her is getting worse and worse . . .

At Christmas and New Year's Eve I was at my sister's. They were very difficult days, the first time I was alone. One only has a mother once, Hennerle. Your mother too was there only for you.—

I am reading Seneca, and it makes me think of how old Herr Mahnert once left his rucksack on the train, and then declared as a distinguishing feature that it contained Seneca's *The Happy Life*. Reading is still the best thing, I always read in bed till I drop off to sleep . . .

Ever your
Fröschlein

3.28

Franz Mahnert, Hans's father, who was so fond of his Seneca, was seventy-five by the time the war was over. He too had been bombed out and had almost nothing to live on. He went to work every day at his old insurance company in order to give himself something to do and to help make ends meet. He lived with his one-time mistress Gerda von Gliszczynski and her daughter Ursel in a house temporarily allotted to them. It appears from her change of name that his mistress had married someone else, but at some stage returned to Franz Mahnert.

As soon as Henny got in touch with her friends in Berlin in the summer of 1946, she sent Herr Mahnert a small gift through the Rabaus, who also lived in Friedenau. He was deeply and decorously appreciative, and wrote to her in English:

My dear Miss Caro,

Just a line to express to you my heartiest thanks for the 50 cigarettes you sent me through Mr. Rabau. It is really *very* nice to have thought of me. You know that we are exceedingly short of cigarettes here, so you can imagine my joy when Mr. Rabau unpacked them! They are *very fine indeed* and I indulge in them to a high degree. Many, many thanks! Much as I appreciate them, I am most sensible of your having thought of me.—

Henny's first reply to him, also in English, refers to earlier letters he wrote, which are not in the file.

Henny Caro   27, Kendal Street,
                                                    London, W. 2.,
                                                    18th July, 1946

My dear Mr. Mahnert,

I was very glad to get your two letters of June 15th and June 23rd from which I could see that you had been in contact with my dear mother and sister in spite of the Gestapo threat and I appreciate this very much. I only wish you are right in your intuition that Lola is still alive!— Only the other day I had a letter from Mr. Wolffsky with whom Lola worked together in the Jewish Committee and who conveyed to me the last greetings of my dear ones. You can well imagine my feelings when I saw the 2 post cards written by my mother and sister which they had sent from the Concentration Camps. I could only recognise their signatures and from the way they wrote these few lines I could see misery, pain and suffering they must have undergone.

It is true that all of us have to die one day, whether we are rich or poor and irrespect of religion or thought and as the Poet puts it in beautiful words:

> Sceptre & Crown
> Must tumble down
> And in the dust be equal made
> With the poor, scythe and spade,

but to die of an unnatural and beastly death as it has been the case with them I can find no solace and peace. You can understand that I hate each and every German who has been connected with the Nazi Ideology. This naturally does not hold good for the people like you who, I know, have always been against the beastly Nazi Regime from the very first day. I know, that some of my old friends changed with the time as the tide changes with the moon and you cannot blame me if I despise such people. I know 'to err is human, to forgive divine', but the way the Nazis have erred is inhuman and *can never be forgiven* and, I hope, never be forgotten.

It is only at the time of adversity that one recognises one's friend, but unfortunately only very few people come through this acid test. I must confess that when I read your first letter for a few minutes I could not place Mrs. v. Gliszczynski, but after a while I did think it could not be anybody else than Miss Garrasch. I am really happy that she proved a good and sincere friend, not only in words but also in deeds and I reciprocate her kind greetings heartily. I personally do not know Ursel, but please also convey to her my best regards . . .

I am often in contact with Arberry's – it was only last Sunday that Dr Seth and myself were invited for tea and dinner at their flat. Naturally we talked about you and be assured, dear Mr. Mahnert, that your relations and your friends – I hope you consider Dr Seth and me as one – will try our very best to help you as much as we can . . .

With kindest regards and best wishes for yourself, and hoping to hear from you soon again,

    Yours

        [unsigned: carbon copy]

315

The lines from the playwright and poet James Shirley (1596–1666), which form part of one of my own favourite poems, are slightly misquoted. The last line should read: 'With the poor crooked scythe and spade'. Herr Mahnert wrote in response to this letter: 'Thanks for the nice poetical verses you quote in your letter, they are beautiful indeed and I shall keep them in memory.' He adds: 'I assure you, we very often think of your dear mother and sister. If we cannot see them again (now there seems to be no hope), let us trust, that they did not suffer too much; they will both be constantly in my and Hans' memory.— '

Mr Mahnert refers several times to his son. He even mentions that Shanti has been in touch with him – 'And how is dear Dr Seth? He has lately written to Hans telling him that the last operation he had to undergo had not the desired effect. We were sorry to hear that.' Not once, however, does Henny refer directly or indirectly to Hans in her correspondence with Mr Mahnert senior.

Mr Mahnert, for his part, never suggests directly that she write to Hans. Both he and Henny realise that only by steering around the rock can they keep the barque of their friendship from foundering.

But in June 1948, one of the Mahnert family's friends – a teacher, Fritz Bruse, whose piano, now destroyed by the flames, Henny used sometimes to play – writes a very informative and even – despite its slightly facetious tone – serious letter on the subject of the Mahnerts, both father and son. He endorses Henny's appraisal of Herr Mahnert as 'a man of honourable character and absolutely dependable, as one is used to with the older generation'. He describes visiting him in his pleasant three-room flat, the only disadvantage of which is that it is on the first floor, 'so that one can literally not understand a single word when a lorry goes past on the road'.

They have also got themselves a little furniture and could live quite snug and contentedly if only Herr M were not quite so tottery. In 1945 he was still studying Russian, quite an achievement, after all, when one considers the difficulties of this language. When I visited him three weeks ago, he had given up this particular quirk in order to sink into *Faust*. He finds consolation in that, as others do in the Bible. As always, I was amazed at his mental agility, but he gets tired very quickly and complains bitterly about his bad nerves. Sleep eludes him and he has no strength for an outing to the Krumme Lanke [a lake near the Grunewald in Berlin]. Frau v. G. looks after him well, but because of that, he is entirely under her thumb. May God preserve him.

Fritz Bruse says that Hans Mahnert is in an office in Munich, working for the American military administration as an interpreter; he chose to go there because 'the West seems to him to offer more security'.

Still, he went only half-heartedly, for he lives there like a grass-widower in the barracks. He has left his two-room flat here in Neu-Westend with all the fittings and likewise his wife. So no one is satisfied with the solution, neither he nor his wife, neither Whisky – his wire-haired terrier – nor I, for I used to visit him frequently. Now the crazy currency business [the postwar currency reform in the Western zones] has come along and spoilt things, so that for the time being he can't come back to Berlin even if he wished to.

Hans's wife works in an elegant ice-cream parlour in Berlin, which is doing 'fabulously well, and she too earns a fair amount of money'.

One has to admit, at any rate, that she's flexible and copes well with life. But the old man complains that she has no affection and no time for him. One flying visit every six months or so. I close with the remark that Hans wishes to emigrate to New Zealand because he feels that nothing much is happening in his German fatherland any more. [Herr Bruse jocularly uses the archaic spelling *teutsch* for 'German']. I think he could have found an easier way of going about things.

And that, dear Fräulein Henny, is the first chapter. Hopefully it will arrive there safe and sound and find you similarly safe and sound in

Merry Old England. The sequel will follow, and until then many warm greetings from your old friend

   Fritz Bruse and wife

Nor does Gerda von Gliszczynski, Herr Mahnert's old friend and mistress, forbear from comment when she writes to Henny. Her letter consists of two long, tumbling, chatty paragraphs cramming the writing-paper to the full; new sentences spring into existence before the previous ones are closed. She writes in the old German script, slanting strongly to the right. Her a's and o's are often left open to the elements, and she never crosses her t's.

Friedenau 15. 1. 47

My dear Fräulein Caro,

   Today I simply wish to thank you very warmly for all the marvellous things that you and dear Dr Seth have sent us. I doubt that one could picture the joy that such gifts produce. Above all, the stockings were such a grand present had they been second-hand ones I would have been just as thankful, hopefully you don't have to go without yourself. Well, may god reward you doubly . . . Ursel and I, we are thank God still in good health and spirits only Herr Mahnert's health has really gone down recently, but one can't after all demand too much, he will be 77 in February. He leaves the house every day at eight in the morning and returns at a quarter to seven at night, it is naturally very hard for him and I feel terribly sorry I'd like so much to go to work instead of him but then it would be even more dreadful because I can still go out now and get potatoes and wood. He would already have starved and frozen if he hadn't had me. *No one* asks after him quite the opposite at best I must keep helping him, one only shows up when one needs one's father's help.

She tells Henny about the adventures of their common friend, Friedel Alexander, who is Jewish and who lived secretly for a long time with various people. She herself put Friedel up in her summerhouse in her large allotment outside Berlin until it and the garden itself were flattened by bombs.

318

Then she went to Hamburg and in fact got accommodation in a Nazi Party model factory as Frau Stephan whose husband had fallen in the war. What utter mockery for a Jew to enter a Nazi factory! But it worked well till the British marched in, then she was Fräulein Alexander once again and went with her brother Klaus who was a British soldier and her sister Ursel to Cape Town.

Henny replies about a month later. She expresses great pleasure at the cheek and courage – chutzpah is the word that probably best describes it – of Friedel Alexander, writing about her and her sister and brother: 'How nice that they are all together in South Africa.' Perhaps one should note that, what with an unequal voting system already in place there and Apartheid soon to be imposed, Friedel Alexander will soon find herself in the position of belonging to the oppressing race.

I remember Shanti Uncle mentioning the blonde-haired Alexander sisters more than once as we pored over old photographs. Until she realised that they were Jewish, their teacher used to point them out as the epitome of Aryan physiognomy. Their mother, a great royalist, used to correspond with the exiled Kaiser.

Regarding the glancing remark about Hans, Henny writes, elliptically:

With respect to the further contents of your letter, it is unfortunately the case in life that one is often disappointed in people. I believe, and I have in the meantime learned, that the best principle is not to expect too much of people, and then one is spared any disappointment.

Another voluble letter from Frau von Gliszczynski follows, containing still more pungent remarks about Hans.

Friedenau, 18. 3. 47

Dear Frl. Caro,

. . . Ursel and I are thank goodness in good health still, only as regards Herr Mahnert we could wish for better he recently had a couple of heart attacks and I was very worried about him, for the last eight days he has been going to work again but it is a big struggle and is really too much for him.

She mentions that all their potatoes have frozen because they don't have a cellar in the house, and that she often gets up at 5 a.m. to search for food, coming back with perhaps just a couple of potatoes after midnight. The farmers sell nothing except for barter and, since she and Herr Mahnert have lost everything, they have nothing to exchange.

I doubt anyone can really imagine what life is like here. But we mustn't give up hope perhaps for us too one day the sun will shine above all I wish it for Herr Mahnert it's not so bad for Ursel and me we'll come through all right. Yes dear Fräulein Caro, who could have thought it in the days when we lay happy and carefree in the sun on the shore of the Sacrower See. Thank you very much once again for the lovely things that you have sent me they *really* gave me a lot of pleasure Ursel too is very happy such a young person apart from that has no pleasures only work and on top of that not even enough to eat. You are quite right one is often disappointed in people I myself have also often found that to be so, the one person who is really sincere and good is Herr Mahnert unfortunately his son doesn't take after him he has nothing of the father in him the father is the very essence of reliability there is no relying on the son I can't write any more but at least you haven't lost anything these words for your eyes only.

Now I have told you something about our lives and not bored you too much I hope. Please give Herr Dr Seth my very warm greetings and tell him I'd like to serve him braised kidneys once again he liked eating them in those days.

3.29

Franz Mahnert by now has decided not to struggle on in his elegantly unidiomatic English:

11 January, 1947.

Dear Fräulein Caro,

I would like to write to you today in our mother tongue. My clumsy English stands out too much against your smooth English, and besides, it'll go faster. We have power cuts here, as before, except that it's usually eight hours now, and we will have to adjust to that, for soon it will be darker than in Egypt during the time of the great darkness.

Henny replies (in English) with her typical mixture of affection, sympathy, generosity and tact. She is sending him some coffee, bouillon cubes, sardines, flour, chocolate, cigarettes and socks; in addition, she says, 'we are afraid that we cannot totally remove the "Finsternis" [darkness] of which you speak in your letter, but we do hope that our birthday candles will bring a little light on your birthday'.

Franz Mahnert's response, typed as usual (and in German), but with shaky underlinings (under the words printed here in italics), came a few days later, in early February 1947.

Dear Fräulein Caro,

Yesterday, to *celebrate* my birthday (the parcel arrived exactly on the day) I received the things sent by you and Dr Seth together with your kind wishes.— I thank you warmly in my name and also for Frau v. Gl. and Ursel, who shared my pleasure. May the good wishes which both of you expressed for me be fulfilled, for in these hard times and this unmerciful winter, cheering up is urgently needed. Such kind lines from you and your friendly and generous gifts contribute to that. *Many, many thanks*.— What you have sent us is extraordinarily beautiful, but the splendid candles in the most beautiful colours cannot be sacrificed to the blackouts, – that's what we *intend* now, but nevertheless we *have to* use them.

He goes on to describe a present from Shanti and Henny that Henny had not mentioned in her letter:

Now try to imagine my astonishment when on my birthday Frau Rabau brought round the (long-sleeved) pullover, which I put on immediately, for here it is still *like the North Pole* – 15 below zero with a raw east wind; the other morning it was 20 below.— For that, I mean, for the pullover, I thank you both *most especially*.— I'm even told that I look very youthful in it – but I'm not old yet anyway!— For the cigarettes, unfortunately, I cannot thank you, someone else will have to do that for me, someone who apparently regards cigarettes as highly as I do. But 'Tout comprendre c'est tout pardonner'.— I'm not resentful or malicious and don't say: 'Let him choke on them.'— Why should someone else not have something!— . . .

Who knows whether we will ever see each other face to face again. In England too, things don't appear entirely rosy; we read today in the newspaper of extensive power cuts. Now goodbye – may things go as well for you as you deserve. Warm greetings, also from Frau v. Gliszczynski and Ursel; and once again MANY THANKS!

    Your ancient
    F. Mahnert

So his letters continued, sometimes cheerful, sometimes fraught with loneliness, for neither Hans nor his wife visited him much. In August 1947 he wrote (in English once again):

Your little parcel was handed to me on the 29th ult. and was a relief: I would have had to use twine for my boots, had you not been so kind as to send me the laces. *Many thanks* also for the other things . . . When you have some time to spare please let us know a little about yourself. Are you accustomed to the climate there and to the people? We are glad to know you have a good and reliable friend there in the person of Dr Seth. He IS a good fellow!— It is not nice, to think that we shall very probably never meet again. Well, we have after all nice souvenirs,— we have lived during a time which the present youth will never see, I suppose, here in Germany. You can hardly form an idea as to how things are here, all people thin and haggard and in fear of the coming winter, without coal (or with a ridiculous small quantity thereof) and, for the greatest part, without window glass!— But never trouble the trouble until the trouble troubles you.— Meanwhile Mrs. v. Gliszczynski does all she can to keep the old man alive.— Please write to us when you have time.

The dignity-preserving laces came, unbeknownst to Herr Mahnert, as a result of a request from Frau von Gliszczyinski, who asked for nothing for herself. Earlier, Herr Mahnert, again asking for nothing for himself but news of his friends, requests Henny (again, in English) to send something for Frau von Gliszczynski:

You were kind enough to ask me in your last letter what we needed here. If I am not abusing your kindness, I would say that Mrs. v. Gliszczynski would thank you very much if you could send her a pair of stockings, *used of course*, and some underwear (undies) also worn, if you have some. She possesses *one* single pair of stockings, in an *awful* state and no means to get any here.— We unhappily lost all and everything by the bombs!

This letter was followed by one handwritten in German on both sides of two smallish pieces of paper. In contrast to the tremulous underlining of a previous letter, this is marvellous handwriting – clear, stylish, economical, full of character; spare and yet rich. But Herr Mahnert is seventy-eight, and in the last year of his life.

His final letter is typed in English during the Berlin blockade and airlift, three months before his death.

Franz Mahnert
Berlin, Friedenau
Rheinstr. 48 I   11 July 1948.

Dear Miss Caro,

I wrote to you last on 21 April.— Having leisure, much more than you have, I just want to drop you a line with a view of hearing about you and dear Dr Seth. We here hope and wish that you are both in good health and spirit. Mine is not good unhappily – Dr Seth will tell you about that ugly illness of heart trouble I am fighting with (angina pectoris).— The worst is that there is no medicine to be had here in Berlin that would release my pains a little when I suffer an attack,— the pains are *awful* indeed and I then wish my life to come to an end.— In spite of that the heart is a wonderful thing,— 300 throbs per minute would make 12,280,000,000 in 78 years! You just see how an old man employs his time! But I know one should not complain if thousands and thousands of other people are equally suffering.

While he is writing, the sky is heavy with noise: three hundred and eighty planes have landed in the last twenty-four hours to help supply West Berlin, which is surrounded by Russian-controlled territory, with food. There seems to be no hope of a diplomatic solution.

The recent monetary reform, as a result of which people had to give up all their cash and received sixty Deutschmarks each in exchange, has left everyone poor except those who own houses or land. Everything has broken down, says Herr Mahnert: salaries can only be paid in part, life insurance policies have dropped to a tenth of their value; bank deposits have, in his view, certainly been lost, people have no money even to pay their rent; and since there are now two currencies in Berlin, it is a juggling act to know exactly when to use the Deutschmark and when the eastern currency, whose derisory name, the wallpaper-mark, reflects its comparative worthlessness. As he remarks, with a sardonic bitterness rare in him:

It's all *very nice*!— You may be glad to be over there, life is worth living there to be sure. It is scandalous here; hungry people, sick people wherever you are.— But it seems that the whole world is not satisfied.— I thought Transvaal to be a little paradise, but it seems it is not, Miss Alexander lately wrote us that she felt unhappy.— From my Cambridge relatives [the Arberrys] I have not heard since months, neither from [my relatives in] Cairo,— may be there are letters blocked by the Russians.—

Weather is very bad here, no Summer at all, rain and rain and *cold*. We are often talking of you both and are sending you our kindest regards, meanwhile all good to you and dear Dr Seth, Mrs. v. Gliszczynski and Ursel join with us.—

Ever your old,

F. Mahnert

3.30

Item: a black-bordered notice sent in a black-bordered envelope to 'The Rabau family, Ber.-Friedenau, Kirchstr.'; it looks as if the address has been written by Ursel. The Rabaus sent it on as a memento to Shanti and Henny.

On Sunday, 24 October 1948,
after a brief but severe illness our beloved father and father-in-law,
our devoted friend and comrade for many years

Franz Mahnert

passed away peacefully at the age of 78.

In deep sorrow

Dr. Hans Rudolf Mahnert
and his wife Wanda
Gerda von Gliszczynski
and her daughter Ursula.

Berlin-Friedenau
Rheinstrasse 48.

The funeral will take place on Friday, 29 October at 2 p.m. at the Friedenau Cemetery on Stubenrauchstrasse.

Am Sonntag, dem 24. Oktober 1948 entschlief
sanft nach kurzem, schwerem Leiden mein lieber
Vater und Schwiegervater, mein langjähriger, treuer
Freund und Kamerad

Franz Mahnert

im Alter von 78 Jahren.

In tiefer Trauer

Dr. Hans Rudolf Mahnert
und Frau Wanda
Gerda von Gliszczynski
und Tochter Ursula.

Berlin-Friedenau
Rheinstraße 48.

Die Beisetzung findet statt am Freitag, dem 29. Oktober um
14 Uhr auf dem Friedenauer Friedhof in der Stubenrauchstraße.

Franz Mahnert's death notice.

3.31

Henny Caro   27, Kendal Street,
                                                 London, W. 2,
                                          28th November, 1948

Dear Frau v. Gliszczynski,

The news of the sudden passing away of our dear friend has struck both Dr Seth and me most painfully, and I can understand only too well your great loss. I would like to express my deepest condolences to you on behalf of both of us. We held old Herr Mahnert in great esteem, and we have never forgotten how, during the terrible days of November 1938, at the risk of the gravest danger to himself, he kept one of our best Jewish friends hidden. We ourselves have the feeling of having lost a true friend, despite the fact that we are far away.

I have heard the details of the funeral from my friends the Rabaus. How good it was that Herr Mahnert had you at his side, so that at least he did not die utterly alone.

I hope that in these difficult days you find a support in Ursula [Ursel]. Please greet her from me. Warm greetings to you, also from Dr Seth.

Your

[unsigned: carbon copy]

Fredy Aufrichtig – of whom Franz Mahnert had enquired in one of his letters when he heard he was in Shanghai – was probably the friend he had protected during Kristallnacht and the days that followed. In September 1949, about a year after the death of old Mr. Mahnert, Fröschlein wrote in a letter to Henny:

Frau von Gliszczynski had a letter from Fredy. Old Herr Mahnert always stored Fredy's things safely for him, although he had said that if Hans demanded them, they had to be given to him, since Fredy had given them to Hans and not to Herr Mahnert for safekeeping. Hans has

had them handed over to himself, and is supposed to have just sold
Fredy's mother's watch. I can hardly imagine Hans would do that, but
his wife, no doubt, has a very bad influence on him. It is said that she
wears the rings that belong to Fredy. But at least these things are still
there. Should I do anything on Fredy's behalf?

Also in the same month, Margarethe Bruse, who, unlike her
husband Fritz, had not met Herr Mahnert after the war, wrote of
his son:

Since the funeral of old Herr Mahnert, we haven't heard anything more
of Hans Mahnert. He seems to be inwardly and outwardly entirely
separated from his wife . . . Hans Mahnert once said to my husband,
'My father often gets letters from Henny Caro, I am really surprised
that she doesn't write to me.' I told my husband that that was a bit too
much to ask. On another occasion, my husband told him, 'When I met
your bride, I knew at once that she wasn't the wife for you.' And he
replied, 'Why didn't you tell me so at the time?' I find him pretty naïve.

Hans Mahnert now largely disappears from these pages.

3.32

A different Hans, for a short while, comes on.

The Dietrichs – Hans and Annerose – were at the heart of the
circle of friends. They have been mentioned before in passing; they
are now introduced in their own right as the last of Henny's Berlin
correspondents.

They are unique among these for a number of reasons. For one
thing, they lived not in the western part of Berlin in a sector administered by the British, the Americans or the French, but in the
eastern part, in the sector administered by the Russians. Nor, unlike
the others, were they within fairly easy reach of the centre. Their

house was on the very outskirts of Berlin, where, as the Rabaus wrote, 'the foxes say goodnight'. At first, only distance and poor transport separated them from their friends; then they were prised apart by the events of history: currency reforms, intersectoral passes, and finally – beyond the chronological range of these letters – a wall.

Second, Hans was a bureaucrat during the war, but neither he nor Annerose ever joined the Nazi Party, though it would have been greatly to their advantage to do so. Later, they would avoid joining the Socialist Unity Party, or SED, which was supported by the Soviet military administration, and were to suffer as a result. Their spirit encapsulates in a sense the struggle of private individuals against the domination of the heavy-handed, inclusivist state.

Third, Hans Dietrichs's personality is a particularly winning one in its straightforwardness and lighthearted nobility; his love for his wife, his affection for his friends, his delight in music, his pleasure in and struggles with nature speak well not only of him but of all those who, like Henny and Shanti, sought or obtained his friendship. His style or, more accurately, styles of writing are also wonderfully lively – whether serious or humorous, formal or colloquial, direct or convoluted (as only German can be).

Fourth, Annerose's love for and memory of Henny's mother help bring her to life.

Even more with the Dietrichs than with Henny's other friends, I feel that I, as writer and intermediator, am somewhat superfluous. Hans and Annerose talk themselves into existence through their words. Anything more than the lightest commentary on their letters would seem ponderous.

Hans Dietrich's first letter begins with a curious tentativeness and formality of language, reminiscent almost of Henry James or Thomas Mann, which, however, does not belie his deep affection for Henny and Shanti.

Berlin-Wilhelmshagen, 30th January, 1947

Dear Henny,

Towards the end of this month a communication from our dear Rose Rabau provided us with a quite particular joy, which has done us a great deal of good in these joyless times. Shanti and Henny, friends from better days, have thought about us and have thereby shown us that the bands of friendship from former times, despite all events, still continue to exist. Our friends now staying in England were not infrequently the subject of our conversation and the cause of the question of whether they would stand by us even today. We are glad with all our heart that this question has now been answered in the affirmative, and to this answer we attach the hope that in the future our friendly relations will be hindered only by spatial separation. On a bitterly cold Sunday morning this year, even before your thoughts about us were made known to us, I stood on the piece of land in Neu-Venedig that still remains ours, and from the shore looked at the children who were enjoying themselves on the shining ice, and my thoughts turned inevitably to how, years earlier, on just such a Sunday, we two went for a winter's walk across the ice when all the other agreed participants from our circle had pulled out on account of the cold in order to remain at home and in bed! Do you still recall that day? We then arrived in Schmöckwitz and travelled homewards hungry and chilled through. Long behind us lies that day; the following years brought blessings to no one in our circle and burdened each of us with his share of hardship and unhappiness in the world.

Hans goes on to describe what has happened to them. In 1939, he was immediately drawn into war service and appointed an administrative officer. In January 1945, their home in Karlshorst was destroyed by an attack from the air. They lost all their possessions. They were excluded from access even to the ruins because the Soviet military government had made Karlshorst its seat. At the time of the collapse of the country, they were separated from each other for weeks until they were almost miraculously reunited in May. At the beginning of 1947, they were living in the attic of the small house that had once belonged to Annerose's parents but was now owned by others. Annerose's mother had been forced to sell her property to help Hans and Annerose survive. Annerose's parents had died shortly thereafter of malnutrition, as had Hans's father.

But, as Hans stoically states, the successor to his former department employed him again, 'and so we count ourselves among the lucky ones who have a home and can live without material need. In addition, we are in reasonable health.'

Annerose writes more colloquially:

My dear Henny,

We have often spoken of you in the last few years, and in my imagination I have written a great deal to you by way of consolation. How great is the gap that our Lola has left in our circle of friends. It will never be closed. The parting from your dear and admired mother was very hard for me. My dear Hennerle, I know what you have lost, and we would give everything if we could have spared you from these events, this terrible news . . . We will never forget the hours that we spent together in your parents' house with your family. The consoling words of your dear mother, 'God gives us no more to bear than we are capable of bearing', have often given me the strength to take heart once more after the nights of bombing and after being bombed out, as I rummaged around in the dirt for weeks on end to see what I could save. Because Hans was not there, and we were also not Party members, I had no help from the state or the Party. But good friends, you know, . . . our Uncle Jazko came daily to help . . . I was very proud that all the things that Jazko and Rose had left with us could be rescued as well as the big package from Lola that she left with me for safekeeping on one of her visits. Unfortunately, all our work was in vain.

Annerose describes how, through bombing and parting, confusion, lack of transport and compulsory relocations, everything was lost, including the parcel from Lola, which, as she says, would have been an irreplaceable keepsake for Henny. She mentions Lili sympathetically; she knows of the breach, months earlier, between her and Henny, but says that when she herself was in misery and despair, it was Lili who had got her released from army employment and transferred to her own firm, which had been moved out of Berlin.

A letter from Annerose, undated:

My dearest Hennerle,

in remembrance of the 23rd, Lola's birthday, our innermost greetings. Hans and I will never forget the time we spent with your family and I am grateful to have these memories – something that no one can ever rob us of. Memory gives one strength and distance from this life, which appears so hard to bear – a wise saying that I owe to your dear and greatly admired mother, whose deeper meaning I only fully grasped in my own times of hardship. Our Lola! We miss her in our circle, we miss her, every one of us. Do you know, I sometimes think, when people who were earlier declared dead return home, that perhaps we too may live to see such a miracle, and that our Lola too will come back . . .

On Sunday we talked so much of the summer of 1938, when Shanti so suddenly surprised us. Do you still remember that marvellous Sunday on the Wannsee and those many happy hours?

It is strange to think that it was on the Wannsee, with all that the name of that idyllic lake was later to conjure up, that Shanti, sick of Edinburgh and homesick for Berlin, surprised his friends in the year before the war. Kristallnacht had not yet occurred, and it appears that Jews were still allowed to go to parks and forests and lakes around Berlin. Or was it that Henny and Lola just ignored the prevailing atmosphere and went about in the security of the company of their Christian friends?

A letter from Hans Dietrich on 17 December 1947, four days after Henny's birthday:

Dear Hennerle and Shanti,

On the pitiful heaps of rubble that are all that is left of our beloved old Berlin, white snowflakes fall ceaselessly down from the sky and announce that it is once again winter; and somewhere in our unconscious we also become aware that Christmas is at the door. This festival, that was at one time celebrated nowhere more intimately and inwardly than here in Germany, will once again make us feel melancholy and wistful when one is forced to think of all that Christmas used to bring us by way of edification and joy and love, and that it now for the third time and to an ever-increasing extent denies us. We look back at the Christmases before 1933 [the year Hitler came to power] and particularly to the wonderful hours that our circle of friends celebrated in familiar togetherness and remember most particularly the loved ones who were with us then and can be so no longer. In this snow our thoughts and all our good wishes are also with you. May the 'Merry Christmas' that we now call out to you two dear ones be fulfilled for you in the truest sense of the greeting.

After discussing the conference then going on among the occupying powers in London, which offered a glimpse of peace and reasonable conditions of life only to break up in bitter wrangling, Hans goes on to say that, as a result, the borders between the various sectors of Berlin might well become as strictly controlled as the borders between the various occupied zones of Germany.

A visit to the Rabaus or to Fröschlein would then make the acquisition of an intersectoral pass necessary, and if the occupying powers were to establish the basis for the issuing of intersectoral passes as rigorously as for interzonal passes, in the future one could just as well live in, say . . . Moscow or Orel or somewhere else in the USSR. Whether it will get to be as bad as this, no one knows; that it has already become worse than one could ever have foreseen, we actually know from all too bitter experience.

It is at about this time that Hans sends Shanti, who must at one stage have collected stamps, an unusual gift, ironic in its echoes of occupying powers:

[It] makes our position easier to bear when we are not always the recipients of the kindness of friends, but can also enjoy the elation of giving pleasure. *That's why* I request you and dear Shanti too to appreciate the gifts enclosed in this letter and to accept them accordingly. I refer to a gift for Shanti, whom we remember among other things for what one might call his 'heated discussions' with Hans Mahnert in his capacity as a philatelist. It is a very great rarity for connoisseurs among stamp-collectors, namely, a postcard from the Boxer Rebellion of 1901, to which the then valid overprinted stamps of all the intervening powers (England, France, Russia, USA, Japan, China and Germany) were attached and on which the individual postmarks of the military postal authorities of every single power were stamped. We hope that Shanti will be made as happy by this addition to his collection as we wish with sincere hearts to make such joy possible.

In the same letter, Annerose offers to help Henny with her business affairs in Berlin, just as Fröschlein has been helping her friends the Haacs.

Did you, Lola or your mother have assets that were confiscated – savings account books, bank accounts, furniture and so on? I only wish to remind you to leave no stone unturned in an effort to rescue something at least . . . It can naturally not bring back to life one's beloved relatives, but you are certainly entitled by law to concern yourself with the estate and the inheritance. If you have not yet given thought to the matter, I will gladly deal with it, and learn whatever is necessary from Fröschlein, who has a sound knowledge in this field. It could, after all, provide you with some savings for your old age.

In due course, as is later described, Henny would indeed take up this matter, though with Fröschlein as her representative and champion.

But the Dietrichs are soon to face their own vicissitudes. Two months later, in early April 1948, Annerose writes to say that Hans has been sacked.

The actual grounds are that he did not join the Socialist Unity Party or S.E.D., the party that is supported by the Soviet military administration in the central administration. Many Nazis prove their true democratic retraining by immediately joining the S.E.D., thus becoming white sheep and innocent angels! We didn't belong to a party earlier and don't want to choose the same system, only under a different name. We are spared nothing; we thought we empathised with all of you and with Uncle Jazko, but when one experiences it oneself it goes much deeper and the empathy is all the more pronounced. For 20 years Hans has built up and worked hard for his job for life, despite all the Nazi hatefulness, as you all know; and in 10 minutes he has to leave the firm and is told he doesn't need to go there any more. Such is the 'democratic freedom' of the eastern half of Germany!

Hans adds a few lines in a hand which is clearly disordered by anger. First he mentions how Henny's gifts have given Annerose great pleasure.

My Annerose has written eloquently about her pleasure. And I am so pleased too, for Annerose's pleasure is just that for me as well; so my warm thanks too.

Then, he analyses his position both psychologically and with economic objectivity:

Annerose has also told you about the loss of my job. I am still pretty stunned, and am filled with rage, the sort one calls a 'stink rage' or livid fury. Well, that in itself won't get one anywhere, and so something must be done. It is going to be hard, because during the last decade old employees have found it difficult to be re-employed, and that's even more true today, now that business in Berlin is crippled – and the disbanding of all the old Reich authorities and banks has naturally itself created an army of older employees seeking work. But one mustn't give in to despair or lose faith in oneself. So I too will bear up! I hope I will be able to send you some better news.

Fondest wishes to both of you dear ones

Your   Hans

There follows an almost pastoral interlude.

Three weeks after his previous letter, Hans, in oddly high spirits, describes his adventures in his allotment, or *Schrebergarten*. Gardens such as these were an institution of social policy dating back to nineteenth-century Berlin; urban people were allotted plots in green belts for weekend use and the planting of flowers, fruits and vegetables. Those who were bombed out during the war often shifted there, especially if they had built a small summerhouse or hut; it was in one such *Schrebergarten* that Gerda von Gliszczynski gave refuge to her friend Friedel Alexander, when she was in hiding from the Nazis.

Hans writes:

I have devoted my involuntary holidays to hard work in the garden; I will tell you something about it. First of all: working in the garden in this really warm and sunny April has given my face a deep-brown tan; I don't look at all like those usually so pale-faced Berliners; my hands certainly resemble those of a lumberjack, they look so cracked and callussed! No matter – it's only external! I have 18 apple trees, 1 pear tree, 3 plum trees, 4 cherry trees, 8 peach trees, 4 hazelnut trees, about 30 black- and redcurrant bushes, 15 gooseberry bushes and several raspberry bushes. The blossoms are almost over; I had an anxious night with a night frost two days ago, but it seems to have passed once again without much damage, and now we hope in our hearts that the heavens will grant us an excellent harvest of fruit. In addition, potatoes, sugar-beets, peas and beans, carrots and other greatly sought-after things have been entrusted to the earth and now it only remains to hope that the heavens reward all the effort and work I have expended. You know that our little garden lies by the water (an arm of the River Spree!). I've used that fact to lay out an improvised fishing-rod – and guess what, yesterday a little eel even felt sorry for me and fell into my trap, or that of my pathetic apparatus! I was very proud of this catch, to which were added a few *small* whitefish, caught in a similar fashion, and Annerose was happy not to have to worry once again about what to cook! . . .

I have also decided to take up the violin again in earnest. Lili Würth will lend me a violin, and Herr Landau (the plump lark!) has promised me printed music and general practice at his home (he is the happy possessor of a piano). With this activity I hope to obtain temporary release from the all too material realities of our German existence.

In the event, Hans, after much effort, found a job with fewer perks but a higher salary and greater responsibility. It had an impressive title too: he became head of the Department for Financial Accounts at the Municipal Housing and Housing-Estate Construction Company. His crop, however, the nursling of his involuntary leave, did not fare well and gave him 'nothing but great sorrow'.

After a marvellous and richly promising season of blossom on fruit tree and bush, there came a nasty night of frost that shattered all my hopes of harvesting and preserving. April and May then brought a serious drought that hindered the growth of all vegetation, and the continuously cold nights and, recently, days as well have hampered things yet further. Instead, pests and vermin of all kinds celebrate real orgies everywhere, and one can't get the better of them because there is still a shortage of suitable chemical pesticides and insecticides. Nevertheless, undaunted efforts are continuing, and hopes are still high that the harvest will eventually recompense one for all one's pains.

So much for us. Surely the time will come again when in our letters we can report predominantly our joys and hopes, and there is less of care and sorrow. Give us the pleasure soon of having some news from you. It is always wonderful to hear from time to time from dear friends that there are places in the world where life is indeed also no picnic but whose inhabitants are permitted, far from the pressures of the all-pervading power of political error and the consequences of a no less insane war, to live as everyone would wish to. Then we can picture for ourselves how wonderful it will be when we too at last reach the same point.

Kind greetings to both of you

Your Hans

The Berlin blockade and airlift, already seen from West Berlin through the eyes of old Mr Mahnert, find Hans Dietrich in a cynical and Annerose in an indignant mood. They get a letter out to their friends by posting it in West Berlin, thus avoiding the Russian censors.

Bln – Wilhelmshagen, 5 August 1948
Wilhelmstr. 68.

Dear Hennerle and Shanti,

With one bold leap over the air bridge this brief letter comes to you to ask after your well-being and to give you a sign of life from us. We haven't heard from each other for a very long time, and it strikes us as time to alter this state of affairs.

That we live in an interesting city is something that very likely the whole world now knows; for us it would be a good thing, however, if Berlin were less interesting, and that life here on the other hand were a bit more uniform and uncomplicated. One might well assume, as 'lucky' inhabitants of the eastern sector of Berlin, that we have been hit less severely by events; the facts, however, show only too clearly that this assumption is false. Two glorious currency manipulations have robbed us of our last freedom of movement, with which we could previously still get around after a fashion . . . For us even the black market is now closed, which is willing to sell things *only* for Deutschmarks,— and those unfortunately we don't have nor can we manage to get, because the rate of exchange between eastern and western money would reduce our income far too much and make any exchange illusory. In short: Berlin is an interesting city – but one should not be condemned to have to live there.

Annerose's letter continues on the same page.

This life is really only worth living if one wishes to wait and see how and whether the Allies muddle their way through to create bearable conditions for us. Until now, with all the squabbling among them, it has been only we who have had to bear the brunt of it. The behaviour and actions of the Russians are classic examples of those crimes against humanity so much denounced in Nuremberg. One notes that Hitler copied Stalin, for Stalin, as we know, came to power first.

Shortly after this letter, the file ends and the Dietrichs fade from view.

3.33

Following Henny's life and the lives of her friends and family in Germany through the medium of letters and documents in German inevitably made me consider and reconsider the part that Germany and the German-speaking people had played in the culture and history of the twentieth century, and even speculate about their possible influence in the present century, a small but bloody shred of which has gone by.

This was particularly so because I had not thought much about the subject earlier. I had no general basis in my early years for placing a story such as hers and Shanti's in a historical context. Throughout my schooling in India, Germany – and, indeed, Europe in general – had been largely ignored; in History, we had concentrated almost exclusively on India, and in Geography on those parts of Asia, Africa and Australasia that had once been coloured pink. As a result, I knew far more about sheep-farming on the Canterbury Plains of New Zealand or the mineral wealth of Nigeria than about the Industrial Revolution or the formative conflicts of European history. Now, as grand-nephew and recounter of

Shanti and Henny's story, I felt compelled to try to work out my own thoughts about the country that had been so central to both their lives.

Needless to say, whole books have been written even on minute aspects of this subject; any brief analysis, such as this, necessarily reduces; and any reduction carries the risk of being too reductive. Some of the argument may seem unjustifiably monocausal or historically determinative. But I feel that this risk is worth taking so that the perspective of the story, told so far mainly through dense description of personal lives, may be opened out. So is the risk that a wider perspective may lead one somewhat far afield from the actual 'Two Lives' of the title and from the web of those they knew.

Hans Dietrich's comment – 'Berlin is an interesting city – but one should not be condemned to have to live there' – makes one think of that double-edged benison, 'May you live in interesting times'. But it also gives rise to the thought that Berlin has been much more than an interesting city; indeed, Berlin, Germany and the German-speaking world at large have been central to the history of the last century. Germany is a merely medium-sized nation, less than 2 per cent of the earth's population. Yet events and currents in Germany, scientific and political theories developed by Germans, and the direct and indirect effect of German arms have been instrumental in moulding events not only in Europe but far beyond.

Berlin shaped the first half of the twentieth century, and epitomised the second. The imperial and National Socialist governments whose capital it was were the prime generators of the two world wars that marked the years till the end of the 1940s; and its own division from then till the end of the 1980s reflected the conflict between the communist and capitalist systems that played itself out across the world.

With respect to the genesis of capitalism, Germany's role has been historically important but not, like that of Britain, seminal. With respect to communism, however, Germany has played a crucial role in both its theoretical and its actual germination: Marx and Engels were both Germans; and one of the major causes of the Russian Revolution was the war with Germany. Had there been no Russian Revolution, it is very doubtful, to continue the counter-factual chain, that there would have been a Chinese Revolution.

As for India and the other colonised countries, their fate was greatly influenced by the two world wars initiated, at least in Europe, largely by Germany. Subject countries that provided soldiers, resources and funds for European-generated wars, ostensibly fought in the name of freedom, more vigorously sought their own. After the Second World War, the main victorious colonial powers, England and France, were financially and physically weakened and increasingly unenthusiastic about sacrificing their citizens' lives in order to oppress unwilling and increasingly militant subject peoples. India became independent almost immediately, and within twenty years, almost the entire apparatus of overt colonialism had gone.

In art, music, literature, drama, architecture and scholarship in the humanities (such as the history of culture or the history of science), great contributions were made by Germany and the German-speaking world in the last century, but similar claims could be made for other countries and language zones. Where Germans and Germanophones made singular contributions was in the fields of science, quasi-science and pseudo-science, all of which, perhaps surprisingly, often coexist in the same country and indeed – as one can see from someone such as Newton – often rattle around in the same head.

To take science first, both theoretical and applied: one salient example would be the allied fields of aeronautics and astronautics. Owing to loopholes in the Treaty of Versailles, while military research into regular aviation was forbidden to Germany after the First World War, rocketry and glider technology were permitted; this is what the German military concentrated on. The V-2 missiles that fell on London depended on advanced German research in rocketry. Hitler's plans for a transatlantic weapons-delivery system that could be used to bomb New York or Washington depended on research both into rocketry and into the design of aerodynamically efficient aircraft greatly influenced by glider design. After the war, when most German scientists came within the ambit of the Americans, the space programme (including that part of it which first put humans on the moon), the missile programme and the design of military aircraft all used and further developed this German research.

To take another example: German physicists, from Einstein to Heisenberg, formed a disproportionate number of those who developed the theories that were to lead to the uses of atomic energy. Here it is almost certain that the relevant discoveries and inventions would have come about anyway, but not quite so soon. Under the impetus of war and assisted by the exile of German-Jewish scientists, this research was most effectively harnessed by Germany's most powerful enemy, and the bombs thus produced used against Germany's not yet defeated erstwhile ally. Thus began the atomic age and, in due course, the nuclear arms race.

When one comes to the quasi-science of human behaviour, one can hardly conceive of psychology, psychiatry, psychoanalysis or psychotherapy without the German-speakers, whether the Austrian Freud, the German Adler or the Swiss Jung.

Finally, the pseudo-science of racial superiority and inferiority was cultivated most assiduously and to greatest effect in Germany and Austria by the National Socialists and their supporters as well as precursors. The working-out of this particular line of study included everything from an emphasis on phrenology to the whole farrago of the classification of Mischlings of different grades and a grid of permissible intermarriages. The actions resulting from such pseudo-science are too well known. The techniques that the Nazis brought to the task included the classification through IBM cardfiles of large sections of their population; propaganda, including film propaganda, for the aggrandisement of one so-called race and the denigration of another; state-organised hatred of designated groups in the population; and the use of terror to ensure the acquiescence of the whole population, many of whom were non-complicit or even opposed to state policy, but few of whom dared actively to organise and resist. These, together with the techniques of immiserization, demoralisation, isolation, concentration and elimination that characterised the Holocaust itself, were powerful contributions from Germany to the political, social and moral life of the past century, though not in all cases unique contributions; under several heads, the Soviet Union could even claim priority.

Many Germans believed that they, by virtue of what they perceived as their superior racial and cultural characteristics, had been chosen by the hand of history or fate or God. The great advantage of being a chosen people is that one can choose to decide who is unchosen, and withdraw sympathy and equity from them. They may be verminised, as the Jews were by the Nazis or the Tutsi by the Hutu; or they may be seen as uncivilised or for some other reason less than fully humanised as, for example, when the imperialist Churchill complained in the 1920s about the squeamishness of some of his colleagues when it came to using poison gas against Iraqi tribesmen; or when the British government offered the Zionists a Jewish home in Uganda, populated mainly by mere blacks, or later, in Palestine, populated mainly by mere Arabs.

Often, such dehumanisations, for all their terrible cost to the dehumanised, may not impinge seriously on the dehumanisers. For example, the atrocities of German colonialism, including in one case a genocidal order against the Herero people in South West Africa announced and effectively implemented in 1904–5, did not cause the German people to suffer any painful repercussions. But it is good to know that sometimes they do.

A large number of factors contributed to Germany's defeat in the Second World War, and one of them was the anti-Jewish actions of its government from its formation in 1933 to its dissolution in 1945. It was not merely the evil idiocy of tying up physical resources, manpower and transport to further an eliminationist policy at a time when a war was being fought, or even the loss of the labour, often highly skilled, of those eliminated; it was also the effect of the earlier loss of scientists who fled the land which they had thought of as home, which they had loved as much as had their fellow citizens, and which they would probably have fought for as fervently. As patriots, just as Jewish airmen could not have objected to bombing Coventry or London, Jewish scientists, had they not been treated as outcasts, would almost certainly have turned their energies to creating weapons and delivery systems on behalf of their homeland. A Jewish scientist, Fritz Haber, had been one of the foremost inventors and developers of poison gas in the First World War. The Second World War could well have seen an effective Munich rather than Manhattan Project, the fruits of which would have been delivered to its targets without qualm at the behest of one who had stated, publicly and with relish, that he wanted to erase the cities of his enemies.

This argument requires the caveat that virulent anti-Semitism, which was a central plank of Hitler's *Mein Kampf*, may well have been essential to the Nazi drive to power and been seen as an indispensable tool for mobilising their cohorts later. But there have been plenty of governments who, once they have succeeded in gaining power, have jettisoned their manifestos when it suited them, or pragmatically tolerated, accommodated or even co-opted those whom they had earlier vilified. There was no inevitability about the way things turned out, even given Hitler's obsessive personality and a system of government in which his underlings vied to outdo each other in interpreting and implementing his stated or perceived will.

Counterfactual speculations, needless to say, should be advanced only with caution; it is always possible, in any given case, that so-called second-order counterfactuals might have kicked in. Even in the absence of German input and the particular events of the Second World War, India might have gained independence and also been partitioned. Even without the particular events of the First World War, there might have been a Russian Revolution that took roughly the form it did. Something else might have caused these and many other events to happen anyway, even if not quite so soon. But for one thing, it is not obvious what. And for another, it matters to people if they are freed or subjugated or murdered or enriched or lauded or reviled in their own lifetimes, not in that of their children or grandchildren.

In this present century, of which a mere quinquennium has gone by, there are a number of areas – and four in particular – in which I think the effect of German history may be played out in a significant way.

One of the greatest threats likely to be faced in this century is that of terrorism; improvements in technology combined with the willingness of people to die in order to inflict damage on their enemies will increase the destructive force deployable by states, small groups of people and even individuals. By far the bitterest cause of resentment in the Muslim world are the actions of Israel against the Palestinians; in all this, Israel has been supported mainly by the United States, regardless of which party is in power there. Here again, many of the historical roots of the situation lie in Germany. Both Zionism and anti-Semitism, including eliminationist anti-Semitism, had deep roots in Germany and, more widely, the German-speaking world. Indeed, it is arguable (though the juxtaposition of the two names is bizarre) that but for Herzl and Hitler – both Austrians who reacted to the plight or perceived effect of Jews throughout Europe and beyond – Israel would not have existed. In this process as well, the two world wars were instrumental. (Even the Balfour Declaration of late 1917, in which a British government approved of and promised to help facilitate the establishment of a national home for the Jewish people in Palestine, could be seen as a by-product of specific aspects of the First World War. And Truman's announcement of support for the merely nascent Israel, which helped give it the legitimacy that enabled it to buy arms to defend itself at a critical time, was partly the result of worldwide sympathy for Jews after the Holocaust.) The formation, situation and policy of Israel have had profound effects on opinion and action in different parts of what can loosely be called the Islamic world, a fifth of humankind; this has continued for fifty years, and is not likely to cease of its own accord.

Unless something happens to create a more just dispensation than now exists, no wall or fence will protect Israel and no homeland security measures, however draconian, will protect a world seen as acquiescing in or promoting continued injustice.

The second area is Europe itself. Germany's crucial role, together with that of France, in the formation of the European Community and its precursors went back not only to the ideas of pan-European visionaries but also, it is sometimes claimed, to the practical experience of cooperation and collaboration between German and French bureaucrats during the Second World War. As the European Community, now the European Union, has grown larger, spreading northwards, westwards, southwards and, most significantly, eastwards, Germany has found itself no longer a divided border state in a Cold War world but a centrally placed European country surrounded by economic and political colleagues. Even its capital has moved hundreds of kilometres east, from postwar Bonn back to an undivided Berlin. The swift decision to unite the two halves of Germany after the collapse of the Berlin Wall may also, through conditions placed by the French on reunification, have led to the swifter introduction of a common European currency, a critical step towards unification.

As Europe becomes a larger zone of economic integration, on the whole, despite internal disagreements, it grows more politically important. This is particularly crucial with respect to its relations with the United States and with Muslim countries. Here it could act as a balancing and ameliorating force with views more nuanced and far-seeing than the extreme reactive and pre-emptive views that have characterised the decision-making circles of the United States government under the younger Bush. Islamophobia, though it exists in Germany, may take powerful hold less easily in a country that has examined with so much heart-searching the effect of past Judaeophobia. Pre-emption may seem less attractive to a country whose attacks on its neighbours brought about two disastrous wars.

In all this, Germany's relationship with Turkey is likely to prove critical. (This relationship is more difficult for Germany than for many other members of the European Union not only because of the complex relationship between Germans and the large population of Turkish 'guest-workers' in Germany but also because Turkey would in time replace Germany as the largest single member and most powerful voter.) With a toehold over the Bosporus and with succeeding governments of different complexions eager to join the European Union, amending their laws and policies to accord with those of liberal democracies – particularly with regard to human rights, where it has a bad record – Turkey has made it clear that it will not accept merely associate or honorary membership of Europe. If, after all its efforts, it is granted full membership, it will be a step towards showing that Islam as such is no bar to full fellowship in close communities of nations. If it is not, it will be clear to everyone that Europe is, and is intended to be, a Christian club. In Turkey, this will create deep resentment born of rejection, and among Muslims in general it will strengthen the widespread perception that they are isolated, beleaguered and victimised.

The third area where Germany has made and will probably continue to make a considerable contribution is in the area of ecological politics. Apart from terrorism and war, the other great threats to humankind in the current century are ecological disaster through human-induced climate change; and biological, chemical or nuclear tampering in the name of industry or science that for some reason goes awry. Despite a daunting clause in the present German constitution (introduced to combat splintering and extremism) which disallows representation in parliament to parties that get less than 5 per cent of the national vote, the Green Party has entered both parliament and, through coalitions, the German government itself. A combination of love of nature and responsibility to the earth and to future generations has fuelled this movement, an unusual and influential one, and a great force for good.

Finally, it may be the case that the terrible tragedies both caused by and inflicted on Germany in the previous century may help us to some extent to avoid them in the present one. In particular, the intensely analysed history of Hitler's rise to power, of the Second World War and of the Holocaust has lessons for the descendants of the perpetrators, of the bystanders and of the victims, and of those who had nothing to do with it at all. It is not only the lessons of history writ large and the avoidance of gross political errors that can be absorbed. (This learning from history could be one reason why, for example, the Second World War was followed not by demands for crippling reparations from Germany but by the reconciling generosity of the Marshall Plan.) It is also the lessons of history writ little that may be taken to heart – the sense that the acts and decisions of ordinary individuals, trivial or momentous, may lead, sometimes by imperceptible gradations, sometimes by sudden jolts, and not even always in the same direction, towards making the world a humane and reasonably secure home for all its denizens or a riven and uncertain place of grief and injustice, fear, hunger and pain.

This may well smack of wishful thinking; all too often one finds among the very people to whom wrong has been done a blindness to the suffering of those whom they are wronging. But at least, more than sixty years after the worst of what happened in Germany was disclosed to the world, the general consciousness still exists of how so many people of a civilised country could be led into a morass of evil or complicity or indifference or inaction.

It is curious that so much leads back to Berlin or Germany or the proportionately small group of German-speakers outside Germany. It is certainly possible to make an analogous case for some other country, but the links would be far more tenuous and contrived. Even the United States, a critical intervener in both world wars, was, for the most part, and certainly for the first half of the twentieth century, more of a reactor than an initiator in international affairs. Later in the last century, apart from armed action in Korea, Vietnam and Iraq, it preferred to topple elected governments that threatened its strategic, ideological or economic welfare, such as in Iran or Chile, by covert action.

Why did Germany play the central role it did? One of the most important circumstances was its position at the geographical centre of Europe. In an age of empires, events in Europe had greater importance than they would otherwise have had, for their effect resounded throughout these extra-European colonies and spheres of influence. Germany's position in Europe hardly mattered when it was not politically unified; and it might not have mattered so much had it been united, as was possible, in 1848 under a liberal constitution; but once it was unified in 1871 in a jingoistic atmosphere and under militaristic and monarchical auspices in the immediate aftermath of a victory over France by Prussia, it became very important indeed. Germany was now the dominant European land power, and this promptly led Britain, with its age-old foreign policy of discouraging single-power domination in Europe, to set up alliances and quasi-alliances with its old enemy France and with Russia in order to contain Germany, which as a result felt itself surrounded. Germany was also resentful that, unlike Britain, France and other European nations, it had arrived late at the scramble for colonies. It now tried to make up for lost time by gouging out a place for itself in the sun. It also built up its navy, which was seen by others as a threatening act. It remained worried, and justly worried, about the possibility of a war on two fronts, a corollary of its central position. This combination of aggressiveness and insecurity was hazardous for peace.

Other answers to the question 'Why Germany?' lie in speculation, somewhat stereotypical, somewhat true, about various aspects of the German character: respect for education and culture, science and scholarship; a tendency towards theorising and the pursuit of theoretical ideas to the point of extremism; a deep and transcendental romanticism and love of nature; industry, fortitude, discipline, and obedience to authority; a sense of mission, of the high seriousness with which life should be taken; a restless unrelaxedness. All these, for good and ill, have had their effect, as, until 1945, did a sense of pride in being distinctively German. This last largely dispersed after the facts of the Holocaust became more fully known:

painful self-examination combined with the contempt of the world made many Germans happier to emphasise that part of themselves that said 'Bavarian' or 'European' or 'world citizen' and to de-emphasise, in their composite identity, their Germanness. Even though, after the long passage of time and the reunification of the country, this is not so true, many Germans, aware of their history, are keen to contain and restrain its impulses within the structure of a wider Europe, one which no single power can dominate.

3.34

This diversion or summation brings us back not to Berlin and Germany but to the world beyond. Specifically, it leads us to the Jewish diaspora – and the prewar and postwar emigrations brought about by the policies of Hitlerian Germany. What happened in Henny's circle of friends was replicated throughout the country and beyond.

Apart from Jazko, saved by the existence of his non-Jewish wife, and the Alexander sisters, who brazened it out in the very midst of the enemy, none of Henny's Jewish friends and none of her family who remained in Germany survived the Second World War. If they were alive at the end of the war, it was because they had fled their homeland.

The Pawels had fled to Sweden, Adolf Berliner to the United States, Fredy Aufrichtig to China. Some of Henny's acquaintances, like Walther Schachtel, who became a bus conductor there, had fled to Palestine. Others, like her brother Heinz Caro, had fled to South America. Even after the war, many survivors left Germany. Friedel Alexander went to South Africa, the Wolffskys to Australia.

In different parts of the world, under the burden of grief and with the memory of fear, still thinking and dreaming in German, they tried to rebuild their lives.

Friedel Alexander, as Franz Mahnert reported, did not find the

Transvaal a paradise. Fredy Aufrichtig, once a solicitor, then a watch-repairer, languished for years in Shanghai, working in a bakery. He wrote to Shanti and Henny in early 1947 about his attempts to get an American visa: 'Just imagine, I have not received an answer now for nine months and have to fear that I will not get a permit *because I am a German*. As this was my only chance to get out of this pigsty, I am in great despair.' When, more than a year later, he got to San Francisco, he lauded the city and its people while denigrating the country that had first given him refuge: 'Where the Chinese were coarse and insolent, the people here are friendly and kind.'

Of all the members of this diaspora, it is Heinz Caro who is the most intriguing; but there is very little information about either him or his relationship with Henny. Even in Berlin, where the two sisters had had many friends in common, Heinz had remained apart; he was only occasionally mentioned in the letters of Henny and Lola's circle. He lived a separate life, waking up late and idling away his time but, being the youngest and a boy, was indulged in all this by his mother. He emigrated to Bolivia in 1938.

During the war, he did not keep in touch with those whom he had known in Berlin and who, like himself, were now refugees. A. G. Belvin (Adolf Berliner) wrote to Henny in January 1942 – in English, so that the censors would not hold up the letter – that he had written to him at his last known address:

Heinz has not answered me, but I 'got' him. I sent him to Bolivia a registered airmail letter with 'Return Receipt' and he signed it! So we see he is alive, but bad enough not to write to anybody.

Henny had no high opinion of Heinz, and it must have plummeted yet further when, after the war, she learned from Ilse that, before emigrating, he had emptied the account intended to provide assistance for his mother and sister. But for Henny, he was still her brother, the only surviving member of her family. She mentioned in a remark to A.G. that she did reply to Heinz's letters, even though most of them were requests that she support him financially.

Only one letter from Heinz survives. He is now attempting to make a go of it in Argentina. The letter is written in a small hand; the final greeting is larger, and he signs off with a giant flourish.

21. 6. 47

My dear Hennerle,

You will be surprised that I am writing to you again today after six months. I ask you, however, not to hold it against me. It is unfortunately my thoughtlessness, I know, but in my heart, despite not writing, I have *never* forgotten you. Now I will write a little about myself, dear Hennerle. Buenos Aires is fantastically beautiful, a really cultured city. But the struggle for existence is very hard. At first I wanted to begin as an office worker, but the salary offers were too low for me to accept. That's why I decided to set up on my own. For four months I have been dealing in women's corsets and face-powder. I am not an agent, but work under my own name on my own account. I have so far acquired a good clientele. Unfortunately here, as in other countries, there is a purchasing crisis, and June and July are the so-called silly season, but in life one has to be an optimist. Apart from that, I am in good health and each month become stouter and fatter. But, as you will remember, I was always 'a schein Jingl' (that is Yiddish); in German we would say 'ein schöner Junge [a handsome lad]'. In my next letter I'll send you a photo of myself.

Now as to you, dear Hennerle, how are you? Don't you think about getting married these days? Or has *the* person whom you want to marry not yet entered your life? From my knowledge of you, dear Hennerle, I believe that you are too choosy. Apart from all this, I hope you are in the best of health. How is Shanti? What happened to your earlier friend, whom you used to see in Berlin? His name is on the tip of my tongue; his father was a high-ranking employee of the firm you worked in. Please write to me about everything in detail.

Now, dear Hennerle, I will close in the hope of receiving a speedy reply from you. I know you will not take me as a model, otherwise I would have a long time to wait. Believe me, when I get down to writing, it is I who reproach myself most.

    With sincere greetings and kisses
      From your
        brother
          Heinz

No copies of any letters that Henny sent to Heinz are to be found. Heinz died six years after this letter, in 1953. It was only then, in a letter to Fröschlein dealing with certain matters of probate, that Henny revealed her feelings for and about her brother, and how his death had affected her.

3.35

Of those Jews who emigrated to England, some, like Henny, remained there for the rest of their lives – though I was to discover, from correspondence between her and the German authorities in the fifties, that she had at first intended to go on from England to the United States.

    But some moved elsewhere after the war. A friend of Henny's, Tilly Reich, went to settle in Palestine in 1947, making the sea journey though she was pregnant at the time. The two letters from her which Henny kept are intriguing; the first one, written while Tilly was still single, is moving and somewhat mysterious.

                         15, Dene Mansions,
                             Kingdon Road
                                 N.W.6
                            Sept. 8th 44

My dear Henny,

    I have been wanting to tell you something for quite some time but it is really very difficult so I decided to write.

    Henny dear, you have been the most wonderful friend to me in all this trouble and I can never really thank you enough for your kindness in every way and most of all perhaps your patience when I was bad-tempered and irritable. I am really very lucky to have you as my friend and I want you to know how much I appreciate it. So never think that I shall just forget about you, now that we don't meet every day. For the time being thanks are all I can give you – but be sure that I shan't forget just how good you have always been.

> Until we meet again,
>> love,
>>> Tilly

The second, an air letter sent from 'T. Reich, P.O. Box 726, Haifa, Palestine', is dated more than three years later, 18 November 1947. It paints a picture far removed from the food rationing of postwar Britain and the freezing and smoggy London winters.

I've been feeling more or less well (there are after all days, when one doesn't feel so grand) in spite of the change of climate and food. Believe me especially the latter is a great change. Any thing can be had and there is no shortage at all. Most people though live rather simply but there are plenty of eggs vegetables and fruit – just those things that are missing in England. Strange as it will seem to you we are having quite summery weather, though not by Palestinian standards.

Tilly gives one a sense of what many young Jewish settlers in Palestine must have felt:

I am feeling very confident as to the future. We won't have exactly an easy life (who has that any way these days) but it can be very satisfactory. There are a great many opportunities for young people, the country is still raw and unfinished in contrast to the polish and sophistication of England. Social standards are different and altogether one must throw a good many English ideas overboard.

Of her feelings for Henny she writes:

England seems very far at the moment but I often remember the days of the V bombs that we spent together and how very good you were to us. Life is like that – one goes some of the way together and then each is taken another way, but I hope very very much to see you once again.

Very much love to you

from Tilly

In February 1947, the British government had abdicated its responsibility for a troubled area racked with animosities between Jews and Arabs by transferring its mandate over Palestine to the United Nations. Less than two weeks after Tilly's letter, on 29 November, influenced by sympathy for the suffering of the Jews under Hitler and despite Arab pleas and protests, the United Nations decided to divide Palestine into a Jewish and an Arab state, with Jerusalem under international control.

War broke out between Arab and Jewish militias; the latter were better led and equipped. By the middle of May 1948, when the mandate was to end, they had won a string of victories. From the city of Haifa, where Tilly had written her optimistic letter, tens of thousands of Arab inhabitants had fled.

Though her sister Lola had become increasingly involved with Judaism, Aunty Henny did not strike me as being particularly religious. She would go to the bar mitzvah of the son of a friend, but would not attend services, even on important holy days such as Rosh Hashanah or Yom Kippur. Nor do I recall her bringing up in conversation the question of her Jewishness or discussing her experiences in Germany – for example, Kristallnacht – or the fate of her family. My clear memory of her searching look and question when she noticed me at the age of nine reading the article about Adolf Eichmann was not complemented by any subsequent discussion, even a decade later, about him or anyone else involved with the Final Solution.

When I lived with her and Shanti Uncle, they had a number of mainly German-speaking Jewish friends, some of whom travelled to Israel and several of whose children went to work on kibbutzim. But I don't think Aunty Henny, sun-lover though she was, ever went there. And the only time I remember her commenting on Israel or the Middle East while I was living at 18 Queens Road was when, after reading an article in the *Guardian*, she said something along the lines of 'It's terrible, what's going on there.'

Partly as a result of writing this book, so much of which deals with the question of Jewishness, I have tried to work out my own views on that most salient manifestation of postwar history, the Jewish state. This was a matter about which I had a very sporadic consciousness while growing up in India. As a schoolboy, I followed the news of the Six Day War in June 1967 between Israel and her Arab neighbours – Syria, Jordan and Egypt – with great excitement, as did many of my fellow students. I simply took the states as given entities, and was happy that one small country had managed to take on and defeat three others.

But now, though I am still glad that Israel was not defeated, I am more concerned about the basic rights and wrongs of the situation. While, at the age of fifteen, I was completely unaware of what had happened to the Palestinians, I have not been able to maintain this ignorance. As for states – democratic or otherwise – that deliberately favour one religion over another in anything more than a nominal sense, I have come more and more to believe that these in effect perpetuate inequality and injustice.

Jewish control of the nation is central to the idea of Israel. Its demographic policy, had it been perpetrated by anyone else, would have been condemned as ethnic cleansing – both the permanent exclusion of Palestinians (some of whose families had lived there for centuries) who fled the terror unleashed on them when the state was founded, and the vigorous encouragement of all those who are Jewish, wherever they are from and however little connection they have with the land, to settle there.

Various justifications for the foundation and maintenance of Israel as a specifically Jewish state have been adduced; none of them takes into account the concomitant injustice to the Palestinians. Historical yearning for certain religious sites or landscapes or a belief that one is divinely ordained to possess a particular part of the earth is hardly an excuse for creating one's own living space at the expense of others. After Hitler came to power in Germany, it could also be maintained that there was a humanitarian imperative for the Palestinian Arabs – as for other people all over the world – to share space with the cruelly oppressed Jews. But that the Jews could then carve out their own state in Palestine does not follow.

The eviction over the decades since 1948 of yet more Palestinians from their land, the building of Jewish settlements in the West Bank and elsewhere, the massacres in the refugee camps under Israeli military control during the Lebanon operations of 1982, the construction of the boundary fence and wall incorporating still more Palestinian land, the assassination of Palestinian leaders, the repeated siege of cities, the razing of entire streets and colonies of houses and the regular humiliation of Palestinian civilians by Israeli troops paint a picture of terror, injustice and arbitrariness either sanctioned or not greatly opposed by the state. Many among the dispossessed and far weaker Palestinians support their own terrorists, who strike with equal injustice and arbitrariness at Israeli civilians. In the fearful calculus of terror, where impulse and response are difficult to distinguish, many more Palestinians have been killed than Israelis.

The litany at the end of the German prayer-book of 1893 reads:

Judaism teaches: 1. the unity of mankind.

It commands us therefore 2. to love our neighbour, 3. to protect our neighbour and his rights, 4. to be aware of his honour, 5. to honour his beliefs, 6. and to assuage his sorrows.

If only this humane ideal could be put into practice – on both sides of the divide.

3.36

Tilly's letters speak of a great tenderness for Henny. And indeed, Henny had the capacity for inducing admiration, or more. Paul Oppler, the solicitor in whose firm she worked during her last days in Germany, and who was later to emigrate, wrote to her in England in August 1939:

Dear Fräulein Caro,
Your letter of 12th August could have been written by no one but you:
outwardly: wonderfully clearly written and without a single error
inwardly: supportive, careful and practical.
My best thanks to you for it.

    After the war, Henny got a fan letter from Holland, written in German, from someone who appears to have been a business, or at any rate, chance acquaintance rather than someone she had met socially. It almost has the quality of a one-sentence declaration of love with multiple clauses.

S.F. Willheim   22 Oct 1946
372 Heerengracht
c/o 'Texwil' N.V.

My dear Miss Hennie! [this greeting is in English]
    Without being too formal, I nevertheless feel the need to tell you—
that I consider it a privilege to have made your acquaintance —
that it gave me great pleasure to be able to chat a little with you in the small café—
that you give the impression of being a courageous and balanced woman— (with a special touch)—
that in you one finds the happy combination of humour and intelligence—

that you possess inward and outward culture—

That is what I wished to say to you personally, but had no opportunity to do so.

Thank you once again for your selfless assistance.

If I can ever do anything for you – please do tell me! I hold the most pleasant memories of you.

> With kind regards,
>> Yours ever [illegible]

3.37

But the most passionate letters of all come from Henny's friend Eva Cohn (not her real name), an Austrian refugee who had also lost her family to the Nazis. Henny and she both lived in the boarding-house in Kendal Street near Marble Arch until, in 1946, Eva emigrated to New York, where she had relatives, and they began to write to each other.

Unusually for such a long correspondence, there is almost no record of Henny's letters.

Eva's letters are in German. Her handwriting is exorbitant: unformed and messy, lively and large, often underlined, sometimes with multiple lines. Her Ds are madly ornate: the time-consuming curl of a small spiral precedes the semicircle and hangs over the top of the vertical. She uses no paragraphs at all and jumps wildly from subject to subject. Her vocabulary is full of Austrian words like *heuer* (this year), Yiddish words like *meschugge* (crazy) and English phrases.

Eva begins to write her first letter as soon as her plane departs from the airport at Bournemouth for the long trip (with stops in Ireland and Canada) to New York.

14th Jan. 1946

My dearest and sweetest Henny,

I've just been up in the air for 5 mins. and I'm not yet feeling bad and I already have the need to write, here is letter no. 1. You are indeed my darling, the *first* [underlined twice] one to hear from me, even though I must send a telegram to my relatives . . . The use of the parachute has just been explained to us, I think I'm going to be sick!? Darling, how will I feel later when already I long for you so much! I weep whenever I think of you. That was the *only* [underlined twice] parting when I felt I died a little. Now I'm crying again! I have firmly decided *never* to have another girlfriend [in German, *Freundin* simply means a female friend], quite apart from the fact that I will never find anyone like you.— . . . Now it is 6.45, and Mr Donath is probably coming back. Do all of you also think of me too? Give my best wishes to Shanti. I am high in the sky and dog-tired. So, darling, that's all for now, be embraced and kissed deeply (unfortunately only in my thoughts) by the one who misses you terribly, your

Eva.

Mr Donath was yet another lodger in Mrs Sherratt's boarding-house, and the second of Henny's 'two men' later referred to by Eva. It is difficult to get a picture of him since, apart from frequent references to him in Eva's letters, he rarely appears in the rest of Henny's correspondence.

New York, 17th Jan. 46

My dearest, sweetest and best,

We've finally arrived and today was my first day here. I will try to describe everything to you, but I don't know, Darling, whether that will be possible, there is too much to tell . . . I already miss you frightfully and when I talk to myself about you, my tears start. I don't know if I

Shanti and Henny just after their wedding in 1951.

Henny's brother Heinz and his stepson. On the obverse is written: 'Many greats from your nephew Harry. La Paz 3rd July 1953'. Heinz died later that year.

Hans Mahnert and his wife Wanda. On the obverse is written: 'To my dear friend Shanti from Wanda and Hans, Berlin, March 12, 1947'.

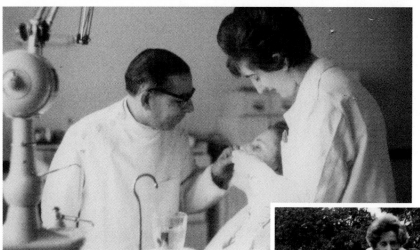

From top to bottom: 18 Queens Road, seen from Hendon Park. Shanti bought the house in 1948 and lived there for fifty years; Henny joined him in 1951; both died at home, she in 1989, he in 1998. The room on the ground floor with the large windows facing the street was Shanti's surgery.

Shanti with Henny (standing in for his nurse) in the surgery. Despite having lost his right arm in the war, he continued to work from the same side of the chair as a right-handed dentist. As a result, he suffered back pain throughout his working life.

Shanti in his dental jacket reading a newspaper in the garden during his lunch break. Henny stands behind him.

Clockwise from top left:
Shanti and Henny with Henry
Edwards – Shanti's best friend –
and his wife Nita and daughter
Susan.

The charming Fred Götte talking to
Henny.

A party at home, with the bridge
tables used alternately for cards
and tea.

An unidentified woman sits on
Shanti's lap while Henny looks
straight at the camera.

WITH FAMILY

Clockwise from right:
My parents (Prem and Leila Seth) in 1951. On the obverse is the inscription: 'Leila and fiancé'.

'Mother-in-law and baby Shantum' was the caption of this photograph taken by the *Evening Standard* when my mother came first in her bar exams. Shanti and Henny, who were childless, wanted to adopt Shantum.

Shanti and Henny (and friends) with my parents in the garden of 18 Queens Road. My grandmother Chanda paid a surprise visit from India; she is shown here holding me on her lap.

My parents with Shanti and Henny in the drawing-room at 18 Queens Road.

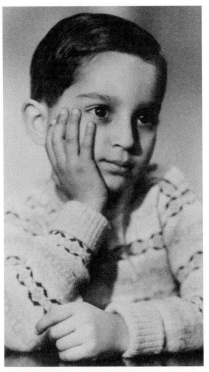

Left: The author photographed on the eve of his departure from London at the age of four.

Below left: The author on a visit to London at the age of nine. He is shown in the company of Jackie, the au pair at 18 Queens Road on whom he had a crush.

Below right: The author with Shanti Uncle and Aunty Henny, when he went to stay with them for four years at the age of seventeen.

Holiday photographs in Switzerland. Very few photographs of Henny survive, because in his grief at her death Shanti destroyed whatever he feared would remind him of her.

Shanti with the *Observer* on his lap.

Henny in late middle age.

Shanti and Henny resting on a bridge.

Shanti, suffering from heart disease, supported on either side as he walks.

With close friends and family at the launch of the author's novel *A Suitable Boy* at the Nehru Centre in London in 1992. This was one of the last social functions that Shanti Uncle attended. From left to right: Sue Hughes, John Hughes, Alun Hughes, Shanti, the author and Michi Seth (Michi Mama) (photograph: Susan Greenhill).

Shanti Uncle in April 1997, a year before his death.

can express myself so well in words as Tilly, Amy, Milli, Fanny etc. etc., but such a friendship as I had with you I will never have again nor do I want to . . .

Eva describes with great zest her first impressions of New York: the shortage of housing, the wonderful plenty in the shops, the long journeys on the subway, a marvellous Viennese confectioner: '– wonderful things!! – I could only eat a little, I was full just from looking at them.'

What are you doing, Darling, do you sometimes think of me? Who's been smitten by you lately? Give Shanti my best wishes. That's all for today and I embrace you and kiss you with the greatest love and longing.

  Your   Eva.

Five months later, in July 1947, she writes:

My dearest Hennerle,

 I have received both your letters, one of them crossed with mine. I am often truly homesick [she uses the English word] when I get these letters. Sometimes I don't really know whether we shouldn't have remained together. I have already parted once before from the people I loved most – and it was not good. Now I have done the same again and parted from the person who is dearest to me. For you too I have the 100% feeling of a sister and regard you as such.— . . .

This sisterly aspect of their regard is something that Henny touched upon in a letter written a year earlier, in July 1946, to A. G. Belvin: 'I have a very good friend in New York, who unfortunately also lost her mother and sister in the same way, and we have lived together for over 5 years here at 27 Kendal St. and have become as close as sisters.'

 Eva goes on to express her forthright views on Henny's generosity towards her German friends:

It doesn't concern me at all *whether* and *what* you ~~are~~ send to people in Germany. But my firm view is and remains that the people you can be sure are 100% are the poor survivors of the concentration camps, who have been through a bit more than the 'poor' 100% Germans. And it would be more sensible to let them have something!! Don't be annoyed that I write like this to you, but whenever this subject comes up, I simply boil over [she writes 'boil' in English] and can't keep my mouth shut.— What are you up to, Darling? And the two men? Today is Saturday and you are probably all together. Do you think of me 'just a little bit'? . . .

I embrace you deeply and smother you in kisses in eternal love, yearning and devotion.

Your longing
Eva

In September, after opening her letter with 'Darling, *how* [underlined six times] I miss you!!', Eva goes on to describe the expensive and rather painful beauty treatment she has been undergoing for her skin, and tells Henny she has just read a very good book, *Gentleman's Agreement*, which deals with the social exclusion of Jews in certain echelons of American society. She continues:

The only one in the whole wide world who is close to me is really you and you alone. I simply don't have any feelings for anyone else. I can't help myself. I often tell myself, it is not good at all to be as I am, but inside me I feel as if I am dead – most of the time. But despite everything, I still take everything too weightily and seriously.— Now my Dearest, enough for today, write to me again. I take you warmly in my arms and smother you with kisses

with love and longing
Your Eva

A month later, still more passionately, Eva writes:

My Hennerle, beloved above all others,

Today is Sunday evening and what could be better than to chat a little with you? What would I not give to be able to do it face to face! To take you once again so truly in my arms and to smother you with kisses!! I know so many people here – – and feel all the more lonely! Darling, I hope you really do miss me just a weenie-little bit! . . .

What do you do on Saturday and Sunday? Tilly is certainly very nice, but I could never get enthusiastic about her. But then – whom did I ever want except you! – How is Shanti? I'll write to him soon. I really have a bad conscience. But here one finds time for nothing . . .

Darling, I hope I'm not boring you too much nattering on like this. But I don't have anyone else and with you perhaps I can find a little understanding, although your letters are rather impersonal.

Where is the photo . . . that you promised me? A pity that I can't peep into the waste-paper basket at Marble Arch! Now I'm going to bed and my thoughts are with you. In my mind I run upstairs – well, and *anyway* you know the rest! I hold you really, really close and kiss you all over

    with the same old love and ever-increasing longing
      Your Eva

Added upside-down under the date is the pertinent postscript: 'Can you read my handwriting?'

A year later, in September 1948, apparently in response to a wish or suggestion of Henny's, Eva tells her:

I too am always so happy when a little letter from you lies on my table. And I think so very much about you! It really was wonderful! How wonderful it would indeed be if we could set up together here just as in London. I would even renounce all men (I get quite disgusted with them from time to time) . . .

    I embrace you deeply and smother you with kisses (quite crazily)
      with old love and longing
        Your Eva

A sudden development:

. . . A few things have happened to me in these last few weeks. You see,
I plan to be engaged in January and to get married in February. Well,
where shall I begin to tell you about it? He is called Rudi (Lippmann)
[not his real name], is 39 years old, no great beauty and also a bit
shorter than me. He is very nice and good-hearted and he would
certainly make me a good husband. I like him very much and like being
with him – he also 'appealed' to me. He is a furrier (very good here) and
earns a lot.—

Eva describes their meeting and sudden courtship and continues:

I see him three times a week and I believe he is very much in love with
me. On Saturdays we always go out together – and he has a marvellous
car – which is of course not so important – but is certainly
convenient . . . I think he would like to have a beautiful wedding – but I
don't want him to spend too much money on it. A simple reception is
what I would like.— . . .

What do you think about all this? What is your news, my Dearest?
How much I think of you . . .

So, my Dearest, I'll close for today, don't be cross with me, write
soon. I embrace you deeply and madly in old love, devotion and longing
Your Eva

In January 1949, Henny wrote a letter to Eva, the shorthand
draft of which she retained in her file. This is the only example of her
words to Eva, so I felt it was important to try to get it transcribed.

Unfortunately, it was written in a form of shorthand which
Henny must have learned in the 1920s and which is extremely
unfamiliar in Germany today; the difficulty is compounded by the
'wild strokes' Henny employs. (I am quoting from the cover-note of
the shorthand expert Hans Gebhardt, whom I should like to thank
for not merely transcribing but in effect decrypting this note.)

My dearest Eva,

Today, on your wedding day, all my thoughts are especially with you. This morning when I woke, I thought of you most deeply and intimately [*innigst*], while you were still in the profoundest sleep (or were you awake all night with excitement?). I can well imagine how you are at this very moment running about nervously here and there making your final preparations (it is 3 o'clock here). When it is 7 o'clock this evening, Shanti and I will raise a glass of wine together and drink a toast to you and ~~your husband~~ Rudi. Once again, I wish you both every happiness on earth – health, love and mutual understanding. I feel as if my own sister were getting married today and my only sadness is that I can't be there.

When you receive this letter, you will perhaps just have returned from your [indecipherable: honeymoon?]. You will surely have spent a wonderful time together, days that will remain unforgettable.

Donath has unfortunately not been too well these last two weeks. He had terrible bronchitis and is still not completely OK. Shanti is fine. We have both been invited today to Dr [indecipherable: Johanni's?].

Evalein, I close for today with my deepest wishes once again for you and Rudi. I embrace and kiss you warmly.

    With old love and friendship,

      Ever your

      Hennerle

Though this is a warm and tender letter, it could not be called passionate; the outbursts of yearning characteristic of Eva's letters are not to be found here.

At the end of June 1949, five months after her marriage, Eva writes to Henny to tell her that she is pregnant and often feels sick.

I believe that in February you will become an 'Aunt'. My feelings are very mixed. It was not planned and I wanted to put a stop to it – but so far I have not found a way.

She writes that Rudi is out of work – things are bad in the fur trade – but he is a very supportive husband and helps her a great deal, in her present condition, with the housework.

What have you been doing, Darling? It is really marvellous that you will be going to Switzerland – how gladly would I come with you!! But now you will probably have to come here first, for before I can come over, a lot of water will have flowed down the 'Thames'. It is terrible how life tears us apart from each other! . . .

    Warm greetings from Rudi, and be
        deeply embraced and covered in kisses
        in love, devotion and longing
            Your Eva

Eva and Henny remained friends through the years. She sent Henny attractive snapshots of herself posing on the beach as well as pictures of her husband and, in due course, her children. When I was studying in California and Henny and Shanti visited the USA, it was with Eva and Rudi that they stayed in New York.

After Henny's death, when Shanti visited Toronto to get away from things, Eva flew from New York to see him. He said: 'I gave her Henny's favourite piece of jewellery. Henny never asked me to, but I knew that was what she would have wanted.'

I wish I had asked Shanti Uncle what this piece of jewellery was. It would have pleased me to imagine it on Aunty Henny and, later, on Eva. Where, though – wrist, finger, neck, ear? What was this emblem of love so tacitly conferred, and through so understanding an intermediary? But how much did Shanti Uncle in fact understand of what Henny meant to Eva, or Eva to Henny? Even if he had been alive, it would have been difficult to pursue this question. Indeed, had he been alive, I am not certain I would have been able to write this chapter at all.

PART
FOUR

4.1

We left Shanti's story at the point in 1948 when he had bought a house in north London and started practising dentistry from the surgery there during the hours when he was not working at the Amalgamated Dental Company. His feelings for Henny were encapsulated in the single birthday card that survives of the many he sent over the years.

Shanti and Henny got engaged in 1949 and married in 1951. I asked him why it had taken seven years from his return to England till his wedding. He replied in somewhat general terms:

After losing my arm, there was always this question, what future did we have? I didn't want to probe this question. Henny and I were always invited together to all our friends; we saw Henry and Nita at least twice a week. In my own mind, I was not sure what the future would be, whether I could give her the same standard of life that she used to have, could I make a living, having one hand only. We used to meet when I was living in a boarding-house. I thought it would be a good idea to have my own house where I could start a practice. It was very difficult.

Everybody took it for granted that Henny and I would sooner or later get married. Nobody invited us separately; the names Shanti and Henny were always together. When I gave a party, Henny used to act more or less as the hostess, but she didn't stay here any time before we got married.

She knew she had nobody and I had nobody.

It was 'Mum', Henry's mother, who helped break this state of uncertain understanding. Henny had always been fond of her. Now, after her own mother's death, they grew even closer. Mum spoke to Shanti – they would have spoken in German, as they always did unless Nita was there – and told him that what he was doing, or rather not doing, wasn't right. 'Either you marry Henny,' she said, 'or give her her freedom.'

Shanti's decision was as sudden as his decision to set off for Germany to study – or to sign up with the army.

The very next day I proposed to Henny and bought her an engagement ring at – what's the name of that shop? – Mappin & Webb of Regent Street. As far as I remember, it had one solitaire diamond of a medium size set in platinum. The next day I took Henny to get the ring. She never took it off her finger.

They celebrated their engagement by having a drink after work at the Regent Palace Hotel near Piccadilly with Henry, Nita and Mum. Shanti would have had his usual whisky; Henny, who according to Shanti 'only liked sweet drinks', would have had a sherry or a gin and lime. As he put it: 'We didn't say anything, I don't know, maybe that's what happens when you know each other so long. We more or less took it for granted.'

They were engaged for two years, during which time Shanti's practice developed in parallel with his work at the Amalgamated. Once again, things settled down into an open-ended pattern until his friends intervened.

Mum probed again, asking, 'When are you actually going to get married?' And Henry and Nita had a chat with me. I told them about my doubts about being able to make a go of my profession, and Henry said, 'If you are not successful in your practice, I will come and help you.' I decided to get married at once – with just two days' notice – under special licence. I was very impulsive.

On my wedding day, 20th July, 1951, I was working at the

Amalgamated. Since I was due to get married at one o'clock, I went to my technical director and said, 'Would you take any calls that come to me from dental colleagues? I want to go home.' He asked me, 'Are you feeling well?' I replied, 'I'm getting married.' He said, 'For heaven's sake, you should have taken a few days off.'

Poor Henry, my best man, was in the house, getting panicky: the bride was there but not the groom. Finally I turned up. The four of us went to the registrar at Burnt Oak and we had a very good wedding. Then we went out and had a meal.

Shanti's matter-of-fact account of this simplest of weddings is rounded out by two small black-and-white photographs from that day. They were taken, either before or after the wedding, in the long back garden at 18 Queens Road; I recognise it from the wooden fence. They show Shanti, waistcoated, suited and button-holed, carrying a glove in his artificial right hand. Henny, leaning towards him, has her arm linked with his left arm; with her other she holds her wedding bouquet to her. She is wearing a jacket and skirt, and a half-veil is attached to her hat. In one photograph, of the two of them alone, they are smiling – though Henny's upper teeth are smudged with lipstick. In the other photograph – which includes Henry, Nita and their little daughter Susan, all three smiling broadly – Henny and Shanti have their mouths firmly shut but don't succeed in looking serious.

Their sudden decision to get married meant that there had been no time to send out invitations. Since both Shanti and Henny were working and had little time to spare, Mum decided to take charge of the wedding reception, which took place in the garden of Shanti's house. To quote Shanti: 'It was a wonderful party. Just by word of mouth there were sixty-eight guests. There was plenty to drink; Derek – Nita's son from her first marriage – and my friend George Little manned the bar. Both of them got drunk, and George broke lots of glasses, four at a time – it was quite funny. It was a fantastic day, with sunshine and everything.'

For their honeymoon, they caught a flight to Switzerland late the same night, arriving in Zurich early the next morning. They decided to go to Flims. As on their previous visits to Switzerland together, they had not reserved rooms in advance.

We would decide on the spot where to go. We'd been to Klosters three or four times earlier. Separate rooms. No hanky-panky till we got married. No, not at all, not like these days.

In Flims they were not so lucky with accommodation. There was a conference on, and not a single room was available in any hotel. Finally, when Shanti in desperation mentioned that they were there for their honeymoon, they were given a room that had been cleared out in the attic of a hotel, but charged the full tariff.

Henny always looked under the bed in hotel rooms – and that's what she did on our honeymoon. This was because when her parents got married, a man who had been hiding under the bed chloroformed them and stole a lot of their wedding gifts and jewellery.

Shanti phoned the proprietress of the hotel in Klosters where they normally stayed to tell her that they had got married. She was very annoyed, said he was a traitor – he had been to her place many times, but was going somewhere else for his honeymoon – and ordered him to take the next train to Klosters. There they were given the bridal suite but only charged for a regular room.

This incident made Shanti cautious in future. He recalled: 'After that I never went to Switzerland without booking in advance. I'd order brochures from four or five hotels. I preferred family hotels. Hotels with directors have to show a profit, family hotels want the same people to come back each year. Like this hotel in Weggis on the Vierwaldstätter See – it's really out of the moon.'

'Out of the moon, Uncle?'

'We should have gone there together, Vicky. But now I can't

climb the hills. What's the point of sitting in a lounge? I may as well sit in the lounge here.'

4.2

'I didn't want to probe this question,' said Shanti Uncle about the matter of his future with Henny. He did not expand much on the subject, and I felt awkward about exploring it directly with him, but I did wonder why. The only reason he gave was that he felt he could not provide properly for Henny until he had set himself up successfully in his practice. But Henny was working too; surely their joint incomes were sufficient for running a home. It is possible that, as with many men and women of his generation, in Shanti's mental template of an ideal marriage the roles of breadwinner and homemaker were separate. There is some evidence of this in the later trajectory of Henny's career.

Did he feel that if Henny accepted him, she might do so out of pity? To obviate this possibility, he might again have wanted to set himself up properly in his profession. It is true that Henny, in a letter to Ilse, had stated almost bluntly that there was no reason to feel sorry for Shanti – he was skilled in the use of his left hand; he made research films; he had even obtained his driving licence – but Shanti might not have been certain of what she felt.

He gave a strong impression of independence and confidence, but he seems to have been somewhat insecure with regard to what he meant to Henny. In the letters he wrote to her during the war he importuned her to give him some inkling of her feelings for him; presumably, he too sensed the slight note of impersonality that even her best friends occasionally complained about. Perhaps he too believed – as he told her her mother had averred – that Henny had no heart: perhaps not 'no heart' as such, but no passionate romantic inclinations – or at least no romantic inclinations for him. As I mentioned before, though he protested that she shouldn't visit him in the hospital in Nottingham, it would have been surprising, had she felt about him the way he felt about her, that she would have stayed away.

And then there was the imponderable question of Hans, now married, and from all accounts, unhappily. Shanti and Hans continued to write to each other, but Henny professed indifference even when Shanti suggested that they meet Hans in Switzerland. But was this merely a mask to disguise her hurt? Did Henny still hold a torch for him? When I asked Shanti Uncle about Hans's marriage, he said, in passing: 'I personally don't think Henny was ever in love with him.' He paused, then corrected himself: 'To tell you the truth, I'm telling a lie – she never discussed it.'

Another unresolvable question – and one to which it is difficult even to ascribe an appropriate significance – is that of Henny's feelings for the exuberant Eva. It seems clear that there was a deep affection between them, and even something of a physical relationship, but whether this was Henny's only passionate friendship is uncertain; in one letter, Eva, with a twinge of jealousy, mentions the names of other women as possible competition for Henny's regard. Shanti Uncle's attitude to relationships between those of the same sex was tinged with facile prejudice; his remarks were sometimes quite unpleasant. But this was not true of Aunty Henny. I remember being surprised when, in the course of one conversation at teatime, while Shanti Uncle was holding forth on the subject, Aunty Henny quietly interrupted and said that there had been a girl in her office who had had a crush on her and had written her letters and poems. She had added that one had to understand these matters and these feelings.

There is another possible explanation for Shanti's delay: that his own feelings had changed over the years. The passionate fusion of mountains and clouds and ecstasy of which he wrote to Henny in 1944 may have been dispersed by quotidian contact with what he had earlier referred to as 'the Kuckuck of flesh' rather than of dreams. But it seems to me unlikely that his feelings had changed so greatly. Whether or not they were as passionate as they had been, they were certainly as deep – and continued to be so. As Henny confided to Fröschlein years later, in 1954, Shanti had told her that he would give his life for her.

Whatever the reason, it is clear that Shanti deferred his proposal of marriage and then, through a prolonged engagement, the wedding itself till both he and Henny were in their early forties – although this deferral carried the risk that they might not be able to have children. In the event, it was Mum's and Henry's intervention that made him propose; and this would have quieted at least one of his possible concerns, for Mum would not have advised him to do so unless she had learned from Henny that she would accept.

As for prolonging the engagement for two years, it is possible that Shanti felt that Henny herself was having doubts; as indeed she was.

Long before the engagement, during the period when it could be said to have been merely an understanding – in fact, on the last day of 1946, the sort of day on which one might take stock of things – Henny had written to her confidant in Atlanta, Georgia, A. G. Belvin:

Regarding Shanti, you are right. I am in a dilemma and don't know what I should do. I like Shanti, I value him, and he is particularly close to me because he is the only one here who knew my loved ones and, I could say, also loved them. That is a great deal, that is indeed a very, very great deal, for no other man can understand me, because he can sympathise so very much less than Shanti with what I have inwardly gone through and what will never again be erased. But I must come to a decision soon. Just as your self-denial, your decision to give up a lot, has gained you something too, so I wish to imitate you, and perhaps that is best for me. Shanti has a good and upright character, and I believe I may say that I also mean something to him. I want to make him happy – he deserves it – even at the risk that I am not 100% happy. But who knows all that in advance? Perhaps I will find happiness in this uncertainty?!

It is pointless to comment on Henny's general analysis of her own perplexity; what could add to such self-knowledge? But it is perhaps worth asking what might have made Henny happier. Two years later, in September 1948, Eva wrote to her: 'How truly wonderful it would be if we could set up together here just as in London.' But whatever this companionship was, it appears that Henny did not seriously consider a continuation of it.

More than a year later, in November 1949, by which time Eva had got married and Henny engaged, Eva wrote to her in a heady mixture of English and German (the English words are here underlined):

How are you, <u>Darling</u>, and what are you up to? I hope you don't feel <u>lonely</u> these days, but you do of course have many friends. <u>Darling</u>, you ask me what I think about marriage. What a difficult question that is. Naturally, your <u>habits</u> are <u>formed</u>. But <u>marriage</u> is a <u>half-and-half proposition</u> and both parties must get used to each other and adapt to each other. That may not be easy at the beginning, but two intelligent people such as you and Shanti should have no great difficulty. You know that I have <u>the highest opinion</u> of Shanti and he is <u>a wonderful person</u>. But whether one can and wishes to live with someone – that you can only sense and find out for yourself. A <u>marriage</u> is never easy. But to have a <u>home</u> and a person to whom one belongs compensates for a great deal. Look, <u>Darling</u>, one cannot wander around in furnished rooms for ever – or <u>even</u> if one has a home – it is nothing if one is by oneself. Naturally, one can't marry for this <u>reason</u> alone. But if one can imagine living with someone, and he is *good*, and one likes him (it needn't be a Romeo and Juliet sort of love), and he has a certain education and income – it is certainly much, much better than to be alone for ever. <u>Darling</u>, I wish I could speak with you, it is so difficult by letter. I do know one thing, that I would be happy to hear you had got married and were content and also had a home. And that you are happy is something I wish with all my heart. Look, after all, we really don't have any family or anyone. And the only home we can have is one we make ourselves. And to be alone is terrible in the long run!— . . .

I kiss and embrace you
with enduring love, devotion and longing
Your   Eva

4.3

My mother's eldest brother Michi and his wife Moyna were visiting England in the summer of 1951; Shanti, still a bachelor,
invited them to stay at his house. Michi and Moyna went to the
continent for a short trip. On their return, they found it difficult
to open the front door. The obstruction was a large pile of con-
gratulatory telegrams. To their astonishment, they discovered that
Shanti and Henny had got married and were away on their
honeymoon.

In India, a rumour grew that Shanti had suddenly married his
nurse. My parents too, years later, mentioned this in passing.
Henny had indeed helped Shanti in his surgery when, for some
reason, his regular nurse had not been on hand to help. But few
had known of her other, entirely independent, job.

My picture of Shanti and Henny's marriage is somewhat
skewed. Shanti talked about his marriage and about Henny at
length. Henny is almost silent. Her surviving letters from and to her
friends disappear at the end of the forties – except for her correspondence with Fröschlein, which, being part of a surviving file
dealing with German officialdom, continues into the late fifties.
There are no letters to and from Eva, for instance, which would
have given one an intimate insight into the marriage, even if one
only had Eva's voluble side of it.

What could fill this hiatus? I sounded out my family about
their impressions of Shanti Uncle and Aunty Henny and will
record their views here, partly because they help flesh out the
portrait I am painting and partly because they illuminate Shanti
Uncle's attachment to the family – an attachment that makes

his behaviour in his final days all the more disturbing and inexplicable.

My mother first heard of Shanti Uncle when she was very little. He was part of family lore. He had been born after his father's death. He had left India when he was young. He had treated her father – his eldest brother, Raj – like a father. He had visited from Germany in the thirties, and brought Michi a toy Zeppelin.

When Raj died in September 1942, in the middle of the war, Shanti had tried to help out, but had been able to do so only in a very limited way, since he was just starting out in his profession. Then, a year and a half later, the family received the news of his war wound. Mama says:

I remember that we were in Darjeeling when we got a telegram informing us that Shanti Uncle was 'critically ill'; this was quite often the precursor to a death notice. I remember Ma being very upset. That day on the street we happened to meet a man who was known to be a Tantric astrologer – he was wild in appearance, though not in rags or anything. Ma said, 'I'm very unhappy. My brother-in-law has had an accident.' He said, 'What is the time?' Ma looked at her watch and told him. He looked up at the sky and said, 'He's not dead. He's lost a limb, but he'll survive.' I remember his words to this day: 'Koi ang gaya hai.'

My parents got married in March 1951, three months before Shanti Uncle and Aunty Henny (Papa was twenty-seven at the time and Mama twenty). Upon their return to India, Michi and Moyna told my parents a little about Shanti, though, since they were preoccupied with their own travels, the picture they conveyed was somewhat hazy.

Another bit of the picture was filled in by Mrs Khaitan, the wife of the chairman of Bata India, the shoe manufacturing firm for which Papa worked. Mrs Khaitan, believing, with some justification (having had previous evidence of extramarital carnality), that her husband's visits to England were not devoted entirely to business, had got a locksmith in Calcutta to open the steel almirah in which Mr Khaitan had kept her passport and had taken a flight to England. Since she knew no one else in London, she had obtained Shanti Uncle's address from my parents. To Shanti Uncle's and, particularly, Aunty Henny's amazement, she arrived on their doorstep directly from the airport, fully bejewelled and dressed to the nines. She wept, she detailed her woes, she tried to trace the errant Mr Khaitan, and she wept once more. Aunty Henny showed her great sympathy; this was high drama, and Aunty Henny always loved high drama. Dinner was offered, but Mrs Khaitan would drink only milk. Eventually, in lieu of Mr Khaitan, who was untraceable, the great Thomas Bata himself came to the house late at night to appease the distraught Mrs Khaitan and to protect her husband from her future vengeance.

Mrs Khaitan's glowing reports of womanly sympathy gave my parents the sense that Aunty Henny was a fairly relaxed and informal person, an impression that was to be undermined when they themselves went to England.

My father was transferred to England in June 1954 by Bata. Because they thought that setting up a household in England would be difficult, my parents left me behind in India with my grandmother and my uncle and aunt, Sashi Mama and Usha Mami. During their three-year stay in London, Papa and Mama grew very attached to Shanti Uncle and he to them, particularly to Mama, his niece. She recounted:

We stayed for a while in a guest-house in Finchley, in order to be near Uncle; we knew no one else in London, and I felt close to him because my mother was so fond of him. Later, after a lot of searching and some difficulty, we rented a tiny house in Hampstead Garden Suburb, 133 Willifield Way, and it was at that stage that we sent for you from India. Of course, by then it had been more than a year.

Mama sounded a bit defensive when she said this, so I asked her how soon after her arrival they'd gone to see Uncle and Aunty. 'Oh, very soon after,' said Mama. 'And what was your very first impression of them?' I continued, pen poised to capture the significant moment. Mama frowned in concentration for a while – the sort of concentration one might evince if one were asked where first one learned the verb 'to be' – and finally replied, 'To tell you the truth, I don't remember. I don't remember at all.'

Papa, on the other hand, remembered their first meeting well.

The nurse opened the door. Uncle was still in the surgery, but he came out for a second. He was very well turned out in his dental whites. I was surprised at his size: he was so short. He put his left hand forward. That shouldn't have been a surprise, but I can't remember if I shook his hand. I took to him immediately. But then, I'm old-fashioned; I'd take to the family because I was married into it. Ma had also given a very good account of him – how he loved the family though he lived so far away, and how she and her husband had brought him up.

Aunty Henny was very well dressed. She was a real German and very particular about everything. An ashtray had to be returned to exactly the same place as before. She was not a very warm person, but she warmed up. Uncle and she were complete contrasts; he was overwhelmingly welcoming.

The house itself had a rather synthesised – I mean sanitised – appearance. The garden was well maintained. I still remember the roses in front and the lawn at the back. Aunty Henny was very houseproud. Even the kitchen was scrupulously clean and immaculately tidy. But the whole house was very warm, unbearably so.

Papa describes their life as 'regular, not to say regulated'.

They had their friends: Henry and Nita, Mia and Peter, Mila and Tony, and so on, and they had their bridge parties and dinners, and everything had to run like clockwork. Punctuality was everything. In fact, the Khaitans were once invited by Uncle to dinner at 7.30. They came at nine o'clock, in the Indian manner, and were offered a sandwich. Uncle and Aunty had sat down an hour earlier and had had their dinner already. Later they upbraided us: 'Are Indian people always late?'

Uncle had in many ways lost touch with Indian norms of behaviour. Mama recalled:

We had our differences about matters of courtesy. Once, two or three days after a Christmas party, he phoned me and asked me quite curtly if I needed any money. I was surprised and said no. He continued by saying that I seemed to lack the pennies needed for a phone call. Everyone else had rung up the next day to thank them. 'But I thanked you profusely when we left,' I said; and indeed, we aren't used to thanking people in writing or by phone the day after a party. But Uncle was very disgruntled. 'Don't they teach you manners in India?' he asked.

But this was a minor incident. Papa describes, with some self-detraction, how fond Uncle was of Mama and how impressed Aunty was by her:

Of course, Leila was Uncle's darling; she had no father, and he had no children. I was something of an appendage, especially for Aunty, who saw me as a useful manual worker, an attachment to her husband's intelligent niece. 'Intelligent': she always pronounced the g as in 'garden'. Aunty was always in awe of intelligence and intellectuals, pseudo or otherwise – just as Uncle always managed to mention that someone was Sir Somebody Something or that so-and-so's father had been the aide-de-camp to the King of Sweden.

That sport of intelligence and channelled aggression, bridge, was something Shanti Uncle and Aunty Henny both enjoyed.

Aunty was a good player, Uncle a better one. I made a bridge stand for him with my own hands – smoothing the leather out with a hot spoon to prevent it from creasing. He prized it; what he liked most about it was that he could arrange his cards without anyone knowing where they were placed. I too learned how to play bridge – one can't avoid it in your mother's family. But Uncle believed in long post-mortems, and I never enjoyed these.

Mama loved Shanti Uncle and he her. He delighted in having someone who looked up to him as a surrogate father. What surprised me when I talked to Mama was her remark that because he was usually so busy, and Aunty Henny was always there when she and Papa called, she hardly ever talked to him on his own. He used to call her 'Pinni' after the small round Indian sweet, and sometimes he would tell her to sit on his knee. It was, as she said, 'a bit strange. After all, I was not a young girl but a married woman. But he was quite innocent about it; Uncle was very mature in some ways, very childlike in others.'

Uncle always tried to protect Mama from anything that might cause her distress. One Christmas dinner, Papa, who had had one pink gin too many, suddenly turned white and slid under the table. Later, while the other guests were playing bridge in the upstairs drawing-room under the gaze of the large ceramic parrot, he lay on the downstairs sofa, fast asleep. When the au pair began hoovering the room, he stumbled upstairs, entered the guest bedroom, lay on the bed near the window, and went off to sleep fully clothed – not even snoring, for once. But, as it happened, this bed was not empty. One of the guests, Elsie Little, who had earlier not been feeling too well, was already in it, fast asleep. She had been wearing a new dress which she didn't want crumpled, so before going to bed, she had taken it off and was now lying asleep in her slip.

Another guest opened the door, which was slightly ajar, took in the amazing scene, and quickly closed it. The news swiftly spread to everyone at the bridge tables except Mama. People peeped in from the game whenever they happened to be dummy or between rubbers, and went whispering away. The next day, everyone, including Henry, Nita, Mum and Mum's sister Auntie Rosie, in fact Shanti and Henny's entire acquaintance, knew about the scandal.

But Shanti Uncle had somehow managed to keep Mama from looking into the room, and only she, and of course Papa and Elsie, had remained blissfully unaware of all the fuss.

The sharper side of Uncle's personality was borne home to my parents quite suddenly; it was activated by an innocent remark by Papa.

Whenever there was a party at Uncle and Aunty's, Leila and I helped out. By nature I'm quite obliging, and willing to put my hand to any job. If this had to be moved, I moved it. If that had to be done, I did it. I shifted tables and chairs from morning till evening, hauled large boxes out of the way, served the drinks, lent a hand where I could, and ran endless errands by car for Aunty, who took it all for granted. When the guests were leaving, Aunty turned to me and said, 'You don't mind – you'll drop him home, of course.' I replied, 'Aunty, I don't think I can do it.' Aunty couldn't believe this and said sharply, 'You are very disobliging.' I responded, 'You must be the first woman in my life to tell me I'm disobliging.' Uncle, whom I had never seen really angry before, heard what I'd said and started frothing – yes, actually frothing and foaming – at the mouth with rage: 'How dare you treat my wife like a charwoman? How dare you call her a woman?' We left quickly. In the car I told Leila, 'You can visit them again if you like, but as far as I'm concerned, I'm never going back.' It was months before we returned, but eventually – I can't remember how – we made up. Well, weeks, maybe.

But by the end of his stay in England, Papa had fully redeemed himself in both Uncle's and Aunty's eyes. For one thing, he could talk to Aunty Henny about shoes, something of an obsession with her; she had innumerable pairs, mostly made by Bally. As Uncle later said, she went for style, not comfort, and, if she could only manage to obtain too small a size of a pair she fancied, she got a local shoemaker to stretch them for her.

When Papa repaired Shanti Uncle's surgical chair and later even put up the garden fence for a total cost of £20 instead of the £200 they had been quoted, Aunty Henny decided that he was in fact very obliging. Still later, when Papa tussled to the ground a drunken Englishman twice his size who had crashed into his beloved Hillman Minx which he had parked outside 18 Queens Road – an incident which got into the *Hendon and Finchley Times* partly because the man, hauled before the magistrate, had complained, 'But he performed ju-jitsu on me' – Aunty Henny, whose love of drama had been titillated, was on the phone to her friends for the better part of a day describing with admiration my father's exploit. He was now seen by her as a Man of Action.

But his real redemption – indeed, transfiguration – in Aunty Henny's eyes came when he began to study law in Mama's wake. Mama had taken up this course of study since it was the only one that was compatible with taking care of the house. She would study at home during the day, go to Lincoln's Inn in the evening to eat her dinners – the only form of attendance that in those days was necessary – and take her exams when they were due, all of which she passed splendidly.

After I arrived in England at the age of two, Papa took care of me in the evenings when Mama was attending her dinners. But when, in the wake of the Suez Crisis of 1956, my parents sent me back home to India, Papa felt lonely, returning in the evening to a spouse-less and childless house, and decided that after his day's work at Bata's he would eat his dinners with Mama at Lincoln's Inn. This meant enrolment at the Inns of Court and a modicum of study.

There were five papers in the first part of the bar exams. I took the first paper – I think it was Roman Law – after studying for about eighty hours in total, and I passed. Aunty Henny was incredulous. 'I can't believe it,' she said. 'I can't believe it. It's very good. Very good. But I can't believe it.'

Then I passed the second paper – Criminal Law, perhaps, or Contract and Tort, or Hindu and Mohammedan Law – and Aunty was shocked. I wasn't shocked. I had a very simple method of study. Bata's had given me a job with an impressive-sounding name, Development Officer, and my job was to study various gadgets, layouts and so on, and to do time-and-motion studies. Every so often in the course of my duties I was required to go to Holland, and the journey lasted several hours. Well, I like a boat trip generally, and I like a drink generally, and I never get seasick, so I'd have a beer or two and read my law book.

When the exams came, I wrote very little. I didn't waffle at all. I always tried to grasp the basic principles of law, not all the complex elaborations. I couldn't expand the picture, but I could portray it. I passed the third paper, and by now even Aunty could not put it down to luck. Then, on just about the same amount of work, I passed the fourth and the fifth. By then Aunty had decided I was a genius, and a Rough Diamond, which is how she took to referring to me.

Two questions that interested me in particular were Uncle's disability and his marriage. When I spoke to my parents about the former, Mama told me about her first encounter with him in a professional capacity:

Two or three weeks after we arrived in England, I had terrible toothache. It was Sunday. I hadn't intended to go to Uncle for dental treatment, largely because I didn't know how good he could be with only one working hand. I had even anticipated what I might have to say in order not to hurt him when I went somewhere else, namely, that the company had insisted on it and that I hadn't had any choice. But the pain must have been pretty bad for me not to have been able to hang on until Monday. I told him I was in agony and he told me to come over at once. Since it was outside regular hours, Aunty Henny assisted in the surgery. I was quite amazed at how good he was, how skilful, how reassuring, how gentle. I never went to anyone else during my more than three years in London.

As for the second question, both Papa and Mama agreed that Uncle and Aunty formed a rather odd couple, but when I asked them to explain what they meant, they hesitated. 'Well, for one thing,' said Mama, 'they looked so incongruous: he short and compact, she tall and thin in her high heels, towering over him.'

'I think it was more a mutual support system than any great love,' said Papa.

'But you could see there was a caring relationship,' said Mama.

'Except when they quarrelled in front of everyone.'

'Yes,' said Mama. 'Whenever they had a fight, they'd lapse into German and snap and shout, and Aunty Henny would say "Muck dash nish", and then Uncle would go out for a walk. We used to think that if they quarrelled so openly in front of us, their marriage must be on the rocks, but for them, raising their voices in German was like quarrelling behind closed doors. They never lost their temper beyond the point of control. I've never seen Uncle really angry.'

'Apart from when he said I'd called Aunty a woman.'

'Yes,' said Mama thoughtfully.

'Of course, a lot goes on in a marriage that no one knows. I think Uncle was quite a lad.'

'Certainly not,' said Mama.

'Wasn't there a problem once?'

'That's absolute nonsense,' said Mama. 'I know Shanti Uncle's nature.'

'I think there was a Swiss au pair once, who complained to somebody that Uncle had tried to—'

'She complained to Henny, and it turned out to be a complete misunderstanding.'

In fact, I had heard – but I can't remember when and from whom – about an incident with an au pair; apparently, she had been tired, and Uncle had said, 'To bed with you,' which she had mentally translated into German and taken to mean something else.

'We were all much closer to Shanti Uncle,' continued Papa. 'Henny could be very abrupt and abrasive. "I don't care what anybody thinks of me," she'd say.'

'Well, I think she wanted to be liked,' said Mama. 'Michi used to call her Hennylein, and she liked it – she became rather coy.'

'She was attractive, and must have been very good-looking when she was young,' said Papa. 'I remembered noticing her legs had little red spots on them, and she was quite self-conscious about this. But she always wore very good shoes, which of course I noticed, and was very elegantly dressed. Silk and cashmere and so on.'

'And she pointed it out as well: "I only wear the best."'

'Uncle dressed well too,' said Papa, appreciatively.

'That's true,' said Mama. 'But I found it exhausting going shopping with him. He was very generous and always bought me presents, but he was so fussy and went to twenty shops and took such a long time to make up his mind. "Should I buy this tie or that one?" he'd ask.'

'Women should never decide what ties men should wear,' said Papa.

About Aunty Henny's family, Mama and Papa had nothing to add to what I knew at the time. Mama had heard from Shanti Uncle (who was perhaps trying to encourage a bond of affection between her and Aunty Henny) that 'Henny's people' had been killed by Hitler during the war and that she had no one left to call family. But Mama, being discreet, never took up the subject with her; and she, for her part, never volunteered anything. Mama added: 'In fact, we didn't even know she was Jewish for quite a long time. Uncle once remarked, after they returned from a trip to Switzerland, "Some Germans were there and it spoiled Henny's holiday." I didn't understand it – after all, she was German too – but I was always reluctant to ask questions.'

When I asked Papa, his response was: 'For my sins, I didn't know. But then, it's the last thing I'm interested in.' This indifference to a person's background was certainly characteristic of Papa. When he was posted to Patna, the capital of the most caste-ridden state in India, even after ten years he scarcely knew the difference between Kurmis and Rajputs and Bhumihar Brahmins – neither the significance of the distinctions nor which of his colleagues was which.

My mother was not much better informed. When she was asked by a colleague in the Bar Library of the Patna High Court, 'Oh, but what caste did the witness belong to?' she could not understand the point of the question. When she learned that people would happily perjure themselves out of caste solidarity, she was amazed. When she later learned that if a case came up before, say, a Bhumihar judge, it was best argued by a Bhumihar lawyer, she was deeply shocked. Her colleagues were amused by her innocence of the ways of the world.

During their early acquaintance with Shanti Uncle and Aunty Henny, the caste structure of Indian society was to enter with a clang into the conversation at the dinner-table at 18 Queens Road. Mama recounted an incident that was of a piece with their ignorance and Papa's cheerful tactlessness:

Henny was talking about Mr and Mrs Khaitan, and Premo mentioned in response to some remark that, well, after all, they came from the Marwari community. 'Marwari? What does that mean?' asked Aunty Henny, turning to Uncle. 'Oh,' said Premo blithely, 'They hold money rather close – a bit like the Jews.' There was dead silence at the table for a few seconds, and Uncle quickly changed the conversation.

On another occasion, Papa, in contrast to his declared lack of interest, said, 'I thought she was a Jew because of her quite prominent nose.' This was news to me, since, if Papa had indeed known, he would never have made the comment Mama mentioned, let alone been surprised by the effect it produced. Papa had never been one for racial physiognomy, and besides, India has almost no Jews, so I didn't see how he could have had a benchmark of any sort; in any case, Aunty Henny's nose was far from the parodic stereotype. But Papa said that a number of his Czech colleagues at Bata had been Jewish – 'Yehudi Morris was one, and Abraham, our famous shipping man, and Louis Weisz, who was so fond of you, and gave you that radio, and I wouldn't be surprised if Vyrol was one' – before Mama cut him off with 'Well, these things never struck me.'

I later learned that before the Germans marched into Czechoslovakia, Thomas Bata had tried to transfer a number of his employees, and in particular his Jewish employees, to places outside Europe – in many cases to India. But in general, Judaism and Jews have not played a large role in Indian history or in the general consciousness of most Indians. There have been small Jewish communities in India over the centuries – indeed, from the time of Nebuchadnezzar. It is also perhaps worth mentioning that a Viceroy of India, Rufus Isaacs, Lord Reading, was Jewish; the fact that this was not considered very significant is itself significant. After the Second World War, most Indian Jews emigrated – largely for economic and social reasons, not because of prejudice or persecution – to Israel or elsewhere, making it difficult, in many places, to form a religious quorum.

But facts such as these are flotsam in the tide of events. The history of the Jews in Europe and the Middle East – with its great cultural complexity and significance, its assimilationist or isolationist currents and its religious antagonisms, often exacerbated by economic issues but inflamed most particularly by the 'Christ-killer' hatreds embedded in Christianity – has not been replicated in India. We have concentrated on our own religious antagonisms, our own historical hatreds, which seem so much more reasonable. The only time I was conscious in a personal way of an old Jewish presence in India was when I went to Kerala for the first time about a decade ago and stood in the intimate synagogue in Cochin, quiet and calm, built in 1568, its interior lined with blue-and-white tiles from as far away as Canton.

4.4

My parents went to Spain for a short holiday in the summer of 1956, and one afternoon in Barcelona at the Hotel Espléndido – as they think it was called – my brother Shantum was conceived. When Mama realised she was pregnant, she got worried, because it was difficult enough to make ends meet even without a second child. Uncle made a suggestion: that when the baby was born, he and Aunty adopt it. They had married too late for children, and both of them were keen to have a child. Mama promised to think about it and Uncle was very pleased.

When the baby was born (with a little shock of black hair, unlike the bald English babies) at Queen Mary's Hospital in Hampstead, Uncle spoke to Mama again. He said that since it was a boy, and not, as my parents had wished, a girl to complement their first child, he hoped that they would go ahead with the adoption. Mama again promised to think about it.

She describes what went through her mind:

He was such a lovely and happy baby, and of course, as he was my child, I loved him. But I kept thinking, would he have a better life if they adopted him? In terms of money, yes – we were hard up – he would definitely be better off with them. And he would be loved and cared for. But not, I felt, in the way I would love and care for him. I was less concerned about Uncle as a father, though he was in his late forties. But Aunty Henny was so highly strung – and with small children, as I thought, it is finally the mother who matters. So Premo and I made up our minds, and when Uncle mentioned the subject again, I kept quiet and didn't say anything – neither yes nor no. He sensed – you can tell these things – that we didn't want to give up the baby.

I could see what Mama meant about Aunty Henny being 'highly strung'. She was not overtly affectionate. She had a high voice and a strident scream of a laugh and an emphatic manner. She seemed indifferent to the importance of Indian family ties. As I have said, she and Uncle would think nothing about bickering openly – as long as it was in German. When a party was thrown, she would be jittery, impatient, even dictatorial about getting things perfect: everything, from her coiffure to the table settings to the amount of paprika in the chicken to the angle of the pencils on the bridge pads, had to be exactly right. At times, her manner was brusque or brittle. Only part of this could be attributed to what she had gone through.

This was all true, and yet I saw a side of her that my parents perhaps only glimpsed – a side that probably revealed itself only because I lived with her and Uncle for days, weeks, months and years. Under all Aunty Henny's professions of indifference and her concern for form and style, she was also protective and tolerant, affectionate, even gentle. Long before I got the chance to read her letters to her friends, I experienced her pragmatism, generosity and 'optimismus'; through her letters to me when I was at Stanford, she encouraged me from afar when I was close to losing heart. Once, talking to Shantum about our cousin Ira, she said, 'I know what goes on in a young girl's mind, how a young girl thinks.' She might well have made a good – and unusually understanding – mother, however irksomely exacting about petty matters any child of spirit might have found her.

For all this, however, and quite selfishly, I thank whatever powers there be that my parents made the decision they did about that baby. While I was writing this, I tried to think of him being adopted and brought up in a distant country – and of my not having him as a brother. It was impossible; I could not imagine life without him.

Because they loved Uncle and he was so disappointed, my parents decided to name the baby Shanti after him, which is how his name appears on his birth certificate. When my grandmother heard about this, she put her foot down, and wrote from India to tell my mother that this would not do.

'You can't name the child after a living relative,' she said. 'It's not our way. If you are angry with the child, it'll be as if you're shouting at Shanti. And besides, Shanti by itself is a girl's name. It has to be Shanti Behari or Shanti Prasad or Shanti Bhushan. You'll have to change it.' Well, as you know, in your case, Vikram, we changed your name from Amit at the insistence of Papa's family. And we couldn't defy Ma either in a matter like this. But the trouble was that if we changed the name completely Uncle would be terribly unhappy. That's why we invented the name Shantum – which incorporated his name, but chimed with yours.

Shanti Uncle was happy about Shantum's name. He took to call-ing the baby 'my baby' or 'my prize baby'.

Mama describes Aunty Henny's reaction to Shantum's birth and to their decision:

I was recovering from the birth, and my law finals were coming up in a matter of weeks, so I was preoccupied. Aunty Henny, who must have been as disappointed as Uncle, was very helpful. She would go shopping with Premo to get things for the baby, and she also gave him lots of presents. She was anxious and very helpful and kind.

4.5

In 2002, when this former baby was forty-five years old and had a year-old baby of his own, I spoke to him about his memories of Shanti Uncle.

Shantum had seen Shanti Uncle for the first six months of his life. He had then returned to India with my parents. Not long afterwards, in December 1957, Uncle visited India for a short trip – his only one after the war. Shantum would then have been eight months old.

Even though I had no memory of Shanti Uncle, I had been brought up from childhood with him as part of our family framework. He had wanted to adopt me, I knew, and I had been named after him. Because my name's so unusual, I've often had to repeat the story of how it came about. That's one thing that's kept Uncle in my thoughts. Also, I think he was meant to be my godfather – whatever that means, since we're not Christian. I don't know if he was fully aware of it, but in my mind I had been brought up with the knowledge of that special link.

Also, he was very close to Amma [our maternal grandmother, Raj's wife], who was the only other person from that generation whom I devel-oped any relationship with. I think we felt deprived of grandparents. Ever since Nandini [Shantum's elder daughter] was born, I've thought about it a lot. Luckily, she has all four of her grandparents and they all dote on her.

The next time Shantum and Shanti Uncle met was in 1975, when Shantum was on his way to Leicester to do what Papa had done many years previously in Northampton: a technical course in footwear manufacture. He stopped in London and stayed for a few days with Shanti Uncle and Aunty Henny. He was eighteen years old, and they were sixty-six.

Uncle opened the door. He was in front and Aunty Henny behind him near the famous coat-rack. I stayed in the so-called Vikram's room in the attic. I remember the eiderdown: golden, shiny and puffy – it always slipped off. Also the little window set quite high in the wall with a view of the garden. What was important to me was that there was a home in England, a reference point: Uncle, Aunty, a house, a garden. I did not feel completely alien, as I might have if I'd gone to study in France or Italy. It was a connection back to India. I didn't feel abandoned or lost.

But it was very different from home. Although Uncle kept overfeeding me in his hospitable way, it didn't feel like an Indian home. There was the rigmarole with the keys and making sure you were back at a certain time. There was the bath drill, down to the removal of any possible ring around the tub, the dabbing up of the last drop of water and the placing of the towel on the boiler in the upstairs corridor. After each meal, there was the washing-up, then the drying-up, then the wiping of the sink. It wasn't exactly relaxing, but after what I faced day after day in Leicester, it was a sort of refuge.

Shantum's life in Leicester had not been easy. Apart from his intensive studies and part-time work, he had had to face other problems.

What was tough was the atmosphere, especially the racial tension and the hatred. I had arrived as a bit of an innocent, but I grew up fast. Once I was walking in the market area in Leicester, in the High Street. It was crowded. Somebody came by and deliberately shoved his elbow with great force into my stomach. I doubled over, and before I could see exactly who it was, he'd made off. Another time, there was this guy who was selling a National Front newspaper, and he just came up to me and spat in my face. I went to the police station to report it, and their reaction was basically, 'So what?'

Probably my worst experience was when I went with my girlfriend Lea to the French Revolution, the only disco in Leicester where you were allowed to wear jeans. We were dancing, Lea and I, when about half a dozen people orchestrated an attack. They were dressed in green army jackets with German flags, and their heads were shaven. One girl in the group pushed Lea and then said, 'Don't push me.' I instinctively put my hand out to protect Lea. Two guys behind me started punching me on the side of my forehead, a very dangerous area. From the way they were stationed, it had clearly been pre-planned. I fell on to the ground and I can't remember what happened: maybe the bouncers pulled them away. When I came round, Lea and I decided to continue dancing but to quickly get out in the middle of the next dance, and criss-cross out of the alleyway to get to the main road.

I had faced little of this kind of thing compared to Shantum. A couple of kids at Tonbridge would delight in calling out to me, 'Boy!' when they saw me walking by myself near the sports fields; at first I was simply baffled by what they meant, but when it became clear that they were trying to be insulting, I was perplexed at a different level. There were a few taunts late at night on the tube when I was with a white girl, some muttered comments in shops and at ticket counters about 'you people', but by and large, in Tonbridge, Oxford and the parts of London I saw as a student, the atmosphere, if anything, was intolerant of intolerance. But the one time I visited Shantum in Leicester, I saw at first-hand what he had to go through. We went to a pub, not one of those he normally frequented, and I asked for two pints of bitter. There was something of an atmosphere of hostility which I couldn't understand. Then a man who was sitting at the counter told the bartender,

'Don't serve them.' I turned to him and asked why, and his reply, addressed again to the bartender, was 'It'll make them smell more.' The bartender was clearly uncertain what to do. I insisted, in retrospect foolishly, on our being served, but Shantum, who had a better sense of the scene, was clearly uneasy. I changed my order to half-pints and we left shortly afterwards.

Shantum also found that he was quite often stopped by the police for no obvious reason, even on the street where he lived; presumably, he had come to the area to rob or to deal in drugs.

As a reaction to all this, Shantum joined an organisation called the Interracial Solidarity Campaign, most of whose members were liberal white people. He later said, 'It helped in not making me anti-white, because that could easily have happened to me.'

He underwent a transformation from the easy-going young man he had been. In his first three or four years in England, from not being interested in much other than clothes and girls and a career and 'making easy money quick' – as he once mentioned to Shanti Uncle and was never allowed to forget – he became, in his own words, 'completely politicised'. He got involved in numerous causes, became anti-nuclear, anti-apartheid and pro-feminist, changed his clothes, girlfriend and thinking, grew his hair very long, took to wearing a turban and got himself an earring.

One of the organisations he joined was the Anti-Nazi League. Despite this, and though he knew that he'd be fighting people for whom blacks and Asians and Jews were the common enemy, Shantum says that he never really understood Aunty Henny's background of ethnic or racial persecution. 'Aunty was very closed about her past. I couldn't relate to it too well. We'd never studied European history at school [in India], though I'd heard, of course, about the persecution of the Jews.'

As for what he himself faced daily in Leicester, Shantum said: 'I didn't talk much about this to Uncle. I didn't want to worry him – or the family, who would probably have heard about it from him.' He may even have faced a sort of bafflement from Uncle, who averred on more than one occasion that he had never faced anything like racism in England, either within his profession or socially.

Shantum often went to London for demonstrations of one kind or another. But because he was now impatient with what he describes as the 'clockwork lifestyle' of 18 Queens Road, he was usually eager to get away and spend time with his friends and fellow activists. Besides, when he visited, he and Uncle usually argued about political issues, with Uncle always taking the conservative view – although, as Shantum put it, they argued without really listening to each other.

Shantum was arrested for protesting peacefully at Upper Heyford in Oxfordshire, where American F-111s armed with nuclear warheads were based. He was tried before a magistrate in Banbury, did not pay (or let any of us pay) his fine for more than a year, and went to prison for a week in lieu of this. He joined the University of East Anglia at Norwich to do Development Studies and became the vice-president of the Students' Union; he lived in a squat and put up a tepee in a symbolic protest against student rent hikes. He participated in rallies in Trafalgar Square against the apartheid regime in South Africa.

Shantum describes Uncle's reaction to his radicalism:

He was more tolerant of my doings than I expected. I suppose it was the *Guardian* and the *Observer* that he still subscribed to, the liberal veneer he maintained. Or maybe, given what had happened to Aunty Henny, they might even have approved of my anti-racial and anti-apartheid activism. Though they were conservative, the only thing they actively disapproved of was the anarchism that at one stage I got involved in. As for my stand against nuclear weapons, Uncle tried to persuade me that there was no need to go to jail over the fine, but he knew that that was me.

He even accepted the hair, the earring, and so on, though you can imagine how that must have grated. Once I came to their door in a poncho with my girlfriend at the time, a redhead who had blued part of her hair. In fact, Uncle and Aunty met quite a few of my girlfriends over the years, and remembered their names long after they weren't so vivid in my memory.

Shanti Uncle liked talking about pretty girls. In fact, he just liked talking, and he'd repeat his set stories and his set theories: all Seths like peanuts, all Seths have a weak ticker, and so on. When Gitu [Shantum's wife] and I went to see him, he really liked her, though both then and ever afterwards he called her Patanjali rather than Gitanjali – I couldn't change this; it was yet another fixed idea.

They were so set in their ways. And yet, when you think about it, if I'd lived such a crazy, unsettled life earlier, I'd want to settle down to some sort of routine, and chill out for a few decades. England was safe: it was a liberal democracy, there was law and justice – OK, maybe not perfect – and respect for the professions, and people hadn't been killed there on a mass scale for centuries. You could live your own quiet middle-class life, without having it ripped apart by madmen.

Shantum fell quiet for a while, pondering what he had just said. I too said nothing; I was mulling over the possibility with a strange feeling of emptiness and anxiety, illogical since it could not retrospectively come to pass, that he might have become Shanti Uncle and Aunty Henny's child, not Papa and Mama's any more.

4.6

This absence of children from their lives, though rarely expressed, was, I think, felt deeply by both Uncle and Aunty, though in different ways. They had full and busy lives; there was no emptiness at the centre, more a sense of something unfulfilled. Henny's letters do not give much away, but from Ilse's letter, in which she talks about the two of them idling away an afternoon cutting out paper dolls for children, or from the photograph, captioned 'Henny's toy', of Henny on a walking trip tenderly holding up a Tyrolean baby, one gets something of a sense of what she felt for children. In

England, for a few months after she was with the Arberrys, she got a job as a nanny for a Canadian family. A little later, in May 1942, Shanti was to write to her from Egypt:

I have also been thinking lately that it would be nice to have a house of my own with plenty of children. We both seem to agree on this point, which is very important indeed.

Shanti Uncle had been brought up as one of eight children, and to have a childless house must have seemed to him somehow incomplete. However, after the suggestion he made to Papa and Mama about Shantum, Shanti Uncle and Aunty Henny do not seem to have followed up the possibility of adoption. For one thing, they may have been too old to be considered seriously as adoptive parents. For another, Shanti Uncle, like many Indians, may have been loath to adopt a child whose parents he would not have known much, if anything, about. But he loved children, and when my friends John and Sue Hughes visited him, he decided that their young sons were 'prize babies' too. A large red double-decker toy bus was presented to them, and he often enquired about them.

When he had to treat children in the course of his work, he was deeply concerned about their possible distress. He kept an extra chair in the surgery so that the mother of any child who was being treated could be present to support him or her.

Once, a child of seven came to see me and wanted to have a tooth extracted. I said, 'Where are your parents?' and he said, 'They're working, but I have a latchkey to get back in.' Needless to say, I sent him home, and told him that either his mother or his father had to be there, or I wouldn't do anything at all. Can you imagine what trauma the child would go through, having his first extraction without mother or father to comfort him?

Though Uncle called me 'Söhnchen', I found it difficult, when interviewing him, to ask him what my living in their home had meant to them: whether I had been too much of a responsibility; whether my going to America had made them lonelier than before; whether it was hard for them to know that I may have been their 'Söhnchen' but was someone else's son.

Uncle, for his part, touched on such questions only sporadically and, because I didn't follow them up, not very coherently. But I could not help being moved when he wandered off from a comment on an entirely different matter to an aside such as this:

We talked a lot about you from your childhood onwards because we didn't have children of our own. If there was a book review or a news item, whatever happened to you, Aunty Henny kept it. I regret I was strict with you, darling, but Aunty Henny was always on your side. Only, she didn't like it when you were scruffy.

4.7

Aunty Henny's *Wahlverwandten*, or 'chosen relations', as she put it in a letter to one of her Berlin friends, were her family. Uncle's was his family of birth with all its subsequent branches. Again and again during my years with him, he talked about the importance of family bonds. Again and again in his interviews, he told me what his grandfather, his eldest sister Hirabehn, his eldest brother Raj and his sister-in-law Chanda had meant to him.

He believed that as an elder of the family, he had the right to be informed about family events, to investigate, to advise and, if necessary, to upbraid. When he discovered that his nephew Sashi, who in his twenties was pursuing an insurance course in London, had been gambling on the horses, he gave him a severe dressing-down (though Aunty Henny subsequently slipped Sashi a ten-shilling note and asked him to place it for her). When I made a date to go to the movies with the daughter of one of his friends, he ticked me off for not clearing it with him first –

though, needless to say, any pleasure or spontaneity would thereby have been lost.

Through his interest in the extended family and his interrogatory style, he was well informed about the currents and undercurrents of life among the latter-day 'Seths of Biswan' – in some ways analogous to Henny's knowledge of her circle of friends in Berlin. But the information Uncle gleaned was not always used tactfully. Michi, Sashi's elder brother, once stated to Shanti Uncle that he didn't think Sashi would amount to much. The next time Sashi visited, Shanti told him what Michi had said and waited for his reaction. Perhaps this was more than innocently tactless; there was a tinge of cruelty and relish in it which hinted at Shanti Uncle's treatment of his family towards the end of his life. Sashi, in the event, rose higher in his profession than Michi did, but he was profoundly hurt by his elder brother's opinion, so deliberately transmitted.

Where did Shanti and Henny belong, if not in the world of a family or a circle of friends? Which country did they belong to? Not Germany any more, not India. Nor did they have a refuge in the religions of their birth. Both Hinduism and Judaism are somewhat 'social' religions, in that dogma and belief are less crucial in practice than rites of passage and social relations. But their religion or the comforting society of their co-religionists did not cocoon either Shanti or Henny. Indeed, how could it have, since either cocoon would have excluded the other partner? Work, that great home, must have given them some sense of belonging. For the rest, it was the physical house itself and its routine and ritual, that clockwork of which Shantum was so impatient, all underwritten by a certain style of middle-class Englishness more or less naturally absorbed, though at no early age. It had its exterior manifestations: 'I have become more English in my appearance,' wrote Henny to Ilse. Shanti, with his devotion to Simpson's and Aquascutum, Jaeger and Austin Reed, attired himself in the subdued taste of his third country. But its interior manifestations were more complex. The ideal of the gentleman, so eloquently enjoined on him by his brother Raj, was imprinted on Shanti's mental constitution, as was the idea of 'fairness', even more than justice, on Henny and her friends in Berlin. There was in addition something in common between the bourgeois middle-class Indian ethos and that of middle-class Germany, perhaps more particularly middle-class Jewish Germany, in its respect for the professions, for education, for savings, for house and home; and all this was compatible with a settled and useful, undisturbed life in England or, at least, in London.

What did the English make of them? Uncle looked a foreigner; and Henny dressed so smartly that she almost had to be one; but either had only to speak for it to be clear that they were not native. On the whole, though, the English do not feel any obligation to make any-thing of anyone. There was no ritual of conformity, no compulsory protestations of patriotism or national affiliation. Thus these two of the many rooted exiles of the twentieth century passed the years and decades of the latter half of their lives feeling neither very much at home nor very obviously foreign in a land that could be seen as either coolly indifferent or blessedly uninterfering, even tolerant.

What they assuredly were not was what they had been. Henny was as relieved to give up her German passport – stamped 'J' – as to receive the stiff blue passport issued under the imprimatur of His Britannic Majesty (to whom, rather than to whose country or con-stitution, she had signed an oath of allegiance). Shanti claimed throughout his life to be interested in Indian affairs, but his views of Indian life and politics were frozen in the early 1930s. Neither he nor Henny could have predicted that they would live in London for most of their lives. Much of what they were they had either shed or let die through attrition and disuse. Shanti over the years lost his ability to speak Hindi, the language in which he would have felt most at ease for the first two decades of his life. Henny still spoke German but read no German books.

Language too is a home and confers belonging – not only to the larger culture group and the community, living and dead, who have

Oath of Allegiance.

I, *Henny Gerda Caro*

swear by Almighty God that I will be faithful and bear true allegiance to His Majesty, King George the Sixth, His Heirs and Successors, according to law.

(Signature) *Henny Gerda Caro*

Sworn and subscribed this 30th day of December 1948, before me,

(Signature) *R.E. Hartigan*

~~Justice of the Peace for~~

A Commissioner for Oaths.

Name and Address
(in Block Capitals)

R.G. HARTIGAN,
106, Finchley Road,
N.W.3.

Unless otherwise indicated hereon, if the Oath of Allegiance is not taken within one calendar month after the date of this Certificate, the Certificate shall not take effect.

HOME OFFICE
11 JAN 1949
REGISTERED

Henny's oath of allegiance to King George VI on the obverse of her certificate of naturalisation.

spoken or written it, but also to the pods and pairs of our intimate lives. For the first few years that they knew each other, at 60 Mommsenstrasse, Shanti and Henny would have spoken nothing but German. Yet in England during the war, with German the suspect language of the enemy, they were compelled to write to each other in English. In the letters he sent to Henny between 1942 and 1944, Shanti even wooed her through English, which must have been an awkward endeavour. But the language spoken at 18 Queens Road – when no one else was present – reverted to German; and part of the reason that I graduated from 'my husband's nephew' to 'my nephew' for Aunty Henny, and from 'my nephew' to 'my little son' for Uncle, was that I had learned to share their language, and nothing spoken aloud at home remained veiled from me.

Shaken about the globe, we live out our fractured lives. Enticed or fleeing, we re-form ourselves, taking on partially the coloration of our new backgrounds. Even our tongues are alienated and rejoined – a multiplicity that creates richness and confusion. Both Shanti and Henny were in the broader sense exiled; each found in their fellow exile a home.

In Shanti's case, the exile was of his making; not so with Henny, though it could in some strict sense be said that she chose not to return when, once again, it became safe to do so. Increasingly from adolescence onwards she would have sensed that she was set apart from her Christian friends – that her position was precarious, even in the city in which she had been born, in the only streets she had known.

Aunty Henny never came to India. Knowing her, and knowing what she missed, this makes me deeply sad. At any time during the almost four decades of her marriage, she could have gone there with Shanti Uncle; it was never more than a day's journey away. I quote without comment Shantum's insight into this phenomenon:

She had a big fear of India – the noise, the crowds, the germs. It's a bit of a pity that they didn't come here. He had very strong memories, but he had a fear too, and he certainly didn't want to expose her to India. You would have thought that if someone married an Indian, they would want to come and live in India or at least to visit, but not in this case. Shanti Uncle first became rather German, and then rather British, and Aunty Henny didn't appreciate the Indian side of him, though she did appreciate the qualities that might have come about as a result. And to go to a place where there was this huge extended family when she had no family of her own. She lived, I imagine, with a lot of memories of the past. Can you think – if something like that happened to us—

4.8

Work too gives one a sense of belonging – not only (if one's work is not solitary) to the society of the office or shop or corps or department and one's clients or customers or contacts or patients but also (whether one's work is solitary or not) to the general category of people who find it easier to see themselves as 'useful'. Shanti's struggles with his profession have been described in some detail. But Henny too worked, from 1926, when she was seventeen years old, almost continuously until her early fifties. Then a stark choice was put to her by Shanti, and she stopped.

In one of three dull-green files of official correspondence with German bureaucracy dating from the 1950s, one finds a summary of Henny's life, somewhat akin in its laconic style to the CV appended to Shanti's dental dissertation many years earlier:

<u>Curriculum Vitae</u>

I was born on 13 December, 1908 as the daughter of the businessman Isaac Caro (born 19 November, 1869) and his wife, Ella Caro née Schmelkes (born 10 November, 1870). [On the Gestapo transport list, Ella's date of birth is given as 11 November 1871, but there her name too is incorrectly recorded.]

Between the ages of 6 and 16, I studied at the Lyceum of the Fürstin Bismarck School (Sybelstrasse), which I completed with my Matriculation certificate (single-year). I then took a one-year course at the Higher Commercial School.

I then obtained a post in the offices of the Mannheimer Life Insurance Company, which I held for many years and was only dismissed from because the company was not allowed to employ any Jewish workers.

I was, as a result, forced, since it was impossible to find a job as a Jew, to emigrate from Germany, which I did on 27 July, 1939.

Since then I have been in England and have acquired British nationality.

I have been married since 20 July [1951]. My husband is a dentist (Dr S.B. Seth) and I live at 18, Queens Road, London NW 4.

London, 10 October, 1952

signed: Henny Seth née Caro

This document is part of a file dealing with a compensation claim against the German state for 'damage to career'. In response to an enquiry by Fröschlein, the insurance company writes on 6 November 1957:

Dear Fräulein Fröschke,

With respect to your inquiry of 26.10.57 we can inform you that Frau Henny Seth née Caro, born on 13.12.1908 in Berlin, entered the service of our company on 17.3.1926. She was employed here until 30.6.1937 and drew a standard salary of RM 256.35 at the time she left. The salary that she might have attained had she continued to be employed by the company, is unfortunately impossible now to say.

We hope to have been been of service.

Yours sincerely,

M a n n h e i m e r
Lebensversicherungs-Gesellschaft AG.

When Fröschlein asks them to state that Henny was let go 'on the sole grounds of the Nazi measures', they fob her off with:

> We regret to have to inform you that we no longer possess the documents that would cover the question of the grounds on which the dismissal of Frau Seth ensued.

Henny next worked as a secretary for the firm of Paul Oppler, a solicitor. She writes in another, more detailed, statement of her career:

> As far as I can remember, I was paid at an hourly rate, and my earnings at this firm fell far short of my income at the Mannheimer Life Insurance Company. My employment at the firm of Paul Oppler ended, as far as I can remember, towards the end of 1938, because Herr Oppler emigrated. I do not know whether Herr Oppler is contactable, since he too was a Jew.

After she emigrated to England in July 1939, she worked for ten months as household help for Professor and Mrs Arberry in exchange for food and accommodation only, and then as nanny for a Canadian family, who later returned to Canada; from them she earned a very small allowance by way of pocket money. Not until February 1941 was she able to re-enter her profession as a clerk/typist, possibly with minor managerial duties, at the company where she was to work for the next two decades.

Shanti explained the situation as follows:

She knew the Weissbergs, who had left Germany well before the war. They owned the Nu Organic Company, a small firm of about fifteen or twenty people which produced and sold pharmaceutical goods, and they gave Henny a job. Margot Weissberg ran things; she was a very nice person, but her husband lived under her thumb because she was the earning member. In due course, Henny became second in command, and later, when Mrs Weissberg became very ill, Henny took charge.

Something of this history is reflected in a document issued by HM Inspector of Taxes for the Hampstead District in December 1957. It was sent to Henny's accountant, Derek Hudson (who was Henry Edwards's wife Nita's son from her first marriage). It would have been issued as supporting evidence for the German authorities.

Dear Sir,

<u>Mrs. H. G. Seth.</u>

With reference to your letter of 29th October 1957, your client's income is as follows:–

1940/41	£19.10.0
1941/42	164
1942/43	164
1943/44	184
1944/45	240
1945/46	282
1946/47	390
1947/48	406
1948/49	450
1949/50	471
1950/51	480
1951/52	356
1952/53	499
1953/54	887
1954/55	1596
1955/56	1527
1956/57	1615

Yours faithfully,
[illegible]
H.M. Inspector of Taxes

D.E. Hudson Esq.

Henny's income from child-minding was clearly nugatory. From the time she joined the pharmaceutical firm, however, it climbed steadily. The dip in 1951/2 might correspond to time that she took off following her wedding. The two steep steps in the early fifties would have corresponded to her taking on senior managerial duties; the second step probably reflected her promotion to the position of managing director. Clearly, a good five years into her marriage she was still working and earning well. When Shanti had been in the Army Dental Corps, he had earned about £1. 5s. a day. Now, after he had resigned from the Amalgamated Dental Company and was engaged fully as a dentist in the National Health Service – one who, owing to his disability, would have worked more slowly than most – he may well not have had an income as high as Henny's. When one considers that the house in Hendon had cost only about £5000 in 1948 and that taxation in the UK was high but not yet as exorbitant as it was later, for a time, to become, one can see that Henny's disposable income would have been substantial.

But her satisfactions from work would have extended far beyond her earnings. She would have had the prestige associated with her title and responsibilities. She would have had, as one can see from her correspondence, the admiration not only of her office staff but also of her business acquaintances. She would have taken pleasure in the exercise and expansion of her skills and her ability to make decisions. She would have had a place to go to every day, quite distinct from the routine of house and shops and social circle. And, judging from the stamps that she collected from her office correspondence and sent me when I was a young boy in India, her work would have opened a window on to a wider world: her horizons would have stretched from Sierra Leone to Iraq, from Iceland to New Zealand.

The stream of exotic stamps thinned out when I was about eleven or twelve, so it must have been in the early sixties that she stopped working. This is what Shanti Uncle had to say about the matter:

After Mrs Weissberg died, Henny continued to run the firm. By now we were married. They wanted to sell the firm to her at a bargain price. I told her, 'It's up to you. If you own the company and are the managing director, you will be mainly engaged in work. Now, you decide whether you'd like that or would rather give it up and stay at home.' She decided to stay at home and she never looked back.

What Henny gave up by this decision was not trivial, either in its substance or in its satisfactions. She had enjoyed working, as she mentioned to me more than once. For whatever reasons she gave up her job – stress, exhaustion, self-sacrifice or an appraisal of the firm's prospects – I think it would have been surprising if she had never looked back.

4.9

The subject of 'damage to career' was only one of the matters contained in these three files. Other subjects, more painful to contemplate and deal with for Henny, were the question of compensation from the German state for the plunder of the family's possessions by the Nazis; and the inheritance issues that arose from the murder in the concentration camps of Henny's two aunts, Olga and Flora Glaser.

Annerose Dietrich had told Henny that she had a right, indeed, a duty to herself and her family, to address such questions, however emotionally difficult they might be, however ponderous or petty the correspondence might prove, if only to help provide for herself later on. Both Annerose and Fröschlein had offered to help Henny handle matters at the Berlin end. After Fröschlein came over to England – invited by Henny, Shanti and Margot – Henny did put matters in train, and it was Fröschlein whose help she sought. (For one thing, Annerose was living in what was now East Berlin, and Henny's home had been in Charlottenburg, which formed part of what was now West Berlin.)

Jews had been required to hand in their silver and jewellery by

February 1939, their radios by September 1939 and their furs by January 1942 to the Pawn Institution, the cynical name for the conduit used by the Nazis for outright appropriation. For the grand silver dinner services, of which, as Jews, they had been allowed to retain just one setting per family member, the documentation had to be found, the weight ascertained or approximated, and the value estimated by local silversmiths. Here, after the passage of much time and the incurral of much expense, Henny's lawyer got the government to pay up.

For the other objects that had been taken from Henny's mother, the postwar German institutions slithered behind a shield of specious legality in order to avoid responsibility. At one stage of the restitution proceedings, in October 1958, thirteen years after the end of the war, Henny was asked to adduce proof for the radio and the fur coat that her mother had owned and had been forced to deliver up. It is worth quoting from the Secretary for Finance (Special Property and Building Administration) in his letter to the Offices for Compensation in Berlin:

A mere supposition that the objects must have been delivered up earlier, because they have not been set out in the property declaration of the victim, suffices as proof of unjust deprivation not at all. [Note the way in which in the German the final word *nicht* explodes the expectation of reasonableness that has been built up.]

I must therefore request the petitioner to furnish proof through witnesses or in some other suitable manner.

For the time being I am compelled to raise an objection.

As Fröschlein writes to Henny:

I don't know how these people can imagine you can furnish proof of the fur and the radio, since the very worst happened to your people. You had already left, and your mother and Lola were taken away; who could provide proof?

Fröschlein nobly takes up the cudgels herself, writing to the Offices for Compensation, Berlin, in January 1959:

> With reference to your letter of 3 November last, together with enclosure, I respectfully inform you that there appears to be almost no prospect of bringing forward evidence other than the previously presented affirmations sworn under oath.
>
> We have here, unfortunately, the sad fact that Frau Seth, as a result of the Nazi measures, was forced to emigrate; and that the only people who could give exact details of the process of the handing-over, namely, the mother and sister of Frau Seth née Caro, were deported and have been declared dead. A fur coat and a radio, according to the statement of Frau Seth, existed. In the property declaration made at the time of the deportation of her mother and her sister, they are no longer listed. It seems to me clear that, in accordance with the legislation then applicable, they were handed over. The sister of Frau Seth, who died as a result of the deportation, last worked in the Jewish Gemeinde. She was exceedingly correct, and it is extremely unlikely that she would have put the life and security of her old and sick mother at risk through the circumvention of such a regulation as existed for the handing-over of furs and radio sets.
>
> I request that the particularly unhappy circumstances set out here be taken into account, so that an unnecessary cruelty may be avoided.
>
> Yours faithfully,
>
> [unsigned: carbon copy]

But how absurd to speak of humanity before the bureaucratic machine. In the end a derisory 50 Deutschmark (less than £5) was granted for the radio, and nothing for the coat.

The documents relating to the furniture and other property in the flat in Bleibtreustrasse in which Henny, Lola and Ella had lived, make melancholy reading.

The earliest document in this file dates to 1 May 1943, when Lola was required to list her property. By then she and her mother had already been taken from the flat and imprisoned in a collection camp in the centre of Berlin, prior to being taken to a railway station and deported to wherever they would have to go.

Property declaration of Lola C a r o – Profession: stenographer and typist— . . .

Furniture	1 table, small	3 chairs	1 couch
	1 carpet	1 waste-paper basket	
	various books	1 glass cabinet	

signed 1.5.43 –   Lola Caro

A few days later, a list of all the property in the flat, room by room, was made, the property being attributed to the mother; and it was stated:

By the Gestapo decree of 1.2.1943 –
Secret State Police, State Police Regional Headquarters,
Berlin, Gruner Str. 11—

the entire property of Gabriele C a r o née Schmelkes – born 11.11.71 – last place of residence Charlottenburg, Bleibtreustr. 19 – has been taken over for the benefit of the Reich.
This decree was served personally on Frau Caro on 14.5.1943.

The property, though confiscated, remained in the flat. Rent continued to be paid, according to the records, but by whom and to whom and for whose benefit is not recorded. It is not clear that anyone was living there. On 15 March 1944, ten months or more after Lola and her mother were thrown out of it, and when both had been dead many months, it was declared that 'the residence of the deported Jew [had been] vacated' by order of the Chief Bürgermeister (Mayor) of the Reich capital Berlin – Head Office for Economic Affairs.

On 30 June 1944, the property was reappraised by order of the Finance Administration of Berlin-Brandenburg, Office for the Evaluation of Property, and its value adjusted downwards owing to 'war damage'. By then the Allied invasion had begun, and Berlin was being steadily reduced through bombing.

A large correspondence deals with Henny's share in the inheritance of her aunts, Olga and Flora Glaser – both unmarried, as they are referred to as Fräulein – whom the German state first robbed, then killed. Henny's mother was one of their heirs. (Though she and her elder daughter Lola were killed much earlier, the date on which they were 'deemed dead' was 31 December 1945.) Ella's and Lola's heirs were Henny and Heinz. Heinz had died in La Paz in September 1953, and his widow Mia was his heir.

Olga and Flora Glaser had once been wealthy women, but their wealth had been thieved from them. The catalogue of forced sales under Nazi duress, the requisitioning of property under false pretences, the freezing of bank accounts, the plundering of loved objects that the two old aunts were forced to hand over because they contained gold or silver, metals forbidden to Jews ('1 ring with 1 diamond, 2 candelabra, 5 dessert spoons, 1 gold chain . . .'), makes difficult reading. When one thinks what the relinquishing of things that were dear to them meant to these two women, and how none of this helped them in the least to avoid the annihilation planned for them, one can perhaps imagine what Henny might have felt as she looked over these papers.

Together with the Glasers' other heirs, Henny and Mia applied to the German state for compensation for the forced sales and the requisitioned funds. They also tried to trace any wealth that the Glasers had managed to get to America before the war. Here, however, they were thwarted at every turn by the harsh laws and interpretations regarding so-called enemy property in force in the United States. In December 1956, more than a decade after the war had ended, their attorney in Berlin quoted from a response to several letters of inquiry he had sent in which he had tried to ascertain the amounts in relevant bank accounts located in the USA:

> In the matter of the American inheritance of Flora and Olga *Glaser*, I have received the following letter from Herr Moser:
> '. . . The Alien Property Custodian takes the view that the confiscated assets are American property, and that therefore there can be no enquiry by [other] interested parties. This official standpoint is indeed very harsh, but in law there is nothing that can be done about it . . . although the owners are Jewish.'

Nothing more regarding this matter appears in these files. Clearly, the heirs just gave up the quest as expensive, frustrating and fruitless. It is hard to believe that so little justice was available on either side of the Atlantic. After a great deal of paperwork, the file ends with the German state disbursing to Henny what, after costs, came to 3000 Deutschmarks, or less than £300. As 15 per cent of the property of two once wealthy women, this was a pitiful amount.

Henny and Heinz's widow were given, in all, 2000 DM for the furniture and other possessions in their mother's house, and 2396 DM, appraised on the basis of its silver content, for the family cutlery and other silverware. It is unclear what, if anything, was given for damage to income. The file ends, and there are no other files to draw on. But Shanti Uncle did tell me that Aunty Henny received a small pension from the German state, which devolved upon him and for which he had occasionally to appear in person. Had that anything to do with this business, or was it something paid after retirement age to all who had been persecuted? I do not know. Nor is it really worth pursuing; it would have been a small amount in any case.

Sometime in the late fifties, Henny seems to have drawn a line under her relations with German officialdom. Unlike her personal correspondence, where the files break off arbitrarily, the official correspondence, except on the question of damage to her career, appears to come to a natural close.

4.10

If Henny had dealt directly with the lawyer in Berlin who was handling her affairs with the authorities, we would have known nothing more than the legal and financial circumstances of the various petitions and processes. But Fröschlein was her intermediary, and so, in parallel with the forms and instructions, arguments and counter-arguments, decisions and postponements, we get a final glimpse into the circle of Berlin friends. From the manner in which Fröschlein conveys this information, it appears that Henny now gets most of the news of her friends through her correspondence with Fröschlein.

By 1954, things had settled down in West Germany, and the terrible conditions of cold and hunger and uncertainty that had prevailed in the years immediately following the war had been ameliorated – in part because of the unprecedented magnanimity of the United States through the Marshall Plan. In East Germany, things were different. But the 1953 uprising in East Berlin and its possible effect on the Dietrichs is not touched on. In May 1954, Henny asks Fröschlein to congratulate Hans Dietrich on her behalf, but doesn't state for what. A few months later, Fröschlein mentions that he has had a heart attack. Ilse, still in Marburg, has had trouble with her lungs and been admitted to hospital. The Rabaus write from the USA, where they have gone for a visit, and rhapsodise about how lovely Inge and her children are.

As for Fröschlein herself, despite high blood pressure and assorted ills, she continues to help Henny in innumerable ways, to send her *Stollen* for Christmas, and to admonish her sharply for lapses in friendship:

To return to your kind letter: I would actually like to say that I will not do the slightest thing for you again, if you don't stop giving me endless amounts of money. Is it that you aren't convinced that I do this work willingly for you with all my heart????? If you weren't, I would be very sad. You have done so much for me already!

Following up onerous legal matters relating to her family while working in a company as managing director, handling the shopping and the housework while often helping Shanti in the surgery, entertaining her nearby friends while keeping up this frequent correspondence with a distant one, must have been physically and emotionally draining for Henny, even without her sad memories and present griefs. Most atypically for an optimist – or, upon the failure of optimism, a stoic – in these letters to Fröschlein Henny reveals the stress and distress that she must have felt continually, for years on end.

Just before Christmas 1954, she describes her physical condition:

Because of all my work – office, surgery, house, shopping, etc. – I am at the moment quite tired, but I'll be back to normal soon. Shanti is well; he is always worried about me because of my heart, but I think it's really just my nerves, which is what my specialist also confirmed to me last year.

A week later, she writes again, and this time we see something of her spiritual state:

It is now almost two years since Margot's death, and I keep thinking of her. I have actually never felt really well since her death. The horrible shock was too much for me and I still can't get over it. Yes, well, life just goes on. Do you know, some people can take it all in their stride, but I can't.

Shanti once mentioned that when Henny first heard about what had happened to Lola and her mother, she developed a condition in which her skin was covered with small red spots – urticaria pigmentosa. Now, once again, and with more profound effect, it was as if her body was succumbing to her grief and trauma. Margot

Weissberg could not have meant what her mother and sister had meant to her, but this might have been one of those cases where lesser tremors against which one is unbraced knock one down when one has withstood – or seemingly withstood – more violent shocks.

On 29 December 1954, possibly inspired by the hinge of the festive season to contemplate both the year past and the year to come, Henny writes a revealing letter to Fröschlein. She has taken on a German au pair two days earlier, but her feelings about Germany are as complex as they were ten, or indeed twenty, years earlier.

I don't always feel so well either. I have pressure on my heart and palpitations too, but I think that it's only my nerves. I work, of course, quite a lot – especially given my condition, for I am no longer so strong. I have gone through too much since 1933, and it's taking its toll. Shanti is very, very good and is very concerned about me. He told me recently (but this is just between us) that he would give his life for me.

We had a marvellous Christmas. On Christmas Eve we had about twenty people over at our house, and on Christmas Day we were invited over by friends. Here one celebrates Christmas very differently from how we used to, more in the spirit of a carnival, and not so solemnly.

Fröschlein, will we see each other this year? Perhaps you can manage to meet us. It would be so wonderful. Otherwise we will have to spend a vacation in Germany some time, but somehow I can't – as you can well understand – bring myself to do that, and I also don't know what sort of effect it would have on me.— Write again soon, and once again, my most sincere thanks for all that you have done for me and are doing for me. With a very big hug, also from Shantilein, and a thousand greetings and kisses,

     Ever your

     Hennerle.

It was no wonder that my parents, who were in England during these years, found Henny 'highly strung'. Whatever protective or self-protective instinct forbade her from sharing with Shanti the feelings she shared with Fröschlein, it closed to her the possibility of solace that could have led, if not to peace, at least to a little calm.

Symptoms of mortality and uncertainty were all around her, and she must have felt more encumbered by loneliness than ever. Soon after she heard about her brother Heinz's death, she wrote:

Dearest Fröschlein,

My warmest thanks for your kind letter. Yes, I cannot get over Hei at all, especially since I had the feeling that he had become a 'richtiger Mensch' [a proper man]. His friend wrote to me to say that he lived in a very happy marriage with his wife (her name is Mia) and that he got along very well with his 15-year-old stepson. I don't know whether he adopted him. I haven't heard from his wife so far, though I wrote at once to her and to Hei's friend. But she is probably so desperately sad that she can't pull herself together enough to write, which I can fully understand. She doesn't know me, after all. Recently, just before our holidays, she sent me a photograph of herself, and she looks very nice. Incidentally, I have postcard-size photos of Hei and also the young lad, who looks quite charming. Hei too looked very good. Yes, Fröschlein, life is often so short, and I must say, this news has really shaken me, for Hei was, after all, the last of my family, and as the English say, 'blood is thicker than water'.

Fröschlein, in my agitation about Hei I completely forgot to thank you for the lovely light-blue organdie handkerchief. Please forgive me for not mentioning it in my last letter, but I was on my last legs. Many many thanks . . .

4.11

One slightly mysterious line of enquiry in this correspondence with Fröschlein leads to Fred Götte, one of Shanti and Henny's friends whom (as I mention much earlier) I got to know and like during my years at 18 Queens Road. Fred was a dentist, and had been a student with Shanti in Berlin. After the war, when Shanti went to Hamburg to give lectures on dental materials on behalf of the Amalgamated Dental Company to students, professors, researchers and practising dentists, Fred had been in the audience. When, afterwards, Shanti stood everyone a round of double whiskies, Fred had come up to him and they had got talking. During the few days that Shanti was in Hamburg, they became friends. Shanti recounted how he got Fred out of Germany, where he was having a hard time:

Fred looked like a half-starved chap and not very smart. [Shanti Uncle laughed affectionately.] I felt sorry for him. 'Can't you get me out?' he asked me. Now I knew someone in the Ministry of Health, Dr, what's his name, the top man, Mr Senior, who was then the Secretary of the British Dental Association, and I approached him and said, well, lied, that I had physical difficulties in my work and needed an assistant, that I had a German class-fellow who I could vouch was not a Nazi, and could they accommodate an officer who had lost his arm?

Well, that got Fred over and, unlike me, he didn't have to take his exams again. But he looked so young that some of my patients said to my nurse, 'Tell Dr Seth that I didn't come to his surgery to be treated by a student.'

Shanti's letter to the Home Office (Aliens Department) with a request on behalf of Fred Götte was dated December 1955. Fred came over on a temporary basis; he started work with Shanti. Because there was not enough work for Fred, he then got a job as a school dentist, and later set up a practice in Wembley, which, however, did not take off. He travelled between England and Germany fairly often.

Henny grew very fond of him. He had undoubted charm – he would have teased her, appreciated her good looks and cooking, and flirted mildly with her. In 1958 – and this came as a surprise to me, given what she had written earlier regarding her feelings about her hometown – Henny wrote to Fröschlein that she and Shanti were thinking of going to Berlin and driving back with Fred. But despite this, when Fred wanted to migrate permanently to England later the same year, Henny asked Fröschlein to make enquiries about him in Berlin.

Please be careful when you make any inquiries about Dr G. He mustn't know anything about this, of course. We see him from time to time; he is so very nice, but somehow or other we don't quite trust him 100%, and it is certainly odd that he would wish to emigrate at his age.

Fröschlein replies that

Dr. G. is something of a puzzle to me. I don't go to the area where he lives. I could only make inquiries through an investigative agency, if you would really like me to. But should one spend money on that?

Henny appears to have let matters rest. Later, she writes laconically:

Dr. G. is still here; he works three days a week in a clinic (a dental clinic for schoolchildren). He doesn't overexert himself.

Shanti was always teasing Fred about how little he liked to work and how much he enjoyed his statutory siesta. I myself remember Fred with affection. He was lively, outspoken, young at heart and easy-going; and, shy as I was when I went to stay with Shanti Uncle and Aunty Henny, I didn't feel awkward in Fred's company as I often did with their other friends. Fred was at the time a bachelor and had not succumbed to the tendency to stodginess that too often comes with being part of a linked pair.

While Fred Götte was lively, Henry Edwards, the other dentist at the core of Shanti and Henny's social life, was solid. If Shanti could be said to have rescued Fred, Henry had been Shanti's saviour.

Where Fred was a single and singular addition to Shanti and Henny's circle, Henry's whole family was drawn into it.

When Henry's mother, 'Mum', died, Henny, who had grown very attached to her after the death of her own mother, drew even closer than before to Mum's sister, Rosie. I remember 'Auntie Rosie' well from my student days; she was someone else whose company I enjoyed. She was in her eighties, had a robust view of life, and loved driving. When they took away her licence for crawling along at twenty miles an hour in the fast lane ('But, officer, I was driving so slowly,' she said by way of excuse), she retook her driving test in Chiswick because the Hendon examiners were notoriously strict. She lived in a luxury flat, but when she later had to move into an old people's home, she became very depressed, refused her beloved whisky and didn't eat. 'Shanti, there are all old people here,' she complained, though in fact she was the oldest.

Henny did not much care for Henry's wife, Nita, whom she thought brittle and uncultured, though she couldn't often bring herself to say so explicitly. 'I like Henry, Henry's my type. I like him,' she would assert emphatically.

Henny and Shanti were both very fond of Derek, Nita's son from her first marriage, whom Henry had brought up from childhood as his own. (It was Derek who later became Shanti and Henny's accountant.) Decades later, in her last illness, Henny kept asking whether he had phoned to ask after her. Henry and Nita were by then both dead, and Derek had had no idea how ill Henny was, since no one had told him.

Henry and Nita's daughter Susan was Shanti's goddaughter. In later years, he often complained of Susan's attitude towards him. 'Susan is my godchild, but do you think she will ever phone me up? She said she'd come to see me, she's sold her boutique, she has time, but . . .'

Why were these two German dentists at the heart of Shanti and Henny's friendships, even in London? Shanti and Henny did have a number of English friends, but they never seemed as intimate with them as with Fred and Henry and Auntie Rosie. To me they were most at home when they were speaking German. It is true that over the years, Henny's German, even her written German, was infiltrated by 'false friends' from English. For 'guilty' she sometimes used *gültig* (which means 'valid'); for 'afford' she sometimes used *erfordern* ('require'). But in contrast to her good but careful and slightly unidiomatic English, there was a great sense of naturalness to her German conversation with her friends, whether face to face or on the phone. She laughed much more in German.

As for Shanti Uncle, he had lived in Germany for only five years, as opposed to twenty-three in India. Yet those Berlin years had been formative years – of achievement through great effort against great odds. They represented his first taste of true independence from his family, some of his happiest recollections of friendship and carefree fun, and warm memories of family life at 60 Mommsenstrasse, his second home. These years and this language brought him and Henny together. Since German was the language they spoke with each other throughout their marriage, it was natural that their closeness to other friends should be most naturally attained as an extension of this.

That Shanti's dearest friends in London were both also dentists may simply be a question of their being thrown together by professional circumstances, but that would account for their initial meeting rather than their close and continuing friendship. Here the explanation may lie in Shanti's love for – indeed, almost obsession with – his work, and it was Henry, above all, who had helped him take it up again. Although their style and pace of work were different from his own, Fred and Henry were both colleagues with whom he could discuss matters that interested him. They understood his professional background and concerns; like him, they came from a tradition of dentistry different from that of British dentists trained at the same time.

Several of these strands are brought together in Shanti's account of two related events separated by several decades:

Henny was quite conscious of how she looked. When I was in Berlin, because she knew I was a student of dentistry, she showed me her front teeth and I noticed that she still had two milk teeth at the age of twenty-five. I later found out by X-ray that the undescended teeth above them – they were canines – were lying in an awkward position and could not descend, so there was no question of pulling out the milk teeth. Now the problem was that these milk teeth were slightly loose, but to make a bridge to keep them in place was very tricky.

Shanti described how he finally found the right person for the job, not one of his famous professors but a dentist in private practice.

It was particularly difficult because he had to make two *Halbkronen* – I'll say it in German – on those existing milk teeth to cover the gap between the firm teeth on either side. He did such a good job that the thing lasted for nearly, let me see, 1934, '44, '54, '64, well over thirty years.

Later, when these milk teeth finally had to be removed, I asked my colleague Fred Götte to perform the procedure, though I was there too. He had to make a small denture to be fitted as soon as the bridge was taken out. Like all ladies, she was vain; but the denture was so well made that no one noticed. A clear plastic piece covered the palate, so well colour-matched that you couldn't tell. On holidays, people would say to her, 'What lovely teeth you have.'

Yes, now I remember how one says *Halbkronen* in English: abutting half-crowns for contiguous teeth . . . Aunty Henny would kill me if she heard all this.

4.12

Work was at the heart of Shanti's life. He enjoyed exercising his skills, he enjoyed solving problems and he enjoyed helping people. Because of the sometimes necessary infliction of pain inherent in the procedures of the profession, a well beloved dentist is as rare as a well beloved traffic warden; but Shanti was certainly one. His patients, whether young or old, felt he cared about them. His nurses too liked him, though he was demanding when it came to punctuality and efficiency.

He retained his enthusiasm for his work long after he had ceased to practise it. In his interviews, he described to me at length how he managed to handle complicated gingivectomies with only one arm, details of which the reader will be spared. But his occupational anecdotes were not limited to dentistry. His thorough grounding in medicine in Berlin helped him on several occasions to diagnose conditions that had eluded others.

On one occasion, he was treating his friend George Little, whose wife, Elsie, was seated on the extra chair in the surgery. Elsie had for some time been suffering from severe loss of weight, sleeplessness, nervousness and hyperactivity, but her doctors, even after sending her to a specialist, had been unable to reach a diagnosis; they had finally put it down to psychosomatic causes. Now that Elsie was sitting still for a few minutes, Shanti's attention was drawn to the fact that a slightly swollen part of her neck was moving up and down. He kept his eyes on her, and George was puzzled and slightly irked that Shanti was looking not at him but at his wife.

I was sure in my mind that it was her thyroid gland that was causing all her problems. I told her that when she next went to her doctor, she should tell him to check her thyroid, but that she shouldn't mention my name. Sure enough, she tells him – you know how women are – 'You couldn't diagnose me but my dentist did.' The tests came out and he did agree that it was a thyroid problem. Elsie had an operation, and felt much better. Her problem was the overproduction of some hormone.

It was Shanti Uncle who told my father, who had come to visit him while on a trip to London, that he probably had prostate problems. After his return to India, Papa went to see a doctor, and found that this was indeed so.

The young student who had recoiled at the idea of spending his life putting his fingers into other people's mouths had, in the course of his career, got to the stage where he would interrupt a Christmas Eve dinner he was throwing in order to do so.

It was Heiliger Abend, and Henny and I had a sit-down dinner for friends. Everyone was having their last course and a cup of coffee when a woman phoned to say that her husband was crying with pain and she didn't know what to do. I told her to bring him around, though there was no nurse. He had a fat face, caused by a very big abscess, and I had to drain it with a drainage tube to give him relief.

Easing pain was half his dental philosophy; the other half was preserving teeth. Unlike many other dentists, he believed that extractions were a last resort. At the age of eighty-five he told me that all his teeth were his own; and this was almost certainly still the case when he died. Patients who came into the surgery intending to have teeth extracted were often dissuaded; in some cases, these teeth were preserved in good order for more than thirty years afterwards. Some complained: 'Dr Seth is a very good dentist, but he is too thorough.' Others, even after they had moved eighty miles away, continued to come to him to be treated.

Had Shanti been able to work, he would not have given it up even in his eighties. But the chronic heart and lung problems that Aunty Henny described in her letters to me eventually forced him into retirement. Shanti recalled:

I found it very hard to retire. I was still practising long after seventy. My heart specialist told me to retire, and I said OK. He told me to rest more, and I said OK. But I thought there'd be no harm in working for just half a day a week, and within two weeks I was back to the old regime, on my feet five days a week – with no lunch till three o'clock if I had a difficult or interesting case.

425

On one occasion, he was at home, waiting in his dressing-gown for a private ambulance to take him to Charing Cross Hospital. A patient rang the doorbell; he was in acute distress. Henny told him that Shanti was too ill to help him. But when Shanti came out of his room and recognised the man, he told Henny that he could not go into hospital without treating him.

Eventually, after he had promised to retire several times but – to the great detriment of his health – resiled each time, Aunty Henny had the dental chair uprooted from the floor of the surgery, so that he could no longer use it; and she later sold it off.

When Shanti did retire, he was certain that he did not want to move house or let out the surgery to another dentist. Nor did he sell the practice. He recounted:

One dentist offered me a few thousand pounds if I would simply tell my patients that the practice had moved physically and that it had been sold to him. I told him, 'I'm afraid I don't know your work.' I considered this sort of sale, where I didn't know the person whom I would recommend to my patients, to be a sort of debauchery.

When his patients asked him where they should go, he found he could not recommend anyone. His friends and any other dental colleagues whose work he knew well had retired already. He could only advise his patients to ask their friends and relations to suggest someone.

Even after he had retired, informed his current patients, and had his brass sign taken down, former patients kept drifting back. One came to the front door and told Henny that the dentures Shanti had made for him twenty-five or thirty years earlier had been so good that he had been able to eat everything with them, from the crunchiest of apples to the stickiest of marshmallows. He was still wearing these old dentures. But because his gums and bones had shrunk with age and the shape of his mouth had changed, they no longer fitted properly.

He lived far away from here; he had tried other dentists, but had not been able to get satisfaction anywhere. Henny told him I wasn't working any more. He didn't believe it. He took out his chequebook and said, 'Write out the amount. Any amount.' I came down from upstairs. I was ill at the time. I had to show him my surgery – even the chair was no longer there – before he believed me.

4.13

Shanti now rarely went into his surgery, which became something of a store-room. I imagine that Henny would not have found it easy at first to have him around all day in the areas of the house that would normally have been her preserve. (They did not agree, for one thing, about what constituted a comfortable level of heating in the drawing-room, though in this part of the house Henny, who liked warm rooms, invariably got her way.) Shanti now helped with the shopping, which he quite enjoyed, and pottered about the house and garden. He decided to supplement the surviving apple tree – one had meanwhile died – with two plum trees at the far end of the garden, and they soon bore prolific quantities of fruit. He also consulted more closely with the gardener, who came in once or twice a week, about the flowers to be planted. (Henny enjoyed only the extremes of wild nature or cut flowers. For her, a garden was for sunbathing in and not much more.)

Shanti used to take a half-day off from his work each week – I think on a Wednesday – to go into town. Now he could go into central London whenever he wished, since he was unconstrained by work. But he did not go more often; his heart had become his constraint. When he took the underground, he tried to avoid exiting or changing at stations where, because there was no escalator, he would have to walk up flights of stairs.

He had never been overly sociable with his neighbours. When, many years previously, a Polish doctor had bought 19 Queens Road, the house next door where Shanti had once boarded, and had decided to keep a cockerel that crowed at three in the morning, Shanti had written him a letter of objection. When this was ignored, he had sent a quasi-legal letter under the heading 'Without Prejudice', stating that unless his neighbour got rid of this cock, measures would be taken that would not be to his liking. This had had the desired effect. Shanti remarked, 'Actually, the man was only interested in getting his hens to provide him with eggs, not chickens. But though he was a doctor, he didn't know that you don't need to keep a cock to get your hens to lay.'

He got along much better with his neighbour at 17 Queens Road, the semidetached house adjoining his. She was the short, frail and elderly spinster Miss Snelling, who was always very correct but friendly; Shanti and she greeted each other courteously whenever they happened to collect their milk from the doorstep at the same time. Miss Snelling was a good-hearted person, but somewhat unfamiliar with the ways of the world. On one occasion, as they talked to each other across the fence, it emerged that her lodger at the time, to whom she had lent a large sum of money, had made off with it. Earlier, he had offered to clear out her attic and had taken away two taxi-loads of objects that he had found there.

During one of my interviews with Shanti Uncle, I told him I'd noticed that the large ceramic cockatoo was no longer in the green room.

'Oh, yes, it flew away,' said Uncle.

'Of course,' I replied, matter-of-factly.

Uncle looked disappointed, then told me that Miss Snelling's lodger, who had been a patient of his, had admired and repeatedly offered to buy the parrot (which he had noticed when visiting the upstairs loo). Shanti did not want to sell it; it had been given to him and Henny by a friend who was a multimillionaire tobacco manufacturer from Hamburg; Shanti liked it and it had sentimental value. But one day, noticing that the front door, which she had left unlocked, was slightly ajar, Henny went upstairs and found that the bird had gone. When the police were called, Shanti did not voice his suspicions, but the man phoned two days later to say, 'Dr Seth, I didn't take your bird.'

Henny was much more sociable with strangers than Shanti.

She was known in Hendon as the friendly lady. She was approachable; she had a friendly style, even on a bus – unlike me; I am much more reserved. Sometimes I would notice someone waving to her or greeting her on the street, and when I asked who that lady was, she would say, 'Oh, she's a shopping friend.'

Across Queens Road lay Hendon Park, but getting to it had become difficult. Once there had been very few cars on Queens Road, but now there was a continuous flow of traffic. Since the road had a blind spot where a curve combined with a rise, this made crossing hazardous. A small pedestrian island had been created, but it still sometimes took Shanti a minute or more to get across.

He walked every day in the park, sometimes more than once a day. When I visited London, we would go for walks together; after we had done a round of the open park, we would go and sit in the small hedge-enclosed flower garden adjoining it. Aunty Henny had no taste for walking around parks. It was only when I read her friends' letters to her that I realised what a nature-lover she had once been.

As before, Shanti Uncle very rarely read a book. He took to reading his newspaper from cover to cover. He watched a good deal of television. Whenever there was a programme that dealt with the Nazis, he turned it off for Aunty Henny's sake.

Cathy, their robust cleaning woman, who had a strong Irish accent, got on well with Shanti and Henny and fussed over both of them. If she saw Aunty Henny looking tired, she would say, 'Now you just sit down, Mrs Seth, and let me make you some tea.' Aunty Henny, who normally did not like anyone fussing over her, did not mind if it was Cathy.

If they wanted to get something fixed in the house or garden, they would phone their younger friend, Colin, who was very practical and always tried to help. His first wife had been one of Shanti's favourite nurses; when the marriage ran into difficulties, Shanti had tried to repair things by talking to both sides. Though the marriage had eventually ended in divorce, Shanti continued to be something of a mentor to Colin. He advised him on his career, encouraged him to educate himself and helped effect a reconciliation between him and his father by convincing Colin that he should make the first move to end their estrangement.

Shanti and Henny's life in retirement had an even tenor, and they kept themselves occupied. They continued to throw the occasional bridge party for their friends, though no longer under the impartial eye of the porcelain cockatoo. Except when Shanti was ill, the institution of their winter and summer holidays continued. As usual, Shanti's birthday, in August, was celebrated with their friends in Zurich.

Some of their friends fell ill; some died. With the death of each friend, something of their world slipped away. They too were now well into their seventies.

Thus the months passed, and the years, until first Aunty Henny died and then, almost a decade later, Uncle.

Although I was with Aunty Henny during her last few days, it was only when talking to Shanti Uncle much later that I understood something of the background to her final illness. About eighteen months before her death, she developed a small ulcer at the back of her neck; when it did not heal, he advised her to go to a doctor.

It turned out to be a rodent ulcer, which I knew was not as bad as real cancer, but it was a cousin, a very good cousin. [Uncle laughed, a little bitterly.] A skin man operated on it and on similar small ulcers near the nose. She felt better, but in my heart I knew it was already the start, though I never told her. For one year she was quite all right. In February 1989 she was tired, and had no energy. A lady doctor told her she was fit – Henny

430

went to see her but didn't tell me till afterwards. Normally, Henny would never see a doctor.

The birthday of one of Aunty Henny's closest friends was in February. Since she was feeling ill, Shanti Uncle tried to dissuade her from taking her friend to a matinée at the Curzon cinema; he told her that the hall would be unheated for a matinée. 'No, no, no, I've promised,' she said. When she came back, her lips were blue and she was shaking. She had diarrhoea and shivered throughout the night. She said in English, 'As it comes, so it will go.'

After three or four nights when neither of them were able to sleep, Shanti told Henny that this was not fair on either of them, and that she should go to a doctor. The doctor asked for a blood test, but Henny refused – 'No, no, no blood.' She had always had a phobia of blood; even when she had acted as a temporary nurse to Shanti, she would turn away if he was extracting a tooth. It was with great difficulty that she was persuaded to have some blood drawn.

Shanti Uncle went on:

Meanwhile, her feet and legs had become swollen. I thought it might be heart, so I spoke to a heart specialist. He said no, it wasn't heart. So I said, 'Lymph?', and he didn't answer.

The cancer had metastasised. Who knows where it began – from the stomach trouble that she often had from eating tasty but indigestible food or from the rodent ulcer in the neck. I told the consultants, 'Please don't mention the word "cancer" in front of her.' They simply told her her red blood cells were being destroyed – some cock-and-bull story. At the end, she herself said, 'I wish I had cancer, then they could do something about it.' She said that if it was cancer she could have chemotherapy. A sweet thought.

I thought this a strange choice of words; but I said nothing, and Shanti Uncle continued:

They gave her a general anaesthetic in order to see the stomach, and she vomited blood and I realised this was the beginning of the end. In order to do a scan, they made her swallow some horrible liquid, which again she refused. I said, 'I fought for you, you fight for me now.' So she went through all of this, but she had diarrhoea again, which was for her embarrassment and pain and torture.

Once, in the hospital, I saw her on all fours on the floor looking for something. Her tablet had fallen. I was paying such a lot of money for the hospital! I said, 'Buzz the bell.' But she said, 'Oh, the nurses are all so busy.' She was always worried about other people.

In the hospital, she said, 'Shanti, let me die.' That's why I brought her home. I knew she was very ill, and close to death.

Two days before she died, at two in the morning she called out my name. 'I'm not sleeping,' I said. Then she said, 'Shanti, help me, help me, you are the only one who can help me. Give me your hand.' We were so well integrated that I knew what she meant, that it was not easy to die. Then she said, 'Don't do anything stupid, promise me. Promise me on my soul you won't do anything foolish. God has brought you here and he will take you back. Now let me go, goodnight.'

There was a hard lump in her stomach, so big, as big as a fist, a blood clot. Her hair hurt, her bones hurt. She was in such a distressed condition, down to four and a half stones. She didn't want to see anyone. Yet she was so happy to see you, Vicky. I'll never forget it.

Finally, the doctors made me agree to morphine. We couldn't do anything more; the time had come; she was in such pain. I told the nurse to quieten her down with an injection. I came back after five minutes and said, 'I hope you haven't given her the injection,' but she had.

The next day she didn't recognise me.

Cathy she did recognise still. She told her, 'If anything happens to me, look after my husband.'

4.14

Thus ended, at the age of eighty for both, this marriage of thirty-eight years and this friendship of fifty-six.

It was, I think, an unusual marriage. Something that puzzled me for a long time was that Henny never spoke to Shanti about the deaths of Ella and Lola. In some ways, it still does. Once, Shanti said to her, 'What a shame that your mother and sister were taken away. If they had survived just a year longer—' before Henny cut him off with 'Let's not talk about it.' On another occasion, when he tentatively brought up the subject, she said, 'Shanti, it's no good going into the graveyard.' He also told me, in a troubled manner: 'When Henny found out they had died, I only wish she had dropped a tear. She never cried. She would never talk about it, not even to me. She never mentioned their names again.' One of the reasons Henny had once given a friend for marrying Shanti was that he, having known her loved ones, could sympathise 'with what I have inwardly gone through and what will never again be erased'. Yet it appears that Shanti did not know how much she had mourned for them, or that her friends received those confidences and that view of her sorrow that were hidden from him.

But perhaps they were spared him. Henny wrote about Shanti, 'I want to make him happy – he deserves it,' and talking about sad events to one with sufferings of his own might not have advanced this aim. Or it may have been that she needed to create in her marriage a zone where she could be at peace, a zone where the pain of the past and its tentacles into the present were not allowed to enter. For if she had once spoken of these matters to Shanti, she might well have thought that he could, at any time, have brought them up again, and that she might, without warning, be overwhelmed with resurgent grief.

I offer these remarks tentatively. No one apart from the two parties concerned understands a marriage and what goes on in it; and often enough, not even they.

Unlike many older couples, Shanti and Henny were not overtly affectionate with each other. They did not kiss when others were around or hold hands or sit close to each other or address each other with terms of endearment. Henny was not effusive; and Shanti's natural demonstrativeness was expressed in public more to others, like my mother, than to her. In some of her letters, Henny can sound brusque and unsympathetic about Shanti's health, as when she writes to Fröschlein: 'It is quite astonishing how such a strong man can, as the result of this sort of flu, suddenly become so weak. The specialist assured Shanti that it was nothing serious, but rather the consequence of the flu that he had neglected.' Yet in her letters to me more than twenty years later, one can see her exhausting efforts and profound anxiety for him when she knows he is seriously ill. That they cared deeply for each other was patent, if not to the casual observer, certainly to someone who lived with them and saw their daily lives. Shanti had told her he would give his life for her. In the end, Henny did something perhaps more difficult; she tried to live on, despite indignity and pain, for his sake.

They were good for each other, even if they did not get from each other all they may, earlier in their lives, have hoped to find. Shanti must always have wondered if Henny had ever loved him romantically as he had loved her – or as she may have loved someone else. Henny was uncertain, as she once wrote, that she would find '100% happiness' with Shanti. 'But who knows,' she had added, 'perhaps I shall find happiness in this uncertainty.'

Once, when they were flying back from a holiday in Switzerland, Shanti suggested, 'Wouldn't it be lovely if the plane crashed and we would both die together?' Henny had replied, 'I don't want to die.' She did not say that she was afraid of death. Her response seems to me to have come more from a sense of contentment or even hard-won happiness in life, ensuing in some great measure from the assurance of Shanti's love.

There were matters deep in her heart that she withheld from

434

him. There was the world of his birth and upbringing that she chose not to explore. There was a great deal they did not understand about each other. They were not soulmates. Theirs was a companionship based on mutual confidence rather than confidences.

They believed in each other's abilities, in each other's character and in each other's love. It may not have been a requited passionate romance, but it was a deep and abiding concern. Beset by life, isolated in the world, in each other they found a strong and sheltering harbour.

What is perfect? In a world with so much suffering, isolation and indifference, it is cause for gratitude if something is sufficiently good.

PART
FIVE

5.1

Shanti Uncle's grief for Aunty Henny showed itself in many ways. He once said: 'For six months I would cry all the time, by myself or whenever people phoned me.' But one manifestation that is painful to contemplate is his destruction of all her papers after her death and every photograph he could find of her.

If he thought he could put her out of mind by removing things that would remind him of her, it did not work. Years later, he was still grieving. Uncle very rarely wrote letters; but when a close friend of my parents, Shanti Prasad Jain, died after a lifetime's struggle with asthma and emphysema, Shanti Uncle wrote to his widow two weeks later.

2.1.1993

My dear Asha,

I wish I was in Delhi to express my feelings of sympathy by putting my paternal arm round you and your head on my shoulder and wipe your tears away.

As a fellow sufferer I know what it feels to lose one's lifelong partner. It is now over 3 years and 9 months since Henny left me but I still miss and mourn for her. It is idle talk to say that time heals. In our case there is no wound to heal, half part of you and more is just not there.

I always admired Shanti Jain's courage to travel abroad and carry out his daily tasks in great stress from anguished pain. I know how he felt. I, as senior Shanti, felt a privilege to meet both of you as Leila's intimate friends.

439

I have great belief in God, without this strong belief I would not exist. Dear Asha, all is not lost – you will see Shanti when caring for the family, in music, in prayer and above all in his memory. I wish I could have exchanged places with your Shanti . . . But Henny rightly said before she died, 'Shanti, do not do anything foolish. Your body is only lent to you from God. You can't despair. He will take it back when the time comes.' Please do not be sad. Keep your chin up.

In case you pass through London, there is always a welcome here for you at 18 Queens Road.

With love, and best wishes for your health,

Yours sincerely,

Shanti B. Seth

P.S. I am sure your friends and your family will keep you company and comfort. The sages said, 'Death is a great mystery and will remain so. Ours is not to question why.'

5.2

> She first deceased; he for a little tried
> To live without her: liked it not, and died.

Henry Wotton's moving epigram, with the pronouns transposed, encapsulates what everyone in the family feared might happen to Shanti Uncle after Aunty Henny's death. But whether it was her admonition or – despite his protestations to the contrary – his intrinsic appetite for life or just the sturdiness of his ailing body, he was to live for ten more years.

About ten years before Aunty Henny's death, Uncle had had his first heart attack, which had been misdiagnosed by his GP, with the result that he had continued to work and made things worse. Five years later, he had a blood clot which almost required the amputation of a leg. A couple of years after that, he was taken to the Royal

Free Hospital for another emergency. This time, his heart consultant gave him only a 15 per cent chance of survival. Six kilograms of fluid had to be drawn from his body in five hours. Uncle said he could see death in front of him; but once again, he pulled through.

He could hardly walk upstairs to the bedroom any more, but he did not want to have his bed moved downstairs to his empty surgery. It was at this point that he was persuaded to have a chair-lift installed in the house. It took him most of the way up the stairs to the first floor, but stopped at a half-landing. He had to negotiate the last three or four steps himself. I found this chair-lift intriguing and enjoyed using it myself.

A couple of years after Aunty Henny's death in 1989, Uncle began to suffer from hypotension with hyponatraemia. He describes it thus: 'I used to fall down suddenly, just like a stone. I knew I was going to fall down, but there was nothing I could do to stop it. They told me I had a heart block; my heart fluttered, it didn't function properly. They had to give me intravenous saline – a pint or more. Both the volume and the sodium level had to be enough.'

Two years later, just four months before I began my interviews, Uncle started bleeding into his stomach, and his blood pressure plummeted to 90/50. Once again he was hospitalised, and the bleeding was controlled.

Often, during these illnesses, Uncle would consult his brother Achal's son Arun, who had been a doctor in London and was now working in Toronto. Arun had formed a close bond with Uncle when he was in London, and continued to make every effort, even from afar, to talk at length to him and his doctors about their diagnosis and his treatment.

In addition to these serious systemic problems, Uncle suffered from chronic back, neck and knee pain, and from headaches, claustrophobia and sleeplessness. He had also been operated on for prostate and for piles.

Even his one good hand gave him a great deal of trouble, not only because he overused it but also because he was somewhat prone to accidents. Once, during the early years of his dental practice, he fell down and hurt his thumb. He said, 'It was Henny who made me exercise it despite the pain, and encouraged me to go on working despite my doubts. Otherwise, I'd really have been a cripple. She always had great faith in me and used to tell me, "You can do anything."' Years later, he tripped over Henny's bag, which she had left on the floor near the bathroom, and injured his little finger and ring finger. His thumb and these two fingers were to trouble him throughout his life. In winter, when he walked to the shops or in the park, they would go white and numb, and he sometimes had to ask strangers to unlock his front door for him.

He once slipped (on a banana peel, as he told me) at a bus-stop near Piccadilly Circus and injured his shoulder – which (since he was off on his annual trip to his beloved Swiss mountains the next day) he insisted be reset, even if in haste and, in the event, not very well. 'Since that day, my shoulder has always been in pain. Turning the page of a newspaper hurts me: you should see the mess I make when I'm reading the papers. I take one page in my hand at a time, and a pile of paper builds up on the floor.'

He greatly enjoyed discussing his illnesses and conditions. As his life became physically more circumscribed, he dwelt a great deal on the claustrophobia that had plagued him from his twenties, ever since he got stuck in a lift in Berlin.

He described what happened during a flight to America.

I was sitting between Henny and another lady when again I had an attack of claustrophobia. I felt like a wild man. I paced up and down looking for a window to jump out from. The chief steward came and asked me what the matter was. I told him I wanted to jump out of the plane. He offered me some medicine to calm me down. I told him I was a medical man, took out a valium and asked for some cold soda water. He told me I should go to the first-class lounge upstairs to relax.

People who don't suffer from it can never understand why a person should get so distressed and panic-stricken and fight to get into the open.

442

I am sitting here now quite happily, but if you close that door and that door there, I will go mad.

Even while he slept, he liked to have the window and door open, something that Henny, who felt the cold a great deal, could not stand. In the winter months, therefore, he kept only the upper half of the bedroom window open.

When ill-health meant that he could no longer travel to Switzerland, he felt hemmed in:

I love the open spaces and am a mountain lover. Henny also liked the mountain air, though perhaps not as much as me, because previously she used to go to sea resorts. But after a few days' walking in the mountains, she used to stop complaining about the cold and felt much fitter.

When I am in the mountains, I really feel free and the nearest to heaven that I can ever reach. Even now I miss my mountains nearly as much as I miss Henny.

5.3

Every so often, Uncle's phone would not work, either because the receiver had not been put down properly or for some other reason. When this happened, I'd go to Hendon to make sure everything was all right. On one such visit in late January 1995, a few months after the interviews, I found that he was quite shaken up. He had gone for a walk in the park and had fallen down. Luckily, he had fallen on the grass; he had a bruise near his eye, but he had not suffered any serious injury and his spectacles were not broken. A few people had passed him by, but a Japanese couple had helped him up and taken him back home.

Towards the end of the year, he fell ill again and was taken to hospital. His heart pressure was low and unsteady, and he was retaining too much water. He was breathless and had to be put on

443

oxygen from time to time. His head lolled a bit and he looked very tired.

'I'll come again soon. But you mustn't excite yourself or talk so much. Just rest.'

'No, darling, you do the talking.'

A few days later, he was back home, but now in the drawing-room there was an oxygen cylinder for periodic use or for when he became short of breath. We sat and watched TV together. He was in his green pyjamas and slippers; his feet had become red and cracked, and his toenails were gnarled and yellow. Moths had got into his trousers, and he wanted to have new ones made at Simpson's. I measured him for them. His high-pitched alarm went off to tell him it was time to take his water-tablets, but he didn't hear it. There was a slight smell of urine.

On television, the Conservative Chancellor, Kenneth Clarke, was announcing some sort of interim budget; among other things, it raised the threshold for inheritance tax. Uncle began talking about money, something he increasingly enjoyed doing.

'Tell me, darling, can I give you anything? Glaxo shares?'

'No, Uncle.'

'No one will be jealous, except one – Michi. Presumptuous! At one stage he said I should give some money to Rajiv [Michi's eldest son]. I told him, "Don't count on anything." . . . I have invested well. My brokers said they hadn't seen anyone with as well balanced a portfolio as Dr Seth.'

By now it was five o'clock, and dark. After a small scotch, Uncle reverted to the theme of money.

'Then how about English cash?'

'No, Uncle. I'm not in need of anything.'

'It isn't a question of need. It's what I want to give. I can see my future. I can give it to you in writing – I won't be here at the end of '96. I've lived too long.'

A couple of months later, my aunt Usha's mother, who had married into the family of the Seths of Kotra, died suddenly in Delhi at the

444

age of eighty-four. After an asthma attack, her heart gave way. The previous evening she had been in good health and had been talking of returning to London for her granddaughter's birthday. She was a wonderful woman, warm and calm, affectionate yet reserved. She had lived with her younger son and daughter-in-law for many years, first in Canada and then – after the slow death of her husband from cancer – for the most part in England. Everyone in the family loved her. Shanti Uncle said of her what he had once said of Henny: 'If she had nothing good to say of anyone, she never said anything bad.'

Uncle said: 'I was about to phone her – I swear on Henny's soul.' He was quiet for a while, then added: 'In one way it is very good. She deserved a quick death. I'm not a bit afraid of death, only of lingering on, like Usha's father.' A few minutes later, he called Usha Mami to express his sympathies.

Usha's mother's death broke Shanti's last link with his furthest past. 'She was the only one I could speak to about Kotra and Biswan,' he said. 'She was of my vintage. Now I can speak to no one about those days.'

5.4

A call from Uncle early in the morning:

'I am coming to the last stretch. I can't cope with it any more. The whole night I didn't sleep a wink. Cathy is ill. What can the blooming doctor do? I could get a girl from the agency, Miss X or Miss Y . . . Last night I wished I could have died. I had to phone Colin, though he's so busy. I am on my own and I had to turn to somebody. The mind goes on and on and on. I only wish I had something to put in my mouth . . . Peace would be nice, but I don't want to let people down . . . Don't forget I'm eighty-seven. I feel so cold. I feel like lying in bed and having my last breath. Come and visit me. I'm a fixture. You don't have to make an appointment.'

After I put the phone down, I lay in bed and thought for a while, then made a note of the conversation as I remembered it. Such notes as I now took were not comprehensive, as with the earlier interviews, but more like occasional jottings. I had imagined that within a few months of my interviews with Shanti Uncle I would begin working on his biography, but a year and a half later I found that I still lacked both impetus and will.

Michi Mama, my mother's eldest brother, came to London for three weeks in June 1996 and visited Shanti Uncle as often as he could. He later told me that Uncle had had a dream. In this dream, Henny had said that she would not visit him again unless he broke off relations with Michi, who should go back home to India at once. Having recounted this dream to Michi, Uncle had had a change of heart and had telephoned him every fifteen minutes to apologise.

A few days later, I heard of a similar visitation. Uncle had asked me to come over. The previous night, he had had a fall by the stairs and had lain on the upstairs landing for more than an hour. He was too frail to get up without help. He had finally managed to push himself against the wall and slowly drag himself upright. He had got to bed and had had a dream about Henny. 'It was so vivid. We were looking for apples in a field, then we bought some in a town, no, it was something between a village and a town, what would we call it, a hamlet? She visited me. And she said to tell your mother that she loves her very much and will be looking down at her from above. That's what she said. I know I don't hear so well, but I'm not gaga.'

Aunty Henny and my mother liked each other, but fulsome expressions of love from above were not at all in Aunty Henny's character.

Uncle next turned to the Michi theme, which had become one of his *idées fixes*. He said that the previous day, Michi, who had come up on him while he was sorting things out upstairs, kept saying, about various objects, that they would suit his wife or certain other people. 'He is still so interested in things,' Shanti Uncle went on. 'I didn't ask him to stay here, and this time he didn't protest. Whenever it suits him, he goes out. He doesn't care for anyone. A panther doesn't change its spots. My little Pinni is not here – she's not in a fit condition to come – I want to see her – I'm a bit sentimental.' At the thought of my mother, he began crying. (My mother had not been able to come because she had had a gall-bladder operation. As for the immaculate panther, it is true that you can't change what you don't have.)

Shanti Uncle was drinking his whisky and spilling a bit of it when the night nurse came in to relieve the day nurse. After the emergency by the stairs, a night nurse had been called in from the agency so that he wouldn't be alone for the next few nights. Everyone except Uncle thought that he should get a beeper so that he would be able to call for help if necessary. One of the nurses said she would speak to the District Nurse about it.

Uncle grumbled, 'I don't want to live.'

I said, 'Yes, Uncle, but why die on the stairs?'

'It's a sign from God. He made me fall. He's telling me I should give things with warm hands . . . Cathy and my gardener are in my will . . . You can tell me, darling, do you have any financial problems?'

'No, Uncle.'

'They don't repair soda siphons any more. Just for the sake of a rubber ring! And I can't open the others.' He lapsed into grumbling about things large and small.

When I visited him two days later, he sounded more cheerful. Cathy had taken him for a walk, not in his beloved park, sadly, but in the garden.

'I am very old and lonely and you must come over,' he told me vigorously.

'But here I am, Uncle. On the other hand, I'm going to Venice tomorrow.'

'Venice? Tomorrow? You must find a lovely girl to take you in a gondola. If one is too much trouble, take two of them . . . God created man, but he was lonely, and then he created woman. From

447

that time neither has God been happy nor man . . . When are you back? The twenty-fourth? Such a short trip? Why such a short trip?'

5.5

In January 1997, when I was visiting him, we had a good conversation, and he joked and laughed. He then suddenly turned serious and said, quite calmly: 'I want to talk to you. First, I am going to die. In three months or so, I won't be here. Dr Evans told me that it would be sudden. The heart has no reserves and is failing. Second, I don't want to live. I've lost my independence. I can't go out. I stare at the walls. I have to be dressed, to be undressed. I loved my independence. I don't have it. Aunty Henny is dead. I've had a good life. How many people live to be eighty-eight? You must admit I'm not what I used to be. So now I want to give things with warm hands.'

'If you're so keen to go, you should stop laughing,' I said.

Uncle laughed once more, but was not to be diverted.

'My will has been drafted by a solicitor. Now I want to give you something with warm hands. You are the only one we have treated like a son, and you're not even in the will.'

I knew that, and wanted it so. Uncle had told the family some years earlier that he had divided his estate, which must have been worth well over half a million pounds, into six equal parts among the four children of his brother Raj – Michi, Sashi, my mother Leila, and Tuttu; and two children of his brother Achal – Anand, who had been a doctor in Banaras before his retirement, and Arun, the doctor in Toronto. Later, Colin had been included as a seventh. Uncle had told me several times over the previous few years that he wanted to include me in his will, but I had resisted this, pointing out that it would create tension in the family and make me unhappy. I was not of the generation whom he had chosen as beneficiaries. There would be a kind of double counting if both my mother and I inherited, and my inclusion might therefore lead to an understandable sense of grievance in the family.

Uncle now told me he wanted to give me some money at once and suggested the figure of twenty thousand pounds, which after forty-five minutes of arguing I beat down to five thousand. I insisted I didn't need it; he insisted that it was not for me to argue. He used the browbeating authority of age and the respect due to one's elders as well as pathetic appeals in the face of impending death; he was wide-ranging and unscrupulous in his arguments. Uncle was a generous man and did not like to be thwarted in his generosity.

Having partly won this battle, he then said that he wanted to give Mama something similar 'with warm hands' as well. I told him that this was not for me to get into. I didn't give his remark much thought at the time, nor did I understand its implications till much later.

Uncle went on: 'And I want your friends John and Sue to have something. Aunty Henny was also very fond of them.'

'I'm sorry, Uncle, but I know them; they won't accept it.'

'Then something for their children. They can't refuse that.' (These were the children described by Uncle as 'prize babies'.)

'That's true,' I said. 'And that's very generous, Uncle. But are you sure you—'

'And I want you and Colin to have priority for buying this house after I'm gone.'

I didn't understand what this meant. I knew that Colin had at one time in the course of his versatile career been a builder and had wanted to do something to the house after Uncle's death. Besides, what did Uncle mean by two people having 'priority'?

I said, 'But Colin expects to be able to make an offer for it.'

'I've told him that you'll bid for it,' said Uncle. 'If he bids £200,000 and you bid one pound more . . .'

'I'll never bid against Colin,' I said. 'You're alive today for us to drink this whisky together because of Colin.'

Uncle went on: 'Colin said to me, "Why does Vicky want the house? I can build and convert it into flats. What does Vicky want it for?" I said that I didn't blooming well know.'

I was becoming rather upset with this pointless discussion. Uncle seemed to be getting some pleasure from stirring things up. I said: 'Uncle, I *don't* want it. And I don't want bad blood in the family. You should pick up the phone and tell him.'

Uncle shook his head impatiently.

In the event, I phoned Colin later that day and assured him that I was not going to be drawn into any competition with him. Even the idea struck me as damaging and absurd.

5.6

Uncle's heart progressively failed. His body retained more and more fluid. His legs and feet swelled up. His skin cracked, causing him great pain. Then the cracks became infected sores. The fluid in his chest gave him a constant and racking cough combined with a wheezing sound. He even had to sleep in a semi-upright position. He said to me, 'I hate to give you bad news, but I've had it. I can't carry on any more. My heart palpitates. Ask the night nurse. There's a time to come and a time to go. Lots of love to my little Pinni. I even told Arun I had no wish to live.'

Arun had come over from Canada, and kept in close touch after he returned. Uncle had been given strong diuretics, first intravenously, then as tablets, and these had been effective. Colin, speaking in front of him, said, 'He's had a glass of wine, and he's looking better. His feet are half the size they were yesterday; he's lost six pounds of fluid in one day. Yesterday he was about to meet his maker. He's still on the water-tablets. Come on, Shanti, you'll be happier if you have a wee.'

'There's no quality to this life,' Uncle said as he was helped up, 'if you go to the toilet and can't wipe your own backside.' So painful were his feet that he had to lean on Colin's shoulder in order to get there.

'Right, Shanti, to the throne.'

'You're trying to kill me.'

'OK, now, I'm the navigator, you're the bomber.'

'Don't press on my toes. It hurts.'

Later, while Uncle watched TV, Colin told me about his train journey and discussed various national and personal ills. 'It cost me twenty-two pounds from Petersfield, the train was forty-five minutes late and I had to stand all the way. The railways are a disgrace . . . I'm all for private enterprise, but did you see the news on TV about this man who bought these transport rights from the government for a hundred thousand pounds and then sold them on a few months later for tens of millions? That can't be right . . .' He went on to tell me how a debt he'd taken out with his bank had ballooned into a huge figure when interest rates rose, then added: 'But it could have been any bank, they're all the same. They would have bankrupted me.'

He asked me what I was up to. I mentioned that one of the characters in *An Equal Music*, the novel I was working on, was going deaf. Colin was interested; he said that his father had been very deaf. A teacher had hit him when he was seven years old, and he had gone 95 per cent deaf in one ear and 85 per cent in the other.

'Have you noticed that I have a loud voice? Well, that's because when I was a lad, we were six kids in a small house with a loud TV and a deaf father. Later, when he retired, he got some kind of hearing device which was connected by a band to his skull. "What's that noise?" he asked when we opened the kitchen door to the garden. It was birdsong.'

Uncle, watching a programme, I think on sheepdog trials, was crunching ice-cubes and taking surreptitious sips of water.

'You are a one, you are,' said Colin. 'I'm trying to get rid of this water, and you're trying to take it in.'

'I may as well enjoy what I can,' said Uncle with relish. 'I'm going to go soon.'

'With all due respect, Shanti, that's not in your hands,' said Colin.

I decided to indulge Uncle's fancy. 'When do you predict?' I asked him.

'By this August,' said Uncle speculatively. This was an improvement on his earlier prediction.

'It could be years,' said Colin. 'I'll camp here if necessary, and spend weekends at home. But nine years ago, he was in an even worse state. Let's see. Spring is coming, winter is over.'

Later, while Uncle was snoozing in his chair, I said, 'Colin, it's really good of you to do all this. You must be so busy – and then your family—'

'Well, Valerie – my old lady – when I told her the state Shanti was in, she said I had to do it. I would be impossible to live with otherwise. But it's not easy. When he wants to do something, he does it even if it's not good for him. He's a stubborn—'

'Ox,' said Shanti Uncle, his eyes still closed.

5.7

In March 1997 I visited Israel for about ten days. This was when I ended up doing research into the fate of Aunty Henny's mother and sister in the archive at Yad Vashem.

When I was back in London I went to see Uncle, and found that his old friend Trüdchen – who, with her husband Oskar, had put me up at their place in Zurich so many years ago – had come from Switzerland to visit for a few days. During this period, I found speaking German a psychological strain, so Trüdchen gallantly spoke English with me.

'You are always staying here at London?' she asked.

'I'm spending a lot of time here now.'

'It is good. I am worried for Shanti. Now he suffers, and is in pain and alone, the nights and the days, he is too much alone. It is very complicated.'

As if all his other ailments weren't enough, lumbago had now kicked in.

'I'm very glad you're here,' I said. 'He misses his old friends. He doesn't have a lot to interest him these days.'

Uncle enjoyed Trüdchen's visit. Henny and Oskar were dead, and their widower and widow had memories in common. They chatted away in German, with Trüdchen's 'Doch, doch!' chiming in frequently.

But it was not only his old friends who gave Uncle's spirits a fillip. I brought my friend Francie Jowell to visit him in late April. When he discovered she was Helen Suzman's daughter, he became very animated, and talked of her and of Nelson Mandela with great admiration. 'I was convinced it was going to end in a blood-bath,' he said of South Africa. 'How wrong I was.'

Nor was it only the middle-aged or old who formed part of the salon at 18 Queens Road. Yossi and Yonni, two boys who lived with their parents at 17 Queens Road (where Miss Snelling used to live), had taken to Uncle, and dropped in frequently. This cheered him up a great deal. Yossi was, I think, sixteen or seventeen, and his little brother, who was Shanti Uncle's particular friend, about nine. Every time Shanti Uncle was hospitalised, Yonni would insist that the family visit him. Yossi suggested rigging up some sort of alarm device that would go through the common wall into their house and that Uncle could pull in an emergency. The family were fairly orthodox Jews. When someone in their family got married, they took the bride over to meet Shanti Uncle, since he couldn't come over to meet her.

Colin had now arranged a shift of three nurses so that there was someone in the house around the clock. Each nurse had an eight-hour shift, but if one of them was late for some reason, the previous nurse was expected not to leave until relieved. Uncle teased them affectionately, and they treated him rather like a trou-blesome grandfather.

'Now sign this form, Shanti,' said Colin. It authorised a monthly expenditure of about £4000 on nursing. 'Is money going to be a problem?' I later asked Colin. 'No,' he replied. 'It's about fifty thousand a year, and he deserves it. Derek says that this can go on for about ten years or so. If it runs out, I'll stay with him myself. He's a tough old bird, but his mind isn't all that clear any more. We want to keep the fluid level down, but then the concentration of urea goes up and he begins to ramble.'

He went on: 'The thing is to maintain not just the quantity but the quality of his life. Unless you're strict with him, get him to walk around the room, help him dress every day, make sure he puts his arm on even if it hurts, he'll turn into a vegetable.'

'At least,' said Shanti Uncle, whose failing hearing had interludes of surprising acuity, 'at least if you're a vegetable, when you die you can say you're used to it.'

5.8

Michi Mama visited London in late May or early June. Uncle told me that he had 'summoned' him, but did not elaborate further; I took this as a figure of speech. When I visited Shanti Uncle, Michi Mama was holding forth on the subject of architecture. He stated that architecture was the soul of a civilisation set in stone and that Indian architecture was Babu architecture; from this he moved on to Indian politicians and gave his dismissive opinion of them. I could sense that there was tension between Michi Mama and Uncle, but I took this as normal.

The next evening, I got a call from Michi Mama. He was in a fury, in fact in such a fury that he seemed to have difficulty speaking. Michi Mama's well known temper was frightening. In recent years, under the influence of his second wife, Mohini, he had mellowed; but now, even from his greeting when I lifted the receiver, I could sense that he was in the grip of uncontrollable rage.

'Can you believe this business with this fellow Colin?' he demanded.

I bridled. I did not care for the resurgence of the old and angry Michi Mama. Nor did I care for the phrase, 'this fellow Colin', with its transparent snobbery and contempt. I knew that Michi Mama had always been suspicious of Colin and that there was no love lost between them.

'Michi Mama, I don't want to get into all this. I trust Colin, and I know he's devoted to Uncle. If you have anything to say about him, please take it up with Uncle. I really don't want to hear anything against him.'

This ended the conversation. I remember feeling angry rather than dismayed by the call. I was even rather glad that I had, in a sense, told Michi Mama off. I saw him in this particular mood as a bully and a tyrant, who had been a figure of fear in my childhood. In recent years, as he had become less abrasive and more affectionate, I too had begun to feel affection for him, but now the old hostility had welled up again.

I was to regret my reactive anger and rather cheap self-satisfaction, and the brusqueness that did not let me hear what he had wanted to say.

5.9

A few days later, there was a frantic call from Uncle. He said that his bank manager had telephoned, that he was overdrawn, and that he had to get back the cheque for five thousand pounds that he had sent some months previously to my mother. I told him that I was sure that it had already been converted into rupees and that, given the foreign-exchange controls in force in India, it couldn't be converted back. I reminded Uncle that he had given me a cheque for the same amount, and assured him that he could have that back many times over. But no, it was Mama's cheque he wanted. I was mystified, and phoned Colin. Colin said that the overdrawn bank account was a fiction in Uncle's head. There was no shortage of money at all.

Uncle had begun to imagine things in other contexts as well. One day in mid-July, I had scarcely entered the door to the room where he was sitting than he announced, 'I had a bad fall last night and I lay on the floor and I shouted and shouted till I was hoarse and the nurse didn't hear me though she has a room next door and I got tired and lay on the floor and Cathy found me this morning but that's the kind of life we lead these days.'

Cathy, who was present, said, 'That's not right, Dr Seth. I didn't find you. The nurse heard you fall and you were put back to bed immediately.'

'That's not right, Cathy,' said Uncle. 'Some people sleep so soundly, they don't hear anything.'

'Didn't you have your beeper on you, Uncle?' I asked.

'Colin told me, "What do you need your lifeline for if you have nurses?" And now my buttocks hurt so much that I can't sit down, but it doesn't matter, darling, I'm being punished for the sins of my past life.' He laughed. 'Where have you been?'

'Up north, researching for my novel, and down here, trying to write it.'

'Who is taking care of you for food?'

'Uncle, I'm happiest when I'm working. Food is just a hassle at times.'

'Yes, darling, thoughts are your food. Come and see me any time you're in the area. When is your Mummy coming?'

'I don't know, Uncle. Mama said she'd spoken to you.'

'But she didn't say when she was coming to England.'

'Well, I'll ask her the next time we speak.'

I was feeling a bit restless, and took a walk in the garden. I noticed there were some early blackberries there, ate a few, and brought some back for Uncle.

The next time I visited, I got him some freesias. I also brought my friend Philippe Honoré to play the violin for him – or at least to practise within his hearing. Though Uncle was constrained in his movements, there was no reason why his senses shouldn't be pampered.

I had wanted Philippe to meet Shanti Uncle for a long time, since I had talked a great deal about each to the other. Uncle told Philippe that the violin was his favourite instrument, and said how much he looked forward to hearing him play. He mentioned that when he was on holiday in Switzerland, he had heard Yehudi Menuhin play in St Moritz. Philippe, who was practising for a concert, first tuned up and ran through his scales in 'my' bedroom in the attic, and then, so that Uncle could hear him better, played in the green room on the first floor.

The 15th of August 1997 was the fiftieth anniversary of India's independence. For a few weeks before, there had been a great deal in the newspapers and on television about the events preceding and following the same day in 1947: the negotiations, the hasty withdrawal of British troops, the ceremonies, the celebrations, the partition of India into India and Pakistan, the terrible and widespread killings of – and by – Hindus, Muslims and Sikhs. In the light of resurgent fundamentalism throughout the subcontinent, I, who was born well after Independence and Partition, wondered what, if anything, we had learned from the lunacy of the past.

I could hardly concentrate on anything else during those weeks. I completely forgot to phone or visit Shanti Uncle on his eighty-ninth birthday. When I called him the following day, he was not as upset as I thought he might be. 'I'm an old man,' he said; 'it's not a birthday, it's a deathday'; and he laughed.

5.10

Fred Götte visited from Germany in August, as he did each year. Fred was somewhat scrawny now with age, and deafish; he mumbled a lot, but then his speech had always been a strange mixture of clarity and mumbling. He was as cheerful and humorous as ever.

Shanti Uncle and he were sitting in the green room upstairs, exchanging jokes and reminiscences and opinions, and teasing each other, and this did not stop when I came in.

'Fred is so lazy. He married his wife because Japanese women do everything for their husbands. She serves the "gnädiger Herr" [milord] his breakfast, then she goes shopping. She takes care of their son and daughter. Fred does nothing.'

'I'm a hobby cook,' said Fred. 'But she won't allow me into the kitchen when she's there.'

'He finds Hanover boring,' said Uncle. 'He was offered a couple of practices in Berlin, one was near the wall, one near Ku'Damm; Hitler used to use one of them. But for Fred, they were too small physically. When he went to Hanover on a visit, a dentist, who was desperate to retire, gave him his practice and flat for next to nothing, and now he's stuck in Hanover and misses Berlin. What has Hanover ever produced except the House of Hanover, and look what's happened to them.'

'Berlin people are cleverer,' agreed Fred. 'They make more jokes.'

'Yes,' said Shanti Uncle, and went on to treat us to one of them: 'A young boy was so naive and silly that he was sent to learn wisdom from the Jews. So he went to this old Jewish man who charged him two hundred marks per visit. The boy had to clean the house, do his shopping, cook his meals . . . At the end of the ninth visit, the boy said, "What is this nonsense? I'm not going to do this any more." And the man said, "Look, he's smart already."'

We all laughed. I wondered what Aunty Henny, had she been there, would have had to say about this. But she liked Fred, and was probably used to this sort of joke from Uncle. Once, at the dining-table when Uncle, Aunty and I were together and they had a heated argument about something or other, I even heard Uncle say, astonishingly, 'Hitler had the right idea,' in order to irk her.

And that is what it did: it irked, rather than infuriated her, and her reaction had been to click her tongue and say, dismissively, 'Ach, Shanti, don't talk nonsense.'

Uncle and Fred were in fine form. 'The Germans are so crude,' said Uncle. 'They tell the crudest and filthiest jokes, and yet they produced Goethe – not that Goethe would have recognised Fred Götte as a family member. And the language is very good for all that. When I was on the way to South Africa during the war, this very nice Swiss chap would walk around the deck with me and we'd tell each other dirty jokes in German. It was a relief to do that, because I shared a cabin with two Jesuits, who were trying to convert me. They were very clever, but I said to them, "If your arguments are so good, how come they aren't accepted in India?" They said, "Hah, the Buddhists got everything from the Christians." I said, "Well you can say your religion is better, but you can't say we got it from you. That's a question of dates and history." They were indignant when I told them that Buddha lived before Christ, and said, "As it happens, we have a bishop on board, let's ask him." So we went to the first-class cabins to see the bishop – who turned out to be the same man with whom I took my walks. "*You're* the bishop?" I said, astounded. The Jesuits made their case, and the bishop told them politely to get out. "Ignorant, ignorant," he told me later. "Bloody fools." We continued to take walks together, but there were no more dirty jokes; well, not so dirty.'

The doorbell rang, and Rose, the West Indian nurse, went downstairs to answer it. It was Yossi and Yonni's sister, who had come to see how Uncle was and to say goodbye, since she was leaving London the next day. She was attractive, and talked a bit like Yossi. She said she was going to live in a kibbutz and study in a seminary. 'Which branch?' I asked. 'Jerusalem,' she replied. 'I meant, of Judaism.' 'Orthodox.' 'Oh, do they allow women in seminaries?' I asked. 'Well,' she said, 'it's a bit leftwards of Orthodox, but it's not Liberal.' Like her brothers, she called Uncle 'Dr Seth', and was clearly very fond of him.

So, clearly, was Rose, who was one of Uncle's favourite nurses, pretty and composed. 'This little girl,' said Uncle, 'she spoils me. She buys me things I shouldn't eat, and then says don't eat them.'

'Salted peanuts?' I said. 'I'm sure he opened a tin for a guest who didn't really want them, and then scoffed them all down himself.'

Rose laughed.

Uncle said, 'I haven't bought peanuts for three weeks now, but I can't help it if people get them for me. I don't go to where the nuts are, my hand does.'

'You're naughty,' said Rose.

Over lunch, Fred and Uncle for some reason spoke in English. They discussed various items of recent news. Uncle said something about the RAF, which Fred misheard or misunderstood as 'the IRA'; he shared his views about this organisation for a couple of minutes before Uncle succeeded in halting him.

'What?' said Fred. 'The RAF? Oh, bombs? The war? I remember the bombs. Eight hundred bombers – they destroyed Berlin on those two November nights – petrol bombs, I could see – then they bombed in the daytime.'

'It was more dangerous for the British than the Americans,' said Uncle. 'They could be shot down during the day.'

Fred and he argued for a while as to whether it was the British or the Americans who had bombed during the day.

Fred said, 'It wasn't easy to shoot them down. They flew too high for our defensive fire, then dived too low for it. The military targets were elsewhere. All Harris wanted to do was to destroy everything.' (Fred was referring to Air Chief Marshal Sir Arthur Harris, the head of Bomber Command.)

Uncle responded with the single German verb, 'Coventrieren.'

This annoyed Fred. 'But in Coventry six hundred died,' he said. 'In Kassel, where my parents lived, five thousand died in one night. In Berlin, thirty thousand. In Hamburg – in Dresden—' Fred shook his head, then said: 'This Harris destroyed in a certain way the culture of Europe.'

'He did what Hitler wanted to do to Britain but couldn't,' said Uncle: '"ihre Städte ausradieren [to erase their cities]".'

Fred was silent.

'Eat, eat,' said Uncle. He then started talking about how dependent Britain had been on the import of food and how the U-boats had destroyed the Liberty ships as they brought food and supplies from the United States. Britain had been alone and weak against a terrifying enemy that ruled over most of Europe.

Fred said, almost regretfully: 'But Britain, unlike the others, did not give in, which in reason it could have thought it should do.' Then, after a pause: 'There is no purpose to war. It is foolish. You have to sign papers at the end, so why not before?'

Uncle nodded. He speared a piece of lettuce with his Nelson knife and lifted it to his mouth.

'Your Uncle,' said Fred, 'is an artist of life. He only has one arm, yet he did all that.'

'Lucky for Fred his countrymen shot off my arm,' said Uncle. 'That's why they allowed me to get an assistant into England.'

I remarked: 'I suppose if you'd lost both your arms, you could have got two assistants into England.'

Fred turned towards me, his mouth open at the heartlessness of this remark, but Uncle was laughing.

Uncle had to have a cataract operation in September, and I went to see him a couple of days later. He was spending more and more time upstairs. He was sitting in a wheelchair in the green room, eating boiled potatoes and peas.

I had come with my friend Francie Jowell, who had enjoyed visiting Uncle before. That morning, she had been helping me sort out my papers. I was sunk in my novel, had had no time for the dishes or the laundry, and had let months' worth of important and unimportant papers accumulate into a huge guilt-pile: electricity bills in arrears, unanswered letters from old friends, uncashed cheques, time-bound demands from publishers, curled and fading faxes relating to literary festivals, outdated travel brochures, urgent charitable

461

appeals, professional requests, dinner invitations, subscription notices, receipts, addresses pencilled on to tiny Post-its, ideas for a play scrawled on a railway ticket. Whenever Francie decided that things had slid far enough, she descended to restore order. If it hadn't been for her, the water would have been cut off, the bailiffs would have been called in, and even the muse would have been unhoused. 'Now sign these cheques; no, it's not so difficult, I've filled in the amounts,' she said, placing them firmly in front of me; and I did.

Uncle rebuked me for not giving him any warning that we were coming, and immediately insisted on feeding us. 'I would have had a proper lunch prepared,' he said. 'Or we would have gone to a restaurant.' Francie and I told him that we had had a snack, but he kept shovelling food off his plate on to a small side-plate and pushing it towards us.

Uncle didn't look bad. His eye operation, which had been quick and painless, had taken place at the St John and Elizabeth Hospital and he kept repeating, 'I'm amazed how the old dump has been so modernised.'

One of Uncle's friends, Paul Martin, dropped in. Paul was an optician, and the only one of Uncle and Aunty's friends whom Shantum had really liked – because, though Paul was an outright Thatcherite and he and Shantum would argue fiercely about the way the country and the world should be put to rights, he was very friendly and had a good sense of humour. He now entered, dressed, as always, in jacket and tie, and sat down without ceremony. 'Sorry to interrupt. I usually come on Saturdays, but since he's had this *major* operation I thought I should pop by.' Paul was clearly his usual sarcastic self, but this time, surprisingly, it was private medicine he would be inveighing against.

Uncle said: 'The nurse keeps calling me up to enquire how I am, and whether there's an improvement in my vision. I can't see any difference yet, but they said it would take a few days.'

'So how do you know they did anything at all?' said Paul. 'They could just send you a bill.'

Uncle grunted impatiently. Paul, as usual, had got him stirred up.

'It's a racket,' continued Paul. 'The whole private medical business is a racket. Of course, if you go to a specialist he's going to say he'll do something. And Shanti's such a hypochondriac anyway.'

'He's a cynic,' said Uncle.

'I'm a realist,' said Paul.

Uncle and Paul had a good exchange, interrupted only by the nurse coming in to give Uncle his little legion of pills.

I mentioned that Francie's father had been a doctor who had had great faith in the efficacy of vitamin pills. He would eat and prescribe huge quantities of them.

Clearly, for Paul, this was another species of quackery. 'Oh, yes, they discovered vitamins in the nineteen twenties,' he said dismissively. 'What did they do before?'

'They died of scurvy,' said Francie.

'I think,' said Paul, 'that they'd already discovered that citrus fruit helped, though they didn't know why. But by now I think they've even found an E vitamin,' he continued with a mirthless grin.

Before we left, I went out into the garden. I bit into a windfall apple from the old tree. Along the fence a few grapevines had taken hold. I plucked a few of the tiny grapes and ate them with the bloom still on them. They were delicious, slightly sour with crunchy little seeds.

Both that day and the day Fred had been here, Uncle had been almost his former self, clear in his mind and full of zest. He was now in his ninetieth year, and I hoped he would see his ninetieth birthday.

5.11

A postcard from Delhi:

11th November, 1997

My dear Shanti Uncle,

Vikram gave me a surprise by turning up on my birthday – and it has been fun with the family esp. as it is Divali time. We have been thinking of you a lot – and hope that your pain is less. We look forward to seeing you next year.

Love,

Leila

When I was in Delhi, Mama had asked me about Uncle's health; his leg had been playing up again and he was in pain. We all decided that on 08-08-98 we would gather in London to celebrate his ninetieth birthday. But Mama seemed curiously upset about Shanti Uncle, as if in some way it pained her to think about him. She hesitated to tell me, but finally did. Apparently, Michi Mama had told her that when he was in England, Shanti Uncle had said hurtful things about her. Mama was almost in tears. 'Michi said he called me "Mack the Knife". Why would he do that? What does it mean? Has he ever said anything like that about me to you? Is he angry with me? What does he think I've done? Does he think I'd ever do anything to hurt him?'

I said he had never spoken that way in my hearing – he was always talking about his little Pinni and how much he missed her. I didn't know what the phrase meant beyond its obvious meaning. Mack the Knife was the notorious hoodlum in *The Threepenny Opera*, but what did he have to do with Mama? It seemed a strange choice of words, consciously hurtful but somewhat bizarre. It certainly wasn't in character with Shanti Uncle, but the alternative, even less likely, was that Michi Mama had misreported it. There had been times during the year when Shanti Uncle had imagined things that didn't exist; perhaps this was one of them.

I knew that for Mama he was like a surrogate father, and that she was upset both for his sake and her own. But precisely because she was so upset, I did not at the time explore the context of his remark and Mama did not offer anything more.

Nor did I take it up with Shanti Uncle when I went back to London. I did not think he would remember what he had said, assuming it had been reported correctly; nor could he possibly have defended such a quirkily vicious insult. It would only distress him if I brought it up. Least said, soonest mended; and I wanted things to mend.

5.12

When I phoned Shanti Uncle to wish him a happy New Year, his voice was an unclear croak. He sounded confused, and his speech was a web of clichés, insights and delusions:

'Thank you for calling, darling, I haven't been too well these last few days, time marches on, I'm going to be a hundred, a hundred and one, best to your friend Sue, I can't write, I didn't write to anyone, my shoulders are in a very bad condition, sometimes I sign a cheque and they refuse to accept it, time is a very precious commodity for me, but you can't have everything, if you're this way, a shining star, a privilege, keep writing in English, nearly a hundred and two in a week's time, a good life, a good wife, good nephews, nieces, can't complain . . .'

He continued in this vein. After a few minutes I told him I had to put down the phone, but would visit him soon.

I had heard that nowadays he sometimes confused Colin with Henry. When he had started talking about Henry and how he was expecting him to come over soon, friends who were visiting him had said, 'But Shanti, Henry's dead.' 'What do you mean?' Shanti Uncle had replied. 'He was here yesterday.' But confusing names was not the same as imagining you were a hundred and two.

Two days after our conversation, I visited Uncle. He looked dreadfully ill; he could hardly raise himself from his chair. He now claimed that he was ninety-two years old, and had been alone for his birthday and for Christmas. Yossi, who was in the room, said, 'No, Dr Seth, I was here. And my mother brought you presents. You were feeling low that day.'

Once again, Uncle asked me to give my best to Sue. He asked me what she was doing these days. I said she'd taken early retirement from the Civil Service and was doing a course to become a librarian.

Uncle leaned forward with interest. 'Oh, she's a Liberian?'

'No, no, Uncle. You know Sue. She's not a Liberian. A librarian.'

'A Nigerian?' asked Uncle hopefully. Since I didn't say anything, he went on, 'What is God? Where are we going to? If we meet again, it is good. Otherwise, give my love to Pinni and Pinna. I don't want anyone at my funeral – like Henny.'

5.13

Uncle phoned to tell me that Colin was very upset with him. Uncle had apparently made various accusations and Colin had said he had had enough. Now Uncle turned to me. 'It upsets me that he is upset. I'm terribly sorry. You start to get hallucinations when you're old. You can't tell what's the truth and what's imagination. If I say things about you, will you forgive me?'

I tried to reassure him. 'Uncle, we at least can be philosophical about these things. But you can't. When some idea has grown in your mind and you believe it, it's upsetting for you. Later, when you no longer believe it, you feel guilty about what you may have said. But our love remains the same.'

'You know I don't believe these things. You have been here as a little boy.'

I thought of him lying in bed worrying, full of doubt and guilt and loneliness and fear. After I put the phone down, I rang Colin.

'To be quite honest, Vicky,' said Colin, 'he's getting very difficult. He's telling the neighbours he's been robbed of seven thousand pounds that was lying under his pillow. He says that someone called Johnny, wearing jackboots, came and took it from him. If necessary, I'll have to get the Court of Protection involved in his care, because otherwise it could lead to all kinds of suspicions against me. I love him like a father and he loves me like a son, but I'm in a precarious position. In law, I'm no more his son than his next-door neighbour. Luckily there's less money lying around the house than before – he's distributed the stuff left behind from the foreign trips he used to take – Swiss francs to his Swiss friends, marks to Fred, some out-of-date pesetas to Valerie, Canadian travellers' cheques to Arun – and Derek, as his accountant, knows about all this. But other people don't know that. For all they know, there may be thousands of pounds lying around.'

We talked for a while, and both agreed that we had to be patient with him. I called Uncle and told him that Colin was less angry than worried.

'When you get old, you get stupid,' said Uncle. 'Write it in your book, no one has ever succeeded in taking money away with him.'

Yet just four days later, I got a call from him with a heightened version of what he'd earlier told the neighbours. Now the thief had emptied his bank account as well:

'Darling, Uncle is bankrupt – I had a letter from the bank – and indirectly what happened – there used to be a man who was close to the nurses at home, more or less – it was under the pillow – he used to go on holiday, he used to look after the house. He must be a great crook, he even knew the Nawab of Pataudi, it came out in the newspapers that he shot himself. His name was John. The bank wrote to me, your account is overdrawn – thirty, forty thousand – I mean, years – they've been honouring cheques, but at the present time I am bankrupt, I have no money at all.'

'When did you start banking with them, Uncle?' I asked, in order to be able to get a factual answer.

'In 1937.'

'And what's the bank?'

'The Royal Bank of Scotland.'

'And all of a sudden they've told you it was overdrawn.'

'Yes, overdrawn. Overdrawn is overdrawn.'

'How did he do it?'

'You see, what happened,' said Uncle, clearly thinking on his feet, 'he took it from the bank, little by little.'

'You mean, by cheque?'

'Yes, he copied it easily. And then he shot himself. Three weeks ago.'

I said whatever pacifying words I could and tried to get back to my novel. When we spoke later in the month, his first remark was again 'I'm completely broke.'

'Yes, but apart from that, Uncle, how are you doing?'

'Oh, not too bad on the whole,' said Uncle. 'Of course, I haven't slept for two or three days. Colin doesn't have the car just now, so he can't come. And I'm very lonely – the nurses are in the house twenty-four hours each day. I only wish I'm taken away quickly. There's no room for me upstairs. Or downstairs.' He chuckled. 'Now you, you work too hard. You'll kill yourself. You must go somewhere nice, enjoy yourself, return nice and fresh. And your books will be written with golden letters, no, with diamond letters, and I'll see from upstairs and downstairs how my nephew is doing.'

5.14

Uncle was by now making accusations against everyone in the family, and when I tried to reason with him, he became furious. He described things that he said had happened on my last visit to him, things that I had supposedly said and done at the behest of the family. I mentioned that other people had happened to be there the whole time, and that he should ask them for the truth of the matter. But I couldn't get through to him. He went on to say something absurd about my mother, and I told him I wasn't going to listen any more. For a week I could not bear to call him. I was finding it almost impossible to work, and it was important for me to get on with things; for the first time, I had sold a novel before it was written, and I had a deadline. Though I tried to be philosophical, and to visualise things from Uncle's point of view, I found myself becoming angry.

One morning, a day or so after I had got back into the swing of things, he phoned up. 'Hello, darling, the whole thing is a fabrication on my part from A to Z,' he began without any preliminaries. 'Don't take the slightest notice. I'm telling you, sometimes I've not been feeling too well. My days are counted. I'm sitting here now. I'm neither dead nor alive.'

'I'll come and visit, Uncle. It's just that I've been working.'

'I phoned Colin – he's on holiday. He told me, "You're mad, this never happened." So, please, darling, accept my apologies. And will you please apologise to your Mummy and explain it to her. I love my Pinni.'

'I'll tell her, Uncle. And I'll see you this afternoon.'

'You don't need to visit just for this.'

'That's not why I'm visiting.'

When I got there, he was eager to tell me about his grandfather. 'You see, after all that, he never set foot in Kotra. That means, indirectly . . .' He paused before continuing: 'And he never spoke a word of English, but he did speak Persian and Urdu and sent all his children to English schools, and he kept a woman openly in the house.'

He turned to Tessa, his Kenyan nurse: 'My wife was my true love,' he said. 'Nowadays, they're looking for sex, but how long does it last?'

He waited for her reply. 'Not long at all,' she said after a few seconds.

He went on: 'They see it in a film. Now when I was younger, it used to be something very special, and you couldn't even talk about it to your grandparents.' Suddenly he was seized with annoyance and turned to me. 'I'll tell you now,' he said, à propos of nothing, 'Valerie pretends to be a big lady, a fashionable lady. But it is Colin I love.'

I said nothing. There seemed no point in following up the comment. So I asked how Colin's work was going. Colin now owned a trailer park in Norfolk and was trying to make a go of it. Uncle was concerned that, though he was very hardworking, he was 'too confident'.

So the afternoon went on. It was my parents' wedding anniversary in a few days, and Uncle wanted to add a few lines to my card.

He wrote six straggling lines with great effort. I had suggested he dictate to me what he wanted to say, but he would not have it. I looked over the card. I could read, with difficulty, five words in those six lines: 'Leila', 'Pinni', 'lots of love'. I asked him to read it out to me, so that I could tell my parents what he had meant to say. He looked at his writing, and tried. 'Unknown places,' he said. 'Lots of love for ever.' But that was all he too could manage.

5.15

Uncle's last scrawl was incomprehensible, but the weakness of his mind and body was the reason. My last record of a meeting with him was also incomprehensible, but with less cause. I was tired on my journey back, and I jotted down a few notes on my tube ticket.

The small pink one-day travelcard is dated 26 APR 98; my writing is at right angles to the print:

- ice
- so weak – chair
- Nikera – Kenya
- money stolen
- marriage: George
- sexy novel?

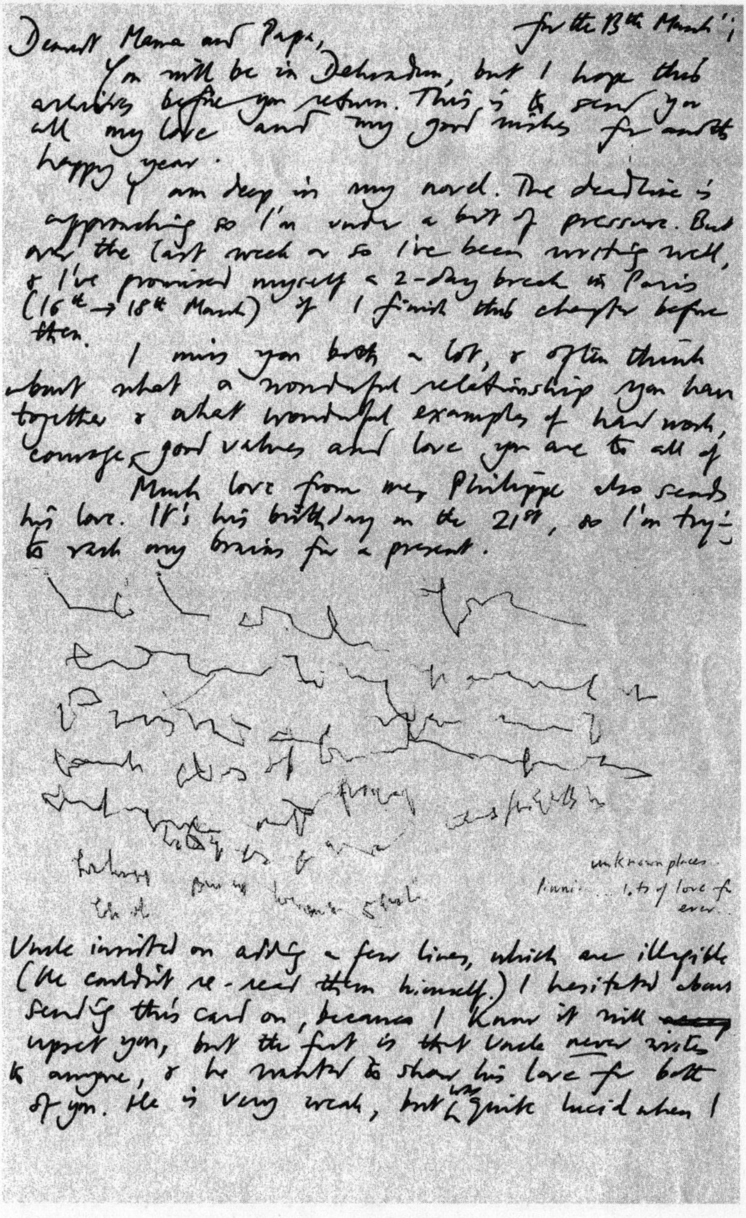

Dearest Mama and Papa, for the 13th March

You will be in Dehradun, but I hope this arrives before you return. This is to send you all my love and my good wishes for another happy year.

I am deep in my novel. The deadline is approaching so I'm under a bit of pressure. But over the last week or so I've been writing well, & I've promised myself a 2-day break in Paris (16th → 18th March) if I finish this chapter before then.

I miss you both a lot, & often think about what a wonderful relationship you have together & what wonderful examples of hard work, courage, good values and love you are to all of

Much love from me. Philippe also sends his love. It's his birthday on the 21st, so I'm trying to rack my brains for a present.

unknown places ...
... lots of love for ever.

Uncle insisted on adding a few lines, which are illegible (he couldn't re-read them himself.) I hesitated about sending this card on, because I know it will ~~[illegible]~~ upset you, but the fact is that Uncle never writes to anyone, & he wanted to show his love for both of you. He is very weak, but was quite lucid when I

Shanti's last lines to my parents.

- swollen feet (raise them)
- you can be heavy when you want to be

I did not elaborate on my notes at the time and I can make little definite sense of them now. It was just an ordinary visit and I hoped to see him again in a few days. Once more, transcribing these notes, I feel sad that I did not know it was to be our final meeting. At least I should have kept a better record of his last words to me.

What could these notes mean? 'Ice' might represent his demand for what he loved to suck and crunch, perhaps because his mouth was so dry. The remark about the chair makes a sort of sense. 'Nikera' might be my attempt to remember 'Nakuru' – possibly the town in Kenya where one of his nurses came from. 'Money stolen' was one of Uncle's themes, but I can remember no new details from this visit. As for 'marriage: George' – could this possibly relate to the story, so often repeated, of how Uncle's friend George Little broke large numbers of glasses while serving drinks at his and Henny's wedding reception? 'Sexy novel' – well, Uncle was always telling me that such novels sell and that I should look into the matter, advice which I always promised to take seriously. The next three remarks are reminders of Uncle's infirmity. The final one is mystifying. Perhaps he was being chided for his wilfulness in refusing to let himself be moved into or out of a chair. Perhaps, just as he practised selective aural acuity, he had learned to practise selective gravity.

In all his powerlessness and dependency, this could have been the last refuge of his resistance: to be heavy when he wanted to be.

5.16

Uncle died less than a week later, on the morning of 2 May 1998. Colin phoned me tearfully to say that he had been with him the previous evening, and that Uncle had been very weak and had wanted to go. The next morning, the nurse had been with him; he had been trying to cough to clear the phlegm from his chest infection, and his heart had finally given in. When the nurse saw what was happening, she called the neighbours, who tried to resuscitate him, but to no effect. Colin had been informed and had returned to the house from Norfolk. He had been working till late, because the village cricket team had been carousing in the bar of the trailer park. When I arrived, he looked exhausted.

We talked to the doctor and the funeral directors and phoned friends and family. Everyone was very upset. When I phoned Fred Götte in Germany, I found it difficult to speak. Fred said, 'This is very bad news. I am really shocked. Lately, of course, he was not happy. He had a good time in life. He was a wonderful friend. No one is left now. I am the only one left.'

In the front garden – almost the only one on the street not tarmacked over to provide parking space – were irises and bluebells. In the back garden, the apple tree was in blossom. The grass was lush and unmown, and dark-red butterflies were hovering over the dandelions. An azalea and a camellia were in heavy bloom.

I wept less than I thought I would. In a way, I was happy for him. This ninetieth birthday celebration would have been more for our sake than for his. Why should he have hung on in pointlessness and pain?

Uncle lay on a green sheet in his striped green pyjamas. He looked calm; a nurse even said it looked as if he was smiling. His hair moved slightly in the breeze; the door to the garden had been left open for fresh air.

On the phone to the funeral directors the next day, in order to bypass questions, Colin referred to Uncle as 'my father' and to Arun, who had arrived from Toronto, as 'my brother from Canada'. Arun said that at the airport he had headed by habit to the duty-free, thinking he was going to see Uncle, before he recalled why it was he had come.

'Throw my body to the dogs,' Uncle used to say; but now, in Hindu style, we raised his body on the stretcher and took him outside into the black van.

I went out and bought the *Observer* in honour of Uncle. Late at night, I tried to occupy myself with the Azed crossword, but my mind kept wandering. A friend of mine from Delhi was in hospital in London and going to have brain surgery in a few days. She was a brilliant academic, full of life and intellectual energy and gossip. Her husband had died some years previously; her illness too had isolated her. When I visited her, she was as lively as ever, but anxious beneath it all. At one point she said: 'You know what Maya said to me before she died? She said, "Dharma, you are really lonely." What a kind thing to say.'

I thought about what Fred had said the previous day, and it came home to me that at a certain point in our lives, if we live long, the living dwindle to a small proportion of those we know. I keep up a conversation of sorts with some of my dead friends. But often there is no response, and the result is an empty sorrow. I keep at it, though, so that they should not be forgotten, and – more importantly – that I should not be left completely without them.

5.17

I kept working on my novel about music – with the help of a pressure bandage, because of a spasming pain in my wrist: this had happened before, and I had been warned against misuse and overuse of my hand. But the deadline was approaching and ideas were once again coming to me and as a result I had ignored the warning signs.

I phoned Colin in case he was in low spirits. He wanted to talk about Uncle: 'He knew me like no one else did – not Valerie, not my parents, not my friends, not my children. I will miss him terribly ... I once phoned him from Monte Cassino, which I visited when I went to Italy. He asked me, "Have you found it?" I said, "What?" He said, "My arm, of course."'

Arun had decided that Uncle should have a Hindu funeral – which was not at all what Uncle had wanted. Some friends and distantly related family who were in London came – again, he would have preferred no one, but there was no way we would have wished to prevent them from coming. With the cremation on the 6th, four days after his death, the news had got around.

We gathered in the familiar chapel in Golders Green Crematorium where Aunty Henny had been cremated nine years earlier. Then a funeral director had taken charge. But now there was a young pandit, or purohit, from a temple in Southall; he was dressed in kurta pyjama and a khaki anorak. Arun and I spoke to him in Hindi, and, where necessary, explained the rites to Colin. The three of us bore the flower-covered coffin into the chapel and laid it on the platform.

Arun performed the rites as if he was the son, while the priest intoned Hindi and Sanskrit in a Gujarati accent: 'Shri Arun Kumar, suputra Shri Shanti Vehari Sheth . . .' and so on. Holy water was splashed from a copper ladle around the coffin. Joss-sticks, dried fruit, invocations to Yama and Agni and the holy rivers Ganga and Yamuna and Saraswati, *swaha* after *swaha*: Shanti Uncle, the sceptic, for whom all this was nothing more than superstition, was not there to object to any of it. The word *shanti* was repeated again and again: 'Unki atma ko shanti pradaan karen [May they give peace to his soul]' or 'Om shanti shanti shanti [Om; peace; peace; peace]'. To most of those present, who did not understand Hindi or Sanskrit, it must have sounded like a keening over the name of the dead.

Colin spoke: 'Forgive me, Shanti, you would not have wanted this fuss. Forgive me these trespasses against your express wishes.' He talked of him as a confidant, friend, adviser, father. He sat down, wrinkles under his eyes, his pink face crinkled in grief. Arun asked me if I wanted to say anything, and I shook my head.

The button was pushed, the casket moved along the rails, the little claw emerged and pushed it through the doors into an antechamber. The crematorium operator was not yet ready, so everyone left the chapel and wandered about the garden among the blossoms and wild grass. It was a clear day, windy and cold. Then the three of us returned to where the coffin now rested. The priest intoned a few words and we pushed the coffin into the furnace. First the flowers burst into flame, then the rest, and then the doors closed.

5.18

Not all of Shanti Uncle's friends came to the funeral. Yossi was there, but it was decided that though Yonni wanted to be there (he referred to Shanti Uncle as his best friend), he was too young not to be upset by the ceremony. At the other end of the age spectrum, Fred Götte, Shanti's contemporary, wrote to me in English from Hanover:

Dear Vikrim,

I am very saddened, that your uncle Shanti passed away. Last week I still talked to him. He often mentioned to me that he didn't want to live any longer. One can understand that, as he could not walk anymore nor read the newspaper or watch the TV properly. I felt very sorry for him. With him I am loosing my last friend and the best one I ever had. Such a good character one finds not so often. He was a reliable and helpful friend. Everybody liked him, he was a good talker and had always jokes present . . .

As your uncle's last will was that not anybody should come to his funeral, I was there present in my mind last Wednesday.

With best wishes and kind regards,

Fred

Uncle had already given me his spare artificial arm, and a few days later I took possession of his Nelson knife, which lies on the table in front of me as I write this.

Uncle wanted me to have his books and bookcases, his old army uniform and so on. But a few months later, I wanted to have little to do with them.

Since Colin had the keys to 18 Queens Road and seemed to be winding things up there, I asked him whether the stair-lift that Shanti Uncle had used could be given to a friend of mine. My friend's wife, though young, found it difficult and exhausting to climb the stairs owing to an illness that had lasted some years. This was exacerbated now that she was pregnant. Colin readily agreed, and my friend hauled the stair-lift away. He installed it in his house in Devon, and it did indeed provide relief. This whole business made me happy both at the time and whenever I have thought about it. There seemed to be a rightness to the fact that, unbeknownst to it, a foetus (soon to be a delightful infant) made the journey up and down on the same stair-lift that had carried Shanti Uncle to the last year of his ninth decade.

Meanwhile, I had a small project on my hands, which took me away from my novel as I neared the end of my first draft. Indeed, when I consider this business in retrospect, I have come to think that I have a fear of completion which tempts me ineluctably towards distractions of this kind. The project was simple: I wanted to get someone to invite Colin to dinner at the Naval and Military Club; and soon.

The Naval and Military Club had stood in vast, Palladian-fronted premises on Piccadilly since 1866. It was the former home of Lord Palmerston, who was Prime Minister during the so-called Indian Mutiny of 1857. It had fifty bedrooms, a ballroom and a library, as well as two gates giving on to Piccadilly, one marked 'In', the other 'Out', as a result of which it was known informally as the In and Out Club. Queen Victoria had been attacked here by a madman, and during the Blitz a German bomb had killed everyone in the dining-room except for a Major Braddell, whose greatcoated ghost continued to haunt the building. The In and Out Club's long lease was due to run out in early 1999, and its Kuwaiti owners were putting it up for sale for the modest figure of £50 million.

When Colin was in his teens, he had trained here as a young chef. He had once mentioned in passing that the club was due to move to new premises in St James's Square. He had always dreamed of having a meal in the dining-room, but of course there could be no question of this unless he was invited by a member.

I felt a great affection for Colin and for all that he had done for Uncle, and decided to make this come to pass.

I knew no one who was or had been in the British army or navy, apart, of course, from Uncle, who would never have been a member; he was the least clubbable of men and, given his views on war, deeply unkeen on army reunions and associations in particular. My first thought was to telephone the club secretary; but I could think of no grounds – other than those of (probably unwelcome) publicity – that I could adduce to suggest that a former trainee chef should be invited to dine there.

But surely I did know someone who had once been in the army; he, or perhaps someone else, had mentioned it at a friend's wedding that we had both attended a few months earlier: Desmond Clarke, who worked at Faber & Faber when they were my publishers, had had some connection with the army. What it was I did not know. I phoned the club, and found out that Captain D. W. R. Clarke was indeed a member. They wouldn't give me his address, so I wrote to him care of the club, asking him to phone me: I had 'a very odd request, which would require too much explanation on paper'. He was on holiday, but when he returned, he did; I put the matter to him, and he generously acquiesced, saying that it would be fun.

I phoned Colin in Norfolk; he was having a quiet drink before opening time at the bar of his trailer park. He told me I was having him on.

The dinner was a great success, though sadly the main dining-room was entirely reserved for the Royal Society of St George, who were having their annual Waterloo Dinner there. (It struck me, annoyingly, that Wellington, like Palmerston, was responsible in an earlier generation for the subjugation of India.) Various members in dinner jackets or uniforms passed by the three of us as we made our way to the buttery upstairs. The meal was excellent in an institutional way, washed down with a white burgundy and culminating in bread-and-butter pudding.

The talk began with Wellington, Blücher and the sounds of the Battle of Waterloo atmospherically transferred on to Hampstead Heath, but soon moved to the streetwalkers who used to greet the sixteen-year-old Colin as he walked back from his shift at the In and Out through Shepherd Market to the number 16 bus back home to Neasden.

Colin's eyes followed the movement of the waiters. He was verifying things he remembered. 'Now you can enter by this door, but not by that one,' he said. 'And what happened behind *that* door,' he continued, 'reminds me of Mr Bevan, the chef. He was quite something. Happy as Larry when Arsenal won and mad as a bear with a sore paw when they lost. What happened was that Ali – he was Trinidadian, and had huge eyes – was carrying a whole roast boar downstairs very carefully, but the stairs were worn and he slipped and the boar went bouncing down the stairs all the way to the bottom. Mr Bevan wasn't happy, I can tell you.'

Speeches floated towards us from the plane-shaded courtyard; it was a lovely summer evening in late June. The toasts were rather funereal and sombre. But after 'The Queen' had elicited gruff responses of fealty, the strains of 'Stardust' drifted gently upwards.

The conversation moved back to affairs military, as became the environment, and Colin and I talked about Shanti Uncle and how he had lost his arm at Monte Cassino. Desmond responded, with pleasing symmetry, that his uncle had lost a leg there.

5.19

Colin invited me to spend some time at his trailer park later that summer, and I accepted.

My parents were in England that year, and I got into conversation with my mother. I asked her in passing what had happened with regard to the probate of Shanti Uncle's will, and she said she didn't know. I said that as a beneficiary that was a bit odd. She replied that she wasn't a beneficiary.

At first I thought I hadn't understood her correctly. Noticing the look on my face, she said, 'But darling, didn't you know? Colin and Arun are the sole beneficiaries.'

My disbelief turned to disgust. I shook my head.

'But I thought you knew.'

'Why should I know? I don't take an interest in these things. I always understood it was to be divided among the four of you and Arun and Anand and Colin. When did Uncle do this? When did he change his will? And why?'

'More than a year ago. He called Michi Bhai over and told him. That's when he made that strange remark about me.' Mama couldn't bring herself to repeat the actual words Uncle had used. I now remembered the conversation with Michi Mama which I had cut off because he began by speaking slightingly of Colin. I felt sick to my stomach.

'Why didn't you tell me?' I demanded.

'Well, darling, I don't like talking about these things. And I thought that Uncle must have told you. Michi said *he* tried to, but you seemed to know about it, and got annoyed.'

'I didn't know about it.'

I cannot describe the deep revulsion of feeling that overcame me after this conversation. It changed my view of – indeed, my faith in – Uncle. I had loved him and greatly respected him. This love was now tinged with anger and this respect with something corrosive. All Uncle's talk about the family and what it meant to him came back to me. The sense of his rejection of the family – and that the remark he had made about my mother was made in this context: it was all too much to take.

We were visiting 18 Queens Road; Colin had just gone out. When he returned, I asked him if what I had heard was true. He appeared quite calm about it. 'Yes, Vicky. It's Arun and me. We're the executors and the beneficiaries, and I have first dibs on the house.'

'And that's it?'

'Yes. Well, we've made sure there's something for Cathy – five thousand pounds.'

'And there's no provision for Michi Mama, Sashi Mama, Tuttu Mama or my mother?'

'None.'

'Or Arun's brother Anand?'

'No.'

'They've been cut out of the will?'

Colin didn't say anything.

'And you knew about all this?'

'It was Uncle's wish.'

I did not trust myself to speak.

For several nights after I heard this, I was hardly able to sleep.

I did go to Norfolk and stayed in one of the trailers in the trailer park, which was just outside a small village. I walked to the Saxon church nearby, and wandered around the village and the flat drained fens. Colin gave me two or three old letters which he had found among Uncle's papers and which he thought would be useful to me. He and Valerie did their best to be hospitable, but there was an acid of dismay inside me that I could not get rid of. I spent an unrestful night. The next morning at breakfast, Colin received a call from Derek, Uncle's accountant, and seemed uncomfortable that I was within earshot. When he returned, I told him I needed to go back to London that same day. We got to the train halt and – rather like hailing a bus at a request stop –

hailed down the train. I can't remember what we said. We parted civilly.

Over the next few months, Colin called me several times, but I pleaded work. The last thing I wanted was Uncle's army uniform or his bookcases. I had very little time for mementoes of a man whom I had once so much admired but about whom I now felt a deep ambivalence. I did not know what to make of it. It seemed that it was someone else that I had known. His love for the family had been much on his lips, but the disjuncture between his words and acts was now distressingly patent. The sense that Arun and Colin had acquiesced in this wretched business made it the more unpleasant.

I often wondered what Aunty Henny would have thought about what Uncle had done.

5.20

Several months after I first heard about the will, I was to discover what had happened that day between Uncle and Michi Mama.

My father and I were having lunch at home in Delhi with Michi Mama and Mohini Mami, who were visiting from Pune. We began to talk about the will at the dining-table. Papa, for the most part, did not enter the discussion.

Michi Mama said that it had been at his instance that the original sixfold division had been expanded to include Colin. He said, 'Uncle told me that Colin was to get a certain amount a month. I said that that was unfair, and that Colin should at least get one share. I even suggested Uncle divide it eight ways and give Colin two shares. But eventually Uncle decided that Colin should have one share like the rest of us – that he should be included in the family. That was fine.'

Michi Mama paused, then continued: 'Uncle loved talking about the family and his will. He said that some of his other relations had written to him protesting love and hoping to be included, but that he had responded to this with a comment to the effect that they hadn't been in touch with him for years and he knew how much they loved him.'

'What happened to make him change his will?' I asked.

Michi Mama continued: 'Well, in January 1997, I had a stroke. Mohini was away, and I was in Pune. I was going for dinner somewhere, and had difficulty tying my tie. Over drinks, I couldn't hold the canapés properly, and at dinner could hardly grip my fork. A lady whose husband was a doctor in Bombay got up and phoned him. He said, "He's having a stroke. Get him to a hospital immediately." I was taken to hospital, and everything was done to dissolve the clot that was forming. In four days I got most of the use of my hand back, and after three or four weeks of physiotherapy, I was almost completely OK, except that I was not allowed to travel for a while. Meanwhile, I got a call from Uncle, in London, summoning me to go and see him. I explained why I couldn't go, but he didn't seem to accept the explanation. Tuttu had earlier said he would go, but his passport was not in order and, as you know, it takes weeks or months to get things sorted out. No one knew Uncle hadn't been at all well. Colin certainly didn't tell me.

'Come May, I went to London. As usual, I spent three weeks near Uncle and about ten days in town, staying at the RAC. The first morning I went to see him, Uncle was obviously dying to say something to me, and suddenly, after lunch, without any preliminaries, he said, "I've cut you out of my will with my own hands." I said, "And the others – Leila too?" "Yes, Leila too," said Uncle. "She is Mack the Knife. Only Colin and Arun are to be my heirs."

'I was surprised, a bit disappointed, and deeply aggrieved. I didn't ask Uncle why he had done it. But he volunteered it. What he said was, "Colin needs the money more than you all; you're well enough off." I said, "Uncle, I never asked you for a justification, but since you've given it, do you think that Arun, as a doctor in Canada, needs it more than Anand?" Uncle brushed this aside. "And Tuttu?" I asked. At this, Uncle said, "I have always given you

483

enough. I give you five hundred pounds when you come here." I said, "Uncle, that is all very well, but if you think we come here for that, you are mistaken. We come here because we love you and want to see you; and, incidentally, it costs me at least five thousand each time I fly to and stay in London. You may also be sure that I am not going to cut short this visit or spend less time with you because of what you have told me."

'I didn't repeat back to him something that was very much on my mind: his often reiterated remarks about how much he owed my father, etc. I thought that was petty, and I wouldn't do it.

'I did, however, ask him if he had left Cathy anything. He said he hadn't, and I said, "Uncle, that's shameful. You must leave her something." Suddenly he became very agitated. "I'll give it to her with warm hands. Immediately. Get some money." I said, "Uncle, you need what cash you have. Leave her something." "Then call my solicitor," he demanded. I replied, "That, Uncle, is for you to do."

'The things he had said to me made my hackles rise, Vikram, and if I was sharp in my manner of speaking to you the next day, that was the cause of it. I should have waited longer before phoning you.'

There was a pause, and I replied: 'No, Michi Mama, I shouldn't have cut you off. If I'd heard what you wanted to say, I'd have known more than a year earlier. The only thing is that I would certainly have spoken to Uncle, and it might have led to an estrangement. Perhaps, in a selfish way, I should be glad I didn't hear, because it didn't spoil my sense of him in his last year.'

Mohini said quietly: 'I think he regretted it. When Michi was sleeping or when he had drowsed off on the sofa, Uncle would often say, "Their father did so much for me. He could have sent them abroad, but he sent me. He always treated me less as a younger brother than as his first child. And I owe my sister-in-law Chanda Bhabhi so much. I must give it back to them," and so on.'

Michi Mama said: 'I asked Colin several times to take me to see the solicitor, but it never happened. I'm not the only one in the family who thinks Colin influenced him.'

'But Michi Mama,' I protested. 'You can't believe that. Colin loved and cared for Uncle. If Uncle had had no money, he would still have cared for him. Influenced or not, Uncle changed his will voluntarily and deliberately. What do you think was the real reason?'

Michi Mama shook his head and said nothing. Mohini said, 'Probably he had grown to depend on Colin so much, and to some extent on Arun. There *they* were, here the rest of the family – for whatever reason – was. He might have felt resentment towards those he saw as absentees. Then, having done it, even if he wanted to change it, he might have found it difficult to tell the solicitor: a sense of pride, perhaps.'

'Strange,' said Michi Mama. 'The very day after he told me about the will business, he said to me, "That fellow, Colin, I don't trust him: he wants me to sign a cheque for more than four thousand pounds every month." I said, "Uncle, he has been taking care of you. He has to pay the bills for food, nursing, etc." A form was created, which Derek audited each month.'

What a sorry business, I thought.

5.21

My mind often turned to Uncle, but my thoughts were now tinged with unease.

I was not, had never been, and indeed had refused to be a beneficiary of his will. Why then was I letting all this get to me? Everyone else seemed to be much more philosophical than I was. But I found it impossible to be philosophical about someone who had greatly affected the way I felt and thought, partly because I had loved him but mainly because I had admired him. I would have been equally upset at his invidious division if the sum had been a hundredfold or a hundredth of what it was, and not in the least upset if he had left it all to charity. I wanted to see the will to discover if it would give me any clue about his state of mind; but since the money itself was not the matter, I wanted to see it only after it had passed the stage where it could be challenged.

When I finally saw it, I noted the date it had been made; this was 26 March 1997, two months after Uncle had summoned Michi Mama to London. It was also two months before Michi Mama was able to come, on which occasion Uncle had told him with such relish, 'I have cut you out of my will with my own hands.'

The cover document from the District Probate Registry in Brighton stated that both the gross and net value of the estate were a little over £800,000. The substance of the will was simple. All previous wills were revoked, Colin and Arun were appointed as executors and trustees, and the property was divided between them. In the fifth clause, Colin was given the first offer to buy 18 Queens Road at the price determined by professional valuation. The will was signed in the presence of two local witnesses.

But that frail 'S. B. Seth' was not the only place on the will where Shanti Uncle's handwriting could be seen. It appeared in two other places.

At the beginning of the third clause he had cut out Colin's full name as an executor and replaced it with Derek's full name. The change had not been witnessed or countersigned, and the hand-writing was even more shaky than in his signature. At the beginning of the fifth clause, above Colin's name, were seven words, again not countersigned or witnessed, which I later pored over but was unable to make sense of, so illegible was Uncle's handwriting at this stage. They read as follows:

[illegible] [illegible] Arun Seth Vikram Seth [illegible]

This second change surprised me. No one had ever written to me about it, though that did not matter. But just to see my name in Uncle's hand gave me a peculiar and disturbing sense of his pres-ence. Though it implied that at some time he had thought about me, and had perhaps in the watches of the night got out of bed to scrawl my name on his will, it was in the delusional context of my being interested in buying or bidding for his house. I had told Uncle clearly that I was not. I had a great many memories of the house, but I did not want to live there.

For many years after Uncle's death, I did not return to the house or even pass by it. I had no idea what had become of it – whether it looked as it once did, whether the front garden still existed, whether the whole thing had been made into flats as planned by Colin. Sometimes I thought back to the time when, as a schoolboy, I first arrived at the door to be greeted by Aunty Henny. The red pillar-box by the gate, the gleaming professional sign: I found myself thinking about these things and shaking my head with pointless sadness. What had once been a happy zone of contemplation was something I now tried to avoid.

I had been unable to tackle this book while Uncle was alive. In the year or two after he died, I tried, more than once, to begin writing it. Each time, I stopped after only a page or two. What he had said about the family had twisted my feelings into a misshapen knot.

I kept the materials for the book – the documents, the letters, the interview notes, the photographs – prominently on a shelf, so that they could upbraid me for procrastination. But I had no taste for them. After a couple of years, I took the materials off the shelf and put them away in cardboard boxes.

One day, without planning to, I began writing again. This time it was not a false start. As I wrote, my feelings towards both Uncle and Aunty revived. As I read their letters – to me, to their friends, to each other – I both relived my days with them and drifted into days and times of which I had no direct experience.

Towards Aunty Henny, there was nothing to resolve except a kind of regret. As I read her correspondence with her friends after the war, I grew to love and admire her even more than I had in life. But it was too late to express this to her, and besides, had she been alive, I would not have known about these letters.

But there was something to resolve with respect to Uncle. In the first draft of this book, when I came to write about his will and his attacks on the family – and most particularly on my mother – my anger and outrage were once again aroused. Friends who read this draft saw something raw and bitter. If I no longer feel what I felt then, it is not because I intended the writing of the book to be cathartic. But being forced to look steadily at what I would rather have averted my gaze from – or made a swift and unsparing judgement about – has, in some manner, helped me come to terms with it.

Though later, clearly, Uncle's mind became clouded, at the time he made his will it was not obvious that this was so. He was old, but most people get to be old. Indeed, just as *in vino veritas*, it is sometimes said that people often reveal themselves in old age, when some of their social constraints and pretences have dropped away. One can then see them as they most truly are: in warmth, in coldness, in generosity, in pettiness, in kindness, in cruelty, in gentleness, in wrath.

But it could be said that, in Uncle's case, old age not only enhanced certain facets of his personality but also distorted them. At the end, he was a sick and insecure man, powerless, frightened and lonely. His occupation had gone and with it his sense both of usefulness and of mental challenge; for him, unlike others, books or music could not fill this void. The love of his life had died, and so had almost all his friends. With them had gone most of his world. There was hardly anyone to whom he could say, 'Do you remember how it was when . . .?' or 'Do you remember when we . . .?' His health had gone. He could barely get to the park unaided, let alone to the mountains that he knew he would never see again. He was in pain and discomfort. He had lost his independence and even his power to run his own affairs. He had lost the dignity of being able to take care of his physical self.

As for his confidence in the love others had for him, it may be that he had always been insecure on this account, and that this insecurity now became more manifest. One wonders in the light of their letters if he was ever completely sure that Henny loved him as he loved her. Perhaps Uncle began to believe that his kinsmen loved not him but his money. When he summoned them and they did not come immediately, he may have thought they were taking him for granted because, as he had endlessly told them, they were in his will.

If so, he would give them a shock. His will was almost the only sphere in which this once active, energetic and determined man could still exercise some power. One other aspect of his personality, his pleasure in seeing the effect of his actions or revelations on those affected, now also came to the fore. This is the only reason I can think of for his actually wanting to tell Michi face to face what he had done.

If this enjoyment of Michi's discomfiture could perhaps be seen as a sad enhancement of an existing trait, what was I to make of his 'Mack the Knife' remark? This was made of his beloved niece, his 'Pinni', the daughter of his dearest brother. But perhaps I was wrong in imagining that Uncle was entirely unclouded in his mind at the beginning of 1997. Unlike Aunty Henny's rapid physical decline, unaccompanied by serious mental impairment, Uncle's slower decline had an insidious effect not only on his body. The paranoia he showed towards the middle of the year could have attacked him episodically earlier. It may have been in episodes such as these that, his mind now having turned against most of the family, he spoke as he spoke and did what he did.

Where did these feelings come from? It is possible that he was in the early stages of dementia, most likely vascular dementia. It is possible that it was uraemia, perhaps aggravated by his medications, that was at work. It is a riddle, and a troubling one – unresolved and probably unresolvable.

But what is surely resolvable is my anger against him. After reading what I had earlier written, my mother wrote to me:

I was not at all unhappy about not receiving anything in his will – in a sense, relieved that there was no bickering among brothers and sisters, since we had all been excluded. I valued and value the love and great affection he had for me – and so I was hurt deeply by his remarks. I hope this book is a success as he loved you dearly. Your own anger seems partly to stem from the fact that you didn't know – you had shut up Michi Mama when he wanted to tell you – and got a shock.

My mother is right; that was part of it. But why should this bitterness have lasted for years? Why could I hardly bear to think about him? Perhaps, if I had not revered him so much, I would not have been so censorious.

The problem lay in this reverence. Shanti Uncle was for me a remarkable man – of great grit, intelligence, affection and family feeling. When I was once asked in an interview which living person I most admired, his was the name I gave. Even Aunty Henny, part of whose philosophy was not to expect too much of people, had high expectations of him. I saw his will and his insults as aberrations, but I did not, in the scheme of my admiration, make any provision for aberrations.

'He loved you dearly,' wrote my mother, and he did. In the perspective of the love he gave me throughout his life and his generosity to me when I was younger, what excuse do I have to vex his shade with righteous reproofs? In the perspective of his whole life, or – even more – the history of his times, what do things like these matter?

What would Aunty Henny have wanted? To this I know the answer. She would have wanted me to be less troubled in spirit. She would have wanted me to think well of Uncle. She would have wanted me to try to make sense of things – but, even if I could not, to get on with them.

5.22

My lens has zoomed in for the most part on my two subjects. But occasionally it has become a wide-angle and touched upon the history of the century they inhabited.

It is true that centuries are arbitrary... other things, by the miscalculated date of ... religion and the number of fingers on our ha... invest these units with spurious significance, they... nificance. Shanti and Henny's lives were almost co... arbitrary unit, the twentieth century. Both were born ...; Henny died in 1989, Shanti in 1998. Many of the great cu... nts and movements of the century are reflected through the events of their lives and those of their friends and family: the Raj, the Indian freedom movement, post-Independence India; the Third Reich; the Second World War; postwar Germany, including the division of Berlin and the blockade and airlift; the emigration of Jews from Germany in the 1930s (with some of Henny's friends going as far afield as Shanghai, South Africa and California); the Holocaust; Israel and Palestine; British politics, economics and society. Many powerful 'isms' – imperialism, Nazism, anti-Semitism, racism, conservatism, liberalism, socialism, communism, totalitarianism – worked through (and sometimes battered) their lives or those of their family and friends. I felt that a picture of these individual lives would be complemented by glimpses of their century, even if these glimpses were mediated by the opinion, perhaps opinionatedness, of the author. Indeed, the lens has also turned around upon its wielder, for this book is memoir as well as biography.

In a double biography, an intertwined meditation, where the author is an anomalous third braid, sometimes visible, sometimes not, there are intriguing possibilities of structure. For one thing, in what order should one recount events? The sequence of a biography with a single subject can be directly chronological. But it would have made little sense to ricochet from one protagonist to the other through their first two decades, before they had even met.

Though I now know where to end this book, I did not at first know where to begin it. There was too large a choice of starting-points: critical events such as Shanti and Henny's first meeting in Berlin; the loss of Shanti's arm; the discovery by Henny of the murder of her family; Shanti and Henny's wedding in London; her death; the revelation of the will. Or else, in order to make explicit from the start my involvement with their lives and the tension between authorial distance and personal immediacy, I could have begun with my first or perhaps last interview with Shanti Uncle, or my mother's suggestion that I write about him, or the actual point where I at last took up the pen. In the event, I chose to start the book with a moment involving all three of us: when, as a boy of seventeen, I went to live with them. It was not dramatic in the grand scheme of things, even if fraught with tension for my more nervous younger self.

Now I am three times that age, and they are dead, and the book is almost written. It has been a voyage not only round their histories but also a sort of pilgrimage of their geographies.

I will end by revisiting a few points along the way.

5.23

Biswan, February 1989
Long before I knew I wanted to write this book, I went to Lucknow to do some research for *A Suitable Boy*. On the way to Mahmoodabad Fort I stopped at the small town of Biswan, the hometown of Shanti Uncle and my maternal grandfather, whom I had never known. I visited unannounced, not knowing if anyone in the family was still there.

Brahma, Shanti's third brother, had stayed in the town long after the others had left. He had involved himself in various farming schemes, but they had been unsuccessful, and now even the site of his house was a heap of rubble, with not a wall standing. Among the thin bricks and the thistles, donkeys browsed; they shied away as we drew near. Brahma's children had left Biswan.

'The land has not been occupied by squatters because we keep an eye on it,' said a more distant member of the family who still lived in the small town. 'When Brahma's son came, he wept when he saw it. He was a good boy. He couldn't stop weeping. Home is home, after all.'

Another member of the family, viewing my approach suspiciously, was told that I was Raj Behari's grandson. He instantly hugged me and drew me into his house. Peas were being shelled inside. Tea was made. Photographs were taken. Feet were touched. 'How long are you staying? Just today? No, that's not possible – that is very wrong. Dipak – that's him – is getting married the day after tomorrow in Sitapur. You must come. You've got to stay. You must spend the night here.'

At one point in the conversation, I asked where a particular town, Mirzapur, was located.

'Between Allahabad and Banaras,' I was told.

'Ah, yes, on the river.'

Sharply, almost angrily, I was rebuked: 'Don't say "river".'

Rather shocked, I corrected myself. 'On the Ganga.'

'On the holy Ganga. On mother Ganga.'

'Yes. On the holy Ganga.'

Monte Cassino, November 1994
Shortly after my interviews with Shanti Uncle I visited Monte Cassino – sacred not only to the memory of Saint Benedict, but also to that of the many dead and wounded who once fought along its ridges, slopes and valleys. I had no purpose in going there except to see where Shanti Uncle had lost his arm.

Bombed into rubble during the battle fifty years earlier, the monastery-fortress had been completely reconstructed in gleaming and somewhat sterile white stone. It looked like a massive hotel, rising sheer from the hillside. Below the parapet, the yellow and red leaves of a vineyard blazed out against the stony soil. To the right was the Polish cemetery. I visited it, and gathered some yellow leaves from among the graves, most of which were marked May 1944, the date of the last battle.

I saw but did not visit the memorial obelisk above the graveyard. On it are inscribed the words that, translated, read:

We Polish soldiers
For our freedom and yours
Have given our souls to God
Our bodies to Italy
And our hearts to Poland

As I copy out these words, I look once again at the brittle yellow leaves pressed together with a sprig of juniper between the glossy pages of a guidebook. On the grey inside cover, plainer and rougher, is the aspiration, translated there as follows:

Benedict man of God
From the praying and industrious peace of this Mount
See us always
Pilgrims along the paths of life
And show us the true Light that is Christ
Our Peace our Salvation

Berlin, August 2003

I have gone to meet various German publishers in Berlin to see if they are interested in publishing this present book. One morning, I find myself with time on my hands. I take a taxi from my hotel, which stands just inside what was once East Berlin. We drive past the Brandenburg Gate and the Victory Column towards Charlottenburg. The taxi driver asks me where I'm from; he himself was born in Istanbul. He asks me my name and, when I tell him, exclaims enthusiastically, 'Oh, Ikram, Ikram!', which is a Muslim name.

I would have liked to continue the conversation, but we have arrived. This is Bleibtreustrasse 19, a handsome building on a prosperous residential street. I open the heavy door and walk into the elegant foyer: veined marble; a female nude in semi-relief on the wall; ditto, a male nude with a panther; a somewhat threadbare carpet on the stairs; a gold-and-white design of twined ivy trailing upwards along the stairwell; an old-fashioned lift.

I look out at the garden: ferns, hydrangeas, tall trees in full leaf. Light pours down into the garden between the wings of the building. This is where Henny spent her last years in Berlin, and her last night with her family. In July 1939 she left for England. In May 1943, her mother and sister were taken from here, through this foyer and this main door, to a collection camp, and thence, respectively, to Theresienstadt and Auschwitz.

I sit on a bench near the lift and gather my thoughts. Every so often, someone walks up or goes down the stairs. Naturally enough, I am glanced at suspiciously. When an older woman comes down, I pluck up the courage to ask her, 'Excuse me, I wonder if you could tell me whether in the Second World War—' She cuts me off: 'I know nothing about that. Nothing, do you understand, nothing.'

On a small board near the lift are listed about twenty names from the ground to the fourth floor of this large apartment building. I feel reluctant to disturb a resident in order to get a glimpse of a flat. But the Pension Kettler is also marked on the board, and after half an hour or so, I walk up and ring the bell.

To my surprise, I notice a very small Star of David hanging from a chain around the neck of the woman who opens the door. She welcomes me in and shows me around the *pension*, which consists of a series of comfortable rooms off a corridor in a private home. The walls of the corridor are covered with eclectic pieces of mainly modern art. With hospitable loquacity, she tells me: 'Business is terrible. There's the Broadcasting Exhibition this week, and you'd expect it to be better, but no. I used to get people from China, Japan, Israel, America, and of course Germany, but the economic situation is very, very bad. In thirty-one years I have never seen it so bad.'

When I tell her about Aunty Henny and her family, she says: 'My husband was much older than me – he was a Romanian Jew. The Nazis beat him up in Prague; they gave him a severe head wound. He escaped to France, but was locked up in a camp near Perpignan. Then he escaped to Spain, and was locked up again.

Then he escaped to Portugal. When the police came once more, he said, "Herr Kapitän, kill us. You can see how we are, starving, lice-ridden, filthy, weak. Kill us. Don't lock us up or turn us back." The captain said, "Last week a law was passed; no one is to be turned back once they have crossed the border." So he lived out the war.'

Not so fortunate were Lola and Ella, for whom Bleibtreustrasse 19 was their last home. In Lola's prayer-book, which ended up in Henny's hands, and thence mine, is a Kaddish for the bereaved that ends as follows:

> ... Praised be the Holy One, who is above all praise. May all the world praise the Lord, whom all the world's praise cannot touch.
>
> May he send out from the height of heaven peace and life over us and all Israel. Amen.
>
> May he, who establishes peace from on high, let peace prevail over us, over all Israel, and the whole of mankind. Amen.

Ella once told Annerose Dietrich, 'God gives us no more to bear than we are capable of bearing.' But in her case and that of her daughters, he appears to have exceeded his brief, as in the case of millions more.

London, March 2004

Before I close this book, I should return to 18 Queens Road. For more than five years, I have had no wish to go back. Now, so that things might come full circle, I will.

My train arrives at Waterloo just before one o'clock. I get the underground, and travel up the Northern Line, emerging into the daylight at Golders Green. At Hendon Central I get out and walk up the steps, thirteen and then five, yes, just as I remember, to the level of the street. It is a cold afternoon, getting cloudier and windier.

The traffic at the intersection is as heavy as ever. But the cinema – or was it a bingo hall? – has changed into a health club, and where I turn into Queens Road, there is a huge black plate-glass façade offering, among other pleasures, aromatherapy massage, botox, microdermabrasion, reflexology and skin rejuvenation. The red double-decker bus number 83 is no longer the old Routemaster that let one hop on and off, but the more economical single-driver vehicle. Graffiti scar the walls here and there. A young man speaking Arabic on a mobile phone passes another young man wearing a yarmulke, also speaking on a mobile phone. Pink quince bursts out on leafless twigs. A few daffodils bloom in one of the two or three front gardens still remaining on Queens Road.

Semidetached houses, sometimes several of them, have been merged into blocks of flats, taller than the houses to either side, with names such as Highview House or Beatrice Court. Beyond the birch trees, as I come to the top of the hill, I see the bright-red pillar-box near Uncle's house. Once again I see Uncle and Aunty standing in the open doorway, and I find myself smiling.

But as I pass the pillar-box, my heart sinks. The familiar low wall, the familiar gate, the path, the front garden, are all gone. Where there was a lawn, there is nothing but a continuation of the pavement, paved over in dull red and black. A dirty yellow van stands where the roses and the burnished professional sign once stood. The house looks much as it used to, except dingier. In an upstairs window, a pane is broken. Bricks are missing from the steps.

The front door, painted in black and white, is much the same. The brass knocker, the brass digits 18, are the same. The small doorbell is the same, but I will not ring it. It was a mistake to come; no purpose would be served by compounding it. I am not even curious about who lives here now.

Yet as I stand and look at the house, I see it reinhabited by people and by things, by voices and by thoughts. I see Aunty Henny picking up the telephone receiver to say, 'Hendon six double three oh,' Uncle spearing lettuce on to my plate with his Nelson knife, my father discovering a cobweb-covered cabin trunk in the attic, my mother listening to Uncle's anecdotes with a quiet smile. I see the surgical chair going out and the stair-lift coming in. I see the porcelain cockatoo, bored with his endless observation of bridge games, flying out of the green room and over the rooftops of Hendon.

Fröschlein comes to visit and returns with news to her friends in Berlin. Hirabehn sees that her early lessons in discipline have borne fruit and that her little brother, now eighty-nine years old, has made something of his life. The sloping roof flattens, and a small boy, playing with his kite on the roof, finds it entangled in a lichi tree. A young man, clutching his bleeding arm, runs through the din and fear of a battle to a surgical tent. An old man, weeping in a crematorium, consigns his wife to the flames. And I hear her voice saying, in German, 'Don't take the black man,' and, after a while, in English, 'Cathy, take care of my husband.'

Behind every door on every ordinary street, in every hut in every ordinary village on this middling planet of a trivial star, such riches are to be found. The strange journeys we undertake on our earthly pilgrimage, the joy and suffering we taste or confer, the chance events that cleave us together or apart, what a complex trace they leave: so personal as to be almost incommunicable, so fugitive as to be almost irrecoverable.

Yet seeing through a glass, however darkly, is to be less blind. That is what has motivated this effort; that is all I have hoped would result. These two people whom I loved and who loved me may not, in differing degrees, have wanted every stroke – sometimes distorted, sometimes overexplicit – of this portrait. But they are dead and past caring; and I want them complexly remembered – in sickness as in health, in weakness as in strength, in secrecy as in openness. Their lives were cardinal points for me, and guide me still; I want to mark them true.

I cross the road and walk for a while in the park. It is a weekday afternoon and the goalposts are empty. The gulls and pigeons wheel around. I had forgotten how windy it was, here, on the exposed high flank of the hill.

I seek refuge in the small garden – now a memorial garden – that forms an enclave in Hendon Park. Here I sit on a bench and close my eyes. The roar of the traffic on the North Circular Road, the mad buzzing of a leaf-clearing machine, the passing noise of the overground tube-train skirting the park, the voices of children, all merge with the images in my mind.

I had better be getting along; I have an appointment in town in an hour. I walk around the garden. Apart from a few crocuses and snowdrops, little is in bloom. An orange-beaked blackbird wanders beneath the sparse pink-white blossom of a prunus. The magnolia buds are closed. Small red goldfish gather at the roots of rushes in a pool.

A sign requesting people to respect the peace of this place is printed in English, Urdu, Chinese, Greek, Gujarati, Hindi and Arabic. As I leave, I glance once more at the gate of the memorial garden. On it, in silver metal on black, is a single word in Hebrew. In a flowerbed to the side, so small as to be almost illegible, is a sign that mentions the Jewish holocaust in the context of more recent events in Cambodia, in Bosnia, in Rwanda, and goes on to explain the single word above the arch: 'Lezikaron. The meaning refers to the importance of looking forward as well as remembering the past.'

As I walk back to the tube, I consider the word in the context of an evil century past and a still more dangerous one to come. May we not be as foolish as we are almost bound to be. If we cannot eschew hatred, at least let us eschew group hatred. May we see that we could have been born as each other. May we, in short, believe in humane logic and perhaps, in due course, in love.

TWO SETS OF PEOPLE

Shanti's family on his father's side

Shanti's paternal grandfather had three sons: the eldest became an accountant, the second became a district and sessions judge, and the third stayed at home to manage the estate.

This youngest son, Manorath Prasad Seth, had four daughters (including Hirabehn, the eldest, and Mangla, who later married Pran Nath) and four sons: Raj, Achal, Brahma and Shanti.

Achal, who became a doctor, had several children, including Anand and Arun; Brahma had several children, who do not appear in this book. Raj, who became an engineer and worked on the Railways, married Chanda (who was called 'Ma' by her children and 'Amma' by her grandchildren). They had three sons – Michi (whose first wife was Moyna and second wife Mohini), Sashi (who married Usha) and Tuttu (who married Neepa) – as well as a daughter, Leila.

Sashi and Usha's daughter was Ira. Leila, who married Prem (whose surname also happened to be Seth), had two sons – Vikram (the author) and Shantum – and a daughter, Aradhana, who married Peter.

Shantum, who married Gitu (or Gitanjali), has two daughters: Nandini and Anamika.

501

Henny's father was Isaac Caro; her mother was Ella (or Gabriele) Caro, née Schmelkes. Henny's (elder) sister was Lola and her (younger) brother was Heinz (or Hei). Olga and Flora Glaser were Henny's aunts.

Henny's fiancé was Hans Mahnert. His father, Franz Mahnert ('Mr Mahnert senior' or 'old Mr Mahnert'), had a high-ranking position in the insurance company in which Henny and Lola worked. Franz Mahnert was long widowed; his wife had been Jewish. Gerda von Gliszczynski lived with Franz Mahnert during and after the war, together with her daughter Ursula (or Ursel).

The schoolteacher Fritz Bruse and his wife Margarethe were friends of the Mahnerts. Fredy Aufrichtig, who had been a solicitor before it became impossible for him to work in Germany, left his family valuables with the Mahnerts when he emigrated from Germany.

Christmas was always celebrated by the circle of friends at the house of the mathematics teacher (later, school inspector) Jazko Rabau and his second wife, Rose. During the war, both were moved into an apartment in the same building as the Caros under the policy of concentrating those whom the Nazis defined as Jews or in 'non-privileged mixed marriages' in 'Jewish houses'. She was Christian, he a converted Christian, Jewish by birth. Inge, who lived in the USA, was his daughter by his first marriage.

Ilse Heydt (née Schmidt) was a close friend of Henny's who, during the war, married Dieter Heydt, a librarian and interpreter. After the war, he was imprisoned by the French occupation forces.

Alice Fröschke (Fröschlein) was originally a friend of Henny's sister, Lola; the record of her correspondence with Henny does not cease in the late forties, as with the others, but continues into the fifties because she undertook a great deal of correspondence with German officialdom on Henny's behalf.

Hans and Annerose Dietrich, also part of the circle of friends, lived in East Berlin after the war. Though Hans Dietrich was an official during the war, he never joined the Nazi Party.

Lili Würth, a close friend of Henny and Lola, was believed by some to have become an apologist for the Nazi regime.

A. G. Belvin (originally Adolf Berliner) was a certified public accountant who emigrated to the USA. Lola worked for him in Berlin for a while after she was sacked from her job in the insurance company for being a Jew.